The Teaching
of
Psychology

The Teaching of Psychology

Method, Content, and Context

Edited by

JOHN RADFORD
North East London Polytechnic

DAVID ROSE
Goldsmiths' College, University of London

JOHN WILEY & SONS
Chichester · New York · Brisbane · Toronto

British Library Cataloguing in Publication Data:

The teaching of psychology.
   1. Psychology – Study and teaching
   I. Radford, John, *b. 1931*
   II. Rose, David
   150'.7   BF77   79–40824
   ISBN 0 471 27665 0

Photoset by Thomson Press (India) Limited New Delhi and printed by The Pitman Press Bath Avon.

Contents

SECTION I METHODS IN TEACHING PSYCHOLOGY

SECTION II TEACHING SUBJECT AREAS WITHIN
PSYCHOLOGY

SECTION III TEACHING PSYCHOLOGY IN DIFFERENT CONTEXTS

Notes on Contributors

TERESA M. AMABILE received her Ph.D. in psychology from Stanford University in 1977. Since that time, she has been Assistant Professor in the Department of Psychology at Brandeis University, where she has taught courses in social psychology, statistics and quantitative methods, and the psychology of creativity. Her major research interests include: (a) creativity, and the social/environmental factors that can influence it, (b) intrinsic motivation and the influence of motivational state upon creativity and other aspects of performance, (c) person perception, especially the biases and errors made by social perceivers, and (d) social psychological factors in education. In addition to research articles appearing in the *Journal of Personality and Social Psychology*, she has written (with Albert Hastorf) a chapter on 'Person Perception' for *Social Psychology*, edited by B. Seidenberg and A. Snadowsky, and (with William DeJong) a chapter on 'Statistics and Methodology' for *Psychology and Life*, by P. Zimbardo.

RICHARD J. ANDERSON was born in New York, received both Bachelor's and Master's degrees from the University of Florida and a Ph.D. from the University of Michigan. During a long-term affiliation with the University of Florida, his teaching duties have included mathematics and statistics, as well as history and systems in psychology, personality, testing and measurement, general psychology and a survey of the behavioural sciences. As Professor of Psychology for the past 23 years, he has been the senior member of the department for sixteen years, and in 1978 was invited to present an address to the Florida Psychological Association celebrating its thirty years, as the only one of the original founders still a member, and the earliest in term of service, of the past-presidents. He has done considerable field research in Guatemala, beginning with a literacy study in 1965–67 and a programme of enrichment of primary education in the early 1970s and culminating in 1978 in a six-year

Basic Village Education programme of communication with remote villages in the interests of promoting social change. He has published several papers on the contributions of Wilhelm Wundt during these centennial years of his original delineation of the new scientific approach to psychology. Other interests include studying several aspects of expressive behaviour, and coverbal responses.

RICHARD BRUCE is Professor of Psychology and Associate Dean, College of Arts and Sciences, University of Alaska, Anchorage. He has fourteen years of college teaching experience in graduate and undergraduate courses in physiological psychology, sensory processes, comparative behaviour, learning theories, and research methods and apparatus, and research experience and publications in physiology, sensation, and learning. He has participated in the establishment of a psychology department in a small, liberal arts college, and is presently assisting in the development of a growing university. He has also been instrumental in the design, furnishing, and maintenance of a physiological–experimental–social psychology laboratory. Professor Bruce is author of *Fundamentals of Physiological Psychology*, New York: Holt, Rinehart, and Winston, 1977, and co-author of a textbook in experimental psychology (Matheson, D., Bruce, R., and Beauchamp, K. *Experimental Psychology: Research Design and Analysis*, 3rd edn, New York: Holt Rinehart and Winston, 1978). His current research interests include computer applications to research and teaching, behaviour genetics, sensory and perception phenomena, development of inexpensive laboratory apparatus, behavioural catalogue of new and exotic laboratory species, and the applications of brain stimulation techniques.

DENNIS CHILD, who graduated from London University in physics, zoology, and psychology, holds higher degrees in education from Leeds and Bradford Universities and is a Fellow of the British Psychological Society. He taught in comprehensive and public schools as a science and mathematics teacher. He then became a lecturer at Leeds College of Education, first in physics, then in education. He moved to the University of Bradford School of Education as lecturer then senior lecturer in psychology of education. At present he is Professor and Head of the School of Education, University of Newcastle upon Tyne. Current research interests include the impact of personality and motivation on academic achievement, and cognitive and affective 'styles' in education and study skills. He is the author of many research papers and articles, several books, and commissioned chapters. These include a basic text on factor analysis, a student–teacher text entitled *Psychology and the Teacher* with an edited companion volume, *Readings in Psychology for the Teacher*. He was a visiting Professor at the University of Illinois with Professor

Cattell producing a joint book entitled *Motivation and Dynamic Structure*. Currently he is general editor of a new series for Blackwell entitled 'The Theory and Practice of Education'.

CARY L. COOPER received his B.S. and M.B.A. degrees from the University of California, Los Angeles, and his Ph.D. from the University of Leeds, UK. He is the only American to hold a chair in a British university in the field of management and is currently Professor of Management Educational Methods (a chair sponsored by the Foundation for Management Education), in the Department of Management Sciences, University of Manchester Institute of Science and Technology. Professor Cooper is currently Chairman-elect of the Management Education and Development Division of the American Academy of Management (the first time a UK-based academic has been elected to this post). Professor Cooper is currently the editor of the international quarterly journal, *Journal of Occupational Behaviour*. He is also on the editorial board of a number of other scholarly journals (e.g. *Group and Organization Studies*). He has published fifteen books and is the author of over one hundred scholarly articles.

ROBERT S. DANIEL has been on the faculty of the University of Missouri-Columbia (US) since 1942. His graduate degrees are from Indiana University. He is currently editor of *Teaching of Psychology*, a quarterly journal published by Division Two of the American Psychological Association. Research interests include teaching and other professional problems, human factors, and physiological psychology. He was chairman of the APA's Publications and Communications Board (1977–79) and was a member of the committee that prepared the Board's *Publications Manual* (2nd edition). In 1978 he received the Unique Contribution to Teaching Award of the American Psychological Foundation in recognition of the establishment of the journal he now edits. He was co-author of *Professional Problems in Psychology* with C. M. Louttit in 1953, edited *Contemporary Readings in General Psychology* (1959, 1965), and has published research papers in *Science*, *Journal of Experimental Psychology*, *Journal of Physiological and Comparative Psychology*, *Psycho-physiology*, and others. The chapter on psychology in Downs and Jenkins's *Bibliography* was prepared by Daniel. Among various teaching responsibilities he has directed a multi-sectioned introductory laboratory psychology course for over thirty years, and has authored the manual for that course (now in its eleventh edition).

WILLIAM DEJONG received his Ph.D. in social psychology at Stanford University. He was, for one year, a National Institute of Mental Health Post-Doctoral

Fellow at Dartmouth College. He is presently an Assistant Professor of Psychology at Brandeis University. His research interests include altruism and prosocial behaviour, the social psychology of physical deviance, and self-perception and attributional processes. He is the author of several research publications.

HARRY FISHER read mathematics and physics at University College London before qualifying as a teacher at Westminster College in 1951. Subsequently he taught mathematics and statistics at Chingford County High School, London. In 1971 he obtained a first-class honours degree in psychology at North East London Polytechnic. At present he is Principal Lecturer in the Department of Psychology at North East London Polytechnic, teaching the psychology of language and statistics. Additionally he is course tutor for the part-time honours degree course in psychology. Since 1973 Harry Fisher has been an Examiner for the Associated Examining Board 'A' level in psychology. His research interests include sentence comprehension and the comparison process.

CLIVE FLETCHER was born in Liverpool, England, in 1945. He obtained his B.A. and Ph.D. in psychology at the University of Wales. After a period of research and teaching in the clinical field, he turned to occupational psychology. He joined the Behavioural Sciences Research Division of the Civil Service Department, where he was a Principal Psychologist before taking up his present post of Senior Lecturer at Goldsmiths' College in 1977. His main areas of research are performance appraisal, career development, and the use of interviews in selection and counselling. Apart from publishing numerous books and articles, Dr Fletcher is actively involved in management training and consultancy with a number of organizations. He is an associate member of the British Psychological Society and a member of the Division of Occupational Psychology.

MICHAEL J. A. HOWE is Senior Lecturer in Psychology at Exeter University. On obtaining his Ph.D. at the University of Sheffield in 1966, he became a Post-Doctoral Fellow at Dalhousie University, Canada. Subsequently he was Assistant Professor of Education at Tufts University, Massachusetts, and Associate Professor of Educational Psychology at the University of Alberta, Canada, before returning to England in 1971. He has written a number of books, including *Introduction to Human Memory* (1970), *Understanding School Learning* (1972), *Learning in Infants and Young Children* (1975), *Television and Children* (1977), *Student Note-taking as an Aid to Learning* (1977) (with Jean Godfrey), and *The Psychology of Human Learning* (in press). He is the editor of *Adult Learning* (1977) and the author of about fifty articles describing research on various aspects of human learning and memory.

DAVID LEGGE was educated at Midhurst Grammar School and University College London, where he took a first-class honours degree in psychology and subsequently was awarded his Ph.D. for research on perceptual-motor skills. He was appointed to a lectureship at UCL in 1961 and taught there until his move to City of London Polytechnic in 1970. Subsequently, as Reader in Psychology at Birkbeck College and most recently as Head of the Department of Behavioural Sciences at Huddersfield Polytechnic, his teaching responsibilities have generally spanned the field of cognitive psychology, ranging from verbal learning and memory to skills and human performance. He has also been heavily involved in ergonomics, experimental design and data analysis. He edited a volume of readings on 'Skill' in 1970 and wrote three titles in the 'Essential Psychology' series (two jointly with Dr P. J. Barber). In 1978 he was appointed to the post of Dean of the Faculty of Education at Huddersfield Polytechnic.

DOUGAL MACKAY is the principal clinical psychologist at St Mary's Hospital, Paddington, London, and is also an honorary lecturer in psychology in the medical school of that hospital. He has taught psychology to pre-clinical, clinical, and postgraduate medical students for twelve years and has also been involved in training courses for nurses, occupational therapists, and physiotherapists during this period. As a clinical psychologist working in a general hospital, he enjoys close professional contact with general practitioners, community physicians, neurologists, gynaecologists, dermatologists, and psychiatrists. His clinical and research interests are mainly in the field of behaviour therapy. Most of his publications have been concerned with the implementation of assertion therapy and social skills training programmes with adult neurotic patients. He has also written papers on the use of behavioural techniques with cases of sexual dysfunction. He is the author of *Clinical Psychology: Theory and Therapy*, published in 1975 by Methuen.

ELIZABETH MCWHIRTER graduated with first-class honours in psychology from The Queen's University, Belfast, in 1967 and obtained her Ph.D. from Stirling University, Scotland, in 1970 after three years part-time research into cognitive development. After a period of teaching educationally subnormal children, and serving as an educational psychologist with the Belfast Education Authority, Dr McWhirter took up a lectureship at the Ulster Polytechnic in 1972. During the next five years she lectured mainly on developmental psychology but also published numerous articles on the psychology curriculum in a range of applied and professional courses in *Social and Health Science*. Since 1977, Dr McWhirter has been lecturer in the Department of Psychology at The Queen's University, Belfast, teaching developmental psychology to both undergraduate and postgraduate students in educational, clinical, and occupational psychology. Her research interests lie within the area of concept development from childhood to adulthood—specifically concepts of proportionality and generally the whole question of ecological validity in developmental research.

MUYUNDA MWANALUSHI obtained his Ph.D. in experimental child psychology at the University of Strathclyde, Scotland. In 1974 he moved to the University of Zambia where he became Dean of the School of Humanities and Social Sciences. He is now Associate Professor of Psychology at the University of Zambia. Currently Dr Mwanalushi is on secondment to the Institute for African Studies, University of Zambia, as a Research Fellow working on a WHO-sponsored international project on Community Response to Alcohol-related Problems. He has published works on the mediational function of imagery and verbal codes, and emotional adjustment in adolescents. His current research interests include the effect of alcohol and psychosocial development in adolescence.

After graduating in history and literature, JOHN RADFORD took an honours degree in psychology at Birkbeck College, University of London, where he also obtained his Ph.D. At North East London Polytechnic (formerly West Ham College of Technology) between 1965 and 1976 he built up one of the largest Departments of Psychology in the UK. In 1976 he became Dean of the Faculty of Human Sciences at the Polytechnic. In 1970 he founded the Association for the Teaching of Psychology. He was largely responsible for the introduction of psychology as a subject in the General Certificate of Education and was Chief Examiner at Advanced level for the Associated Examining Board from 1970 to 1979. Since 1978 he has been Chairman of the Psychology Board of the Council for National Academic Awards. John Radford is co-author of three books: *Thinking: Its Nature and Development* with A. Burton (Wiley, 1974); and *The Person in Psychology* and *Individual Differences* both with R. Kirby (Methuen, 1975, 1976). He is co-editor of two books apart from the present one: *Thinking in Perspective* with A. Burton (Methuen, 1978) and *Textbook of Psychology* with E. Govier (Sheldon, in press). John Radford is a Fellow of the British Psychological Society. Among his more exotic interests are the relationship of psychology to music, to Zen Buddhism, and to science fiction.

COLIN ROBSON took a degree in physics at Manchester University and after teacher training at King's College, London, spent three years teaching electronics as an Education Officer in the R.A.F. He then taught physics in London secondary schools for several years, taking a degree in psychology at Birkbeck College, London, by evening study. After graduating, he joined the lecturing staff at Birkbeck, teaching courses in statistics, experimental design, and learning, and completed a Ph.D. in the field of discrimination learning. He has been at Huddersfield Polytechnic since 1971, where he was at first Head of the Education Department and then piloted the development of an innovatory joint psychology/sociology degree, becoming Head of a newly formed Behavioural Sciences Department. For the past three years he has been Director of a D.E.S. funded research project seeking to develop and evaluate new approaches to teaching the severely mentally handicapped. His research interests include the analysis of teaching behaviour and discrimination learning in humans and animals. He is author of the Penguin text *Experiment, Design and Statistics in Psychology*, and has recently contributed a chapter on 'Language Training the Severely Mentally Handicapped' in the *Handbook of Mental Deficiency* (Ellis, 1979).

DAVID ROSE graduated with a first-class honours degree in psychology from North East London Polytechnic in 1969. Subsequently he worked at the Medical Research Council Unit on Neural Mechanisms of Behaviour at University College London and obtained his Ph.D. on the role of the neocortex in learning in 1975. At present he is Principal Lecturer in Psychology at Goldsmiths' College, University of London, and an Associated Research Worker at the Medical Research Council Unit on Neural Mechanisms of Behaviour. Since 1973, Dr Rose has been the Editor of *Psychology Teaching*, the journal of the Association for the Teaching of Psychology. As well as publications on the teaching of psychology, he has published a number of papers on his main research interest, brain–behaviour relationships.

ROBERT SERPELL is Associate Professor of Psychology and Director of the Institute for African Studies at the University of Zambia. He was born and educated in England, but has spent most of his professional life in the Republic of Zambia of which he is now a citizen. After graduating from Oxford in psychology and philosophy, he first went to Zambia in 1965 as a Research Fellow in the Human Development Research Unit of the Institute which he now directs. In 1969, on receipt of his doctorate from Sussex University, he joined the University of Zambia's Psychology Department, and served as its Head from 1974 until 1977, when he returned to the Institute. He has also worked for shorter periods at the Hester Adrian Research Centre for the study of learning processes in the mentally handicapped at Manchester University, at the Laboratory for Comparative Human Cognition at Rockefeller University, New York, at the East West Centre, Honolulu, and at Howard University, Washington. His main research interest is in cognitive processes and abilities in children, especially perception and language. His publications include, as well as technical reports in various scholarly journals and books, an introductory text entitled *Culture's Influence on Behaviour*.

Teaching has been, and is, PETER SHEA's favourite professional pleasure, and he has experienced a great variety of it. He began teaching in inner London and gained deputy headships as he moved from primary to comprehensive to special school education. He then took a headship in a new town setting. After some years, when he began to be aware of the routine of the school year, he took a senior lectureship in a college of education. He had taken a degree in psychology at Birkbeck during the 1950s and parallel with his school experience had been teaching adults in W.E.A. and university extra-mural classes and summer schools. When he felt that he could not go on teaching trainee teachers without recharging his first-hand school experiences, he transferred his full-time interest to the education of adults by becoming the Staff Lecturer in Psychology for the University of London's Department of Extra-Mural Studies.

JOHANNA TURNER obtained both her M.A. and her M.Ed. from the University of Edinburgh. In 1969 she was appointed Lecturer in Education at the University of Sussex, a post which she held until 1974 when she took up her present appointment of Lecturer in Developmental Psychology at the University of Sussex. Her research interests include social interaction and cognitive development in primary school children and the interaction between cognitive development and personality development up to the age of seven. Among her publications are *Cognitive Development* (Methuen, 1975), *Psychology for the Classroom* (Methuen, 1975), and *Made for Life: Coping, Competence and Cognition* (Methuen, in press).

Foreword

I am a great believer in common sense, in relying on the good sense of mankind to 'get it right'. It generally does—in the end. But the fact that common sense may have had it wrong for a few preceding millennia does mean that we need to be on our guard and not be too hasty over the certainty of any answers. For example, at one time everybody knew we lived on a flat world; it was self-evident until someone went to the edge and did not fall off. About the same time, everyone knew that the sun charioted around the earth each day, whilst the earth was the centre of the universe, and so on. As we have come to accept, blood has to be spilt before common sense accepts change, but eventually it does and yesterday's heresy becomes today's credo, whilst common sense forgets that it was ever otherwise.

The pivotal point for the onlooker is to get his history right, that is, to assess where the time in which he lives occurs in the changing cycle. Man may trundle along for centuries during which no serious challenge is made to a universally accepted doctrine; but constant vigilance is essential if it happens to be a time when such a challenge occurs. And the results linger on. For example, it is now over a century since Darwin's *Origin of Species* produced its major upheaval of man's view of man. Today, there is lip-service acceptance of it, insofar as most scientists would accept the general theory of man's evolutionary development from the animal world, but the essential thinking underlying that acceptance has hardly permeated our everyday world. It is not part of the texture of our culture to see or to think of man in this pattern of inheritance linking him to the animal kingdom.

If this seems somewhat removed from everyday tasks, we should bear in mind that the implications are everywhere, as in the field with which we are concerned —teaching and learning. On the one hand, man takes over a phylogenetic frame that links him as a species to many thousands of years of development and ties him through his ancestry with other creatures to many millions of years of evolution. On the other, man's ontological development is so swift and has been completed within such a short time—a few years only—that we have scarcely begun to understand it. It is obvious that the two stages overlap one another and necessarily interact. But we have little knowledge of the processes underlying such learning. Even so, lack of understanding has rarely prevented man from facing the challenge of new intellectual demands; he pushes forward with a boldness that has so often been a hallmark of his history. Today he acquires and uses more and more symbolic materials, until eventually most of his life is contained in their transactions. Hitherto such intellectual tasks have been restricted to a small proportion of the population, but now through a deliberate policy of education for everybody, the problem is extended until it concerns the whole population. The recent campaign for literacy conducted through the British Broadcasting Corporation's programmes was a striking example of the public's reaction when it learned that so many of its members had not achieved this 'basic' skill of translating verbal symbols, our so-called reading and writing. Man has launched himself in this country on a gigantic exercise in which he expects everybody, irrespective of background, to learn how to manipulate the tools of his invention—symbolic material.

It would be misleading to pretend that we always know what we are doing in the world of learning and teaching. Man's ability to learn may link him phylogenetically with his fellow creatures but the stress which he now places on the use of symbols of all kinds—languages, mathematics, music, technology—has given him such powerful tools that he operates on a different dimension from other animals. Can we assume that the same rules govern his learning as theirs? At certain fundamental levels, it may be so. The contiguities of time and place still operate so that events occurring at the same time and/or the same place are, for no other reason, mentally associated. But that form of conditioning does not take us very far in man's world of symbols. The association of many ideas is only understandable in terms of their related meanings and this takes us into quite a different area of learning.

The increasing complexity of human learning is illustrated in the field of motivation where, as George Miller has said, 'the central problem of education is to make the students want it'. A library has been written about motivation, and some scholars have read it, but the subject still baffles us. It is tempting to think that with motivation all things are possible; certainly without it, most are not. Motivation is often discussed in terms of a reward system on the analogy of an animal learning to associate a response with the delivery of food, but often that is an inadequate description where motivation has become an integral part of the learned action. For example, little Johnny learning to kick his football is 'rewarded' by the kick itself, just as eventually the scholar's satisfaction in his accumulated knowledge is its own reward. The psychologist appreciates that the continuum of motivation, if indeed it is a continuum, is long indeed and that the variations along the dimension match its length.

When we turn to teaching we find that within the area of higher education there has been a long tradition that its teachers do not require training. Unlike other sectors of education where staff undertake long practice sessions, in the higher echelons of the educational world they have not done so. Apparently by reason of their understanding of their subject, new staff can immediately begin to communicate satisfactorily to their students. The rationale seems to be that at this level the gap between student and teacher has narrowed; both are participating in an on-going learning exercise, both are students, both are teaching as well as learning.

I am not here to quarrel with this view, except to doubt whether it is enough. We can surely not only smooth the road in the early stages but make it more efficient. Psychologists are actively concerned, and ought to be, in the teaching of any subject and at any level, and in spite of a limited understanding of how we learn they have improved many teaching methods. It is natural enough that they should give special attention to their own subject, for the teaching of psychology presents both new and old problems. Many modern subjects are made up of a number of different disciplines and psychology, which ranges from neurophysiology to social groups, from statistics to clinical problems, is broader than most. It often happens that a student who is good at, and interested in, one field may fight shy of another that to him is totally unrelated. The student with an arts background may be prone to give up at the sight of a few statistical formulae or an unfamiliar physiological vocabulary. Motivation rears its head again.

This book is not a revolutionary text. Indeed its strength is the very opposite. Its editors are practising teachers who have had long experience in their craft and have had to think about its development. Hence the book presents admirably what is available to staff in the different branches of psychology. It covers an enormous range of subjects, well represented by the various experts in their different fields. It will be of obvious value to new staff whilst tempting the established lecturer to compare his priorities with those in this selection.

The book examines the kinds of questions students ask of their subject and the questions teachers should ask of themselves. In teaching psychology everyone faces the issue that what is taught is not only a part of the world, as is all knowledge, but that the subject itself is changing that world and changing the individual who learns it. In one respect it is a process of understanding ourselves and our relation to the world, akin to the age-old philosophical questions that have been asked about the nature of our perception of the real world. Psychology brings these questions sharply into focus. Here is the process by which every individual perceives (see, hears, touches, smells, etc.) this world. That process is subserved by common mechanisms transforming physical energy into coded signals that are in turn received in a neural network where subsequent translation is very much determined by the individual's previous experience. We are making the world in our image; fallibility is all around us.

Now many students read psychology with hopes that go beyond the context of seeking knowledge: they specifically expect to increase their understanding of themselves or their society, or both. There is much to applaud in this attitude and psychology would be a poor subject if it did not make a contribution to such ends. But reading psychology can lead to doubts and sometimes to disillusionment. In the areas of personality and social psychology there are no quick answers, no easy solutions and often no firm conclusions to the kinds of questions such students pose. A student has to accept the ambiguity of uncertainty, the indecision of an on-going, unfolding discipline that has now made considerable progress but still has an immense way to go. If, however, we are tempted to think that progress is too slow then there is here (see p. 169) a happy reminder of how Cambridge University, only a hundred years ago, turned down James Ward's request for a laboratory to study psychophysics on the grounds that it would 'insult religion by putting the human soul in a pair of scales'. Yes, common sense has moved on.

8 February 1980   HARRY KAY

Introduction

JOHN RADFORD

As far as the Editors are aware, this is the first book devoted to the teaching of psychology in general. Our intention has been to draw together authors with a range of experiences and points of view; our hope is that the book will have something to offer to teachers in a wide variety of situations.

We gave our authors some guidance as to the content of their chapters, and we particularly urged them to keep to the same approximate lengths. However, we did not seek to impose a uniform style or level. Thus each contribution is a discussion or review from an individual point of view. Authors are, naturally, more familiar with their own subject areas; their own institutions; and their own countries' educational systems; than with others: and much of what they have to say must be considered in that light. Nevertheless we think the contributions reveal more things in common than differences, and we hope that each adds something to the others.

Our idea is that the dimensions of method, content, and context between them cover a large number of the issues that arise in teaching psychology. We hope that the whole book will be found worth reading; but also that teachers with specific interests will be able to select appropriately.

All our authors but one are British or American; and all are trained in the relatively homogeneous tradition shared by these two countries. We are very well aware that this does not represent the whole of psychology, even when defined fairly narrowly. 'Our' psychology exists as a teaching subject almost world-wide, both in English-speaking and in non-English-speaking countries. Both of these make massive contributions of their own to psychology as a science. Both, perhaps particularly the non-English-speaking, have their own patterns of education with peculiar problems for the teaching of psychology.

If at this point I [JKR] may drop the editorial 'we' in order to express more personal views, I may suggest also that probably every advanced culture throughout history has dealt in some measure with problems that we in our culture have somewhat arbitrarily grouped together as 'psychology'. It behoves psychologists, perhaps more than other scholars, to be aware of the relative nature of their discipline. It appears to me that psychology is not likely to be as objective a study as physics or chemistry. The behaviour and experiences of human beings, with which we mainly deal, are clearly the product of interaction between genetic endowment and environment, of which the most important part is almost certainly cultural. But psychology, indeed every sort of study, is itself part of that culture: it helps to form it, and is formed by it. A wider cultural awareness has fairly recently come (or perhaps some would say, come back) into psychology: for example in the work of the Harvard school of experimental anthropology, and in various more-or-less systematic attempts to compare Western psychology with that of the East (e.g. Ornstein, 1973; see Radford, 1976, for further references).

How far these changes may go is outside the scope of this book. In the particular culture in which the psychology with which we are dealing has emerged, it exists as a science or study; as a profession; and as a teaching subject. These are not completely separate activities although at times they may seem so. And even within this more limited psychology we can distinguish many different traditions, not necessarily all of the same conceptual status nor the same historical impact: the introspective, the behavioural, the psychometric, the depth analytic, the phenomenological, the 'humanistic', have perhaps claims to be considered distinct. And it may be suggested that there have also always been exponents of an eclectic approach drawing on several of the more strict doctrines at any particular time.

Psychology, in reality, has always been a conglomerate. Beloff (1973) refers to 'a loosely-knit collection of psychological sciences'. This collection has had a somewhat curious public life, attracting both indiscriminate praise, and obloquy probably equally undeserved. Freud's theories were at first shocking, then accepted uncritically, by many at least, and certainly absorbed into the culture. Watson's *Behaviourism* (1930) was called 'perhaps the most important book since the Bible'. Behaviourism now is one of the most popular creeds for general attack.

The relatively few studies that seem to have been made of public attitudes to psychology suggest both ignorance and ambivalence (e.g. Philips, 1968; see also Atkinson, 1977; McKeachie, 1972).

On the one hand, psychology seems potentially or actually a powerful body of almost esoteric knowledge promising control over human behaviour; on the other, it appears trivial and futile. Both of these may be either good or bad, and any combination seems tenable. The opponents of intelligence tests appear to think that they are both ineffective and dangerous; academic psychologists can be found who avow the uselessness of what they do, yet persist in it (perhaps for purely financial reasons). One of my hobby-horses is the way in which such ambivalence has, I believe, been faithfully reflected in popular thinking in the unique medium of science fiction; but I will not ride it here (see Rose, this volume).

The vicissitudes of psychology as a science and as a profession deserve separate treatment and indeed have books and papers devoted to them (see for example Koch, 1975; Peterson, 1976; Broadbent, 1973; Heather, 1976). As a teaching subject psychology has also experienced ambivalent attitudes. In some circumstances, its right to exist at all has been bitterly opposed. This was true when it was introduced at first-degree level. Boring (1950) tells us that when Ward and Venn attempted in 1877 to establish a laboratory of psychophysics at Cambridge, a mathematician objected that they would 'insult religion by putting the human soul in a pair of scales'. The attempt failed. The University of Oxford waited to create its first Chair in Psychology until 1947. At a lower level, psychology made its first appearance as a pre-college examination subject in the United Kingdom in 1970. In the General Certificate of Education students commonly take up to eight or so subjects at Ordinary level, and up to three two years later at Advanced level. For school students the approximate ages are sixteen and eighteen; but many are older, and not at school but at semi-adult colleges. The modest attempt (which took almost ten years) of one Examining Board to establish psychology as an option at 'A' level aroused strong opposition and, apparently, strong fears: that it would make students 'introspective' or, perhaps, infect them in some more pathological way; while (some) university teachers dreaded an influx of ill-taught students to their courses. Many other countries had taught psychology to comparable students for years (Snellgrove, 1974) and it is possible that the British educational system is more reactionary, or alternatively wiser, than others. Perhaps psychology had been adopted with more initial enthusiasm elsewhere.

On the other hand it seems that psychology has sometimes found itself, as it were, drafted in where it might have been thought to be somewhat unfitted. This is particularly so in a number of applied fields, above all perhaps education. Universal education in this country began, later than several others, in 1870, and throughout its existence as a separate discipline psychology has generally been regarded as an essential component of teacher training. Many of the most eminent psychologists have written specifically for teachers or been directly involved in school education: James, Binet, Burt, Wertheimer, and Bruner, for example.

It is hard to know whether the effect has been, on balance, beneficial or otherwise. Many psychological theories have subsequently been abandoned by psychologists, while they were still being enthusiastically propagated, perhaps in debased form, to new generations of teachers (an effect reflected in science fiction since Frankenstein's poor creature ran amok). It has become axiomatic that any course for teachers of anything must have a substantial

psychological component. Too often, what has been presented could be cari-
catured as simply the chapters of a general textbook with the words 'in the
classroom' added to each: Perception in the classroom; Motivation in the
classroom; and so on. It has been hard for drafted psychologists to realize,
and announce, that on any particular educational issue, their discipline may
or may not have anything useful to contribute at its particular stage of development. The fact that psychologists have studied learning for many years does
not of itself guarantee the relevance of what they have to say to education,
even though that too is manifestly concerned with the learning process.

It is also the case that students of applied disciplines not unnaturally tend
to want facts rather than theories, certainty rather than doubt, and useful
techniques rather than methods of investigation. Yet it may be that it is the
latter in each case that is the most appropriate (if not the only) contribution
that the psychologist can make. What the discipline shows quite often is not
exactly how children are motivated, in a quantitative way, but that there are
many different ways of conceptualizing motivation and many complexly
interacting factors in the individual child; and something of the ways in which
these might, in principle, be teased out.

Similar arguments apply to many other applied professions, such as medicine,
nursing, social work, personnel management, etc. (see, for example, Dacey
and Wintrob, 1973; Tait, 1973; Weinman, 1978; Rachman and Philips, 1975).
In this book we have chosen for discussion what seem to us perhaps the leading
contexts in which psychology is taught. In any context, the needs of the students,
and the personal preference of the psychologist, may lead to the presentation
of one particular theoretical framework as though it were in itself, 'the psychological approach'. Perhaps the most popular has been that of Freud, or
some version of it. This popularity has no doubt been one contributory factor
to the lay view of that approach as a kind of woolly do-gooding of little practical
effectiveness. The fact that Freud sought causal explanations, not excuses,
and that most psychologists probably reject his analysis anyway, go for little.

Be this as it may, if there is a case for teaching psychology in any context
either as a single discipline or as a component, it is necessary to have some way
of classifying the areas from which material might be drawn. General textbooks
have often adopted fairly traditional chapter-headings, modified to a greater or
lesser extent to reflect shifting interests in research and application or to render
the presentation more accessible to students. The current edition of what is
by all accounts the most popular general psychology text ever produced, that
of Hilgard, Atkinson, and Atkinson, has the following:

1 The nature of psychology
2 Biological basis of psychology
3 Developmental psychology
4 Sensory processes

While Hilgard *et al.* are very aware of changing views in psychology, such a list does on the face of it suggest a particular perspective: a traditional one in which psychology arises from physiological studies, moves to sensation and then to cognitive processes, discovers emotion and motivation, develops practical applications in testing and psychopathology, and finally realizes that man is a social being and that psychology has social implications—almost the history of nineteenth-century psychology.

Such headings also reflects a problem in teaching, that psychology appears to lack a logic of the subject. There is really no intrinsic reason why perception should be taught before learning, or vice versa. Second or third year students sometimes ask why they could not have started with what they are doing now, as they understand it so much better than what came first. Having experimented with many different orders I believe the relative ease derives not from the topic but simply from its coming later rather than earlier.

Whatever the sequence, it seems desirable to impose some structure on our conglomerate subject, for a number of reasons. One is the practical necessity of devising syllabuses and timetables. One is the hope of aiding the student to make some sort of sense of the whole thing. And another is the wish to avoid relying entirely on tradition, or on fashion; to consider, at least, what appear to be major aspects of the subject-matter for possible inclusion.

One starting point that might be used is the concept of levels of explanation. It can be argued that a psychological account, to be complete, should be consistent at the physiological, individual, and social levels. The distinction goes back at least to the work of Hobbes (1651). Few psychological theories attempt this, and indeed grand general theories are currently unfashionable. Contrariwise, however, it is possible to suggest that most psychological material in practice centres on one or other of the levels. This led me to suggest as a structure for one single subject degree, five streams or groups of studies: the other two were 'practical' and 'contextual and integrative' (including history, general theoretical issues, etc.). This structure was probably more useful as an organizing device than as an intellectual aid. It did perhaps have the merit of causing people to question the traditional lists of topics. We have adopted a derivative of this classification for this book.

Another classification I have found helpful is as follows. It seems to me plausible to suggest these as relatively distinct areas of enquiry:

(a) The biological basis of behaviour: structure and functions of the nervous system, the special senses, the endocrine system, mechanisms of genetics.

(b) Information processing: the acquisition, retention and manipulation of knowledge about the world; processes of sensation, learning, memory, thinking, language.

(c) Individual differences: the measurement and explanation of the range of abilities, capacities and traits; individual and group differences; comparisons within and between species.

(d) Interaction: processes that occur between two or more individuals.

(e) Causes of action: motivation and emotion; needs, drives, wishes, feelings, and their effects on behaviour.

(f) Disorders: psychopathology, behaviour and character disorders, subnormality.

(g) Development: processes of growth and change.

(h) Historical and theoretical issues: the nature and progress of psychology as a study and a profession.

(i) Related studies: other disciplines existing in their own right such as anthropology, sociology, ergonomics, etc.

(j) Psychological methodology: techniques of investigation; skills such as interviewing and testing; experimental design, statistical analysis.

This list, or any similar list, is not a syllabus for a particular purpose. Most simply, it is an *aide memoire* for use in planning. It may be suggested, however, that a qualified psychologist who had *completely* neglected any one of these items throughout his education would to that extent be deficient as a psychologist.

Planning of psychology courses (indeed most higher education) has traditionally been mainly in terms of content. I have suggested elsewhere (Radford, 1978) that we ought to give much more deliberate attention than hitherto to two other aspects. This attention needs to be paid whether psychology is to be provided as the main vehicle of a higher education or as a component of a programme based mainly on other disciplines.

In the first case, my opinion is that psychology is in many ways peculiarly well fitted for that purpose. In the second, we have to ask what psychology has to offer. In either case, psychologists are self-confessed experts on human behaviour and experience. They may modestly claim to have established little with certainty, but we cannot disavow the attempt to be explicit. I label the two additional aspects experiences and skills.

Opinions differ on the extent to which higher education should deliberately plan for the experiences a student may be expected to get. There seems little doubt that when educational systems have been most effective they have either explicitly or implicitly arranged that students should receive quite specific and intense experiences. One may instance Greek education in the classical period (Beck, 1964) or the English public school and Oxbridge systems. Some of these even seem to share some techniques of personality change with religious and therapeutic systems (Radford, 1976). As far as psychology is concerned, the experiences I suggest we should consider include the following:

(a) Communication with
   (i) high-grade practitioners of the discipline;
   (ii) a variety of students: various both in personal characteristics and in subject areas;
   (iii) possibly others, e.g. non-academics.
It may be felt that communication occurs best when it is spontaneous. Spontaneity however has to some extent come to be regarded as a virtue in itself (as in the 'creativity' boom of the 1950s and 1960s). The chances of spontaneous communication can be increased by appropriate timetabling, by arrangements for eating and drinking, by open rather than closed doors. It requires, in my experience, a deliberate policy of always being on the look-out for means of making communication easier. The doubtless apocryphal American college announcement 'from Tuesday it will be a tradition that . . . ' arouses British laughter; but traditions can be created, and they can also disappear without constant attention.

(b) Tackling issues which are in some sense basic or fundamental, at least in the context of a particular discipline. This is a relative matter, but it may be considered an educational virtue of psychology, not a failing, that it spends quite a lot of time on such matters as the nature of science and of scientific explanation, and the assumptions we hold about human nature. At a level perhaps slightly less fundamental, the nature–nurture issue, for example, is not just a King Charles's head, turning up periodically and irrelevantly: it occurs in a context of prevailing attitudes, which it helps to form. It is partly for reasons such as these that some historical account seems essential for any but the most superficial course in psychology. Much of psychology's theoretical and still more of its experimental material has the air of being ephemeral. An historical background may help the student to see how far this impression is justified.

(c) For at least some period, being called on for the best intellectual efforts of which one is capable. This sort of notion has perhaps been somewhat unfashionable of late. But if education is of value in personal development, this is surely an important aspect. Psychology, it may be suggested, makes quite a wide range of intellectual demands. The student must handle material ranging from apparatus through to conceptual theories. He must try to integrate very disparate material, while at the same time resisting the temptation to include everything in a vast but nonsensical whole. He must be able, as Boswell said of Johnson, to argue close or wide as occasion demands. There is something to be said, besides tradition and convenience, for the system of a final examination, like a race in which talent and training are put to a real test (real, inter alia, because the prizes are real). There is something to be said for the four-questions-in-three-hours examination paper. A good examination paper should be a fair sampling of a syllabus; a set of questions about issues of some psychological importance. Giving a coherent, integrated, informed reply to four of them is, it may be argued, not such a bad measure of at least one important sort of psychological competence. Of course other skills require other assessments, which can also be intellectually demanding.

(d) The opportunity to develop some independence, increase the range of life experience, and so forth. This is perhaps a matter more for the institution than for the discipline. Within most institutions, however, it is often possible for a discipline to structure courses so as to make use of work or other experience before, during, or even after study. In principle psychology is particularly well equipped to do this inasmuch as it deals, at least nominally, with people. In practice, achievement has been patchy. For a particularly interesting programme, see Hutchison (1977) and Krasner (in press).

(e) The opportunity to extend familiarity with one's own culture (or adopted culture); to gain a sense of political, historical, aesthetic identity. This too is partly an institutional matter, but psychology with its obvious role in social history can certainly be one vehicle for this sort of personal development.

In both (d) and (e) I have used the word opportunity. Individual students may not wish to take up such opportunities. An institution which fails to provide them, however, seems to me lacking as a centre of education. And within an institution, it may be hoped that particular courses of study contribute to what makes education complete. It does not seem to me too bizarre to suggest that among the potential causes of student dissatisfaction is the fact that opportunities of this kind have, at least in newly created institutions, been often ignored or left to chance.

None of these experiences is unique to psychology. I suggest, though, that psychology can be shown to have specific interactions with each of them. Furthermore, psychologists are supposed to be, however inadequately, the experts on human behaviour and experience. As teachers, it seems logical that they should plan for the behaviour and experience of their students.

As for skills, it seems to me that the graduate from a course in psychology might reasonably expect, and be expected by others, to possess some competence in a number of areas. After three years doing little else, as in the British single honours system, he might perhaps expect all of the following. In shorter courses, less; and there are programmes specifically centred on one or more of such skills. To attempt all is rare. Much is left more or less to chance, or ignored; and this is somewhat odd, in that among the relatively better established parts of psychology are some simple facts about the learning of skills: they are better taught explicitly rather than implicitly; they improve with properly planned practice and feedback:

(a) Interaction.   Competence in social situations as a professional person dealing with people. A psychologist, even a very new one, may be expected to conduct a simple interview; and to communicate with all sorts of people as investigator, persuader, rapporteur, which includes writing and speaking correctly and effectively (see Bender, 1974; Pettifore, 1971).

(b) Measurement.   At least since Galton, measurement has been one of the main characteristics of a psychological approach, and sophisticated techniques have been developed. Many of these are often reserved for advanced courses; there is virtue in introducing at a basic level practice in use of tests, questionnaires, survey methods, observational techniques. This is partly because they are an important part of a psychologist's repertoire; partly because they are so commonly used and influential. Learning psychology should give increased understanding of the influence of the social sciences in our culture.

(c) Experiment.   This often forms the core of major courses in psychology. In these, however, a problem may be encountered of matching experiment to theory. Where experimental work is not included, there is a danger of not understanding the foundations of what is being taught. Psychological findings, and theories based on them, are often presented in a way like convenience foods, as though fish came neatly in fingers. Experiments in practice are rarely smooth, subjects are heterogeneous and contrary, even simple reflexes are not 100 per cent reliable. In some cases, experiments in idealized form have become enshrined in the textbooks for many years before replication was attempted. It may be suggested that almost any teaching of psychology should include some practical, preferably experimental element, to give first-hand experience of the method that above all differentiates this discipline from others concerned with human beings. It is by no means impossible, even when all one has is a large and static lecture class, and no apparatus. Something at least can be done with questionnaires incorporating different conditions; staged incidents; simple learning tasks; etc. Ideally, any more than trivial courses should incorporate some competence in the general principles of experimental investigation, hypothesis formation and testing, experimental design and analysis, statistics (see Regula, 1971; Fisher, this volume).

(d) Knowledge.   Much of a student's time is necessarily spent in the acquisition of knowledge, and the skills appropriate to this are likely to be required in most areas of work that are more or less 'psychological'. There are, of course, general habits of study (again, perhaps, a concept in recent disfavour). There are also more specific skills concerned with the use of sources; with extracting and summarizing information without distortion; with collating information of different kinds; with recording and storing. These skills are both internal and external; cognitive and physical. The two interact in ways that have been noted but perhaps not fully explored. For example the actual cross-referencing record system that is adopted affects not only the accessibility of material but possibly its significance in thought. The effect of serendipity has often been observed; the journal article actually searched for is less useful than the one printed next to it.

(e) Manipulation. A word to refer to, first, use of apparatus and preferably some skill in its construction; at least, some understanding of what it is reasonable to ask of apparatus. Graduate students often have to discover this through trial and error. Second, use of calculating devices (formerly log-tables and slide rules, now pocket calculators) and more particularly of computers. For psychologists computers are not, of course, just large calculators. Other uses such as simulation, control of experimentation, and computer-assisted instruction, need to be considered. Third, physiological techniques: measurement, dissection, implantation, etc. Clearly not every student on every course would master all these. Course planners should at least think about them and, as with experiment, even a little first-hand experience can be revealing.

(f) Self-development.   There are skills that can be taught but which are generally acquired, if at all, haphazardly. Take the choice of a career: it is possible to do this in a more or a less informed way, and a psychologist above all should have the latter available. Students must not only interview but be interviewed. There are ways of studying and working more effectively. There are even, dare I suggest, skills of social competence ranging from use of cutlery through language and conversation to general confidence. English public schools have long taken such training for granted (see also Pollack, 1972).

I have not listed separately a group of skills that might be labelled 'thinking'. This might include such activities as decision making, problem solving, logical argument and logical presentation, creativity. I am less sanguine than many writers (e.g. De Bono, 1971) about the possibility of teaching the generation of good new ideas. Logical procedures might be included under 'knowledge', and making decisions, insofar as that can be taught, under 'self-development'.

The foregoing may suggest a programme so vast as to be unworkable. Or it may suggest an unwarranted interference in matters which are none of a teacher's business. In my view, however, there is still remaining a rather narrow view of education which results, at its worst, in psychology consisting of the learning of a textbook or, at a higher level, of strings of recent experiments. Psychology, with its combination of human and scientific concerns, is well suited to be a component, or even the main vehicle, of a broader and really more liberal education. But I see no contradiction between liberality and practicality. The skills, knowledge, and experiences that psychological education can offer are fitted to produce, not just a good citizen but a very employable one (Korn and Nodine, 1975; Binder, 1972). There is perhaps still a feeling among some academics that the real object of their teaching is to produce more academic psychologists (see Halpern, 1971; Byrne, 1971). That is, indeed, one valuable object; but a far greater proportion of students will not take that route. The majority, probably, of the very large numbers who take psychology as a major component of education (Nazzaro, 1976; Straker, 1976; Clarke, 1972) will work at things that are more or less psychologically related. A few will become researchers and 'pure' academics; rather more enter the restricted psychological professions; while at the other end of the distribution some will turn to almost wholly non-psychological work. A common cry among those who select students is that so many want to study psychology for the wrong reasons: they want to understand themselves, or they want to work with people. Certainly such applicants need to be disillusioned of too rosy a picture of psychology's achievements. Certainly academic courses will not immediately satisfy those ambitions. But are the ambitions, in themselves, so unworthy, or so irrelevant to psychology? If they are irrelevant, in which discipline are they to be satisfied?

It might be thought that I wish psychology to move further in the direction of the humanistic/third force/experiential, and away from the disciplines of scholarship and empirical investigation. This is not so. Psychology as we recognize it is still a novel enterprise in the history of ideas. At the moment of writing, the first experimental laboratory still wants a few months of its centenary. Possibly the most important part of what is novel in psychology is the attempt to apply the methods of objective investigation to human behaviour and experience. This can be said to have united Wundt, James, Galton, Freud, Watson . . . . The attempt has turned out to be far more difficult than it first seemed.

The possibility of objectivity in any science, above all ours, is no longer taken for granted. But the attempt has had, and continues to have, profound effects; many would say, important successes. Until fairly recently though, it may be suggested, psychologists imposed limitations upon their own attempts, ruling out of bounds specific areas, or specific methods; each school having a different set of rules. Some still do this.

What is being urged is the sort of eclectic attitude that indeed many psychologists have always possessed (MacLeod, 1971). Eclecticism does not imply lack of system or rigour or the abandonment of academic standards; it implies openness and freedom of choice. The ideal psychologist, as perhaps the ideal scholar in any field, would be expert in far more studies than would fill a life-time. In practice the best attainable is probably jack of many trades and master of some.

Similar remarks could well apply to teaching methods. It is sometimes a matter of surprise to students that psychologists who, they think, know about learning, should rely so exclusively on traditional methods of teaching. Such surprise is only partly justified. Hard evidence on the efficacy of the traditional methods has not always been available (see Howe, this volume). Alternative methods are often both unproved and considerably more expensive. We should, at least, be aware of a range of methods, and try to use the most appropriate.

It may be asked why psychology should be taught at all. The question can arise in a number of contexts. While in some circumstances, as suggested earlier, psychology may be drafted in, in others it may be necessary to argue for it. Teaching is probably (though not certainly) better if there is some belief in the value of what one does. Students may legitimately query the worth of what they are being taught.

The least satisfactory sort of answer, in any of these circumstances, is probably 'because it's there', that is because it is part of a syllabus, because it is required for qualification, because I am employed in a Department of Psychology, etc.

A more satisfactory answer may be in terms of practical application: the student wishes to be a psychological or other practitioner (or indeed, as suggested above, to understand himself); and what is being taught can be shown to contribute to this. This sort of answer is far from being always available.

Another sort of answer, which some might find the most valuable, would demonstrate the educational value of psychology. Others may think the attempt absurd or unnecessary.

What is educationally valuable is itself an unsettled question, with answers depending upon culture, belief, and individual predilection. In the case of psychology, the attempt might begin with the modest observation that the subject does seem to interest considerable numbers of students. There are fashions in such things, and this may change; less rapidly, perhaps, if we think out what we have to offer. Interest, while not synonymous with value, is by no means a bad starting point.

It might then be suggested, as above, that psychology has at least some practical application to ends that are, in themselves, desirable: medicine or teaching, for example. It might be suggested that, for better or worse, psychological techniques and theories have, largely through such practical applications, contributed much to the nature of our society. This contribution is perhaps less obvious than that of technology, but not less pervasive. There can be very few individuals in technological societies who are not affected by schooling, medicine, social services, mass media and advertising, occupational selection and training. All these and more are themselves largely shaped by psychology and closely related disciplines. It may well be argued that it is better for the individual to understand something of such forces; how they work or at least are supposed to work.

More grandly, it might even be hoped that psychological knowledge will contribute to the improvement of society (Miller, 1969). The evidence thus far is patchy, but if there is any virtue in the attempts of psychology to investigate human behaviour and experience more objectively, more empirically, then the balance, in the long run, must be favourable.

More grandly still, these attempts, however futile they seem at times, can be regarded as part of man's search for understanding of his universe and himself. This search seems, to some at least, to run through the whole history of man as a distinct species. At times it is pursued with vigour, at times it falters, is suppressed or reversed, but as yet it has not ceased altogether. The tendency towards such a search appears therefore to be a fundamental attribute of the human species, and one which can be regarded as originating, persisting, and developing for reasons consistent with an evolutionary theory of biological survival. Psychology, moreover, both in its major theories (Freud, James, Piaget, for example) and in its detailed experimentation (on infantile competence, for example) itself begins to shed some light on certain aspects of the tendency.

What is the nature of the understanding that is sought, is a further question too complex to debate here. A personal preference is for an analogy in which changing psychological views are very like the changing views of a traveller through a landscape. Dreams before Freud, for example, seemed to be oddities, or prophecies: on turning the corner of *The Interpretation*, they appeared to fall into place as part of the determination of all psychic activity. Since then we have attained still other perspectives. Such an analogy does not deny the reality of the phenomena, but it does emphasize the relative nature of our knowledge, including the most recent. The psychological landscape is even less fixed than the physical one. Dreams change with the culture and even with the analyst. I do not necessarily suggest that there is here more than a useful metaphor.

Even should there be nothing more to it, I would wish to suggest that there is value in the gaining of new vantage points. Psychology provides us with some of the means of doing so, and some of these means are, it can be argued, peculiarly psychological. No discipline has a prescriptive right to be part of education, but psychology has a good case. There is point in discussing the teaching of it.

Part of the teaching is the continual attempt to re-think what is being taught, and how, and why. We hope this book will make a small contribution to the attempt.

REFERENCES

Atkinson, R. C. (1977). Reflections on Psychology's Past and Concerns about its Future. *American Psychologist*, **32**, 205–210.

Beck, F.A.G. (1964). *Greek Education 450–350 BC*. London: Methuen.

Beloff, J. (1973). *Psychological Sciences*. London: Crosby Lockwood Staples.

Bender, M. P. (1974). Psychology: Industry or Scientific Craft? *Bulletin of British Psychological Society*, **27**, 107–115.

Binder, A. (1973). A New Context for Psychology: Social Ecology. *American Psychologist*, **27**, 903–908.

Boring, E. G. (1950). *A History of Experimental Psychology*. 2nd edn. New York: Appleton Century Crafts.

Broadbent, D. E. (1973). *In Defence of Empirical Psychology*. London: Methuen.

Byrne, N. (1971). Psychologism: A Psychology or a Politic? Some Reflections on Mr Halpern's Paper. *Ontario Psychologist*, **3**, 215–222.

Clarke, A. M. (1972). Current Issues in the Training of Psychologists. *Australian Psychologist*, **7**, 90–94.

Dacey, M. L., and Wintrob, R. M. (1973). Human Behaviour: The Teaching of Social and Behavioural Sciences in Medical School. *Social Science and Medicine*, **7**, 943–957.

De Bono, E. (1971). *Practical Thinking*. London: Cape.

Halpern, H. (1971). How the University Student is Systematically Converted to Psychologism. *Ontario Psychologist*, **3**, 203–214.

Hilgard, E. R. Atkinson, R. L., and Atkinson, R. C. (1975). *Introduction to Psychology*. 6th edition. New York: Harcourt Brace Jovanovich.

Hobbes, T. (1651). *Leviathan*, reprinted 1976. London: Collins.

Heather, N. (1976). *Radical Perspectives in Psychology*. London: Methuen.

Hutchison, W. R. (1977). Behavioural Training Methods in a Higher Education Programme. *Bulletin of British Association for Behavioural Psychotherapy*, **5**, 89–95.

Koch, S. (1975). Language Communities, Search Cells, and the Psychological Studies. *Nebraska Symposium on Motivation*, **23**, 477–559.

Korn, J. H., and Nodine, B. F. (1975). Facts and Questions Concerning Career Training of the Psychology Major. *Teaching of Psychology*, **2**, 117–119.

Krasner, L. (in press). *Environmental Design and Human Behaviour: A Handbook of Theory and Application*. Oxford: Pergamon.

MacLeod, R. B. (1971). The Teaching of Psychology. *American Psychologist*, **26**, 345–249.

McKeachie, W. J. (1972). The Psychology Department and Society. *American Psychologist*, **27**, 643–646.

Miller, G. A. (1969). Psychology as a Means of Promoting Human Welfare. *American Psychologist*, **24**, 1063–1075.

Nazzaro, J. R. (1976). Identity Crisis in Psychology. *Change*, **8**, 44–45.

Ornstein, R. E. (1973). *The Nature of Human Consciousness*. San Francisco: Freeman.

Peterson, D. R. (1976). Is Psychology a Profession? *American Psychologist*, **31**, 572–581.

Pettifore, J. L. (1971). A Further Comment on Re-afferentiation in Psychology. *Canadian Psychologist*, **12**, 432–434.

Philips, N. (1968). Unpublished undergraduate thesis. West Ham College of Technology.

Pollack, D. (1972). Experiential Learning in College Psychology. *College Student Journal*, **6**, 100–104.

Rachman, S.J., and Philips, C. (1975). *Psychology and Medicine*. London: Temple Smith.

Radford, J. (1976). What Can We Learn from Zen? A Review and Some Speculations. *Psychologia*, **19**, 57–66.

Radford, J. (1978). Skills and Experiences in First Degree Courses. *Bulletin of British Psychological Society*, **31**, 42–43.

Regula, C. R. (1971). Some Suggestions for Improving the Psychology Laboratory Course Experience. *American Psychologist*, **26**, 1020–1021.

Singer, B. (1973). A Practical Annotated Bibliography on College Teaching and the Teaching of Psychology. *Catalog of Selected Documents in Psychology*, **3**, 34–35.

Snellgrove, L. (1974). International Pre-college Psychology. *Behavioural and Social Science Teacher*, **1**, 143–145.

Straker, D. (1976). The Training and Employment of Psychology Graduates. *SSRC Report HR2954* (available in National Lending Library).

Tait, I. (1973). Behavioural Science in Medical Education and Clinical Practice. *Social Science and Medicine*, **7**, 1003–1011.

Weinman, J. (1978). Integrating Psychology with General Medicine. *Bulletin of the British Psychological Society*, **31**, 352–355.

SECTION I

Methods in Teaching Psychology

There is of course no one way of teaching psychology or any other subject. Nor, probably, is there any systematic relationship between any dimension— such as novelty—on which techniques might be measured, and success rate. Some teachers can make anything work, others nothing. Psychology is taught so widely, and to such a heterogeneous audience, that almost certainly a large variety of methods is desirable. Psychologists might reasonably be expected to command at least a sample of them. They often are expected to know which is best. That is less reasonable, but at least they can apply some of the principles of the discipline: to be aware of possibilities, to look at whatever facts there may be, to examine systematically.

The following chapters attempt this. The division of material perhaps approximately reflects its importance at the present time, but the main aim has been to include a fairly wide range of what is, we hope, generally useful.

The Teaching of Psychology
Edited by J. Radford and D. Rose
© 1980 John Wiley & Sons Ltd.

1

Conventional Methods

MICHAEL J. A. HOWE

In the present chapter we shall discuss some of the traditional methods of teaching and learning that are encountered in psychology courses. The aim of teaching is always to help people learn, and the methods that are chosen to teach psychology generally reflect views and beliefs about the effectiveness of particular ways of learning. Academic courses that aim to instil an understanding of modern psychology are constructed from a number of components. All of the ones discussed in the following pages are likely to be present in a conventional degree course followed at a university or polytechnic. A shorter non-degree course, or a lower-level course in psychology would probably contain some of these components, but not all of them.

First, there will be lectures. We shall consider some evidence concerning their effectiveness, and we shall examine some research investigating a student activity, note-taking, that is typically undertaken by learners at the same time that the teacher is engaged in delivering the lecture. In addition, there will probably be some tutorials. These can take many forms, but they nearly always involve two-way communication between a teacher and a small number of students. Written materials provide another instructional component. The student acquires knowledge from reading various written materials, including books and journal articles. The 'teaching' element of such instruction is evident at the stage of the writing and preparation of the materials, but often the learner will have no direct contact with the teacher who communicates through the printed word, and not all printed materials encountered in a course will have been prepared with specifically didactic purpose in mind. In addition, most conventional courses in psychology will contain practical elements, intended to enable the learner to acquire skills in, for example, experimentation, experimental design, the use of statistics and test construction and use. We shall ignore practicals in the present chapter, since they are considered elsewhere in the book. However, each of the remaining components will receive some attention.

The use of the term 'method' to describe ways of instructing or ways of learning is a source of possible confusion. There is an illusory air of precision about a phrase such as 'the lecture method', which may lead us to neglect the fact that alternative uses of lectures, or of any other kind of instruction, may be utterly different from each other in standard, approach and style, and in numerous other ways that can influence what a student actually learns. The fact that one particular lecture is effective or otherwise does not provide any basis at all for statements about the effectiveness of lectures, or 'the lecture method' in general, any more than the success of one particular book indicates that all books are effective for instructing students.

Why do many teachers continue to depend upon conventional methods, despite the fact that newer procedures are available? There are at least two different, although not mutually exclusive, ways of answering such a question. For some teachers, adherence to older, traditional, methods may indicate a belief in their value, perhaps coupled with ignorance of alternative methods, or inexperience in using them, and a dislike in what might be regarded as 'new gimmicks'. In this case it is clear that using traditional procedures reflects a decision to follow them in preference to alternative ways of helping students learn.

A second kind of reaction to the above question is implicit in the fairly widespread feeling that methods and techniques of instruction, as such, are not always particularly important as determinants of what students actually manage to learn. Many lecturers consider that the particular techniques that are followed for instructing students have relatively small influences upon the effectiveness of teaching and learning, and that teachers would be better advised to direct their energies to other matters than worrying about which teaching techniques to adopt. A teacher who agrees with this view might well decide to follow the methods of teaching that are most familiar to him, and in the absence of firm evidence that alternative approaches to teaching are actually more successful such a position is eminently reasonable. Many of the personal and intellectual qualities that underlie good teaching have relatively little to do with instructional methods. The good teacher does not only communicate knowledge and skills, but he also encourages students to share in his enthusiasms, his interests, and his feelings for the subject. As Bruner (1966) has remarked, much successful teaching involves elements of identification, in which the student comes to share some of the teacher's attitudes towards and feelings about the field of instruction, and in some respects models himself upon the teacher. These outcomes of teaching, which are less tangible and harder to define and measure than the acquisition of knowledge, are perhaps especially important in a subject like psychology. Imparting knowledge is only one of the aims of teaching. In psychology it is at least equally important for the student to acquire the skills and habits of mind that enable him to engage in the activities and processes of psychological investigation, for instance by using research methods to investigate problems, or by developing ways to assess human attributes. If students are to learn to think and to act as psychologists it is highly desirable that the teacher is himself actively engaged in exercising psychological skills, either as a researcher or as a professional practitioner. If the teacher regards his role as being simply to pass on a body of knowledge the outcome is likely to be a dull, uninteresting approach, whatever method of instruction is employed.

LECTURES

The lecture method is frequently criticized, but the fact that it has managed to survive so long in the face of many technological developments in communicating knowledge should deter us from writing it off as a means of instruction, and alert us to possible strengths that are neglected by its critics. Samuel Johnson was among the earliest in a centuries-long succession of great scholars to suggest that lectures are outmoded. He studied at Oxford University, and compared lectures there unfavourably with books as a medium of instruction. He admitted that lectures might have been useful in previous eras, but thought that by his day, 'when all can read', lectures were unnecessary. One disadvantage, he noted, was that if a student did not attend to a particular part of the lecture, the point would be lost, and it would not be possible to go back to it in the way that is done when one is learning from a book.

Charles Darwin was a milder and more tolerant person than Dr Johnson, but his views about the lectures he attended at the Universities of Edinburgh and Cambridge were harsh and overwhelmingly negative. He wrote that the lectures he attended at Edinburgh were intolerably dull and, like Johnson, he argued that compared with reading, lectures had no advantage and many disadvantages. His geology lectures at Edinburgh, Darwin claimed, were so dull that at the time he became determined never to read a single book on the subject. (Fortunately he later changed his mind.) Sir Richard Burton, the scholar, explorer and translator, who went to Oxford University, found the lectures there to be very unsatisfactory, and he described the ones he was expected to attend as being incomprehensible or useless. Doubtless the list of eminent people who have regarded lectures as a poor means of instruction could be extended almost indefinitely.

The findings of empirical research into the effectiveness of lectures do not strongly contradict these views. The evidence has been surveyed by McLeish (1968) and Bligh (1972). Most evaluative studies of the lecture method take the form of comparison experiments, in which measures of students' learning following attendance at lectures is compared with learning following exposure to the same material via an alternative means of instruction. Many such studies report an absence of significant differences in learning between the alternative methods being compared, and since comparison studies in which no significant differences between conditions are observed are less likely to result in publication than investigations in which differences are found, the relatively large proportion of published studies in which it is reported that lectures and alternative methods resulted in no statistically significant differences in learning almost certainly underestimates the proportion of actual investigations in which such a finding occurred. Of the published comparison studies surveyed by Bligh, twenty-four found lecture methods to be more effective for imparting information than alternative methods (including, for example, discussion, reading, 'problem solving', and private study), twenty-one found lectures to be less effective, and sixty-one observed no significant differences in learning between lectures and the various alternative instructional procedures with which lectures were compared. Especially when we allow for the probable under-representation in the published reports of findings showing no differences in the effectiveness of different methods, it appears that whether the lecture or an alternative means of instruction is chosen is unlikely to have much effect upon what is actually learned.

As Bligh points out, imparting the kinds of knowledge that can be assessed in tests measuring the degree of learning is not the sole goal of education. Other important aims include stimulating thinking in students, and changing their attitudes. Furthermore, it would be useful to know how the lecture method compares with others in its popularity with students. If two methods are equally effective as direct aids to learning, there is a case for choosing the one which learners most enjoy. Bligh's survey included comparison studies relating to all three of these additional outcomes. Concerning the effectiveness of lectures at stimulating thought (measured in a variety of ways, a fact which makes it necessary to be cautious in accepting the comparability of the different studies) Bligh found that in none of the studies were lectures more effective than the alternative methods with which they were compared, whilst there were twenty-one studies in which lectures were found to be less effective than the alternative (discussions, seminars, reading or 'student-centred teaching') and five studies in which lectures and the alternative method were found to be equally effective. For changing attitudes, lectures were again generally unsuccessful. In only one of the twenty-five comparison studies surveyed by Bligh was the lecture method found to be more effective, whereas alternative teaching methods changed attitudes to a greater extent than lectures did in fifteen studies and in the remaining nine comparison studies no significant differences were found in the effects of the methods that were compared. Furthermore, Bligh's survey also indicated that lectures are relatively unpopular. Out of fifteen comparison studies, only three found lectures to be liked by students more than the alternative ('essay work', audiotapes and seminars), nine found that the alternative methods were liked to a greater extent than lectures, and in three comparison studies no significant differences were observed.

In short, the evidence would appear to indicate that lectures are doomed!

However, Dr Johnson appeared to reach a similar conclusion two centuries ago, but despite all the objective criticisms that have been raised to their use as a means of instruction, lectures continue to survive and prosper. The long survival of lectures cannot be explained away as a simple instance of educational inertia. Were that to be the case we would expect that lectures would be used more often in the older, 'traditional', disciplines—for which they once formed the sole practical means of teaching large numbers of students—than in subject areas such as psychology and other newly founded disciplines, which hardly existed at all before books became widely available. Certainly, there are some educational institutions, such as the Open University, in which lectures play only a small part. But in most fields of instruction, and certainly in psychology, lectures continue to be in widespread use, despite the ever-increasing variety of available alternatives, which, as Bligh's survey makes clear, are at least equally successful at meeting important aims, and often more so.

Why do lectures go on surviving? In addition to the disadvantages we have already mentioned, it is clear that they are a somewhat inflexible way of instructing students and one that cannot be justified on grounds of economy. The fact that the lecturer and all the students have to attend a particular location at the same time brings difficulties associated with finding room space, timetabling and transportation. A system in which knowledge is provided in hourly bursts at weekly intervals is inevitably inflexible, and most alternative methods of learning give students a greater degree of freedom to decide on times, place and rates of learning that are better adapted to the needs of the individual.

To understand why the lecture method does continue to thrive, despite all the objections we have raised, it may be necessary to seek for reasons that are not directly 'educational' in the obvious sense of having an immediate impact upon learning as such. I suspect that lectures help meet some important needs of the individual learner. First, they provide a social function. Learning is largely a private activity, and students may often feel isolated and lonely. The lecture may have some of the attributes of a social occasion, in which the student is reassured by the presence of others who share some of his anxieties and aspirations, and it may serve as a meeting-place for the discussion of matters of mutual concern. Second, once he has decided to attend a particular lecture, the student is relatively free from distractions and from the need to make further decisions about how study time is to be allocated, which bedevils individual study. Once a lecture has begun, the easiest course of action is to attend to it, whereas the individual studying on his own may be tempted to spend his time on alternative activities that appear to be more fascinating or less prone to induce anxiety. Third, lectures may serve to meet a ritual function, which we might term 'putting learning on display'. The delivery of a lecture makes it apparent to all concerned that the students are properly engaged in the activity of learning, the teacher is meeting his obligation to communicate knowledge and the educational institution is quite properly filling its role as a market place for education. In consequence, everyone receives the concrete reassurance that educational aims are being pursued.

NOTE-TAKING

Note-taking provides an important element of traditional forms of higher education. We tend to associate note-taking with instruction through lectures, but of course students often take notes relating to materials they read. Most students depend heavily on the notes they have made, especially in the period immediately preceding examinations, as is evident from the great distress that is apparent on the rare occasions when an individual loses his notes.

The functions of students' note-taking activities fall into two main categories. First, taking notes provides a practical way to record information that the student needs to have at his disposal. Second, note-taking activities may have effects that facilitate learning relatively directly, or contribute to educational goals in some other way. In the present context we are concerned with the second category of functions. However, the practical outcome of providing a record of necessary information is not unimportant, and although note-taking is not so indispensible as a way of achieving this aim as it was in the days before Xerox machines and other technological devices for providing quick and cheap reproduction of printed and written materials were available, even now there are many situations in which the most effective and convenient way for a student to provide himself with a permanent record of information from a lecture, a book or an article is to make notes on it. The fact that in taking notes the student is able to select those aspects of the available information which he needs, and can write it down in a form that is optimally useful to himself, adds to the value of note-taking, compared with alternative means of reproducing knowledge.

Does note-taking make a contribution to the learning of psychology, apart from providing the learner with information he requires? It is difficult to give a universally applicable answer to this question, because so much depends on the particular circumstances and the particular individuals concerned. First, people differ, and one individual may receive great benefit from a technique that is not at all helpful to another person. Second, a great deal depends upon the kind of material on which notes are being taken, its standard, the extent to which effective representation of the important content depends upon literal reproduction of the content, and other aspects of the nature of the materials, the characteristics of the learner, and the impact of the particular materials on the particular student involved. The fact that these variables exert large influences makes it impossible to make statements about the impact of note-taking on learning that are both simple on the one hand and widely applicable on the other.

A number of research investigations have compared learning by following conditions of learning which did, and did not, include provision for note-taking. However, as in the research comparing the effectiveness of lectures and alternative instructional methods, there is no clear consensus of findings indicating that note-taking procedures are invariably either superior or inferior to the alternatives. In a survey by Howe and Godfrey (1977) the authors note that in a number of studies note-taking procedures have been found to have no appreciable effects on learning. Thus McClendon (1958) found no differences in learning between university students who took detailed notes, brief notes or no notes at all as they listened to short lectures. Eisner and Rohde (1959) found no evidence that note-taking during lectures produced more learning than note-taking which was delayed until the lecture had finished. Crawford (1925) observed some very small differences in recall between note-takers and individuals who did not take notes, but whereas subjects in the former group performed slightly better on recall tests administered some days after the lecture, the individuals who did not take notes obtained higher scores on a 'true–false' recall test administered immediately following the lecture. A number of further comparison studies, for example by MacManaway (1968) and one conducted by Jones (1923, cited in Hartley and Marshall, 1974), also yielded insignificant differences. In an experiment by Howe (1970a) students listened to a short extract from a modern novel, and 14 days later they were asked to attempt written recall. No differences in performance were observed between subjects who were told to take notes and students instructed simply to listen.

Some investigations have yielded findings favouring note-taking. Di Vesta and Gray (1972) found that individuals instructed to take notes as they listened to 500-word passages on unfamiliar topics recalled a greater number of the ideas presented in the passages than subjects instructed merely to listen. Weener (1974) describes an experiment by Berliner in which it was found that subjects who made notes during the presentation of a 45-minute videotaped lecture retained the content more accurately than subjects who were simply told to pay attention. Fisher and Harris (1973) found that students who made notes during a lecture and were subsequently permitted to use them for review purposes performed better than students in other conditions. Similarly, Peters (1972) found that subjects who took notes during a taped presentation performed better on a multiple-choice recall test than individuals who were not permitted to take notes, and he also describes similar findings of an experiment conducted by McHendry.

Unfortunately, neither in psychology nor in other areas of instruction do clear patterns of findings emerge concerning the circumstances in which it would be safe to predict that note-taking will either facilitate learning or restrict it, as was found in some studies reported by Peters (1972) and McLeish (1968).

A limitation of the comparison studies summarized above is that they take little or no account of the individual differences that, as we have suggested, may partly determine whether or not note-taking will aid a person to learn.

Another problem with these findings is that they tell us very little about the direct outcomes of taking notes. If we discovered that in one experiment note-takers learn more than individuals who take no notes, we would remain in the dark concerning the precise manner in which note-taking activities exert their influence upon learners.

There are a number of possible ways in which note-taking activities might directly influence the human learner. One is by simply helping the person to attend effectively to the material being presented to him. The student who is listening to a lecture is placed in a somewhat passive role in certain respects, and opportunites for taking initiatives and being active are somewhat limited. Furthermore, the evidence suggests that prolonged physical immobility may be incompatible with effective functioning. Note-taking can provide a valuable function simply by giving an opportunity for the learner to be active and to behave in a manner that is relatively independent. Simply enabling the learner to *do* something that is under his own control, rather than just receiving the information to which he is exposed, may make it considerably easier to sustain attention to the main task.

The activity of note-taking may also contribute to learning in other ways. For example, in order to transform lecture or printed materials into note form it may be necessary for a student to organize and recode the information, and some findings suggests that the cognitive activities involved in doing so can strongly influence the probability that the information will be retained (Howe, 1970b). Furthermore, as we noted earlier, the fact that in producing his notes the learner may have expressed the content in the way that makes the greatest sense to himself as an individual can result in him possessing a version of the material that is especially well adapted to his needs.

In one study, Howe and Godfrey (1977) examined the notes made by students attending either of two psychology lectures. Previous findings (Howe, 1970a) had established that there was a statistically significant positive correlation between the amount of learning by different students and the extent to which, in making notes, they were able to communicate the maximum number of meaningful ideas in the minimum number of words. Furthermore, when students took notes as they listened to a passage, those parts of the content that were reproduced in a particular student's notes were about six times more likely to be recalled by that student than parts of the passage that did not appear in his notes. This was despite the fact that the experimenter 'borrowed' the students' notes as soon as they had been completed, ensuring that they received no opportunity to refer to the notes up to the time when retention was assessed. Howe and Godfrey decided to undertake a naturalistic study, in which the notes made by students attending one first-year psychology lecture and one second-year psychology lecture were reproduced and carefully examined. The students were subsequently tested to assess their retention of information from the lectures, so it was possible to look for relationships between what a student actually learned and the contents of his notes. Since no prior warning was given either of the test or of the fact that the experimenter would ask permission to copy the notes (a request that was never refused) the circumstances of note-taking were quite normal, so far as the students were aware at the time.

There were some large individual differences between students in both the amount and the form of the notes made, but few systematic relationships were observed between learning and patterns of note-taking. In one lecture the number of words appearing in students' notes ranged from eighty-nine to 1167, the mean number being 601, and in the other lecture the average number of words in students' notes was 555, the range being from sixty-five to 836. For one lecture, but not the other, the correlation between scores on the test of learning and number of words in notes ($+ 0.31$) verged on statistical significance, but for the other group there was no significant correlation. The test scores of subjects who spent some time reading or copying their notes were significantly higher than the scores of students who did not. Many students increased the content of their notes by making use of abbreviations, and there was a positive correlation between the number of abbreviations used and the number of words appearing in an individual's notes. Students varied considerably in their use of definite and indefinite articles, which were not essential for comprehension of the lectures. Some students used no articles at all, but others used them as many as thirty times.

Inspection of the contents of the notes revealed that many students copied down anything that was written on the blackboard, irrespective of its real importance. During the course of one of the lectures, there was a short anecdote, concerning a man called Preyer. Although this name was of no significance in the context of the lecture it appeared in most students' notes, often underlined. The lecturer was surprised that students had taken so much notice of this item, and in trying to account for the reason he remembered that he had absent-mindedly written the man's name on the blackboard. Writing words on the blackboard does appear to give the lecturer one way of exercising some control over students' note-taking activities. The same lecturer noticed that a negative statement made in his lecture very frequently appeared in students' notes without the negative. For instance he carefully explained that the human infant is '*not* like some ball of clay, infinitely malleable . . . ', but a number of students reported the opposite.

TUTORIALS

Tutorials form another element in the teaching of psychology. Contributing to the difficulty of generalizing about their effectiveness is the fact that to even less an extent than in the case of lectures can tutorials be said to constitute a single method of instruction. Tutorials in psychology can differ from one another in a bewildering variety of ways. For a start, much depends upon the personalities, aptitudes and the knowledge possessed by the lecturer and the participating students. The number of students involved, which may be only one or as many as eight or ten, has a large effect on the patterns of communication that are possible. Some students and some lecturers are much more at ease than others in the relatively informal and loosely structured situations characteristic of most tutorials. Discussions may involve roughly equal contributions by all students, or one or two may dominate. The extent to which the students participating are similar or different from one another in intelligence, experience and knowledge can make large differences in the way in which a tutorial proceeds. Apparently humdrum considerations such as the shape of the room and the pattern of seating can have important influences.

Partly because most of the above factors are only to a limited extent under the control of the lecturer, it is often almost impossible for him to know in advance the form a particular tutorial will take, or to predict whether or not it will be broadly effective or not. It is common for lecturers to remark that both their most rewarding teaching experiences and their most frustrating experiences of failure take place in tutorials, and I suspect that the sheer unpredictability and uncontrollability of tutorials is a key reason.

In many respects it is desirable that tutorials should take an open and flexible form, with emphasis on spontaneity. The more structure that is deliberately imposed by the teacher on the form of the tutorial, the more predictable the outcome, and the more control the lecturer has over what happens. However, a highly structured tutorial tends to be 'teacher-centred' rather than 'student-centred' and it can be argued that the most effective use is made of learning occasions involving a lecturer and a small number of students in those informal face-to-face contact situations in which the students are given a fair amount of freedom to make use of the lecturer as a 'teaching resource' in whatever way they, the students, think fit. In such circumstances the student is regarded as being an active individual who uses the lecturer's experience to answer questions and to give advice that the student requires. However, not every student has the social or the intellectual skills to make effective use of his teachers in this way, however convincing this conceptualization of the tutorial appears to be, and many tutors find themselves in an uneasy compromise between trying to ensure that tutorials maintain a lively flow and avoiding playing too dominant a role.

In addition to the variability in the form of tutorials that is dictated by the individuals participating in them and by the limited degree of structure imposed by the teacher, tutorials also vary considerably in their actual content. Tutorials can be used in a variety of different ways, and a particular tutor may attempt to maintain roughly the same format for each of his tutorials or he may vary their structure as well as their content from one week to the next. A tutorial may involve the reading of essays by students. In this event, a student reads his essay, and the lecturer and (less often) other students may interrupt with questions or comments. This kind of activity is characteristically encountered in traditional 'teacher-centred' tutorials, and it is often excruciatingly boring for all concerned.

More commonly, the object of the tutorial will be to discuss an agreed topic. Typically, each student will have read certain materials, and individuals will be expected to 'introduce' the topic under discussion. Depending on the above-mentioned personal and intellectual characteristics of the teacher and the students, and the extent to which they have taken the trouble to prepare for the tutorial by acquiring sufficient knowledge to make constructive discussion possible, tutorials of this form can be extremely lively and useful, or they can be very dull. For better or worse, it is common experience that psychology students find it much easier to engage in discussion on those topics that concern the more 'personal' and clinical aspects of the subject—dreaming, schizophrenia, etc.—than on 'hard science' aspects of psychology that the teacher may well feel have more to contribute to the students' education. The degree to which the teacher and the students take the trouble to become informed about the topic to be discussed is clearly important. In the absence of adequate preparation, discussions can easily degenerate into the sharing of ignorance.

Various additional activities can aptly take place within a tutorial session. Sometimes the time will be used for discussing forthcoming examinations, or the group might read through some previous examination questions, and the lecturer may provide specific advice about answering questions or general advice about effective examination strategies and techniques. Students are naturally concerned about future examinations, and they appreciate the opportunity to talk about the things that worry them in a small group consisting of a lecturer and some other students. At the same time—and this applies to all tutorials—the teacher has an opportunity to observe any signs of undue stress, panic or acute anxiety on the part of a particular student, and a tutor who has established satisfactory personal relationships with his tutees will often be the first member of the teaching staff to become aware of important personal problems that are not straightforwardly academic. The support that a tutor can give will vary and may range from arranging for an exam-phobic student to have opportunities to 'practice' examination techniques under conditions of low anxiety, to simply listening sympathetically to problems and offering occasional advice or useful information, and to helping students gain access to appropriate helping agencies for counselling or, occasionally, psychiatric help.

The list of tutorial activities could be extended further, and the considerable flexibility of tutorials, which is perhaps the greatest single strength of this kind of learning situation, makes it virtually impossible to evaluate tutorials as an instructional method. One prerequisite for measuring the effectiveness of a teaching method is specifying the aims it is intended to achieve, but the legitimate aims of tutorials are clearly numerous. Practically the only generalization

that can be made about all tutorials is that they provide opportunities for relatively informal contact between a lecturer and a small number of students. This
is valuable for many educational aims, so it is hardly surprising that tutorials
serve a number of useful functions.

OTHER ACTIVITIES

Institutions which depend upon conventional forms of instruction in psychology
place varying degrees of emphasis on the importance of reading and written
work. Many university teachers assume that reading provides the primary
means to acquire the knowledge on which students are examined, the main
roles of lectures being to provide necessary guidance and structure, to direct
students to sources of detailed information, to integrate information encountered in different sources, and to make students aware of unfamiliar topics and theories, rather than being to provide detailed information. It is felt that reading
provides the best method for the learner to acquire detailed knowledge, and
that students enter university having already acquired the basic skills necessary
for learning from what they read. Guidance in locating books, journals and
abstract materials within the field of psychology is often provided, formally
or informally, either by lecturers or by library staff.

The assumption that students who enter on a degree course have previously
acquired the general reading skills they need may be a correct one for the majority of students. However, there are instances when considerable guidance is
required. For example, many students who are used to reading at a rate that
is appropriate for most of the materials they have encountered in, say, history
or english literature find it difficult to appreciate that in order to comprehend
unfamiliar materials in the more technical fields encountered in a psychology
course, for example in statistics or in physiological psychology, it may be
essential to reduce the rate of reading very considerably. Some students have
a tendency to read something through once, at their normal reading rate, and
on discovering they have not understood it, leap to the conclusion that they
are quite incapable of understanding the content. These people can be helped
considerably by a tutor who explains the need to read the passage much more
slowly than usual, a sentence at a time, and to repeat the same passage until
the meaning gradually becomes clear. Many students are quite surprised to
realize that when they do proceed slowly and repetitively they can begin to
understand something at first appeared to be quite outside their grasp. A small
amount of guidance in this matter can often do a great deal to increase a
student's confidence in his ability to learn from unfamiliar printed materials.

All institutions involved with teaching psychology experience problems in
trying to ensure that students can have ready access to the library materials
they require. The difficulties are somewhat greater in psychology than some
other subjects, owing to the fact that so large a proportion of the information

that post-elementary psychology students need is to be found in journals rather than in books. The purchasing powers of most students being limited, it has to be assumed that the greater part of the reading matter a student encounters will be from a library. A major problem is to try to ensure that all students can have access to materials of which the library has only one or two copies. There can be few lecturers who have not heard the complaint that all the library materials a student wanted to use for an essay were unobtainable because other students were borrowing them.

The various ways of trying to ensure that many students can gain access to a small number of library copies all have disadvantages. The usual compromise situation is to have some kind of a 'temporary loan' system, in which the period for which a book or article can be borrowed is strictly restricted, typically to a day or so, or even to just a few hours. This is not desirable from the point of view of the student who wants to study a long book in detail, but it does at least ensure that the book is not monopolized by a tiny proportion of the people who require it.

It is generally assumed that writing skills, like those of reading, have been satisfactorily acquired by the time a student enters university, but students who manifestly lack the ability to express themselves in good written English are by no means uncommon. Practice in essay writing can lead to improved writing skills, but most teachers of psychology consider that this aspect of general education should not be one of their main concerns. However many students' essays demonstrate an inability to communicate effectively what the individual intends to express, and deficiencies in writing ability continue to be a cause for concern.

REFERENCES

Bligh, D. A. (1972). *What's The Use of Lectures?* Harmondsworth: Penguin Books.
Bruner, J. S. (1966). *Toward a Theory of Instruction.* Cambridge, Mass.: Harvard University Press.
Crawford, C. C. (1925). The Correlation between Lecture Notes and Quiz Papers. *Journal of Education Research,* **12**, 379–386.
Di Vesta, F. J., and Gray, G. S. (1972). Listening and Note-taking. *Journal of Educational Psychology,* **63**, 8–14.
Eisner, S., and Rohde, K. (1959). Note-taking In or After the Lecture. *Journal of Educational Psychology,* **50**, 301–304.
Fisher, J. L., and Harris, M. B. (1973). Effect of Note-taking and Review on Recall. *Journal of Educational Psychology,* **65**, 321–325.
Hartley, J., and Marshall, S. (1974). On Notes and Note-taking. *Universities Quarterly,* **28**, 225–235.
Howe, M. J. A. (1970a). Using Students' Notes to Examine the Role of the Individual Learner in Acquiring Meaningful Subject Matter. *Journal of Educational Research,* **64**, 61–63.
Howe, M. J. A. (1970b). Repeated Presentation and Recall of Meaningful Prose. *Journal of Educational Psychology,* **61**, 214–219.

Howe, M. J. A., and Godfrey, J. (1977). *Student Note-taking as an Aid to Learning*. Exeter: Exeter University Teaching Services.

McClendon, T. (1958). An Experimental Study of the Relationship between Note-taking Practices and Listening Comprehension of College Freshmen during Expository Lectures. *Speech Monographs*, **25**, 222–228.

McLeish, J. (1968). *The Lecture Method*. Cambridge Monographs on Teaching Methods No. 1. Cambridge: Cambridge Institute of Education.

MacManaway, L. A. (1968). Using Lecture Scripts. *Universities Quarterly*, **22**, 327–336.

Peters, D. L. (1972). Effects of Note-taking and Rate of Presentation on Short-term Objective Test Performance. *Journal of Educational Psychology*, **34**, 43–50.

Weener, P. (1974). Note-taking and Student Verbalization as Instrumental Learning Activities. *Instructional Science*, **3**, 51–74.

The Teaching of Psychology
Edited by J. Radford and D. Rose
© 1980 John Wiley & Sons Ltd.

2

Experiential Methods

CARY L. COOPER

WHAT IS EXPERIENTIAL LEARNING?

The ever-increasing use of personal growth groups in the USA was highlighted in 1969 by *Newsweek* magazine. They described a one-night introduction to an encounter group in San Francisco in which 200 participants had paid $5 to take part in a 'relatively leaderless, structureless, agendaless "be in" intended to express human feelings and to cultivate close emotional ties between people'. They went on to say that the experiential movement (encounter groups, *T*-groups, gestalt groups, body-awareness training, etc.) 'is involving Americans in their biggest emotional binge since VJ Day'; and that, as Carl Rogers (1970) observed, 'these groups are the most rapidly spreading social phenomenon in the country'. This article, like many others in recent years (Koziey, Loken and Field, 1971; Appley and Winter, 1973) emphasized the role of experiential learning in helping the 'normal neurotic' to gain greater self-understanding and awareness and ultimately to be more behaviourally adaptable. The focus of this attention is on the individual and how he benefits from direct personal involvement and experience within a group context. Although these personal growth groups attract a great deal of publicity and tend to create the image for all group training activities, there are a vast number of people who use group techniques more pragmatically, in the context of teaching psychology, under-standing human behaviour, and changing and making people aware of organi-zational problems and interactions. Over the last five to six years more and more psychologists, sociologists, organization theorists, etc., have been designing and adapting experiential learning groups to meet teaching and train-ing needs.

The following excerpt (Mangham, Hayes and Cooper, 1970) from a session of an in-company *T*-group for a top management team will hopefully illustrate the dynamics of experiential learning groups. It was felt that it might be worth-while to incorporate a description of one of the basic experiential group methods, in this case an organizational team-building *T*-group, for those readers coming to the subject area without any previous knowledge of it. I chose the *T*-group because this form of training led the vanguard for all subsequent experiential techniques—it was the metaphorical 'pollen' of techniques ranging from gestalt and encounter groups to organizational development.

This description is a real-life account of the use of experiential methods in resolving 'people problems' in a large heavy manufacturing plant in the north of England. The work roles of the various people featured below are: *Eric*, plant director; *John*, joint deputy plant director; *Bill*, joint deputy plant director; *Nicholas*, works engineer; *Harry*, commercial manager; *Consultant*, *T*-group trainer and management consultant.

> NICHOLAS: You [Bill] say that John and Eric are on the beam all the time, I'm not too sure, I wonder if John really does think like Eric, often John seems to agree with Eric a little too readily—so quickly, that he cannot really have thought about it at all.
>
> ERIC: No, that's quite unfair, I don't see the relationship with John in the same way you do, Nicholas. I feel that I sometimes follow John. Often when I reflect at the end of the day I realize that it's John who has got his way and not the other way around, not a case of him coming in too early, a case of him leading me along.
>
> CONSULTANT: What is it that you are saying, Eric? Are you explaining that what Nicholas feels is not the way it is? If I were a full-time member of this group I'd be a little concerned about the relationship between you two.
>
> JOHN: Yes, it's a good point that Nicholas brought up. He sees the role I play opposite Eric as being different from the role I play opposite other people. Sometimes in the short run I might appear to go along with Eric—that's while I think it through, in the long run, you know, I sometimes disagree.
>
> NICHOLAS: This may be so, but on occasions I have felt that you have gone along with Eric even when you didn't agree. In short I feel that Eric can control this group; the two of you together are a formi-dable force.
>
> JOHN: I do feel more sympathetic to Eric than to others; Harry would come at the bottom of any hierarchy of sympathy, in between is Bill and you, Nicholas. I have sympathy with Eric because he works bloody hard. I have a sense of values and this is damned important to me— working hard; but secondly, he's an effective thinker, therefore I listen

to him, I try to understand, whereas with Harry, after listening for a long time I certainly can't understand him.

NICHOLAS: However, with me, occasionally you have been jocular and sort of down-putting, and this bloody irritates me.

JOHN: Well, why don't you say so at the time?

NICHOLAS: Because I feel blocked out, by you two sitting up there smiling at each other, in the know, in each other's pockets all the time. It's bloody difficult for anyone else to get a point of view across. It does surprise me sometimes, that you had been putting pressure on Harry. I remember two or three weeks ago I got bloody angry toward you, John, about some issue, but basically it was because I saw you as putting a hell of a lot of pressure on Harry.

JOHN: Well, you seeing that sort of thing upsets me because I honestly didn't know we were putting that much pressure on Harry, really I didn't, Eric might have noticed it but I did not.

ERIC [returning to the issue of the special relationship]: I can't quite see how this special relationship that John and I are supposed to have can cause problems for the rest of the group. It might be useful to have a look at other people's relationship with me in the group, as I see them anyway. Maybe they'd like to say something about it after I've finished. Bill—you see I'm really very neutral towards you, Bill—this could be one of the problems that's facing this group. As I see it, you don't appear to have built any relationships within the group—you have some sort of relationships outside. There's no meaningful ones within the group. Harry, well, we've said a lot about that relationship. You Nicholas, well, there have been a few problems, not many. You're learning you know. You've made a few mistakes, for example with the shop stewards. You made me mad on occasions but you're doing all right, you're coming along.

CONSULTANT: Nicholas, how do you feel about that?

NICHOLAS: Like a schoolboy being patted on the head by the headmaster. It's as if Eric is saying to me 'you're an up and coming young lad, not yet in the same league as John but you're doing all right'.

ERIC: Well, that's the way it is, I'm sorry—you know, in my opinion, Nicholas, you have done well, in my opinion you aren't yet dealing with the same issues, thinking in the same way as John and I. If it's a question of you being in this group then I'm one hundred per cent for it.

JOHN: And this is really what we're still discussing, whether or not we want this group to exist at all, and if so, who's to be in.

CONSULTANT: Well, it seems to me that the two people you are very uncertain about, and who are uncertain about their own position

in all of this, are Bill and Harry. Before you try to gain their full commitment to the group or to imply their rejection, it might be useful
if you could spell out the pros and cons of their commitment. What's
in it for them?

ERIC: I said before and I'm going to repeat it now, that really the
only way forward is to make a frank assessment and I expect the same
and am willing to accept the same being done on me. As I see it, Bill
and Harry have little to gain in terms of promotions, so this group isn't
going to be a stepping-stone to anything else. The only reward can
be intrinsic, neither Bill nor Harry have a future outside this plant
as far as I know, unless they leave the company altogether. For John—
I would say he is the company's next plant director, and there's no
doubt about that. He's very intelligent, a very capable man and he's
just about the right sort of age. He's got all the energy, all the drive,
everything that's necessary to make a plant director. He'd make a hell
of a lot better manager here than I do. Nicholas, well again, very unsure:
young enough, has got enough ability, but the whole role of the engineer,
and the whole company structure is, as you know, currently in turmoil.
Could be that this group will be very useful for him, to help him move
into the area of general management, so it can make the transition to
assistant plant director, or even to plant director at some stage, much
easier for him. So for two of the people, Bill and Harry, the group holds
no attractions in terms of extrinsic rewards, it holds the attraction
of being in something that makes the decisions, that implements them,
that looks ahead, and that works in the very ambiguous area of general
management. But the reward must essentially be inside themselves.
Is this the sort of thing they really want to be doing with their time?
For the other two it can clearly be of intrinsic and extrinsic use—it
can give them satisfaction, it can also provide a platform for moving
on. Now I can understand how many pressures there are, especially
as you get older; when you're young your wife doesn't mind so much
the long hours. They're expected if you're going to get on, but
remember they become less sympathetic when you've reached your
career ceiling. When that happens it is time to make the decision. I see
this group as being one that has to meet frequently, one that has to
make big decisions, one that has to take time, one which has to check
out, one which has really got to learn to work together. Make no
mistake about it, I basically want to work together, you see, people are
one of my problems. I have accused John earlier of being unemotional
but I feel that really unemotional one is me. I have to work with lots of
people and I keep getting in the same sort of problems we've been
taking about—these last two or three days. I just keep getting in these
problems and I want to get out of them, and this group can help me do

that. They can help me understand me, and they can help me become a better plant director.

CONSULTANT: Well, you've said something about what might be in it for other people, Eric, what's in it for you?

NICHOLAS: That's the question I was just about to ask.

ERIC: Well, what's in it for me? I'm not viewing the success of this group as some sort of vehicle for promotion, no, I'm well past that sort of position, I'm not even sure that if it were offered to me I would want to take it. In some ways this group idea runs counter to what the company thinks about the way to work. In general, the boys upstairs think we should just tell people what to do. We shouldn't discuss things with them, we shouldn't try to talk things through, so I don't think they would look very favourably on it. Even if I were in the position to be promoted, anyway—and I am at the point of not really wanting to go further, not wanting to do anything else, other than just be a good plant director here—team work would not be viewed favourably. What will it do to me in other ways? I think it will make life a hell of a lot easier, because being at the top in an organisation like this is—it's a cliché, I know—a bloody lonely job, and I just want to be able to talk to people to get things sorted out, to be able to get good and honest advice. That's what I want out of it, to be part of something, not trapped in a cold image of the boss, somebody who tells you to do things. You see, I think that at the top it should be a sort of 'we' thing, not an 'I'. We should want to do something, we should agree to it, not 'I want you to do something for me'.

This short description of a particular organizational *T*-group highlights some of the major characteristics of experiential methods in general. First, as can be seen from the above example, the training is primarily 'process-orientated' as distinct from 'content-orientated'. That is, the primary stress is on the *feeling* level of communications between people rather than on the informational or conceptual. Individuals are encouraged to deal with their feelings about themselves and others and to explore the impact they have upon one another. Second, the heart of experiential learning is found in their use of the 'small group', allowing a high level of participation, involvement, and free communication. The case above shows how open and uncluttered communications can be achieved in a small group. Third, these groups are directed toward developing the individual, both as a person and as a person in a particular work role; helping him to become more aware of himself and his impact on others, to behave more effectively in face-to-face situations, and to reassess his fundamental interpersonal approach (specifically in relation to his needs of power, affection, identity, aggression, etc). Fourth, that these group methods can help to *develop* the organization by encouraging team-building within a work group. And finally, in the early days of experiential groups (i.e. *T*-groups), the training design tended to be *unstructured*, that is, the trainees themselves decided what they wanted to talk about, what kinds of problems they wished to deal with, and what means that wanted to use in reaching their goals. The group leader acted as a facilitator who drew attention to behaviour as it developed in the group. More and more, however, there has been a movement away from unstructured, non-directive groups toward predetermined exercise-based ones. Unstructuredness and non-directiveness are no longer characteristics that one can associate with experiential learning groups (as discussed in detail in Cooper, 1976).

In summary, although there are a wide variety of experiential methods in use, they all have the common *objective* of developing the individual and/or his work group/organization in the common *learning dynamic* of emphasizing the 'process' or feeling level of communications between people, and the common *vehicle* of utilizing the 'small group' for achieving the desired objectives.

FOR WHAT TEACHING OBJECTIVES ARE EXPERIENTIAL METHODS APPROPRIATE?

As you might be able to predict, there are a number of possible outcomes of experiential learning methods. Miles (1960) summarized a number of these as increases in:

> *Sensitivity*:   the ability to perceive what is actually going on in a social situation (including both behavioural events and inferred feelings of other persons).
> *Diagnostic ability*:   the skill of assessing ongoing social situations in a way that enables effective action; the employment of appropriate explanatory categories to understand reasons for presented interaction.
> *Action skill*:   the ability to intervene effectively in ongoing situations in such a way as to maximize personal and group effectiveness and satisfaction . . . .

All these experiential method goals have one thing in common: they are directed toward developing the individual; helping him to become more aware of himself and his impact on others, to behave more effectively in face-to-face situations, and to re-assess his fundamental interpersonal approach (specifically in relation to his needs of power, affection, and aggression). In addition to these objectives, there are at least two others. First, as Gottschalk and Pattison (1969) emphasize, in an issue of the *American Journal of Psychiatry* dealing specifically with this form of training, *T*-groups can increase one's understanding of the psychology of group and intergroup behaviour. In this context, the concepts of role differentiation, group normative structure, and authority relationships can be explored in the course of the development of this ongoing self-analytic group. Thus, the skills of people in observing group and intergroup behaviour can be enhanced.

And second, another primary aim of experiential learning is 'to improve team-work within the organization'—to develop the organization as a team rather than the individual as a person, as in the illustration at the beginning of this chapter. In this situation, one would assemble for discussion of inter-personal problems on the job, an ongoing work group; the group might include, for instance, an industrial manager and his subordinates; or a senior social worker and his/her social workers under supervision; or any other group of people who work together and whose interpersonal relationships may be or are preventing them from performing their work effectively. This area of interest is commonly referred to as 'organizational development'.

Broadly speaking, therefore, the experiential methods can and have been used to achieve a number of different outcomes which can crudely be divided into three categories: learning about one's self, learning about group and intergroup dynamics, and improving work group relations. These objectives are not achieved by relying on a standard teaching design, although a number of constituents of the method described earlier are common to all such designs. This form of training requires careful specification of the goal or problem in a particular situation and the creation of a training design which will meet these goals or resolve problems. In addition, the training programme required to achieve a particular goal can vary greatly from situation to situation. For example, a training programme to improve work group relations among a group of waiters and waitresses might differ substantially in design from one for undergraduate students on a psychology course. The objectives of the training may be relatively similar—to reduce interpersonal obstacles and improve the work group climate—but the approach employed may, within limits, differ in quite a number of ways: in the balance of conceptual and experiential learning; in the inclusion or exclusion of boss, subordinates, colleagues, or related staff; in the orientation of the training staff (person-centred vs. group-centred), etc.

EVALUATION OF THE EFFECTIVENESS OF EXPERIENTIAL METHODS

Positive Effects

A large number of studies (Cooper, 1979) have been carried out evaluating the effects of experiential methods and they come up with roughly the same kind of conclusions. The earliest follow-up study was conducted by

Miles (1965) and involved thirty-four American elementary school principals who had participated in two-week T-group laboratories. He used two control groups of untrained principals for comparison, one randomly chosen and the other nominated by the trainee principals. All were asked to describe, via an open-ended change-description questionnaire, the ways in which they had changed their job-centred behaviour over an eight to ten months period following the T-group. These self-reports were compared with similar descriptions completed by a number of their work associates; 73 per cent of the T-group trained participants, in comparison to 29 per cent and 17 per cent of the nominated and random control groups respectively, were reported to have changed.

To further test the generality of Miles' findings, Bunker (1965) studied a sample of participants (mainly managers) from six different training laboratories conducted by the National Training Laboratories (NTL). His basic methodology followed Miles in that he used a matched-pair control group obtained by participant nomination of work colleagues. Bunker used a total of 346 subjects, trained and controls. He found that 66.7 per cent of the T-group trained participants as compared to 33.3 per cent of controls were reported by their work associates to have positively changed. As with the Miles' study non-trained subjects were also perceived to have changed. A later study by Valiquet (1968) supported Bunker's results with sixty participants from T-group type programmes run *within* a company for its managers. He found roughly the same results as Miles and Bunker that nearly two-thirds show positive change but that controls also show some change.

The only British study (Moscow, 1969) to use work colleagues' perception of change and which replicates the above studies, has shown that T-group participants (drawn from management) show changes very similar in type and frequency to those reported by Miles (1960, 1965), Bunker (1965) and Valiquet (1968).

Finally, Boyd and Ellis (1962) made a further contribution by comparing the effects of T-group type training with the effects of a more conventional programme of human relations training built around case discussion and lectures. Both forms of training lasted for two weeks and were part of an in-company training programme for a Canadian Utility company. There were forty-two subjects, in three different groups, participating in the T-group training programme; ten subjects in the lecture/case discussion programme, and twelve untrained nominated controls. The evaluation was made six weeks and six months after completion of the course and was assessed by interviewing work colleagues about behaviour at work; 36 per cent of the work colleagues of the non-trained control managers reported positive change for them, while 52 per cent did so for the lecture/case discussion participants and 70 per cent for the T-group trained participants.

In all these studies it was found that approximately 65–70 per cent of the participants show positive change as a result of experiential group training. Campbell and Dunnette (1968) in their comprehensive review of the effect of *T*-groups concluded 'while *T*-group training seems to produce observable change in behaviour, the utility of these changes for the performance of individuals in their organisational roles remain to be demonstrated'. Although most experiential groups are run on a 'stranger basis' (e.g. managers sent by different companies on a 'cultural island' type course), an increasing number are now organized within organizations and the results from the most recent studies examining the fade-out effect of learning from these latter programmes suggest they are more durable. Smith (1975) in his most recent survey of the field summarizes his review by saying 'the highest rate of follow-up change is found among organisational groups who meet for training and remain intact thereafter', and that 'having discovered their ability to achieve certain goals within the sensitivity training setting, they are more likely to be able to continue doing so in their habitual settings'.

Adverse Effects

There are only two studies which have found high casualty rates among participants in experiential groups. Gottschalk and Pattison (1969) reported that in a sample of three groups of thirty-one participants, there were eleven 'obviously acute pathological emotional reactions' (six of these occurred in a single group). The symptoms they noted among the eleven casualties were psychotic reactions (two), acute anxiety and temporary departure from group (two), isolation and withdrawal reactions (four), depressive reactions (two), and sadistic-exhibitionist behaviour (one). The authors acknowledge that their groups may have been atypical and, in addition, that the effects may have been only transient since they were reporting on behaviour 'during' training.

Although their figure of 30 per cent adverse effects is very high, there are several aspects of this research we should take into account. First, the assessments of trainees was carried out on the completion of the training, so we don't know what the long-term effect was, particularly in the participants' family and work environments. Second, the judgements of pathological emotional reactions were made by the authors themselves, who were psychiatric clinicians, and there may be a tendency for psychiatrists to attribute greater clinical significance to behaviour than is warranted. For example, Weiss (1963) found differences between a group of fifty physicists and fifty-one clinical psychologists on their ability to predict future behaviour of several people on whom they were given data. The physicists' predictions were consistently more accurate when checked against actual subsequent behaviour of the persons judged. The clinical psychologists significantly more often overestimated the difficulties the person would encounter and underestimated their ability to cope with them. And, finally, behaviour such as 'isolation and withdrawal reactions' in a group context could have quite different significance than a two-person psychotherapeutic interview—a situation these clinicians are more used to (Smith, 1975).

The second study which found a relatively high proportion of casualties is the most widely publicized, by Lieberman, Yalom and Miles (1973) in which they claim 'no less than 9 per cent of participants in the 18 groups studied became casualties'. Immediately after the group experiences they reported something like 8 per cent casualties and 8 per cent negative changers (defined as such if they showed negative changes on three or more psychometric and ratings criteria), a total of 16 per cent. Six months after training they found a 10 per cent casualty rate and an 8 per cent negative changers rate for a total of 18 per cent.

There are several reasons why we should be cautious of these results as well. First, the random assignment of students to groups may have increased the risk of psychological disturbance. Second, the decision to categorize the 'suspect' students into 'casualties' was based on subjective criteria, that is, self-report by the students and the authors' judgements of 'psychological decompensation' and not on measurable observed behaviour. No evidence is given to validate the authors' judgements, as in the Gottschalk and Pattison study. Third, it is arguable that informing experiential group participants about the possibilities of 'considerable emotional upsets' before the start of the experience minimizes the psychological risks to participants. It may in fact have the reverse effect of creating an expectation of intensive psychotherapy, which may not have been established without this intervention. Fourth, they had data which indicated that 23 per cent of their control group were negative changers immediately after training and 15 per cent six months later. This is as high, if not higher, than the experiential groups. Although we have to be cautious when drawing conclusions from this study, as we must from any large-scale study in this field, it still provides evidence of casualties as a result of experiential training.

A large-scale study by Cooper and Bowles (1977) found, however, a much lower rate of adverse effects than the above two mentioned studies, from roughly 5 per cent just after training to less than 2 per cent seven months later. In addition the majority of participants showing negative effects up to six weeks after training were seen to significantly change in a positive direction seven months later. Their results were more in line with those of other studies which show smaller casualty rates. Ross, Kligfeld and Whitman (1971), for example, carried out a survey in the city of Cincinnati, Ohio, a community with extensive experiential group activity. They sent questionnaires to 162 psychiatrists asking them to report any cases in which a patient's 'psychotic reactions or personality disorganisations, whether transient or long-lasting, seemed to be consequent to participation in non-structured groups (e.g. *T*-groups, etc.) in the preceding five years'. Of the 91 per cent of the psychiatrists who responded only nineteen separate patients were reported as becoming psychotic or acutely disorganized after group training. The authors were given figures for numbers of persons participating in such groups over the preceding five years, which totalled 2900. Thus, the nineteen represented 0.66 per cent of the population thought to be 'at risk'. Of the participants thought to have been through T-groups (150 in all) fourteen were identified as casualties, an adverse effect rate of 1.2 per cent. This is very close in the follow-up rate in the Cooper and Bowles (1977) study.

In another study, Batchelder and Hardy (1968) carried out an evaluation of group training among 1200 YMCA participants. Interviews with known critics of experiential small group training in the YMCA turned up four cases of allegedly severe adverse effect. After further in-depth work with these participants, trainers, work colleagues, etc., the authors came to the conclusion that in at least three cases the ultimate, long-term outcome was beneficial rather than harmful. This is consistent with Cooper and Bowles' follow-up data on the twelve participants originally identified as potential casualties just after their training. National Training Laboratories (1969) also report some thirty-three participants out of 14,200 (less than 1 per cent) who may have been 'at risk' from their training. These later two studies are very weak ones indeed but the one by Ross *et al.* provides some very important large-scale support for low casualty rates from experiential learning groups.

EXPERIENTIAL METHODS AND THE TEACHING OF PSYCHOLOGY

There are a variety of teaching contexts in psychology in which experiential methods are most appropriate. The most obvious one is in learning about small group behaviour. T-groups (Cooper and Mangham, 1971; Cooper, 1975; Cooper, 1979) and other experiential learning groups (Gazda, 1973) provide a unique opportunity for students to 'learn through experience' about many of the central concepts of social psychology: interpersonal influence, conformity, leadership, decision-making, power, communication networks, roles, social deviance, etc. Because students get involved in these types of groups and because T-groups and other experiential group techniques focus on the dynamics of the group and are concerned with examining their own behaviour, students become very aware of what happened in the group and can easily think of it in the same terms that social psychologists think of social behaviour. In addition, if lectures on relevant conceptual and empirical material can be brought to bear at an appropriate time, one can enhance the intellectual learning as well as the emotional or 'gut' learning.

In addition to using small group techniques one can utilize a variety of other experiential tools in a psychology curriculum. Levine (1973) highlights the ways in which role playing and other experiential events can be used as a learning experience for social science undergraduates. He gives a number of examples to illustrate the range of possibilities:

(1) To illustrate group decision-making: Have five members discuss a problem for 20 min. and come to a decision. Other members sit around and act as observers. This is a very simple but effective way of introducing an emphasis on group *process* to students. If you instruct the observers, for example, to 'pay attention to behaviours that help the group come to a decision and behaviours that inhibit the group from coming to a decision', then they will concentrate on watching how the group is going about their decision-making, and not just on what they are saying.

(2) To illustrate group conflict in decision-making: Take the same situation, but build in external obligations. 'You must defend this position, because your organization believes in . . . . Under no conditions are you to agree to . . . .' In this case, the participants' freedom to act in the situation is limited by the obligations. Conflict is an almost inevitable result with a decision being far more difficult to reach. This exercise is very useful for developing a discussion on the limits to freedom of action, the existence of conflicts in social life, and the way in which organizations can perpetuate positions through their actors, even though the actors may disagree with the position.

(3) To illustrate the effect of hidden feelings on group process: Set up a committee of seven to discuss an 'important' issue (e.g. money to be spent). Two members are to be 10 min. late. Explain that the exercise is to examine the effects of late members on group process. When the two late-members have gone out of the room, explain to the others that: 'Whoever sits in this seat is to be the favoured member. And whoever sits in that seat is to be totally ignored. The group then acts out the situation, and with the observers at the end, they discuss the effect of acceptance and rejection on the late-comers' behaviour (after informing the two members of the deception, of course). Typically, rejected members tend to either withdraw from the situation and become bored, or else they get angry and try to fight their way into the situation. The favoured member often becomes very involved and interested in the group's activities. This is a good example for illustrating how individual feelings are very often responses to assumptions made by other people.

(4) To explore male–female stereotypes: Have members act out their stereotypes of men and women. For example, have one member be the 'male' and the other member the 'female'. The male then telephones the female in order to ask her out to a cinema. This can be done sitting next to each other and the actors pretend to telephone each other. If sex roles are actually reversed (i.e. men play women and

vice versa) substantial insight can be achieved into the stereotyped roles. Another variation is to have a male and a female apply for the same job. Even though the 'interviewer' may be trying to act neutrally to both, the implicit sex stereotypes come out.

(5) To illustrate teacher–student roles: Have one member play a 'teacher' and another a 'student' who is complaining about an exam mark. Even though the student playing the teacher may never have been a teacher before, he nevertheless acts like one. This is a good example for discussing how people learn social roles and how they often learn the reciprocal of the role, as well as the role itself.

(6) Role playing can be created around fantasy and the effect is often very liberating. Here is one that I did once. To one student in a class, I handed an imaginary ball of string. 'Here, hold this end of this string'. I then unravelled the 'string' to still another student. 'Here, you take the string and tie things up'.

After a few minutes of hesitation, the room became criss-crossed with imaginary lines of string that people were stepping over or crawling under. Because of the projective nature of the exercise, a number of issues will come up in discussion: how people can accept a fictitious definition of a situation, how group behaviour revolves around a sense of consensus rather than necessarily something tangible, how people are able to show emotional identification with things, why people feel happy and liberated in the situation (which they usually do), and what is the nature of play and fun.

(7) To illustrate a basic experience of dependency: Two students feed each other salad and the lecturer asks the participants to act like 'parent' and 'child'. Televise the occasion and then play it back in order to provide another dimension to the discussion. The situation is excellent for discussing feelings of parent–child relationships, what it feels like to be dependent, how trust or mistrust grows out of the situations as it develops (some 'parents' create trust in their 'child', while other create mistrust), and what it feels like to be publicly visible in a dependent position (i.e. the TV).

This list should be sufficient to illustrate the wide diversity of experiential learning situations that can be created for psychology students. For a more comprehensive set of experiential exercises for particular psychological phenomenon see Pfeiffer and Jones' (1972–1979) *Annual Handbooks for Group Facilitators.*

CONCLUSION

There are several reasons why experiential methods are growing in popularity in the teaching of psychology in the USA, the UK, and the West generally

(Aronson, 1972). First, students are demanding more active forms of learning. Students are beginning to understand that they must *participate* to learn, and that this leads to interdependence in the learning process as well as stimulating creativity. Second, it provides students with more *affective* data about the behavioural world around them. Experiential learning techniques encourage empathy and the understanding of feelings, as Levine (1973) suggests, 'they require that an individual identify with what is happening and to become aware within himself of his feelings in a particular situation, and it is this emotional identification which allows him to understand why people do what they do'. Third, these techniques require interaction between participants, a fundamental ingredient in understanding human behaviour. They provide a possible source of 'real-life' data about the psychological theories and empirical work which usually serves as the sole basis of most taught psychology courses. We now have the educational technology to go beyond lectures in psychology, to use and explore the transactions between ourselves as vehicles for learning our trade. As Levine (1973) summarizes, 'participation methods of learning are one small development towards a more relevant and active educational experience; and while they certainly do not constitute answers to all problems, they, nevertheless, represent a step forward'.

BIBLIOGRAPHY

Blumberg, A., and Golembiewski, R. T. (1976). *Learning and Change in Groups*. London: Penguin. Blumberg and Golembiewski's book is an attempt to provide behavioural scientists with information about experiential learning groups, with emphasis on *T*-group education. This book is a short, snappy account of laboratory education and the distinguishing features and concepts of *T*-group learning. It also explores the role of the *T*-group trainer, the individual learner/participant, the controversial issues in the group movement and discontent outside the learning group movement. It also, briefly, explores some research fields evaluating the effects of group training but this is better done in *T-Groups: A Survey of Research* (see below).

Cooper, C. L., and Mangham, I. L. (1971). *T-Groups: A Survey of Research*. London and New York: John Wiley & Sons. This book was originally published in 1971 and provided a review of all the *T*-group research up until 1970. The book was reprinted in 1973 and still provides one of the best comprehensive sources of *T*-group research. It examines the effectiveness of *T*-group in producing on-the-job change and before/after studies of *T*-group change. At the time of publication it was premature to explore fully the effects of *T*-groups as a vehicle of organizational change, but a subsequent book by Professor Cooper, *Group Training for Individual and Organizational Development*, has filled this gap. There is, however, in this book, a short review of the work done on organizational change, followed by an interesting example of the impact of organizational training laboratories by Frank Friedlander. Incidentally, this book is uniquely organized in that the authors have reviewed the major areas of research first and then included one study in full that they considered represented the best work, at that time, in that area. After assessing the effects of *T*-groups the authors then focus in on the impact of the *T*-group trainer, *T*-group composition, intragroup dynamics, and the course of development in the *T*-group.

Cooper, C. L. (1973). *Group Training for Individual and Organizational Development.* Basle, Switzerland: S. Karger. This book is an attempt to provide applied behavioural scientists with case studies of the use of group training in a variety of organizational contexts. The chapter titles of this book illustrate the comprehensive spread of environments in which group training has been used: improving social skills in restaurants; group training with students in higher education; the development of group training in the Civil Service; group training within an OD project in an industrial company; group training for community relations; group training as an aid to staff development in psychiatric institutions; group training in understanding society; and group training for social workers. This book provides a variety of examples on UK applications of experiential learning and attempts to highlight the advantages and disadvantages in these different contexts.

Cooper, C. L. (1975). *Theories of Group Processes.* London and New York: John Wiley & Sons. This book is the only book of its kind in the experiential group field. Although a great deal of empirical work has been done in evaluating and assessing group dynamics, very little work has been done in developing conceptual models of experiential learning and group development. The editor of this book invited some of the leading scholars in the experiential field to develop comprehensive theories of experiential learning. The book includes originally conceived and written theoretical chapters by such distinguished authors as Chris Argyris, David Kolb, Robert Blake and Jane Mouton, Robert Golembiewski, Martin Lakin, Richard Mann, Sam Culbert, G. T. Barrett-Lennard and W. Breendan Reddy. This book has now provided the group field with the theoretical foundations that are likely to lead to a new spurt in research and development over the next decade.

Cooper, C. L. (1976). *Developing Social Skills in Managers: Advances in Group Training.* New York: Wiley; London: Macmillan. This book attempts to up-date practising group leaders and researchers on advances in group training over the last decade. It starts by describing the evaluation of experiential learning groups and also recent developments in experiential group methods in the USA. The next section of the book answers the question 'What makes an effective group?' This is broken down into chapters which explore group leader effectiveness, the use and misuse of structured exercises, and why successful groups succeed (the implications of *T*-group research). The third section looks at experiential group design. It focuses in on the use of the Tavistock type design, experience based designs in organizational development, and organizational role analysis *à la* Grubb Institute. The final section examines some applications of experiential group methods for management development. It includes chapters on team development in industry, a new approach on interpersonal skills development, and personal growth and career development. The final chapter, by the author, examines how experiential methods will develop in the next decade or two and emphasizes the greater application of these techniques to industrial democracy and worker participation.

Cooper, C. L., and Bowles, D. (1977). *Hurt or Helped: A Study of the Personal Impact on Managers of Experiential Small Group Training Programmes.* London: HMSO. This research monograph is the most comprehensive study of the potentially negative effects of experiential small group training. It was sponsored by the Training Services Agency and it examined the training programmes run by five major experiential training organizations in the UK. It explored, in depth, the effects of extensive experiential training on over 225 managers. It not only identified the extent of casualties as a result of these programmes, but also the beneficial effects of them as well. In addition, it tried to discover the group dynamic variables responsible for either positive or negative outcome, that is, trainer behaviour, participant personality, type of group orientation, etc.

Cooper, C. L., and Alderfer, C. P. (1978). *Advances in Experiential Social Processes: Volume 1*. London and New York: John Wiley & Sons. This is the first book in a series of volumes examining developments in experiential learning processes. In the first volume, we have contributions examining some of the following topics: experiential psychotherapies, videotape feedback, experiential learning for lawyers, peer consultation for school improvement, Tavistock work in the USA, improving the quality of community life, etc. The purpose of this volume, and subsequent volumes in the series, will be to highlight advances in the use of experiential methods as well as in the development of research and theory.

Gazda, G.M. (1973). *Human Relations Development: A Manual for Educators*. Boston: Allyn & Bacon. The main purpose of this volume is to provide educators with a manual for human relations development in educational systems. It provides educators with a comprehensive background of information that they will find useful in propagating experiential learning in learning situations.

Golembiewski, R. T., and Blumberg, A. (1977). *Sensitivity Training and the Laboratory Approach*. Illinois: Peacock Publ., third edition. This is the third edition of this volume. Each edition has changed substantially and provides the reader with increasingly more relevant research and practice in sensitivity training. The book starts with a section 'what is a T-group' and is then followed by another on 'what happens in a T-group'. More specific information is provided by chapters examining 'who leads a T-group and how', what concerns are there about T-groups, where can T-group dynamics be used, and finally, how can T-group dynamics be studied. This volume essentially reprints articles that have been published previously in the wide variety of journals that have been used by applied behavioural scientists. Most of these chapters are up-to-date and relevant and, therefore, provide the reader with a fairly useful compendium of experiential work found in different disciplines.

Lieberman, M. A., Yalom, I. D., and Miles, M. B. (1973). *Encounter Groups: First Facts*. New York: Basic Books. This book was the first major attempt to study the negative effects of a variety of experiential groups on university students in the USA. The book is essentially an account of the study carried out by the authors at Stanford University. It describes, in very great detail, the impact of different types of encounter groups on students in a university setting. The conclusions of this study have attracted a great deal of criticism and controversy, particularly due to some of its methodological weaknesses, but also probably because it was one of the first to systematically explore this touchy topic. For anybody interested in examining the potentially deleterious effects of experiential methods, this book, and the one by Cooper and Bowles, are essential reading.

Pfeiffer, W., and Jones, J. (1972–1979). *Annual Handbook for Group Facilitators*. La Jolla, Calif.: University Associates. These volumes are annual handbooks which started in 1972. To date, therefore, there are eight volumes available. These books contain a number of standardized sections on experiential learning: structured exercises, instrumentation, lecturettes, theory and practice, and resources. These books are designed for practitioners of experiential group methods and fulfil this role very well indeed. They provide the group practitioner with information about possible exercises he could use, research and other instruments, possible lectures, and potential theory input. With the complete set of these handbooks one could easily design an experiential learning situation for just about any client system, that is, students in psychology, managers in industry, social workers in the field, etc. In addition to the annual handbook they also produce some smaller and more compact volumes of exercises which are entitled *Structured Experiences for Human Relations Training*.

Rogers, C. R. (1970). *On Encounter Groups*. New York: Harper & Row. Carl Rogers' book on encounter groups provides a philosophical and conceptual framework for the development of experiential learning. This book not only provides one with information on the evaluation and development of encounter groups but also makes explicit the underlying assumptions and values of both practitioners and counsellors. It is an important book to read if one is attempting to understand how and why these methods have grown in popular use over the last decade.

REFERENCES

Appley, D. G., and Winter, A. R. (1973). *T-Groups and Therapy Groups in a Changing Society.* San Francisco: Jossey Bass.

Aronson, E. (1972). *The Social Animal.* San Francisco: W. H. Freeman.

Batchelder, R. L., and Hardy, J. M. (1968). *Using Sensitivity Training and the Laboratory Method.* New York: Associated Press.

Boyd, J. B., and Ellis, J. D. (1962). *Findings of Research into Senior Management Seminars.* Toronto: Hydro-Electric.

Bunker, D. R. (1965). Individual Applications of Laboratory Training. *Journal of Applied Behavioral Science*, **1**, 131–148.

Campbell, J. P., and Dunnette, M. D. (1968). Effectiveness of *T*-Group Experiences in Management Training and Development. *Psychological Bulletin*, **70**, 73–104.

Cooper, C. L. (1975). *Theories of Group Processes.* London: Wiley.

Cooper, C. L. (1976). *Developing Social Skills in Managers: Advances in Group Training.* London: Macmillan; New York: Wiley.

Cooper, C. L. (1979). *Learning From Others in Groups.* London: Associated Business Press; Conn: Greenwood Press.

Cooper, C. L., and Bowles, D. (1977). *Hurt or Helped: A Study of the Personal Impact on Managers of Experiential Small Group Training Programmes.* London: HMSO.

Cooper, C. L., and Mangham, I. L. (1971). *T-Groups: A Survey of Research.* London and New York: Wiley.

Gazda, G. M. (1973). *Human Relations Development: A Manual for Educators.* Boston: Allyn & Bacon.

Gottschalk, L. A., and Pattison, E. M. (1969). Psychiatric Perspective on *T*-Groups and the Laboratory Movement. *American Journal of Psychiatry*, **126**, 823–839.

Koziey, P. W., Loken, J. O., and Field, J. A. (1971). *T*-Group Influence on Feelings of Alienation. *Journal of Applied Behavioural Science*, **7**, 724–731.

Levine, N. (1973). Group Training with Students in Higher Education. In Cooper, C. L. (ed.) *Group Training for Individual and Organizational Development.* Basle: S. Karger, pp. 40–68.

Lieberman, M. A., Yalom, I. D., and Miles, M. B. (1973). *Encounter Groups: First Facts.* New York: Basic Books.

Mangham, I. L., Hayes, J., and Cooper, C. L. (1970). Developing Executive Relationships. *Interpersonal Development*, **1**, 110–127.

Miles, M. B. (1960). Human Relations Training. *Journal of Counselling Psychology*, **7**, 301–306.

Miles, M. B. (1965). Changes During and Following Laboratory Training. *Journal of Applied Behavioural Science*, **1**, 215–243.

Moscow, D. (1969). The Influence of Interpersonal Variables on the Transfer of Learning from *T*-Groups to the Job Situation. *Proceedings of the International Congress of Applied Psychology*, International Association of Applied Psychology, 380–386.

National Laboratory Training (1969). *News and Reports*, **3**, 4.

Pfeiffer. W., and Jones, J. (1972–1979). *Annual Handbook for Group Facilitators.* La Jolla, Calif.: University Associates.

Rogers, C. R. (1970). *On Encounter Groups.* New York: Harper & Row.

Ross, W. D., Kligfeld, M., and Whitman, R. W. (1971). Psychiatrists, Patients and Sensitivity Groups. *Archives of General Psychiatry*, **25**, 178–180.

Smith, P. B. (1975). Controlled Studies of the Outcome of Sensitivity Training. *Psychological Bulletin*, **82**, 597–622.

Valiquet, M. I. (1968). Individual Change in a Management Development Program. *Journal of Applied Behavioral Science*, **4**, 313–325.

Weiss, J. H. (1963). The Effects of Professional Training and Amount of Accuracy of Information on Behavioral Predictions. *Journal of Consulting Psychology*, **27**, 257–262.

The Teaching of Psychology
Edited by J. Radford and D. Rose
© 1980 John Wiley & Sons Ltd.

3

Experimental Methods

HARRY FISHER

The methods considered in this chapter are set in different teaching contexts which are experimental in that they provide for active involvement in problem solving situations related to the process of psychological experimentation. It is a convenient, if artificial, arrangement which divides teaching activities in the traditional course into those relating to 'findings' and those relating to 'techniques'. The objectives of the several methods to be considered are that they should contribute to the teaching in both areas and demonstrate their interdependence. The contexts chosen are, of course, only a selection of those possible, and the examples described within them merely illustrative of a wider range. Some have the support of evaluative research, others are commended by their wide usage. Their common feature is the utilization of the educational potential of various aspects of experimentation in the teaching of psychology.

The methods might be considered as natural extensions of some of the activities carried out as part of the conventional laboratory course, which may be used to the same educational end. To use the laboratory course only as a means of acquainting students with the methodological and analytical skills of the discipline is to underrate the contribution it is capable of making (Regula, 1971; Wells, 1972; Miller, 1976), for it may be used to serve an integrating function over the diverse content of the course. Each field covered rests on its own conceptual basis and methods. While the relation between them is designed to deal with questions peculiar to that field, the more general issues raised may also apply to different concepts, and in other fields. What the student learns within the laboratory class of the ways in which information is obtained— together with their attendant limitations—is of immediate relevance as the basis for the development of an evaluative approach across the spectrum of psychological activity.

These several experimentally based methods thus provide approaches to the teaching of psychology which offer routes to some important objectives, namely, that students might become not merely well informed and technically competent, but critical and creative in their approach.

SOME SPECIFIC APPROACHES

If the practical course is to be used to afford insight into psychology at large, and to serve as a means of linking its diverse interests, it will demand careful planning in respect of both methods and content. There is something to be said for the direct, no nonsense approach, which by way of introduction involves the student in an experiment in one way or another, and then sets him to give an account of it within the structure of the formal report. All this with only the minimal prescription of the detail to be included. It has the advantage of directness and provides an active learning experience. With appropriate feedback the student stands to learn much about both experimentation and report writing. There is also much to be said in favour of a contrasting highly structured approach, where the student is shepherded through each stage of the experiment and each section of the report, so that in the process of several repetitions he acquires an intuitive grasp of the total process. The traditional practical class in psychology has been taught effectively using either method—sometimes both—as the staple approach throughout the course, modified in detail only to meet the requirements of particular topics.

The alternatives or supplements to these approaches to be outlined are, with a single exception, devices for directing attention to some of the separate contributions of the total process, or for affording opportunities for the practice of specific basic skills and judgements. For example, in any serious piece of research it is necessary to look beyond the general textbook accounts in order to review the range of alternative conceptualizations of the problem area. This involves the experimenter's skill in drawing on the published literature, and one of the approaches to be considered suggests ways in which this might be developed.

Another approach to be considered is the contribution to be made in an introductory course of non-laboratory observational methods. The ends in view include affording direct insights into the ways in which subject (Silverman, 1977) and experimenter (Barber, 1976) expectations may confound data gathered in a laboratory context and lead to spurious conclusions; in addition, to indicate the ways in which basic techniques are used in conducting research in naturalistic settings outside the laboratory.

An important element in the practical course is the opportunity to discuss, in a specific context, methodological issues which arise in decisions affecting, say, the population sampled—the value, for example, of the random sample (Eysenck, 1975)—or the strengths and weaknesses of specific and popular designs, e.g. repeated measures designs (Poulton, 1973). A variety of ways will be considered of providing opportunities for both discussion and experience in making evaluative judgements of design features.

This, then, is the sort of detail with which the several approaches will deal. Their overall purpose is to produce learning situations in which various aspects of detail can be examined in context. To make time available for drawing attention to particular detail, other aspects of the total process are truncated or suitably covered in some of these approaches. Some consideration of the content of the experimental work will be made together with the methods. Following this some organizational variants of the practical class will be considered.

Non-laboratory Research Methods

Experimentation in psychology is complicated because it involves people. While this should surprise no-one, the extent and complexity of the influence of social factors in this area might. The newcomer to experimental psychology might be allowed to become aware of these with growing experience. Alternatively, a systematic introduction might be presented prior to laboratory based experimentation, and it is this course which is to be considered first in this section. Following this, brief consideration is made of the approach to psychological research by studying behaviour in its natural setting.

One way in which the student may be made aware of the range of social interactions which can materially affect the outcome of an experiment is by using the experiential methods described in Chapter 2. Another way is to exploit the most basic research method, observation, and, where appropriate, asking questions. Questions may be put in an interview situation, or in writing on, say, a survey questionnaire, or standardized psychometric instrument, such as a personality inventory or attitude scale.

At an early stage in one undergraduate course on field methods students observe and report on one family eating together, the observation being made on four successive weekly occasions (Rossan and Levine, 1974) while in another students observe, as an early project, single individuals, pairs, groups and themselves in interaction with others (Stevens, 1977).

Interviews may be structured or unstructured and it is valuable for students to have experience of both interviewer and respondent roles. Similarly it is useful for students to try their hands at compiling ad hoc questionnaires as well as filling them in. Much is to be gained from such experiences if they are carefully planned before and well discussed afterwards. Some limits need to be prescribed for observations, however broad, and it should be clear what information is required from the interview or questionnaire, so that the report of the exercise may serve as the basis for evaluating the methods used. Follow-up seminars are considerably enhanced if videotape records of interviewing sessions can be studied, so that the original participants can be fully questioned about their contributions.

A course of this sort might be expected to contribute to the early stages of a course in a number of different ways. Thus one might expect to see development in the individual of the use of professional skills, from an increasing awareness of the vulnerability of the information gathered to the selectivity of his own perceptions, and the expectations and whims of his subjects. It might also be expected that in at least some students considerable social development should take place, enabling them to find the necessary balance between establishing rapport with subjects and gathering the information required without loss of objectivity. A third area in which changes might be expected is in those attitudes which relate to scientific integrity, shown in an increasing awareness of the experimenter's ethical responsibility in respect of subjects, his department and the discipline.

The study of non-laboratory methods as a means of directing attention to some of the difficulties and limitations of laboratory experimentation is one good reason for its inclusion in the practical course. The methods are, of course, worthy of inclusion in their own right. For those who hold that the better controlled the experiment, the less likely it is to apply to real life, these methods, suitably refined, offer means of carrying out productive research outside the laboratory. Thus while students are engaged in the evaluation of their own attempts at naturalistic observation, there is a useful opportunity for considering some of the features of both the ecological and ethological enterprises. For example, the notion of the research enterprise: the naturalists methods ' . . . are conditional; they are ways of getting into the phenomena, ways of jogging nature into a response . . . . Where the task of the theorist is to explain data, the special task of the naturalist is to generate data' (Gutman, 1969). It is also of interest to consider the nature of the findings made available in this way. The ecologists have presented accounts of behaviour patterns typical in specific settings, the scout camp, the drug store and the like, and have further provided information about the way in which behaviour varies with the environment—childrens' behaviour has been studied in communities of different sizes, considering this both in terms of an individual community (big school vs. little school) and of a more remote setting (city vs. town). Details of the methods and equipment used in order to obtain objective data are of considerable interest here, together with a consideration of the limitations and advantages of ethological studies of humans as well as animals.

The Class Experiment

This approach may be used to advantage in the context of a practical class or as part of a lecture. The tutor acts as experimenter and some, or all, of his class as subjects. In the former context it is usually associated with the production of a written report, while in the latter it is used for the impact and insight which can be gained from participating in such an enterprise. As a means of providing the basis for an experimental report it has the advantage that the student, relieved of the responsibilities of planning, is the sooner in possession of data for analysis and interpretation. Involvement means that he is in a good position to appreciate the value of the data, and to identify areas where methodological inadequacies affect its reliability. The data produces a useful if unorthodox starting point for discussion. How can it be analysed? What can be deduced from it? Can anything further be drawn from the objective deductions? Thus the psychological content can be considered late in the process, together with the design used and possible alternatives. If the gathering of the data and its dissemination to class members is accomplished efficiently, more time is available for the discussion of these details as the material from which a report is to be made. The class experiment is thus particularly convenient for use in the earlier part of the course, when it is desirable to consider the total process, from planning to report, within a limited time span. The writing of clear, unambiguous reports can be a daunting challenge, especially to the beginner. Support, swift feedback and opportunity for discussion can be well invested at this stage, and may provide much needed encouragement to many whose anxieties are often revealed in repetitive and overwritten reports.

The use of this method in either of the contexts suggested is associated with a number of limitations. These include the general weakness of the controls which can be exercised in the classroom situation, and the wide subject variations from one time to another, which place constraints on the sorts of effect which can be used, particularly if the warming glow of a significant result, or even one in the right direction, is desired. A useful source of suggestions for class experiments is the 'Gimmickry' section of the APA publication *Periodically*, to be discussed later. There is, however, no substitute for compiling a stock of class experiments which *usually* work with one's *usual* population.

The Design Seminar

This involves the joint efforts of a group of students, with one or more leaders, experienced in research, to describe the means by which answers to a specific psychological problem might be obtained. It may be seen as an end in itself, and give rise to no experimentation. Alternatively it can be seen as a means of generating a group of experiments in the same area, the findings of which may be considered at a future meeting. The design seminar plays a useful role as part of a practical course in that it provides opportunities for the discussion of design problems in a specific context, thus providing an insight into the interdependence of these aspects in a way which is not always so apparent when experiments are carried out replicating a prescribed design. The values of group discussion in problem solving, as well as its general educational usefulness in providing an active learning situation are well known. This approach draws on those features to provide, within a limited context, an outline of the way in which psychological science progresses, from the generation of hypotheses to the interpretation of the information gathered.

Its flexibility in use and organization commends it as a valuable teaching device. It may be used to advantage with beginners or advanced students; as a means of introduction, or of revision or of preparation for a specific project; or as a means of drawing attention to specific issues of content and related research problems. For example, beginners might be invited to suggest ways of providing an answer to the following. 'When throwing three successive darts at the bull, is consistency of aim related to the interval between throws?' Provided with a given task, and left only with the definition of consistency of aim, by way of preliminaries, discussion may be focused on a range of broad design and analysis problems (difference tests with independent groups, or repeated measures; trend or correlation analysis?), sampling problems (occasional players, novices, experts), and related procedural issues (how the interval is to be timed, number of trials, etc.). As the aim is to provide data which will answer the question, discussion of the psychological content can be deferred.

A wider range of discussion might be expected from a question which left the experimenter to decide the question of dependent variables. For example, 'Is mental alertness related to sleep deprivation?', where the decisions about measures of mental alertness and sleep deprivation and their validations need to be made, would serve to focus attention on the need for operational definitions as a preliminary to further design considerations. For advanced students interested in a specific area, the exercise might further be widened to include the generation of hypotheses, as a preliminary to the design of alternative approaches to a single problem (McGuire, 1973).

The design seminar affords a flexibility of organization which further commends it. Discussion may centre on the production in a class setting of an experimental design in the manner considered above, or on the discussion of proposed designs presented in prepared papers. A further variant may take the form of a discussion, following a written evaluation against a number of explicit desiderata, of either a paper presented by a member of the group or one from the literature (Easting, 1976).

This approach provides useful opportunities for stifling the urge to gather data without well-defined aims, and the consequent 'what-can-be-done-with-this-data?' syndrome. In its place the inculcation of an interest in the generation of testable hypotheses and a willingness to consider the theoretical consequences of a range of possible outcomes might add to the discrimination the individual brings to bear on his own and others' experiments.

It is rarely possible to maintain a formal and structured approach throughout a session of this sort. The interdependence of the issue involved—and the appearance of the occasional red herring—may bring contributions which are at cross purposes. It is perhaps the most significant weakness of this approach that a session's work may produce only a list of incoherent notes and diagrams; for this reason it is useful that leaders, in addition to being seasoned researchers, should also be able to act as firm but sensitive chairmen.

Computer-based Experiment Simulation

One of the important objectives of the practical course in psychology is that the student should gain direct experience of as wide a range of experimental designs as possible, applied in a similarly wide range of contexts. The single most common obstacle to its realization is undoubtedly the time required to run the experiments. Computer-based experiments offer a solution to this problem as well as providing a way of making available a wide range of experimental contexts.

Stored in the computer is a range of models which reflects currently available findings in the fields of enquiry to which they relate. Models in current use include some which relate to motivation in an industrial setting, imprinting, and the aetiology of schizophrenia, together with a number of more conventional laboratory topics. Each model will generate data in terms of a range of relevant variables both dependent and independent. Having followed an introductory course in a given area of enquiry, and equipped with some knowledge of scientific method, the 'experimenter' feeds the details of his design into the computer and obtains a print-out of the data generated, together with the appropriate statistical analysis. The 'experimenter' is thus left with the tasks of interpretation and evaluation of the findings, the assessment of the usefulness of the design, and possibly the formulation of further hypotheses. This, rather than the conduct of the experiment and the analysis, is his major task, attention being effectively concentrated on the psychological content of the enterprise and its relation to the design employed. It is not unknown, particularly in early reports, for traditional students to neglect these aspects in favour of the somewhat easier task of detailing the weaknesses of the experimental procedure. The use of an 'analogue' laboratory (Hoffman, 1962) has recently been adopted by a number of universities and colleges in the USA. At Michigan, where much of the initiative for the recent development was in the hands of Dana Main and her colleagues, the reported findings of simulated experiments were used as the basis of a class 'literature' (Main, 1972), drawn on and contributed to by all those experimenting in the same area.

The saving of time spent recruiting and running subjects is a clear bonus. Since no apparatus is needed there is a further possibility for saving time; sometimes availability and serviceability of apparatus may present hazards in respect of initiating as well as running experiments. But computers have their running troubles, so that in this case the bonus is not so clear. Nevertheless, it seems likely that on the whole this approach confers a significant saving of time, and this means that a larger number of experiments can be performed, and that in each of them the experimenter's attention is focused on the elucidation of the relations among proposed hypotheses, the analysis of the data generated, the design employed and the psychological context in which the study is set. It thus offers to extend the range of experience of the student in respect of both content and design in a way not possible with the traditional approach. However, recruiting and running real subjects is an important part of the psychologist's business, and any course which does not provide for experience in this area would be deficient. It is the practice among users of this approach to present it in the second year of a four-year under-graduate course, following introductory content courses and instruction in design and analysis but prior to experimentation involving apparatus and subjects, on the grounds that these latter resources are of more value to those better equipped to understand the total process.

A further advantage over conventional methods is the variety of data which can be made available. This may include some clinical data, for example, not normally available since clinical patients are not accessible to undergraduate students. Similarly, data from animal studies, frequently time consuming to obtain and often outside the resources of a small department, can be made readily available in terms of a data-generating model.

Since these models typically involve a number of variables, not only do they open the way to a range of designs from simple to complex, they offer the student the opportunity of planning a sequence of experiments in the same area. In this way something approximating to a realistic view of the wider problems of research may be acquired, particularly where students are set to work within prescribed limits to computer time. In institutions where this has been used, not only has it drawn attention to the differences in efficiency among a range of possible designs, but it has also encouraged the formation of research teams who have pooled their resources in order to increase their experimental investment (Miller, 1976).

In view of these, and other, advantages it is not difficult to understand the enthusiasm of the innovators who see the approach as a 'pedagogic break-through'. Attempts to evaluate its effectiveness have offered some encourage-ment (Kiesler, 1974).

Among what appear as possible limitations are some which relate to the models used, and others to the resources necessary for implementation. A given model can reflect only a selection of the variables researched in a given area, and simulation experimenters must perforce choose within these, a limita-tion which may well be seen as a constraint on creative experimentation. Whether these constraints constitute difficulties different in degree or kind from those arising in the traditional approach, based as it is on a literature which itself sets forward models which are developing and typically less than adequate, is debatable. The serious student is likely to question the assumptions of a model whether it appears in explicit form in the literature or in the implicit form of a data-generating programme.

As to resources, few colleges can be without access to computer services, and, in a period when these are expanding, the modest requirements of experimental simulation should present no great difficulties. The first models were restricted in use to the planning institution. In recent years in the USA there has been an increase in model sharing through computer links, and subscribers can draw on a very wide range of models. The necessary human resources relate to the roles of teacher, model builder, and programmer. The teacher carries the general managerial burden of matching the students' preparation to the range of possibilities existing within the model, and guidance in the choice of research strategies.

In 1976 there were over forty installations in the USA providing computer-based data-generating systems. Many of these were used by several different universities and colleges drawing on a range of models both pure and applied from both physical and human sciences. A common obstacle to the establishment of experiment simulation facilities is the still common reluctance over the use of computer technology. Among the institutions where it has been successfully adopted, considerable ingenuity has been brought to bear to ease the problems of the computer-naive. Programme MESS (Michigan Experiment Simulation Supervisor) corrects spelling and typing errors and adjusts for column entry error—among other supervisory functions (Stout, 1974). Experiment simulation should not be confused with other computer-based means of experimentation, where the computer is used as apparatus, or as experimenter (Stang and O'Connell, 1974).

The Individual Research Project

The educational value of the individual project is attested by its widespread use and by the resources in course time and hardware expended upon it. Most honours degree students of psychology, at some time in their course, embark on an enquiry for which they take, under supervision, a dominant share of the initiative for its completion. Its value to the student resides partly in this overall responsibility with the insights into the total process it affords, together with opportunities for drawing on knowledge and skills acquired earlier, and of learning new procedures for dealing with new problems. With adequate planning and supervision it can provide considerable personal satisfaction as well as a profitable educational exercise. While it is typically a required part of the course, since the matter under investigation is chosen by the student, it is usually surrounded with interest and anticipation. Careful planning is required to ensure that the necessary work can be completed within the time available and without undue interference with other work. It is rarely found difficult to identify questions of interest, which offer worthwhile projects, but advice may be needed in restricting the scope of the project. The published literature provides useful pointers for the content of projects, which ideally would aim to test hypotheses drawn from existing models, using a small number of subjects within an elegant design and apparatus which is freely available and dependable. Another useful approach is to replicate an earlier study with some significant methodological modification—in design, apparatus or subject characteristics for example—with a view to examining the extent to which the earlier findings will generalize (Regula, 1971).

Among resources, advice—academic and technical—is an important item, and should be available without overmuch delay, particularly in the planning stage. After that, weekly opportunities for consultation can be useful in limiting crisis calls. Contact on a regular basis provides valuable support for weaker students, and can be just as valuable for the competent and enthusiastic. Even brief contact can afford an opportunity for discussion and a way of avoiding gross errors. It can also be useful to define a number of sub-goals, each associated with more extensive supervision. Even when students are carrying out individual experiments under normal laboratory class conditions it has been found useful to oversee the completion of the work in two stages, the first containing material up to and including the procedure, and the second the remainder of the work, the experiment being run only after any further necessary discussion of the first section (Zenhausern, 1972). In the case of a project this might be further subdivided.

From a departmental point of view, projects draw heavily on both materials and manpower; supervision can involve more than a single person, and the provision of apparatus with a minimum of delay can place heavy demands on technical staff. The disposal of resources needs to be carefully planned, and the demands likely to be made upon them known as early as possible. For some, the production of the project report is an end in itself, for which course credit is given: others have the opportunity of presenting publicly an account of the work to their peers and tutors. This can be an awesome prospect, but worthwhile in terms of the feedback a wider scrutiny may afford.

The individual research project provides a context of considerable educational usefulness both at college and pre-college levels. Drawing largely on student initiative and enthusiasm, set in a one-to-one tutorial relationship with regular discussion, and the opportunities for critical comment at all stages, it provides an ideal opportunity both for creative experimentation and a thorough scrutiny of the several processes involved in experimentation.

The Literature Search

As in other disciplines, it is important that the student of psychology should, with as little delay as possible, be able to draw on the accumulation of original work recorded and stored in various ways. Failure in this respect can impair any research undertaking, original or replicative, in a number of ways, stemming from a general failure to draw on information already available on the topic under investigation. This may result in a number of adverse consequences, including one or more of the following:

(a) Omissions in respect of the consideration of alternative conceptualization of the topic.

(b) Restriction in respect of the formulation of alternative hypotheses.

(c) Failure to incorporate necessary controls established by previous work.

(d) Discussion of findings limited by absence of critical considerations.

It is thus of considerable value that guidance and practice in the use of available resources should be available early in the course. In view of the relation between established findings and the research enterprise, the practical class offers a suitable context for the introduction to both resources and strategies. While such an introduction will reflect the sophistication of both the available resources and the student population, it seems important that the pre-college student with limited library resources should be introduced to the strategies of information retrieval, as well as the honours degree undergraduate.

A number of approaches have been proposed, varying in sophistication with the level of instruction envisaged. These include the following:

(a) Direct instruction, involving the listing and description of the available resources together with organizational details, and demonstration of the way in which they may be used to obtain information for a sample research project (Parr, 1978).

(b) Various types of assignment designed to promote familiarity with available library resources, and described as a 'scavenger hunt' (Le Unes, 1977), 'treasure hunt' (Matthews, 1978), and 'hypothesis verification' (Gardner, 1977) assignments.

(c) Computer information retrieval.

(d) Assignments designed to result in the production of comprehensive bibliographic lists in respect of specified projects.

All approaches clearly invite the co-operation of subject and library staff.

What evaluative research there is (see, for example, Matthews, 1978) lends some support to the notion of the value of course-related library studies. While the research enterprise clearly stands to benefit from the inclusion of such instructions in the introductory practical class, the skills obtainable from it have course-wide relevance.

Some Organizational Variants

In many courses the traditional practical class is a feature of the entire course; time is set aside for experimentation in each year of the course. The content of practical classes is in some cases closely, in others, more loosely related to the course content. While some of the experiments relate to current interests others may be included as vehicles for the presentation of particular design or analytical methods. Other courses may concentrate the practical part over a much shorter period of time, and yet others integrate sections of the practical class within the teaching of specific topics. Such alternative approaches afford interesting comparisons with the traditional methods. Those to be considered here will be dealt with under two headings as follows:

(a) *The modular practical class.* Here the course in psychology is divided into sections which are more or less discrete and separate in a number of ways. They are separate, for example, in respect of content, and there is thus a social module, a developmental module, a cognitive module, and so on. These modules are often also distinct in large departments in terms of the people who teach them, and it would be unusual to find the same person involved in, say, the social and the clinical module. Further distinctive features arise as a result of the methodological demands of the several subject areas, and there may thus be considerable differences in the approach to practical sessions between the different modules. At some level the several modules are related to the extent that overall planning has been successful in subsuming an acceptable course in psychology under separate headings, such that allowed combinations of modules meet prescribed educational requirements. Among the more obvious advantages offered by this approach is the integrity of the practical work within the content of the module. Practical and other 'theoretical' work may, within the narrower confines of a scientific field of interest, be the more comfortably planned to complement each other. Since, as it frequently happens, modules are taught by those having research interests in the field, educational and professional desiderata may be maintained at a high level, sensitive alike to changing emphases and methodologies on the one hand and student benefit on the other. As a long-term plan there is thus much to commend this approach. Among the opponents of this approach are those who see the 'water-tight compartments' as a threat to an integrated discipline and as uneconomic in practice in respect of duplication which can be difficult to avoid if the 'autonomy' of the modules is to include a degree of internal flexibility. This is perhaps most likely in the teaching of statistics and design if this is to be carried out to any extent within modules. An early module in this area can be useful in establishing common terminology and notation.

(b) *The intensive practical workshop.* Under certain circumstances practical work for a group of students may be planned to occupy a period extending from a few days to several weeks. These include practical workshops for pre-college students and summer schools for students to whom the availability of laboratory equipment is normally limited since the bulk of their course work is completed at home. For these students it is clear that the advantage of such courses is the provision of the necessary facilities and support which will allow them to complete the practical work prescribed in the course they are following. Beyond this the intensive practical workshop approach has some benefits which have prompted its use among those working within a normal setting. The repeated application of experimental procedures, and the considerable volume and variety of work included in such sessions, within a setting in which help and advice is readily available, provides a wealth of active learning situations. Over the course of a week or more problems may recur in different forms, and the student has the opportunity of developing his own strategies for solution in a context rich in the support needed.

It is often found convenient to divide the students into two groups such that one is comprised of separate investigators gathering data, those in the other may be writing reports and acting as subjects. Thus not only are there opportunities for 'comparing notes', but supervision is available for both experimenters and report writers. Such workshops may also provide opportunities for more general coverage of statistics and design issues. In this way they provide coverage of the various elements which enter into the total process in a context in which their interdependence may be appreciated.

As with other 'total immersion' educational methods, the advantages to be won depend not only on careful organization but on the motivation and preparedness of the students. While an intensive workshop provides a stimulating atmosphere, the average experimenter is usually able to produce more data than he can comfortably analyse and report in the time available, and the workshop will end for many with some loose ends. The availability of computer facilities which will deal with the standard analyses can be of considerable value.

It is, needless to say, a physically and mentally strenuous enterprise for all concerned. To some extent, the work completed by the student is self-paced, but as a member of an experimental group he is inevitably involved in the planning and running of experiments, and is exposed to the pressure to move as quickly as is expedient from one experiment to another. He will likewise find his writing-up time disturbed from time to time for service as a subject. If he is keen to write while the day's details are still fresh, he may find that evenings as well as days become well filled. In spite of these rigours—perhaps because of them—the intensive workshop is both a popular and a highly valued approach to practical psychology.

BIBLIOGRAPHY

Journals

A number of journals and other publications regularly devote space to matters of direct relevance to the practical course. All contain other material of interest. Suggestions made vary in sophistication and apply to different student populations. Some are based on the authors' own views and experience in the classroom, others are evaluative research reports.

American Psychologist. The journal of the American Psychological Association includes articles of practical interest from time to time: these are frequently to be found in the 'Comment' section.

Behaviour Research Measurement and Instrumentation. Published by the Psychonomic Society and concerned principally with the application of computer technology to psychology, including calculating and experiment simulation functions, the use of the computer as an item of apparatus capable of a wide range of uses, and the computer in the role of experimenter.

Periodically. A pamphlet from the APA Clearinghouse on pre-college psychology. It runs from 1970 to 1977 (to Volume 8), then expands and changes format to become *High School Psychology Teacher.* Under the heading 'Gimmickry' these eight volumes contain a large number of suggestions for class experiments mainly of the paper and pencil kind. They are of varying degrees of complexity and well worth looking at. Some make good class experiments, others, useful individual experiments, and while some are concerned with replication of earlier work, others propose novel ways of drawing on more recent work. Contributers include pre-college and university teachers of psychology. *High School Psychology Teacher* includes this feature under AIDS (Activities, Inquiries and Demonstrations).

Psychology Teaching. The bulletin of the Association for the Teaching of Psychology first published in 1973. Membership of the Association reflects all levels of teaching and the bulletin contains a correspondingly wide approach to practical issues. Since the development of the bulletin has been contemporaneous with the establishment of school courses in psychology for examination at Advanced Level *GCE,* 'practical' contributions relate mainly to this level. It has no section which regularly carries articles relating to the practical course. Particular volumes carry contributions relating to the teaching of 'A' level psychology; for example, Volume 3, No. 1 focuses on this and contains a range of experimental syllabus suggestions and reports from teachers in schools and colleges: other volumes carry reports of experimental workshops and conferences.

Teaching of Psychology. This is published four times a year by Division Two of the APA. First issued in 1974, it is a continuation of a *Newsletter* issued since 1951. It carries a range of contributions relating to teaching issues in general at both school and university level, some of which are research reports. It has a standing 'Methods and Techniques' section in which items relating to the practical course are published. Much of value in this context is also to be found in other sections of this journal.

Laboratory manuals

Much has been written here and elsewhere about the misuse of the laboratory manual. This notwithstanding, most contain material which may be of value to course organizers: since they tend to date quickly, only a small, idiosyncratic, sample of recent manuals are noted here.

Brown, G., Charrington, D. H., and Cohen, L. (1975). *Experiments in the Social Sciences.* New York: Harper & Row. This contains details, together with necessary materials such as word lists, for twenty-one experiments covering some major features of introductory psychology syllabuses. Designed for classroom use with relatively small numbers (sixteen to twenty students), they require no special laboratory equipment. The statistical tests recommended are well within the capabilities of the average 'A' level or first-year university student. Detailed examples of all the tests suggested are provided in an extended Appendix.

Gardiner, J., and Kaminska, Z. (1975). *First Experiments in Psychology.* London: Methuen. This small volume provides full introductions to eight experiments, in terms of background material, methodological detail, the way in which results should be treated and points for discussion. Statistical background is covered in a further volume in the same series. Two of the experiments require laboratory apparatus.

Matheson, D. W., Bruce, R. L., and Beauchamp, P. L. (1970). *Introduction to Experimental Psychology.* New York: Holt, Rinehart & Winston. Much more than a laboratory manual, and aimed at a somewhat higher level than the two above works. It provides a thorough introduction to the research process and statistical testing. It introduces twenty research projects but provides little further prescriptive detail outside a short but useful Bibliography. The reader is left to make any further decisions. Most of the areas covered suggest that access to a well-equipped laboratory would be required.

Jung, J., and Bailey, J. H. (1976). *Contemporary Psychology Experiments: Adaptations for Laboratory,* second edition. New York: Wiley. Each of the eighteen experiments covered is introduced with a review of previous research; suggestions for designs and analysis are given. This volume also deals briefly with methodological and ethical issues, and with report writing.

Kantowitz, B. H., and Roediger, H. L. (1978). *Experimental Psychology. Understanding Psychological Research.* London: Rand McNally. This new book is much more than a laboratory manual. It attempts a thoroughgoing integration of methodology and content at the level of the first-year undergraduate. Each of the ten content sections includes a suggested demonstration experiment which needs little or no equipment, and discusses in detail practical points of experimentation relating to a specific piece of research.

REFERENCES
Anderson, B. F. (1966). *The Psychology Experiment*. Wadsworth.

Barber, T. X. (1976). *Pitfalls in Human Research*. Oxford: Pergamon Press.

Bell, J. E. (1977). *A Guide to Library Research in Psychology*. Dubuque, Iowa: Wm. C. Brown Co.

Dobson, C. B. (1976). *Experiments in the Classroom—Schools Council General Studies Project, Interplay Collection*. Harlow: Longmans.

Dobson, C. B. (ed.) (1976). *Psychology Collection—Schools Council General Studies Project*. Harlow: Longmans.

Dobson, C. B. (1977). A-Level Psychology in Schools. *Trends in Education*, **4**, 42–48.

Easting, G. (1976). A Check-list Method for Teaching Evaluation of Research Articles. *Psychology Teaching*, **4**, 28–30.

Eysenck, H. J. (1975). Who Needs a Random Sample? *Bulletin, BPS*, **28**, 195–198.

Gardner, L. E. (1977). A Relatively Painless Method of Introduction to the Psychological Literature Search. *Teaching of Psychology*, **4**, 89–91.

Gutman, D. (1969). Psychological Naturalism in Cross Cultural Studies. In: Willems, E. P., and Rausch, H. L. *Naturalistic Viewpoints in Psychological Research*. New York: Holt, Rinehart & Winston.

Hergenhahn, B. R. (1970). *Self-Directing Introduction to Psychological Experimentation*. Monterey, California Brooks/Cole.

Hoffmans, H. S. (1962). The Analogue Lab: A New Kind of Teaching Device. *American Psychologist*, **17**, 684–694.

Kiesler, G. R. (1974). Evaluation of Computer-based Laboratory Simulation Models. *Behaviour Research Methods and Instrumentation*, **6**, 124–126.

LeUnes, A. D. (1977). The Developmental Library Search: Can a Nonsense Assignment Make Sense? *Teaching of Psychology*, **4**, 86.

McGuire, W. J. (1973). The Yin and Yang of Progress in Social Psychology: Seven Koan. *Journal of Personality and Social Psychology*, **26**, 446–456.

Main, D. B. (1972). Towards a Future Orientated Curriculum. *American Psychologist*, **1972**, 245.

Matthews, J. B. (1978). 'Hunting' for Psychological Literature. A Methodology for the Introductory Research Course. *Teaching of Psychology*, **5**, 100–101.

Miller, J. (1976). Understanding the Total Process. *Change Magazine*, **8**, No. 2, 46–49.

Murphy, L. E. (1974). The Division on the Teaching of Psychology. ATP's Counterpart in the United States, *Psychology Teaching*, **2**, 200–205.

Murray, F. S., Pasternack, T. L., and Rowe, F. B. (1972). An Informal Self-scheduled Laboratory for Introductory Psychology in a Small Liberal Arts College. *American Psychologist*, **27**, 1200.

Parr, V. R. (1978). Course Related Library Instruction for Psychology Students. *Teaching of Psychology*, **5**, 101–102.

Periodically. From APA Clearing-House on Pre-college Psychology.

Poulton, E. C. (1973). Unwanted Range Effects from Using Within Subjects Experimental Designs. *Psychological Bulletin*, **80**, 113–121.

Regula, C. R. (1971). Some Suggestions for Improving the Psychology Laboratory Course Experience. *American Psychologist*, **26**, 1020–1021.

Rosenthal, R. (1966). *Experimenter Effects in Behavioural Research*. New York: Appleton Century Crofts.

Rossan, S., and Levine, N. (1974). Field Methods: A Course for Teaching Non-laboratory Research Methods. *Bulletin, BPS*, **27**, 123–138.

Silverman, I. (1977). *The Human Subject in the Psychological Laboratory*. Oxford: Pergamon Press.

Stang, D.J., and O'Connell, E. J. (1974). The Computer as Experimenter in Social Psychological Research. *Behaviour Research Methods and Instrumentation*, **6**, 223–231.

Stevens, R. (1977). D305—The Social Psychology Course of the Open University. *Psychology Teaching*, **5**, 177–186.

Stout, L. S. (1974). Modelling and the Michigan Experimental Simulation Supervisor: An Overview and Some Prospects. *Behaviour Research Methods and Instrumentation*, **6**, 121–123.

Wells, A. M. (1972). Ways in Which a Psychology Course Was Improved. *American Psychology*, **27**, 1075–1076.

Zenhausen, R. (1972). Further Suggestions for the Improvement of the Undergraduate Psychology Laboratory. *American Psychologist*, **27**, 1074.

The Teaching of Psychology
Edited by J. Radford and D. Rose
© 1980 John Wiley & Sons Ltd.

4

Alternative Methods

DAVID ROSE

INTRODUCTION

Typically the question is first asked after five or six weeks of the course, and typically the course is a lecture course on the psychology of learning. The question is very often a little hesitantly put, reflecting slight incredulity and perhaps mild embarrassment, but always it is, in essence, the same. How can teachers of psychology (of all people), in the presentation of their courses, so consistently ignore almost everything that research has told us about the principles of learning? If this rings a bell, so too will the usual replies in terms of shortage of staff/ money/time/facilities, etc., and of course unconvincing as they must seem to the questioner, there is more than a little truth in such answers. Nevertheless the general point that psychologists should, where appropriate in their teaching, practice the psychology they preach cannot be ignored.

In Chapter 1 Michael Howe discussed the use of the conventional methods in teaching psychology. The purpose of the present chapter is to review some alternatives which might be considered in teaching contexts where the lecture, seminar and tutorial have traditionally been the preferred methods. These alternatives have developed, at least in part, out of perceived inadequacies in the more conventional teaching methods and represent an attempt to develop aspects of the instructional process so as to take closer account and make greater use of our knowledge of the psychology of learning. From this knowledge it is clear that in order to optimize the learning process one must consider both the nature and presentation of the material to be learned and the characteristics of the learner. Broadly the alternative methods to be discussed here have developed in response to one or other consideration and can thus be considered under the two headings of 'learner-centred' and 'content-centred' developments. Specifically it is intended to concentrate on the latter category of developments although brief mention will be made of 'learner-centred' methods as well.

Before embarking upon this review it is perhaps sensible to make clear the author's own evaluation of this general category of 'alternative methods'. To label a teaching method as an 'alternative' implies that it might be substituted for some other teaching method without loss to the overall educational process. However, even putting aside the questions of staffing and resources this cannot be realistically claimed for many of the methods to be discussed here. Most of these methods are, I think, best regarded as potentially valuable adjuncts to other methods discussed in this section of the book. Thus 'supplementary methods' might be a better title than 'alternative methods' for the present chapter. Additionally we must be wary of applying the term 'method' too readily. This label has already come under scrutiny in Chapter 1 for the 'illusory air of precision' it may afford (p. 20) and the point is well taken. However, in the present chapter the greater concern is that some of the ideas to be discussed are much too specific in their applicability to merit the label of 'teaching method'. For example the recommendation to students of certain types of literature in an attempt to bring home to them the blunt psychological reality of suffering from a mental illness, may prove invaluable in a course on clinical psychology but it hardly constitutes a teaching method. Certainly 'methods' as such will be reviewed here, but 'didactic devices' might more appropriately describe some of the ideas to be discussed.

But enough of labels.

LEARNER-CENTRED DEVELOPMENTS

The traditional 'teacher-centred' mix of lectures and seminars more often than not casts the student in a passive—rather than an active—role, and certainly tolerates very narrow limits of individual difference between students in terms of learning ability. However, as noted above, the characteristics of the learner and the nature of his role in the learning process must be taken into account if learning is to be optimized, and methods of tuition are now available in which their importance is regarded as axiomatic. We may collectively refer to these as 'individual instruction methods', or 'learner-centred' methods (as distinct from the more traditional methods which are 'teacher-centred') but they can be more specifically classified. Hartley (1974), for example, has distinguished four major categories of 'learner-centred' methods in psychology teaching, programmed learning, Keller-type procedures, Ferster-type procedures and computer assisted instruction.

Of these programmed learning has the longest history (Skinner, 1958). However, the most extensively investigated method in recent years has perhaps been the personalized instruction method (PSI) developed by Fred S. Keller.

A brief discussion of PSI will perhaps suffice to give the reader an idea of the general character of individual learning methods.

Keller's method is summarized by Hartley (1972) in the following way:

> A student taking a Keller-type course works at his own pace through a number of instructional units—these may be reading assignments, programmed texts, laboratory exercises, etc. He must demonstrate mastery (usually by taking a short-answer and/or objective test) of each unit before proceeding to the next. His readiness to take the next unit is assessed by a teaching assistant (a student who took the course before and got an 'A' grade). Teaching assistants are themselves monitored by advanced teaching assistants or 'proctors'. Teaching assistants obtain credit for their part in the course. Failure to demonstrate mastery is not held against the student and many opportunities are provided for the student to make up any such failure. His progress through the units is usually displayed on a wall chart. Lectures and demonstrations are used as vehicles for motivation rather than for passing on critical information. They are not compulsory and they are only given when a certain percentage of the class has reached a certain point in the course.

Thus whilst incorporating the basic active involvement and self-pacing characteristics of earlier programmed learning methods, Keller-type procedures additionally emphasize the use of the written word, the need for the student's mastery of one unit before proceeding to the next, and the use of student proctors. Significantly, lectures are regarded only as a means of motivating the student. Keller-type methods are not specific to the teaching of psychology, of course, and have been developed within a variety of contexts and for a variety of purposes. Furthermore, general discussion of their advantages and disadvantages can be found in general texts on educational methods as well as in more specialist sources such as Ryan (1974). Consequently it is intended here to do no more than indicate to the reader interested in the use of PSI in psychology courses a way into the appropriate literature.

Essential reading is the original paper by Keller (1968). The development of PSI over a 10-year period is traced in a further paper (Keller, 1974) and the variety of application of the PSI method in psychology teaching is indicated by a bibliography by Hess and Sherman (1972) covering some 261 papers. Many evaluative papers on the use of PSI in psychology courses have been, and continue to be, published. Sometimes these take the form of objective comparisons of PSI and more conventional course formats (for example Johnson, Zlotlow, Berger and Croft, 1974; Riedel, Harney and La Fief, 1976; Mack, 1977). Alternatively they evaluate one or more of the factors (self-pacing, unit mastery, proctors, etc.) identified by Keller as essential (for example

Calhoun, 1976; Caldwell, Bissonnettee, Klishis, Ripley, Farudi, Hochstetter, Radiker, 1978). Another category of evaluative papers has been concerned with predicting student performance on courses employing PSI (for example, Born and Whelan, 1973; Allan, Giat and Cherney, 1974; Henneberry, 1976; Roberts, Meier, Santogrossi and Moore, 1978). These evaluative papers are too numerous to list but those wishing to investigate this literature further should pay particular attention to three journals: the *Journal of Personalized Instruction*, the *Journal of Applied Behaviour Analysis*, and *Teaching of Psychology*.

Whilst PSI methods have been chosen to illustrate the general nature of individual, as opposed to 'teacher-centred', learning methods, as noted above there are a number of other individual learning methods. Discussion of them is beyond the scope of the present chapter but the reader who wishes to investigate the relevant literature further will find an excellent starting point in three annotated bibliographies by Hartley (1972, 1973, 1974).

CONTENT-CENTRED DEVELOPMENTS

With individual instruction methods in which the student determines his own rate of progress, it is argued that the problems of getting lost (resulting from too fast a presentation of material), and becoming bored (resulting from too slow a presentation of material), are by definition avoided. Thus the student's interest is maintained. Additionally it is claimed that by enforcing active participation by the student the efficiency of the learning process is enhanced. Others have sought to achieve both these objectives by manipulation of the context in which the psychological content is presented, and in terms of which it is discussed by the teacher.

The Use of Context

Specifically the argument is that presenting psychological concepts in a context which is both to some extent familiar to the student and intrinsically interesting serves to facilitate the learning process in the following ways. First, the familiar context provides a memory framework in terms of which the new material can be organized; a structure to which previously unfamiliar facts and ideas can adhere. Second, the intrinsic interest of the context helps to maintain sufficient attention to the new material for it to be learned.

Teaching the history of psychology provides a good illustration of the way in which context can be used in this way. Some consideration of the historical development of psychology forms part of most academic psychology courses. Usually it is seen by the teacher as a means of showing the student how different areas of psychology relate to each other and why particular approaches to the subject have evolved. In other words it is in order to explain the state of psychology today that courses on historical development of the subject are usually regarded by the teacher as important. To the student, however, such courses often seem very dry and indeed irrelevant to the sorts of immediate issues which probably first interested him in the subject. Inevitably it is not until the student has progressed some considerable way through the course that he can appreciate the integrative value of a knowledge of the history of psychology, which is of course the teacher's reason for giving the course. In the meantime he is confronted with seemingly endless lists of apparently tenuously linked names, dates and views. Interest flags before the point of the course can be appreciated. However, this need not be the case. Interest need not flag if the names and dates are presented in a context which is already interesting and meaningful to the student, and since most students have some knowledge of history before embarking on a psychology course psychology's history can be presented within this wider historical context already familiar to the student. Of course it can be argued that if the student has already been made to think of history as boring as a result of earlier educational endeavours this strategy will merely compound the problem. On the other hand so much of psychology's development has taken place in relatively recent years that the wider historical context is likely to have intrinsic interest for most students.

One attempt to enliven the context for teaching the history of psychology by working the names and dates of psychology into the wider sphere of world history was reported by Swain (1976). The main part of Swain's paper is a suggested chronology for students spanning the period from 1800 to 1960. Entries for 1925–1929, for example, are:

1925 FISHER: "STATISTICAL METHODS FOR RESEARCH WORKERS" (BRITAIN)
1926 Baird invents television (Britain)
1927 First talkie film (U.S.A.)
1928 Fleming discovers penicillin—the first antibiotic (Britain)
1928 Disney's first animated cartoon (U.S.A.)
1929 BERGER DEVISES TECHNIQUE (E.E.G.) FOR RECORDING ELECTRICAL POTENTIALS OF THE BRAIN (GERMANY)
1929 HULL COMMENCES WORK ON HIS LARGE-SCALE HYPOTHETICO-DEDUCTIVE THEORY OF BEHAVIOUR (U.S.A.)
1929 LASHLEY: "BRAIN MECHANISMS & INTELLIGENCE" (U.S.A.)
1929–32 World Economic Depression

In other parts of the chronology we are reminded that Pavlov's death occurred in the same year as the start of the Spanish Civil War, and that Hebb's *Organi-*

zation of Behaviour' was published in the year that saw the beginning of Mao Tse-Tung's Republic of China. In 1956 Tommy Steele's rise to stardom and the first large-scale trial of oral contraceptives had to share the limelight with George Miller's publication of the classic *Psychological Review* paper 'The Magical Number Seven Plus or Minus Two'. Certainly Swain's paper provides a most useful starting point for anyone wishing to develop this idea.

Most attempts to enliven the context in which psychology is presented have made use of literature. It can, of course, be argued that a consideration of literature is not merely a 'didactic device' but an essential part of studying psychology. Certainly the view has often been expressed that literature and objective psychological description simply constitute differing representation of a single reality. Indeed no less a psychologist than Donald Hebb recently made this point in an interview (Rawles, 1976, p. 50):

> It seems to me that much of what we know about human beings is learned from novels, plays, ... I don't think that there is any prospect for a thousand years perhaps of scientific psychology giving a study of character as impressive as that produced by Joseph Conrad in *Lord Jim*.

But whether or not the consideration of literature is regarded as an essential part of the psychology student's activities, there can be little doubt that the literature context can be very valuable. Its value lies both in providing an interesting and often familiar framework for the student's learning of psychological principles and a realistic and readily available world within which to predict, observe and question the operation of these principles.

Nor is this notion new. Shrodes, Van Gundy and Husband (1943) published a collection of literary excerpts which purported to illustrate various psychological principles. However, in recent years there has been a considerable growth of interest in the contextual value of literature in the teaching of psychology. Since 1971, for example, several lists of 'psychological thrillers' have been published (McCollom, 1971, 1973, 1975; Le Unes, 1974; Benel, 1975; Swain, 1977; see also the *APA Psychology Teacher's Resource Book*, 1973). A 'psychological thriller' is a book of demonstrated popularity which is more readable, 'softer', and 'lower key' (Le Unes, 1974) than the student's usual textbook diet, but which is sufficiently relevant to some aspect of the student's psychology course for it to be regarded as valuable supplementary reading. The lists quoted above, which contain suggestions for both undergraduates and postgraduates, include many psychology books as such (for example, *Psychology the Science of Mental Life* by Miller) as well as titles from non-psychological literature. Furthermore they are general lists in terms of the aspects of psychology for which they form useful supplementary reading. However, there are now several publications in which the emphasis is clearly laid on the use of non-psychological literature in illustrating specified areas of psychology such as *The Abnormal Personality Through Literature* (Stone and Stone, 1966); *Child Development Through Literature* (Landau, Epstein and Stone, 1972); *Social Psychology Through Literature* (Fernandez, 1972), and *Adolescence Through Literature* (Burden, 1974).

One category of literature which has become particularly popular as a backdrop for the teaching of psychology in the last decade is science fiction. Indeed science fiction appears to have achieved a certain degree of general popularity in the teaching of academic subjects, at least in the USA. Williamson (1975) (quoted by Oshinsky and Anderson, 1977), for example, has listed over 1000 science fiction related courses at American colleges and universities. The increasing popularity of the science fiction approach to psychology itself is evidenced by the increasing number of publications devoted to it.

It is, I am sure, almost as perilous for an author to attempt to define science fiction as to define psychology itself. However, the range of science fiction stories used for the purposes of teaching psychology would seem to necessitate the adoption of a fairly broad definition. For example, the authors of the first reasonably comprehensive reader in this area (Katz, Warrick and Greenberg, 1974) have adopted for selection of their stories the simple criterion that they 'explore the concepts of psychology as they function in fictional worlds'. To put it in the Sci-Fi enthusiasts' terms, and undoubtedly to the horror of the purists, Skinner's *Walden II*, is just as much regarded as science fiction as Asimov's *Foundation* trilogy, or Frank Herbert's *Dune*.

The use of science fiction, like the use of other types of literature in psychology teaching, helps to maintain the student's interest because it allows psychology to be presented in an intrinsically interesting context. However, the ways in which psychological concepts are highlighted by the contexts of science fiction and non-science fiction literature are, I think, very often different. The value of literature in psychology teaching is usually that it provides a situation, albeit fictitious, within which the widespread and complex effects of various psychological factors upon people's overall behaviour patterns can be observed, and thus their relevance in explanation in real life, be appreciated. An interesting and detailed consideration of the precise ways in which literature can assist learning in the social sciences has been published by Sedeberg and Sedeberg (1974). However, in summarizing the position as far as psychology teaching is concerned we might say that the literature context provides ready-made and conveniently packaged units of 'everyday real life experience' in terms of which the student can judge the reality and relevance of psychological concepts.

Science fiction, on the other hand, is of value to the psychology teacher in a slightly different way. The packaged unit of context the teacher derives from science fiction, far from being simulation of real life, typically represents life intentionally 'stretched' or altered in one or more significant respects. For example, the action often occurs on another planet which differs from our own in its physical characteristics, or some particular advance in technology on our own planet is assumed, or, alternatively, a change is assumed in the structure or function of the 'people' in the story. The essence of science fiction lies in tracing the implications of these assumed modifications of our present situation. For the psychology teacher the most valuable stories are those in which the implications for society of changes in psychological processes, or for our psychological processes of political, social, technological or environmental changes, are considered. Generally, however, the value of science fiction is not in illustrating the relevance of psychological processes to man's present situation, but in focusing attention on the psychological processes themselves by exploring the way they might operate in an altered situation. Rather as a hall of mirrors, by systematic distortion of our reflection, can draw attention to certain of our physical features, so the imaginary systematic distortions of our social, technological, political and environmental situation, as occur in science fiction stories, can highlight the nature and implications of our psychological processes.

As mentioned above the first major reader based on the science fiction approach to psychology was published in 1974 by Katz, Warrick and Greenberg. There is now a second edition of this (Katz, Greenberg and Warrick, 1977) but there are also a number of other books based on the same approach. Of these perhaps the main ones are by Jones and Roe (1974), Estrada and Estrada (1977) and Melvin, Brodsky and Fowler (1977). These and related publications on the nature of the science fiction approach to psychology have recently been reviewed by Saeger (1979). Whilst there have been some attempts at evaluating the use of science fiction in this way (Oshinsky and Anderson, 1977; Saeger, 1977), no firm conclusions can be drawn as yet. However, the popularity of the approach among students has frequently been noted and as a means of enlivening the usual fare of textbook and journal it merits serious consideration.

So far this discussion of the use of literature in teaching psychology has been confined to a consideration of fiction. In the category of non-fiction the most useful publications for the psychology teacher perhaps come under the heading of 'first-hand accounts'. These range from straightforward biographical and autobiographical material to accounts of illness and handicap and coping with them, written by sufferers and their relatives.

White (1974) has reported the successful use of life history material in the teaching of personality. Although much of the course followed a traditional format of lectures and seminars, life histories were 'given prominence and taken seriously as a means of studying personality' (White, 1974, p. 69). Some of the materials used by White for his course were published in book form in 1952 (White, 1952), but ordinary published biographies and autobiographies were also employed. The students' own autobiographical details were also used in the course on occasions.

This latter type of material has been used to good effect as an adjunct to more general psychology courses by Hettich (1976). In this case students kept a 'journal' which was defined (Hettich, 1976, p. 60) as:

> neither a diary (i.e. a continuous, intimate, spontaneous out-pouring of important events) nor a log (i.e. an account or record of events). Rather ... it is a topical autobiography: a short, discontinuous personal document which represents the excerpting from an individual's life of a special class of events—in this case events constituting a psychology course.

As Hettich observed, the student's twice-weekly entries in their journals were relatively short, averaging about five sentences. Nevertheless the journal proved to be a successful vehicle for relating formally taught psychology and the students' own thoughts, feelings and experiences.

At the risk of straying from the point slightly, one specialized category of autobiography perhaps merits a brief mention here. However, in this case the suggested references are intended primarily for the perusal of the teacher rather than the student. These autobiographies are of famous psychologists themselves. Boice (1977) in a brief but entertaining article in which he introduces quotations from the autobiographies of Skinner, Webb, Krech, Hunt, Allport and Beach, among others, ably substantiates his claim that 'A rich supply of understanding and appreciation (and, incidentally, some good lecture material) can be had from psychologists' autobiographies' (Boice, 1977, p. 55). For those who become addicted, the references at the end of Boice's article will provide a useful introduction to this literature.

By far the largest group of non-fictional works which are of obvious relevance to the teacher of psychology are the first-hand accounts of handicap, illness and treatment. In recent years a number of excellent annotated bibliographies of such works have appeared (Rippere, 1976, 1977, 1978; Pearson 1977). These cover accounts by parents and relatives of coping with a variety of mental and physical handicaps and illnesses, as well as delinquency in children, and also accounts by adults of their diseases and disabilities (for example, schizophrenia, depression, epilepsy, Parkinson's disease, cancer, heart disease and blindness), and of treatments they have undergone. Altogether the four bibliographies include over 200 references. The major relevance of this category of literature is clearly to those involved in teaching clinical, abnormal and developmental psychology although these four bibliographies are well worth the attention of those devising more general psychology courses.

The value of first-hand accounts in the teaching of psychology is not only in increasing the intrinsic interest of the materials the student is required to study, but also, and most importantly, in providing the student with an all-round view of depression or schizophrenia or whatever, which is all too often unavailable from conventional, 'objective', textbook accounts. The first-hand account helps to redress the balance in favour of a 'whole-person' approach to psychology which almost inevitably gets overshadowed by objective, scientific analyses of psychological processes.

In the preceding pages a number of types of literature have been reviewed from a psychology teaching viewpoint. Clearly the value of introducing such non-psychological literature to the student's reading list varies from course to course. For example, whilst the use of science fiction in a conventional academic undergraduate programme might be seen by the teacher only as providing relevant light relief in an otherwise heavyweight reading list, the teacher of clinical psychology will probably regard at least some titles from the 'first-hand accounts' literature as an essential part of the students' reading. At an intermediate stage the teacher of psychology to non-psychologists (nurses, social workers, probation officers, etc.) may regard the use of literature as necessary in their courses, not because it is the only way to cover the relevant parts of psychology, but because it is one way of maintaining the interest of students whose main interest lies in subjects other than psychology.

Thus it is difficult to formulate any general advice to the teacher. However, there are, perhaps, two points to be made. First, as a didactic device, literature is very demanding of the time of both student and teacher. Clearly the student's private study time must be increased by the introduction of non-psychological literature to the reading list. But even when all concerned are familiar with the work in question, a considerable time typically is needed for small group discussion in order to 'tease out' the psychology from this sort of material and ensure that its relevance to other course work has been appreciated by the student. Second, before becoming too committed to literature-related approaches to psychology, the teacher should perhaps reflect upon the nature of literature as source material in science. The point can perhaps best be made by quoting further from the interview with Donald Hebb (Rawles, 1976), an excerpt from which began this discussion of the uses of literature in teaching psychology:

RR: This means that novelists, writers and artists are providing psychological insights although they are not yet in a scientific form.
DH: And perhaps never will be. You can define psychology as you like. You can define it as inclusive of all psychological insights and that would include, for example, literature and painting. Or you may define it, as I think it more suitable to do so, as the scientific study of the human mind and human behaviour; so that from my definition I would exclude *Lord Jim*. I would exclude it, but by no means down-

grade it. I would prefer to say here is the ally, not the competitor, but the great ally of psychology.

This perhaps brings us back to a distinction previously drawn between teaching 'methods' and 'supplementary didactic devices'. Works of literature, although often concerned with the same problems as psychology do not constitute scientific documents. Thus to attempt to teach psychology entirely through literature—to give literature-related approaches to psychology the status of a teaching method—is surely inappropriate. The use of literature as a didactic device supplementing a rigorous scientific approach to the subject can, however, be of great value to the teacher.

The heavy time commitment involved in literature-related approaches to psychology teaching can be reduced somewhat if the literature is presented in an abridged, cinematic form. Already a number of annotated bibliographies of commercial feature films which may illustrate some aspect of psychology have been published (Thomas, 1975; Cox and Coulson, 1976; Bolt, 1976). Of these, the paper by Cox and Coulson is the most comprehensive, listing almost 200 films and the nature of their psychological interest (adolescence, alcoholism, amnesia, attitudes, depression, drug-taking, generation-gap, handicap, homosexuality, imprisonment, leadership, marriage, 'mass' psychology, mental illness, occupational stress, old age, phobia, therapy). Of course, whilst it may take the student less time to watch a film than read a novel, the teacher must still make allowance for subsequent discussion time. There is also the additional organizational burden of hiring film, projector, projectionist, room, etc., to be considered. With regard to the extent to which it is advisable to include such material in psychology courses, the same cautionary note must be sounded as with the use of literature. Film, like literature, can supplement, but cannot replace scientific data in the teaching of psychology, and as Bolt (1976, p. 190) says

> Our intent in using the film [is] not to replace scientific knowledge but to illuminate it through the insights of the artist, and to place the theory and concepts of the discipline in a context which more closely reflects reality as it is experienced.

The Presentation of Content

In addition to involving less student time, film may be of more use than literature to the psychology teacher because it allows for a more immediate and vivid presentation of psychological content. So far in this section of the chapter we have been concerned with 'alternative teaching methods' in which the student's interest and involvement are maintained by manipulation of the context in which the psychological content is presented. Let us now briefly consider alternatives to the conventional lectures, seminars and tutorials in which interest and understanding are fostered by some particular mode of presentation of the psychological content itself. Such consideration need only be brief because the modes of presentation in question are audio and video cassettes and film, the general educational advantages and disadvantages of which are discussed in detail in many an educational technology text.

The value to students of providing demonstrations of the phenomena they are studying is obvious. However, in psychology such demonstrations can often prove difficult to carry out. Even to demonstrate a rat's learning of a simple operant response in a Skinner box involves considerably more time and effort than one might imagine, and to set up demonstrations of many of the phenomena discussed in social and developmental psychology can present insurmountable difficulties. Furthermore, many demonstrations raise ethical issues. For example, more than a minimal use of many of the techniques of the physiological psychologist for demonstration purposes alone could certainly be considered unjustifiable. Happily the problems can be resolved by the use of film to make permanent and repeatable records of demonstrations. In this way the actual number of demonstrations set up can be kept to a minimum, and, furthermore, the demonstrations can often be carried out by an expert in the use of the techniques in question. There are now a great many films on psychology available for hire or purchase; indeed so many that the compilation of a central register is perhaps somewhat overdue.

However, some attempt has been made to list relevant film catalogues and addresses of suppliers by two organizations:

(a) *In the USA*
American Psychological Association,
1200 Seventeenth Street, NW,
Washington DC 20036.
   (b) *In the UK*
British Industrial and Scientific Film Association,
26 D'Arblay Street,
London W1V 3FH.

In addition, new films are reviewed from time to time in both *Psychology Teaching* and *Teaching of Psychology*.

The increasing access of teachers to video recording equipment, of course, means that it is possible to make a permanent record of demonstrations designed specifically for a particular course, rather than having to rely on the sorts of films referred to above. General advice on the use of video equipment in teaching is easily available from college and university audio-visual centres, of course, but more specific advice on its use in the teaching of psychology is contained in two recent papers (Summerfield, 1978; Apter, 1978). A number of authors have published accounts of psychology courses in which heavy reliance is placed on the use of videotapes (e.g. Ingalls and Moakley, 1971; Walker and Inbody, 1974), and the relative values of live, filmed and video-taped lectures are discussed by McKinney and Miller (1977). Summerfield (1978) has listed a number of uses of video in the teaching of psychology, but nevertheless (p. 21) suggests a cautious approach on the part of the teacher:

> The making of educational videotapes is immensely time- and labour-consuming. Would-be producers should first ask themselves the following questions. Is the material to be presented otherwise unobtainable or only obtainable with great difficulty? (There are a range of commercially produced scientific films.) Will this video-tape save as many hours of my time as it has taken me to make it? Will the videotape allow me to present material to a whole class which would only be seen otherwise by a few students? If the answer to all these questions is NO, you would probably be better off spending your time in other activities. A picture may be worth a thousand words, but a videotape is not necessarily worth a thousand transparencies.

Audio cassettes as well as video cassettes have become quite a popular aid in psychology teaching in recent years. Most of the commercially produced audio cassettes take the form of lectures, interviews or discussions involving the 'famous names' of psychology. Certainly interest can be added to a course if the student is able to listen to Skinner or Pribram or Melzack directly, and being relatively cheap these cassettes make useful supplementary materials. A brief survey of psychology cassettes available in the UK was published by Rose (1977). For sources of such materials in the USA the reader is again referred to the *APA Psychology Teachers Resource Book* (1973). In addition, new cassettes, and also films and videotapes, are reviewed from time to time in both *Psychology Teaching* and *Teaching of Psychology*.

Of course the main vehicle for presentation of psychology remains the text-book. There have been great improvements in the last twenty-five years in the presentation of content in psychology texts, as an examination of successive editions of Hilgard's famous *Introduction to Psychology* will show (Hilgard, Atkinson and Atkinson, 1975). However, psychology text presentation, first seriously examined by Stevens and Stone (1947), has come under ever-increasing scrutiny in recent years (*Peanuts'* observation that 'no book on psychology can be any good if one can understand it' perhaps touched a sensitive spot!). For example, two directories of current introductory texts and reviews of them have been published recently (Johnson, 1977, 1978) and both *Psychology Teaching* and *Teaching of Psychology* specialize in the review of psychology books from a teaching point of view. Furthermore a number of papers have focused attention on readability scores, human interest scores and student ratings of introductory texts (Ogdon, 1954; Gillen, 1973; Landrigan and Palladino, 1974; Gillen, 1975; Quereshi and Zulli, 1975; Quereshi, 1977), social psychology texts (Bamber and Nolte, 1974; Stang, 1975; Stang and Solomon, 1976; Gillen, Kendall and Finch, 1977), educational psychology texts (Hofmann and Vyhonsky, 1975; Eson, 1976; Hofmann, 1977), developmental psychology texts (Feldstein, 1977), biological psychology texts (Rose and Vinegrad, 1979) and texts on behaviour therapy (Kendall, Finch and Gillen, 1976).

Clearly there is room for improvement in many cases, but this increased interest in the presentation of textbook material is to be welcomed as one way of facilitating the student's learning of psychology.

IN CONCLUSION

In recent years there has been a very considerable diversification of the contexts in which psychology is taught. Not only has psychology become an accepted part of many vocational and professional courses, but also within the academic context itself there has been a considerable increase in the number of levels at which it is taught. Psychology, therefore, is now taught to students of widely varying abilities and primary interests. Consequently sole reliance on the traditional teaching methods of university academic psychology courses (lectures, seminars, tutorials) is perhaps less than ideal for a considerable proportion of those studying the subject. Furthermore, even within the narrow context of university psychology the threat or actuality of falling student recruitment on both sides of the Atlantic has provided an impetus for reappraisal of these conventional teaching methods.

Psychology teaching in many present day contexts has been much improved by the introduction of other approaches reviewed in this section of the present volume (Experimental and Experiential). However, there are contexts and content areas for which these approaches are themselves inappropriate or unworkable. The teacher is thus forced to adopt some variant of the lecture method, after all, and in any case, there are still contexts in which the lecture method is entirely appropriate (see Chapter 1). The suggestion contained in the present chapter is that where the conventional teaching methods of lecture, seminar and tutorial are adopted, for whatever reason, the lecturer will find the sorts of 'didactic devices' reviewed here a valuable supplement.

The individualization of learning, the highlighting of content and the underlining of the context and relevance of that content, to which such devices contribute must, after all, improve the efficiency of the educational process.

REFERENCES

Allen, G. J., Giat, L., and Cherney, R. (1974). Locus of Control, Test Anxiety and Student Performance in a Personalized Instruction Course. *Journal of Educational Psychology*, **6**, 968–973.

American Psychological Association (1973). *APA Psychology Teachers Resource Book*. Washington DC: American Psychological Association.

Apter, M. J. (1978). Some Experiences with the Construction and Use of Video Cassettes for Undergraduate Psychology Teaching. *Psychology Teaching*, **6**, 25.

Bamber, R. T., and Nolte, M. N. (1974). The Impossible Dream: How to Outscience Physics. *Teaching of Psychology*, **1**, 28.

Benel, R. A. (1975). Psychological Thrillers: Thrilling to Whom? *Teaching of Psychology*, **2**, 176.

Boice, R. (1977). Heroes and Teachers. *Teaching of Psychology*, **4**, 55.

Bolt, M. (1976). Using Films Based on Literature in Teaching Psychology. *Teaching of Psychology*, **3**, 189.

Born, D. G., and Whelan, P. (1973). Some Descriptive Characteristics of Student Performance in PSI and Lecture Courses. *Psychol. Rec.*, **23**, 145–152.

Burden, R. (1974). Adolescence Through Literature: A Novel Approach to an Age-old Problem. *Psychology Teaching*, **3**, 251.

Caldwell, E. C., Bissonnettee, K., Klishis, M. J., Ripley, M., Farudi, P. P., Hochstetter, G. T., and Radiker, J. E. (1978). Mastery: The Essential Essential in PSI. *Teaching of Psychology*, **5**, 59–65.

Calhoun, J. F. (1976). The Combination of Elements in the Personalized System of Instruction. *Teaching of Psychology* **3**, 73–76.

Cox, M., and Coulson, A. (1976). Psychology Teaching and the Cinema II. *Psychology Teaching*, **4**, 122.

Croll, W., and Moskaluk, S. (1977). Should Flesch Counts Count? *Teaching of Psychology*, **4**, 48.

Eson, M. E. (1976). A Critique of Hofmann and Vyhonsky's Evaluation of Introductory Educational Psychology Text-books. *American Psychologist*, **31**, 256.

Estrada, J., and Estrada, D. (eds) (1977). *The Future of Being Human: Psychology Through Science Fiction*. New York: Harper & Row.

Feldstein, J. H. (1977). Reading Ease and Human Interest Scores of Thirty-two Recent Child-Developmental Psychology Texts. *Teaching of Psychology*, **4**, 43.

Fernandez, R. (ed.) (1972). *Social Psychology Through Literature*. New York and London: Wiley.

Gillen, B. (1973). Readability and Human Interest Scores of Thirty-four Current Introductory Psychology Texts. *American Psychologist*, **28**, 1010.

Gillen, B. (1975). Readability and Human Interest Scores of Thirty-two Introductory Psychology Texts: Update and Clarification. *Teaching of Psychology*, **2**, 175.

Gillen, B., Kendall, C., and Finch, A. J. (1977). Reading Ease and Human Interest Scores: A Comparison of Flesch Scores with Subjective Ratings. *Teaching of Psychology*, **4**, 39.

Hartley, J. (1972). New Approaches to the Teaching of Psychology: An Annotated Bibliography. *Bulletin of the British Psychology Society*, **25**, 291–304.

Hartley, J. (1973). New Approaches in the Teaching of Psychology: An Annotated Bibliography. *Newsletter of the Association for the Teaching of Psychology*, **5**, 11–30.

Hartley, J. (1974). New Teaching Methods in Psychology: A Supplementary Annotated Bibliography. *Psychology Teaching*, **2**, 206.

Henneberry, J. K. (1976). Initial Progress Rates as Related to Performance in a Personalized System of Instruction. *Teaching of Psychology*, **3**, 178–181.

Hess, J. H., and Sherman, J. G. (1972). *PSI Psychology Course Catalog*. Harrisonburg: PSI Clearing House, Eastern Mennonite College.

Hettich, P. (1976). The Journal: An Autobiographical Approach to Learning. *Teaching of Psychology*, **3**, 60.

Hilgard, E. R., Atkinson, R. C., and Atkinson, R. L. (1975). *Introduction to Psychology*. New York: Harcourt Brace Jovanovich, sixth edition.

Hofmann, R. J. (1977). Simple Readability as a Comparative Index and its Application to Introductory Texts: Psychology and Educational Psychology. *Psychology Teaching*, **5**, 58.

Hofmann, R. J., and Vyhonsky, R. J. (1975). Readability and Human Interest Scores of Thirty-six Recently Published Introductory Educational Psychology Texts. *American Psychologist*, **30**, 790.

Howe, M. J. A. (1979). Conventional Methods. This volume, p. 20.

Ingalls, R. E., and Moakley, F. X. (1971). Systems Approach to Development of a Complete Psychology Course of Study. *Audio Visual Instruction*, **16**, 78.

Johnson, M. (1977). Directory of Introductory Psychology Texts in Print. *Teaching of Psychology*, **4**, 15.

Johnson, M. (1978). Directory of Introductory Psychology Texts in Print: 1978. *Teaching of Psychology*, **5**, 26.

Johnson, W. G., Zlotlow, S., Berger, J. L., and Croft, R. G. F. (1975). A Traditional Lecture Versus a PSI Course in Personality: Some Comparisons. *Teaching of Psychology*, **2**, 156–158.

Jones, R., and Roe, R. L. (eds) (1974). *Valence and Vision: A Reader in Psychology*. San Francisco: Rinehart Press.

Katz, H. A., Greenberg, M. H., and Warrick, P. (eds) (1977). *Psychology Through Science Fiction*. Chicago: Rand McNally.

Katz, H. A., Warrick, P., and Greenberg, M. H. (eds) (1974). *Introduction to Psychology Through Science Fiction*. Chicago: Rand McNally.

Keller, F. S. (1968). 'Good-bye Teacher . . .'. *Journal of Applied Behaviour Analysis*, **1**, 89–99.

Keller, F. S. (1974). Ten Years of Personalized Instruction. *Teaching of Psychology*, **1**, 4–9.

Kendall, P. C., Finch, A. J., and Gillen, B. (1976). Readability and Human Interest Scores as Objective Aids in Behaviour Therapy Text Selection. *Behaviour Therapy*, **7**, 535.

Landau, E. D., Epstein, S. L., and Stone, A. P. (eds) (1972). *Child Development Through Literature*. Englewood Cliffs: Prentice-Hall.

Landrigan, D. T., and Palladino, J. J. (1974). A Reply to Gillen. *American Psychologist*, **29**, 571.

Le Unes, A. (1974), Psychological Thrillers Revisited: A Tentative List of Master Thrillers. *American Psychologist*, **29**, 211.

Mack, D. (1977). Personalized Learning in the Introductory Psychology Course. *Bulletin of the British Psychology Society*, **30**, 312–314.

McCollom, I. N. (1971). Psychological Thrillers: Psychology Books Students Read When Given Freedom of Choice. *American Psychologist*, **26**, 921.

McCollom, I. N. (1973). Let's Get Them to Read Psychology Books. *Newsletter, APA Division on the Teaching of Psychology*, December, 1973.

McCollom, I. N. (1975). Readings Readers Recommend. *Teaching of Psychology*, **2**, 42.

McKinney, F., and Miller, D. J. (1977). Fifteen Years of Teaching General Psychology by Television. *Teaching of Psychology*, **4**, 120.

Melvin, K. B., Brodsky, S. L., and Fowler, R. D. (eds) (1977). *Psy Fi One: An Anthology in Science Fiction*. New York: Random House.

Ogdon, D. P. (1954). Flesch Counts of Eight Current Textbooks for Introductory Psychology. *American Psychologist*, **9**, 143.

Oshinsky, J. S., and Anderson, S. J. (1977). Science Fiction and the Didactic. *Psychology Teaching*, **5**, 17.

Pearson, A. (1977). More First Hand Accounts of Coping with Handicap, Illness and Deviance. *Psychology Teaching*, **5**, 145.

Psychology Teaching. The Bulletin of the Association for the Teaching of Psychology.

Quereshi, M. Y. (1977). An Updated Content Analysis of Introductory Psychology Textbooks. *Teaching of Psychology*, **4**, 25.

Quereshi, M. Y., and Zulli, M. R. (1975). A Content Analysis of Introductory Psychology Textbooks. *Teaching of Psychology*, **2**, 60.

Rawles, R. E. (1976). D. O. Hebb on the Teaching and Uses of Psychology. *Psychology Teaching*, **4**, 49.

Riedel, R. C., Harney, B., and LaFief, W. (1976). Unit Test Scores in PSI versus Traditional Classes in Beginning Psychology. *Teaching of Psychology*, **3**, 76–78.

Rippere, V. (1976). First Hand Accounts of Copying with an Ill, Handicapped or Deviant Child. A Short Bibliography for Use in Psychology Teaching. *Psychology Teaching*, **4**, 158.

Rippere, V. (1977). Personal Accounts of Mental Disorder and its Treatment: A Short Bibliography for Use in Psychology Teaching. *Psychology Teaching*, **5**, 26.

Rippere, V. (1978). Experience of Illness, Disability and Treatment. A Short Bibliography of Personal Accounts for Use in Psychology Teaching. *Psychology Teaching*, **6**, 57.

Roberts, M. C., Meier, R. S., Santogrossi, D. A., and Moore, D. A. (1978). Relationship of Student Characteristics and Performance in a Personalized System of Instruction Course. *Teaching of Psychology*, **5**, 118–121.

Rose, F. D. (1977). Cassette Psychology: Audio Cassettes for Teaching Psychology. *Psychology Teaching*, **5**, 54.

Rose, F. D., and Vinegrad, M. D. (1979). Readability and Human Interest Ratings of Recent Texts in Physiological Psychology. *Psychology Teaching*, **7**, 33–38.

Ryan, B. A. (1974). *Keller's Personalized System of Instruction: An Appraisal*. Washington DC: American Psychological Association.

Saeger, W. (1977). Science Fiction as a Teaching Tool in Social and Environmental Psychology. *Psychology Teaching*, **5**, 154.

Saeger, W. (1979). Literature and Learning: The Art of the State. *Psychology Teaching*, **7**, 3–12.

Schrodes, C., Van Gundy, J., and Husband, R. W. (eds) (1943). *Psychology Through Literature*. Oxford: Oxford University Press.

Sederberg, P. C., and Sederberg, N. B. (1975). Transmitting the Non-transmissible. The Function of Literature in the Pursuit of Social Knowledge. *Philosophy and Phenomenological Research*, **36**, 173.

Skinner, B. F. (1958). Teaching Machines. *Science*, **28**, 969–977.

Stang, D. J. (1975). Student Evaluation of Twenty-eight Social Psychology Texts. *Teaching of Psychology*, **2**, 12.

Stang, D. J., and Solomon, R. (1976). Predicting Student Ratings of Social Psychology Texts. *Teaching of Psychology*, **3**, 138.

Stevens, S. S., and Stone, G. (1947). Psychological Reading, Easy and Hard. *American Psychologist*, **2**, 230–235.

Stone, A. A., and Stone, S. S. (eds) (1966). *The Abnormal Personality Through Literature*. Englewood Cliffs: Prentice-Hall.

Summerfield, A. B. (1978). The Uses of Video in Teaching Psychology. *Psychology Teaching*, **6**, 20.

Swain, R. (1976). The History of Psychology and Related Events 1800–1960. A Chronology for Students. *Psychology Teaching*, **4**, 31.

Swain, R. (1977). Psychological Thrillers. An Irish List. *Bulletin of the British Psychological Society*, **30**, 135.

Teaching of Psychology. Division Two of the American Psychological Association.

Thomas, J. B. (1975). Psychology Teaching and the Cinema: An Annotated Checklist of Feature Films. *Psychology Teaching*, **3**, 181.

Walker, L. D., and Inbody, P. W. (1974). A Different Approach to Teaching Introductory Psychology. *Teaching of Psychology*, **1**, 29.

White, R. W. (1952). *Lives in Progress: A Study of the Natural Growth of Personality*. New York: Holt, Rinehart & Winston.

White, R. W. (1974). Teaching Personality through Life Histories. *Teaching of Psychology*, **1**, 69.

Williamson, J. (1975). *Teaching SF*. Portales, N. M.: Jack Williamson.

SECTION II

Teaching Subject Areas Within Psychology

The division of the content of psychology has already been discussed at some length. Divisions for teaching purposes tend to be largely practical. The present arrangement is derived partly from practical experience, and more tenuously from theoretical considerations. Experience suggests that a single honours or major course *could* organize most of its material in these headings. We do not imply that it should. Where psychology is a component of something else—which might be a modular degree, or an applied training, or a liberal study—it is again not unlikely that one or more of these would form the core. And there is at least some case for regarding them as distinctive areas historically and in practice.

While the first five are relatively familiar, the 'Contextual, Integrative and Ethical Issues' heading is perhaps less so. Such issues may well, in teaching programmes, be shared among all the teachers and between different syllabuses. Here, we felt it essential to have a specific discussion of the way in which psychology fits with other studies, of what makes it hang together, so far as it does, and of the wider implications of psychology in its social setting.

5

Biological Psychology

RICHARD L. BRUCE

BIOLOGICAL PSYCHOLOGY

Biological psychology represents the convergence of the traditional functional emphasis of psychology and the structural emphasis of biology. Although researchers in both biology and psychology have dabbled in this intermediate zone for years, it now can claim a separate status and identity. Biology has established a background of knowledge and methodology for studying the structures in the nervous system. Psychology, for its part, contributes a store of behavioral observations and procedures which can be used to determine functional activity. Of more importance to a psychologist, biological research methods have now established means to observe the activity of the structures within the nervous system.

Psychology as a discipline appears to have arrived at a plateau in its growth. The study of the behaviour of an individual organism is yielding exciting 'breakthrough' discoveries with decreasing frequency. Rather, traditional psychology seems to have become a science of consolidating existing laws or polishing specific hypotheses. The advancing areas of psychology can be described as leading in three significant directions. One of these is the emergence of psychological engineering which represents the practical application of psychological knowledge. This emphasis on pragmatic application represents a new level of maturity in any discipline in that the theories have sufficient empirical support that they now can be applied to accomplish desired changes. The second major growth area in psychology is into the area of social psychology. Expanding the scope of interest beyond that of the mere individual into a study of the interaction between two or more individuals has yielded many exciting discoveries in recent years. The third 'leading edge' area in psychology is biological psychology. Psychologists are finding it useful to peer into the 'black box' to try to understand the contribution of the various components therein.

In its role as one of the 'leading edge' areas, biological psychology is also a leader in terms of new discoveries per unit of time. In fact, one of the significant problems to any instructor of biological psychology is to stay current with new discoveries as they are announced. I typically announce, in the first meeting of one of my physiological psychology classes, that some of the facts that will be learned during the semester will probably have to be modified before the semester closes. The growth is so rapid that some of the knowledge will be obsolete by the end of the semester. This rapidity of development provides a vexing problem to the instructor, namely, an inability to provide definitive answers to the questions from students. The best one can hope to do is to provide the most appropriate answer for the present time. However, one is constantly aware that a better answer may emerge in the near future. Another problem is that of keeping appraised of developments; journals, conventions, personal communications and the popular press are all possible channels for new data.

A sample of some of the new technological developments which contribute to the proliferation of new concepts will help to explain the phenomenal growth in biological psychology. One of the more important technological contributors has been developments in the fields of electronics and solid state physics. Since the nervous system appears to work on electrical activity, these technological developments allow the observation and precise measurement of the activity in the nervous system. The development of the transistor allowed the first reliable measurement of tiny electrical signals thus opening the way to directly measuring brain activity. This combined with the oscilloscope so that high speed electrical events could be displayed and recorded for accurate measurement provided the basic observational tools for many neurophysiological discoveries. With the recent emergence of micro-miniaturization, electronic technology now allows unprecedented sensitivity and simultaneously new vistas in terms of more complicated and comprehensive recording. For instance, it is relatively common for a modern researcher to utilize a computer to program the experimental parameters as well as analyse the complicated signals measured in the nervous system. This brain activity is then summarized in terms of the major activity components extracted from combining hundreds of individual trials. Thus, electronic technology allows us to measure previously invisible small signals, and at the same time allows the possibility of measuring and assimilating huge masses of information simultaneously.

Another extension of electronic capacity is the utilization of radio telemetry. Whereas a preparation sometimes can be conveniently measured by wires leading directly to the electronic instrumentation, nowadays it is possible to obtain such measurements from a free ranging animal through the use of radio transmitters implanted in the animal so as not to restrict movement. A final electronic tool can be found in the invention and development of the electron microscope. With this device it is possible to directly observe structural characteristics of the nervous system that had previously been invisible. Hypothetical structures are literally confirmed by photographic evidence via this device.

Another area of rapid growth which contributes directly to advances in biological psychology is that of understanding the chemical activity within the brain. Because of the extensive use of chemical compounds in altering brain functioning it has been said that we have entered an era of drug culture. The initial impression surrounding the phrase 'drug culture' involves the non-systematic use of drug compounds by individuals to artificially alter states of consciousness. Systematic study of some of these psycho-active compounds is providing insight to the chemical steps involved in the operation of the nervous system. Another major dimension to this growing body of knowledge is the legal prescription of compounds which less drastically affect the functioning of the brain. Mental institutions rely heavily on the use of drugs to control the emotional levels of the patients. In addition, tranquilizers, stimulants, and/or sedatives constitute a major category in the pharmaceutical industry. Research into brain chemistry, both for its own sake as well as for understanding the action of mood altering drugs, is another active area. Thus, we find that knowledge about the chemical characteristics supplements the electrical information that has been gained through electronic technology.

Psychological knowledge also contributes considerable insight to the functioning of the nervous system. The plateau previously ascribed to the discipline is sufficiently high that considerable information has been accumulated which may be applied to the functional analysis of the brain. Behavioural data and the research methodologies developed to discover them can be applied directly to a functional investigation of the nervous system. An added dimension towards the understanding of the brain is accomplished through the contribution of comparative psychology and/or ethology. The compilation of phylogenetic animal behavioural capacities is a useful basis for comparison with the nervous system structures found in various species. In many ways, the comparative approach represents only a supplementary source of information to understanding the functioning of the human brain; however, one must keep in mind that many of the surgical procedures employed in neurological research necessitates the use of lower animal forms.

Finally, there is a significant contribution towards understanding the functioning of the brain via the new knowledge obtained about the genetic mechanism. The discoveries surrounding DNA and the elucidation of the mechanics of genetic inheritance provide a rich basis for explaining the growth and development of neurological structures. It appears that many of the neurological circuits follow some kind of genetically coded template with the capacity for modification as dictated by the outside environment. The more that is learned about the genetic mechanism, the more can be applied to the wiring and functioning of the brain. Although it is not a necessary conclusion, there is also emerging a distinct trend to re-examine the possibility of behavioural genetics. That is, if the genetic mechanism actually determines the wiring of specific circuits in the brain as is generally assumed, the close association between brain circuitry and behaviour provides a strong basis for this possibility. This trend is epitomized in the USA, at least, by the theory of sociobiology which proposes that a behaviour is maintained within species according to its survival value to the gene which contributes to that behaviour in the total species gene pool. Although it is difficult to ascertain how far the behaviour genetic trend may go, the investigative procedures employed in traditional genetic research are being applied to behavioural criteria with some success. Whatever the eventual conclusion, biological psychology will be greatly effected by the result of these investigations.

We find, then, that biological psychology appears to be situated at a unique confluence in the history of ideas. That is, new knowledge is rapidly becoming available in a number of allied academic areas. In addition, new technologies have recently emerged which allow spectacular improvements in our observational capacity. Possibly as a result of the preceding two factors, or possibly contributing a third impetus of its own, biological psychology has emerged as an attractive area in the popular interest. It is not unusual to find that one of our more important sources of new information is frequently the popular press.

BIOLOGICAL PSYCHOLOGY IN THE PSYCHOLOGY CURRICULUM

The decision to add biological psychology to a psychology curriculum should not be taken lightly. This area is so specialized, both in its content and its aim, that it is a difficult area to service adequately. The most significant problem is that of schooling a faculty member to the necessary level of knowledge that a high level of instruction can be provided for the students. Although there are superb textbooks available, some of which are accompanied by excellent teaching aids (both for the student and the teacher), an ill-prepared teacher is simply not able to competently deal with the questions asked by bright and enthusiastic students. As is the case with any area, encountering an uninformed or an unenthusiastic instructor is a distinct disservice for all involved. The student will assume that he has encountered a representative sample of the area and found it wanting. Unfortunately, the instructor cannot take a single course in order to obtain a solid foundation for teaching biological psychology. This situation is exacerbated by the problem of remaining current to new developments in the field. In addition, the material in biological psychology does not transmit well in the abstract. Even though a well-organized textbook with special attention to illustrative material gives the impression that one is experiencing the non-didactic aspect of the field, there is nothing that will replace the actual experiential knowledge obtained in a laboratory setting. This means that a course in biological psychology really ought to be taught with a full laboratory section to accompany it. If a lab is unavailable, then a careful selection of demonstrations and models and tissues samples are a necessity. This laboratory experience puts an additional expectation on the instructor. That is, the instructor in order to be able to deal appropriately with students' questions both in and out of the laboratory often must fall back on his/her own laboratory experience.

If one has decided to add biological psychology to the psychology curriculum, then the problem becomes where should such a course be located? If the department has the resources, then one possibility would be to add an entire discipline of biological psychology. That is, to add a sequence of several courses, all of which deal with physiological aspects of understanding behaviour. Although there is sufficient material to fill a student's degree programme, this level of commitment is usually greater than the typical psychology department is willing or able to make, especially in a single step.

Sometimes, a satisfactory solution can be attained by establishing a co-operative programme with a biology department. The psychology department may contribute a course which includes considerable emphasis in neurophysiology but focuses on a functional presentation with regard to the related behaviours. Other dimensions which may be included in such a psychology–biology consortium would be animal behaviour courses which emphasize the comparative differences throughout the phylogenetic scale. Another dimension for the psychology department would be to provide courses in sensory structures and/or perceptual material. The biology department can contribute traditional courses in anatomy, physiology, and neurophysiology. In addition, many biology departments have individuals who have interests which include the study of behaviour. The European tradition of studying animal behaviour via ethology stems from the biological base and this facet can contribute valuable information to a co-operative programme.

The psychology department considering adding biological psychology to its curriculum is seldom in a position to jump into the area with a full-blown programme. Occasionally it is possible to hire a full-time faculty member with this specialized training who can offer a number of courses both at the upper and lower levels within the programme. More frequently, however, the department is confronted with a choice of where to insert a representative course within the total curriculum. The pros and cons for placing such a course early or late in the curriculum present an interesting conflict situation. My personal experience was one of encountering this facet of psychology relatively late in my academic career. When I finally encountered this material, it filled in a number of significant gaps and provided many answers to a list of frustrating questions that had been compiled over the years of studying within the traditional approaches to psychology. Thus, biological psychology provided a timely framework on which I could organize the extensive psychological information I had accumulated. This new area offered sufficient promise that I was willing to undertake the learning of the considerable technical material necessary to realize its full potential. There is the distinct possibility that had I encountered this approach early in my career, I would have been so over-whelmed by the knowledge that was required, and the approach might have been written off as hopelessly complicated.

In spite of my own personal history, I am now convinced that a biological psychology course should be offered relatively early in student's psychology curriculum. The advantages of such a placement are as follows:

(a) The student is exposed to a potentially convenient structural framework for organizing the material in subsequent psychology courses.

(b) The student will have a valuable working vocabulary which can be applied to other psychology classes.

(c) The student is exposed to a dynamic 'leading edge of technology' facet of psychology.

(d) The student is exposed to a potential area of specialization at a time when such options may still be convenient.

The disadvantages of an early emphasis on biological psychology in a psycho-logy programme are:

(a) The technical level and vocabulary required to understand this area even at an introductory level can appear overwhelming.

(b) This approach is definitely a legitimate one in psychology but too strong an early emphasis may 'turn off' good potential psychology students whose interest lies in other facets of the discipline.

(c) If the course fares well the department may find itself being moved into one of the more expensive facets of psychology.

A COURSE OUTLINE FOR BIOLOGICAL PSYCHOLOGY

A one-semester, introductory level course in biological psychology presents an interesting problem to the instructor. One must establish a working voca-bulary of nervous system structures and neurological functioning in order to then apply these concepts to the understanding of behaviour. It has been my personal experience that it is barely possible to pack the requisite knowledge for this course in to a single semester. In fact, part of the opening remarks in the first-class meeting identifies this specific problem and informs the student that there is little room for adjustment in the syllabus that has been distributed. A major portion of the early half of the semester is spent acquiring a basic vocabulary of terms and concepts in order to address problems that are of interest to a psychologist. Thus, we must resist the temptation to lag too far behind the course outline because it will inevitably displace some of the most interesting material; that for which the course is being offered.

The following course outline represents the present evolutionary state of my own introductory level class. The seven sections represent major categories of knowledge to be covered in the class. The thirty-three topics, on the other hand, are essentially descriptive titles for lectures which may be given in the one-semester class. Obviously, material can be inserted, deleted, compressed, or expanded according to the temporal logistics of any particular situation. I have found this outline to be surprisingly robust in its application to such a course in a wide variety of applications. The level of difficulty of the textbook and/or the expectations of the instructor can adapt this outline between a simple introduction and a comprehensive survey.

The outline will be annotated on a section-by-section basis as follows: first, the topics to be covered in the section; second, a short commentary as to the content and location of the material within the context of the overall class; and third, a list of references which are appropriate to the material in the section.

Section 1 Basic Concepts

TOPIC 1: Historical Developments. Pre-scientific Speculations; Early Discoveries and Theories; Milestone Phenomena and Important Names; Contemporary Issues and Trends.

TOPIC 2: Survival Terms. Directional Terms (anterior, lateral, etc.); Nerve Cell Components (cell body vs. axon); Central Nervous System Landmarks.

TOPIC 3: Methodologies. Recording; Stimulation; Ablation; Phylogeny; Ontogeny; Stereotaxic Procedures; Histological Methods.

Comments

I find a significant hurdle getting a course underway, particularly one with the technical content of a course in biological psychology. It is difficult to be able to present some of the exciting dimensions of an area when the students lack a fundamental working knowledge of some of the basic ideas, terms, and methodologies. These three initial topics are intended to provide such a basic conceptual framework. The use of the historical format for the initial plunge allows the opportunity to explore a number of ideas which simultaneously are interesting to the student and provide a bit of flavour about the content they are going to encounter. Early concepts can be selected for their interest value to the student as well as providing a medium to subtly introduce some fundamental concepts which will be encountered in greater detail later in the course. Simultaneously, the historical perspective allows an opportunity to examine a growing science in terms of historical trends, a mechanism which is useful in putting recent developments in perspective.

Probably one of the most formidable characteristics of a biological psychology class, from the point of view of the student, is that of acquiring and understanding the new vocabulary that must be mastered. I have entitled Topic 2 'Survival Terms' in exactly that context. In this lecture, I attempt to provide the student with a fundamental working vocabulary and at the same time share the rules which were used to establish that vocabulary. Since the study of the brain began with simple description, most of the structures in the brain can be translated into some version of their appearance and/or their geographic location. Thus, learning the names of some of the major landmark structures in the central nervous system and terms which describe a direction from that landmark will frequently decode a structure that the student may never have encountered previously. This capacity to 'demystify' some of the complex terminology alleviates considerably the distress when encountering new terms. In addition, it is worthwhile to clearly demark the difference between the cell body of the neuron as opposed to the axonal portion. This dichotomy coincides with the descriptive nomenclature for central nervous system structures, but it is worthwhile to establish this difference early because it is fundamental to understanding the action of individual nerves as well as the complete nervous system.

Finally, the student needs to know the basic methodologies that are used in the functional study of the central nervous system. In the outline provided, the first three are of major importance, while phylogeny and ontogeny deserve mention but are relatively minor. The application of stereotaxic procedures to locate a specific structure within the brain of a living animal, as well as the histological methods used to confirm the location, is very important to the student's appreciation of the geography of the brain. A significant factor in presenting this information is the capacity to transmit information in three-dimensional terms. Most textbook illustrations are remarkably clear in two dimensions but not at all sufficient in the third. This problem frequently exists even when there is a laboratory to help the process.

References

Depending on the level of expertise of the instructor and the competence level of the students, additional material beyond that presented in the textbook for the class may be useful to the instructor. To resolve ambiguities in the class text, it is frequently necessary to compare with the presentation in an alternative textbook. Thus, the lists of textbooks, laboratory manuals, and edited readings presented toward the end of this chapter also identify candidates for the reference shelf of the instructor. The sources itemized here fall into two categories: experimental psychology texts which include a substantial portion related to biological psychology, and handbooks aimed specifically at the biological psychology area. If selection opportunities are limited, the choice should be made on the basis of emphasis, availability, and date of publication.

(i) Neurology handbooks

Field, J., Magoun, H. W., and Hall, V. E. (eds) (1959) and (1960). *Handbook of Physiology.* Vols. 1, 2 and 3. Washington DC: American Physiological Society.
Quarton, G. C., Melnechuk, T., and Schmitt, F. O. (1967). *The Neurosciences: A Study Program.* New York: Rockefeller University Press.
Schmitt, F. O. (1970). *The Neurosciences: Second Study Program.* New York: Rockefeller University Press.
Schmitt, F. O., and Worden, F. G. (1974). *The Neurosciences: Third Study Program.* Cambridge, Mass.: MIT Press.

(ii) Psychology handbooks

Kling, J. W., and Riggs, L. A. (1971). *Woodworth and Schlosberg's Experimental Psychology.* New York: Holt, Rinehart & Winston, third edition.
Osgood, C. E. (1951). *Method and Theory in Experimental Psychology.* New York: Wiley.
Stevens, S. S. (1951). *Handbook of Experimental Psychology.* New York: Wiley.

Section II Basic Neuroanatomy

TOPIC 4: Central Nervous System. Brain Stem (homeostasis and reflexes); Brain Core (conditioning and emotion); Cortex (cognition).

TOPIC 5: Neuronal System. Hypothalamic Centres; Reticular Activating System; Limbic System; Autonomic Nervous System; Peripheral Nervous System.

TOPIC 6: Non-neuronal Components. Protection (meninges and skeletal structures); Nutrition (circulation and blood–brain barrier); Endocrine System; Ventricular Structures; Glial Cells.

Comments

As indicated in the title, this section is intended to acquaint the student with the more important structures found in the central nervous system. It will provide a more elaborate structural scheme than that provided in Topic 2 but follows closely enough in time that the presentation will serve as both a review and an elaboration. To most psychology students, this section appears to be exclusively neuroanatomy. In actual presentation, it is useful to temper the neuroanatomy with a liberal sprinkling of functional applications and illustrations. By the end of this section, the student should have a fairly clear picture of the central nervous system along three important dimensions: the basic geography including the names of predominant structures (Topic 4), the existence of interwoven functional systems (Topic 5), and the location and contribution of 'non-neural' components (Topic 6). The latter are often overlooked in a discussion of the central nervous system, but recent evidence indicates they are important to understanding nervous system activity.

References

Bannister, R. (1969). *Brain's Clinical Neurology.* Oxford: Oxford University Press.
Curtis, B. A., Jacobson, S., and Marcus, E. M. (1972). *An Introduction to the Neurosciences.* Philadelphia: Saunders.
Gardner, E. (1975). *Fundamentals of Neurology.* Philadelphia: Saunders, sixth edition.
Guyton, A. C. (1974). *Function of the Human Body.* Philadelphia: Saunders.
Krieg, W. J. S. (1957). *Brain Mechanisms in Diachrome.* Evanston, Ill.: Brian Books, second edition.
Netter, F. (1968). *The Ciba Collection of Medical Illustrations.* I. *Nervous System.* New York: Ciba.
Walton, J. (1966). *Essentials of Neurology.* London: Pitman Medical, second edition.

Section III The Nerve Cell

TOPIC 7: The Living Cell. Nucleus (DNA); Cytoplasm (cellular work); Membrane (interface with outside world); Substructures (functional components within the cell).

TOPIC 8: The Neuron. Membrane (ionic flow and electrical potentials); Sodium Pump; Cell Body and Dendrites (data collection); Axons (data transmission).

TOPIC 9: Neuronal Activity. Generator Potentials (electrotonic spread); Action Potentials (spike propagation); Summation and Axonal Coding; Excitation and Inhibition.

TOPIC 10: Neuronal Communication. The Synaptic Mechanism; The Axon Bouton; Post Synaptic Receptor Sites; Transmitter Chemicals; Other Chemicals involved in Synaptic Action.

TOPIC II: Drugs. General Action of CNS (synaptic junction); Depressants; Stimulants; Tranquillizers; Antipsychotic Drugs; Psychoactive Compounds.

Comments

This section is intended to acquaint the student with the characteristics of the individual nerve cell, the fundamental building blocks of the nervous system. Topic 7 and Topic 11 could be considered superfluous to the presentation at this point in the course. If time permits, however, these two topics add a dimension and perspective which contributes to the understanding of the activity of the cell and prevents the section from becoming overwhelmingly neurological.

References

(i) Neurons

Eccles, J. C. (1957). *Physiology of Nerve Cells*. Baltimore: Johns Hopkins Press.
Eccles J. C. (1964). *Physiology of Synapses*. New York: Academic Press.
Iversen, L. L., and Schmitt, F. O. (1970). Synaptic Function. *Neurosciences Research Program Bulletin*, **8**(4).
Lehninger, A. L. (1964). Cell Membranes. *Neurosciences Research Program Bulletin*, **2**(2).
Mercer, E. H. (1962). *Cells: Their Structure and Function*. New York: Doubleday.
Robertson, J. D. (1965). The Synapse: Morphological and Chemical Correlates of Function. *Neurosciences Research Program Bulletin*, **3**(4).

(ii) Drugs

Black, P. (ed.) (1969). *Drugs and the Brain*. Baltimore: The Johns Hopkins Press.
Jarvik, M. (1967). The Psychopharmacological Revolution. *Psychology Today*, **1**, 51–59
Julien, R. M. (1975). *A Primer of Drug Action*. San Francisco: W. H. Freeman.
Matheson, D., and Davison, M. (eds) (1972). *The Behavioral Effects of Drugs*. New York: Holt, Rinehart & Winston.
Medical Economics Incorporated (1971). *Physicians' Desk Reference to Pharmaceutical Specialties and Biologicals*. Oradell, N. J.: Litton, twenty-fifth edition.
Smythies, J. R. (1970). The Mode of Action of Psychotomimetic Drugs. *Neurosciences Research Program Bulletin*, **8**(1).

Section IV Neuronal Circuitry

TOPIC 12: Transducer Cells. Stimulus Characteristics (quality, quantity, extent, duration); Transducer Characteristics (thresholds, dynamic range, fidelity); Biological Transducers (radiant, mechanical, chemical).

TOPIC 13: Sensory Coding. Excitatory and Inhibitory Connections; Evoked Potentials; Adaptation; Receptive Fields; Stimulus Encoding.

TOPIC 14: Functional Units. 'On-off' Cells; 'Straight Line' Cells; 'Movement' Cells; 'Direction' Cells.

TOPIC 15: Organization into a System. Specialized Cells and Stimulus Priorities; Data Concentration at Higher Levels; Data Dispersion from Lower Levels; Multiple Channels; Priorities and Redundancies.

Comments

With this section we begin to combine the fundamental building blocks, that is the neurons, into functional systems. At the present time, the sensory systems provide the most convenient data for this construction. More to the point, the visual system provides the basic data for this section. The advantages of a precisely specified and controlled stimulus along with the capacity to measure the resulting neural activity provides exciting glimpses into the organization of the nervous system. The discovery of visual cells which respond to stimuli in such a way that they can most aptly be described as functional units has forced a revolutionary interpretation of the organization of the brain. This section is intended to take full advantage of this development by providing a scenario where the student can share the build up and appreciate the significance of the functional units; then to project the implications of their existence in the form of general organizational principles. In some ways, the location of the discussion of transducer cells might be more appropriately placed in the following section where sensory systems are presented. Although transducers are not absolutely essential to the development of this section, I have found it convenient to begin with the translation of an external stimulus into neural activity as a means for developing a discussion of the various feature detectors. Thus, the proposed location of this topic in this outline.

References

Many of the references for Section I include extensive material related to sensory coding and/or neural connections. The references suggested below focus on sensory phenomena, especially feature detectors.

Biedler, L. M., and Reichardt, W. E. (1970). Sensory Transduction. *Neuroscience Research Program Bulletin*, **8**(5).
Bekesy, G. von. (1967). *Sensory Inhibition*. Princeton: Princeton University Press.
Hammes, G. G., Molinott, P. B., and Bloom, F. E. (1974). Receptor Biophysics and Biochemistry. *Neurosciences Research Program Bulletin*, **11**(3).
Hubel, D. H. (1963). The Visual Cortex of the Brain. *Scientific American*, **209**, 54–62.
Hubel, D. H., and Wiesel, T. N. (1962). Receptive Fields, Bionocular Interaction and Function Architecture in the Cat's Visual Cortex. *Journal of Physiology*, **160** (1).
Kuffler, S. W. (1960). Excitation and Inhibition in Single Nerve Cells. In: *The Harvey Lecture Series No. 54*. New York: Academic Press.
Lettvin, J. Y., Maturana, H. T., McCullock, W. S., and Pitts, W. H. (1959). What the Frog's Eye Tells the Frog's Brain. *Proceedings of the Institute of Radio Engineers*, **1959**, 47.

Section V Sensory Systems

TOPIC 16: The Visual System. Sensory Location and Structure; Transducer Characteristics; Neural Pathways; Cortical Region; Selected Sensory Phenomena (with neural interpretations).

TOPIC 17: The Auditory System. See organization of Topic 16.

TOPIC 18: The Gustatory System See organization of Topic 16.

TOPIC 19: The Olfactory System. See organization of Topic 16.

TOPIC 20: The Tactual System. See organization of Topic 16.

TOPIC 21: Internal Sensory Systems (including pain). See organization of Topic 16.

Comments

Depending upon the interests and knowledge of the instructor (or possibly the students) a discussion of the sensory systems could be the predominant unit in a course in biological psychology, or it may be simply a topic mentioned in passing. Whatever the priority given to the section, the treatment of the individual topics will not be as uniform as is implied in this outline. Probably 90 per cent of the data available on sensory systems is devoted to the visual system. The conclusions reached on the basis of visual research are then typically generalized to encompass the other sensory systems. Thus, in preparing a syllabus, do not be lulled into scheduling equal time for each of the systems in this section. If your sense of symmetry dictates such an equal time allotment, be prepared to devote considerably extra effort for the latter four topics. In fact, my experience has been to combine these latter four topics into two lectures equivalent to the first two topics in the section.

References

Perkel, D. H., and Bullock, T. H. (1968). Neural Coding. *Neurosciences Research Program Bulletin*, **6**(3).
Vallecallu, E., and Svaetichin, G. (1961). The Retina as a Model for the Functional Organization of the Nervous System. In: Jung, R., and Kornhuber, H. (eds), *The Visual System: Neurophysiology and Psychophysics*. Berlin: Springer-Verlag.

Section VI Behavioural Systems

TOPIC 22: Motor Control. Muscles; Nerve–Muscle Connections; Motor Pathways; Cortical Region; Muscle Coordination; Motor Control.

TOPIC 23: Ontogenetic Development. The Genetic Code; Cellular Replication and Growth; Cellular Specialization; Development of a Nervous System; Neuronal Proliferation; The Growth of Connections; Maintenance and Repair; Aging.

TOPIC 24: Phylogenetic Comparisons. Evolution and Species Differentiation; Phylogenetic Distance; Major Levels on the Phylogenetic Scale; CNS Structural Characteristics at Each Level; Implication Towards CNS Functioning.

TOPIC 25: Behavioural Genetics. Genetic Principles (chromosomes and genes, gene expression, Mendelian inheritance, etc.); Sexual Selection; Research Methods (genealogies, population studies, selective breeding); Behaviour as a Selection Criteria; Behavioural Research Data; Sociobiology.

TOPIC 26: The Brain and Behaviour. A Tripartite Proposal (brain: brain stem, brain core, cortex; behaviour: reflexes, conditioning, learning; function: survive, cope, explore); Functional Organization Principles (lower centres: control or respond to specifics; higher centres: choreograph and coordinate lower centres; importance of inhibition); Overview (the nature-nurture issue, present trends and probable developments).

Comments

This is the most controversial section of the entire course and much of the material suggested herein could be skipped entirely without significant loss to a course entitled 'biological psychology'. On the other hand, these topics also represent some of the most exciting and contemporary developments within the field. The topics in this section are contemporary not only in terms of their research emphasis but they also are very contemporary in terms of issues which confront today's society. If you choose to increase interest in the class through the mechanism of exploring controversial topics, this section provides extraordinarily fertile material. If, on the other hand, a more traditional role is preferred, one might consider collapsing Topics 23, 24, and 25 into a single unit for cursory examination. Topic 26 is based on a presentation by Altman (see reference section). Altman's organizational scheme appears to be extremely useful, at least an an introductory level. In fact, his tripartite theory extends considerably beyond the three dimensions mentioned in this outline.

References

Altman, J. (1966). *Organic Foundations of Animal Behavior*. New York: Holt, Rinehart & Winston.

Bermant, G. (ed.) (1973). *Perspectives on Animal Behavior: A First Course*. Glenview: Scott, Foresman.

Denny, M. R., and Ratner, S. C. (1970). *Comparative Psychology: Research in Animal Behavior*. Homewood, Ill.: Dorsey Press.

Hirsch, J. (ed.) (1967). *Behavior-genetic Analysis*. New York: McGraw-Hill.

Kuo, Z. Y. (1967). *The Dynamics of Behavior Development: An Epigenetic Approach*. New York: Random House.

Laughlin, W. S., and Osborne, R. H. (1967). *Human Variation and Origins: An Introduction to Human Biology and Evolution. Readings from Scientific American*. San Francisco: W. H. Freeman.

Lerner, M. I. (1968). *Heredity, Evolution and Society*. San Francisco: W. H. Freeman.

McClean, G. E., and DeFreis, J. C. (1973). *Introduction to Behavioral Genetics*. San Francisco: W. H. Freeman.

Smith, D. W., and Bierman, E. L. (1973). *The Biologic Ages of Man: From Conception Through Old Age*. Philadelphia: Saunders.

Winchester, A. M. (1966). *Heredity: An Introduction to Genetics*. New York: Barnes & Noble, second edition.

Section VII Psychological Topics

TOPIC 27: Consciousness. The Reticular Activating System; Sleep; Altered States of Consciousness; Internal Clocks and Biological Rhythms.

TOPIC 28: Motivation. Gratification Centres; Motivational Systems; Hypo-thalamic Functioning; Limbic System Involvement.

TOPIC 29: Emotion. Physiological Concomitants of Emotion; The Poly-graphy; Adaptive Characteristics; Maladaptive Dimensions; Psychosomatic Illnesses; General Adaptation Syndrome.

TOPIC 30: Environmental Adjustments. Adaptation and Habituation; Orienting Reflex; Imprinting and Critical Periods; Ontogenetic Interactions with Environment.

TOPIC 31: Learning. Short-Term Memory; Long-Term Memory; Rever-beratory Circuits; Classical Conditioning; Operant Conditioning.

TOPIC 32: Memory. Cell Assemblies; Changes in the Neutron; Changes in the Synaptic Space; Changes in the Surrounding Cells.

TOPIC 33: The Human Brain. The Neo-cortex; Split Brain Phenomena; Organizational Implications; New Models for Cortical Functioning.

Comments

At last, we reach the topics which are of primary interest to the psychology student. Although the preceding material is interesting in its own right, most psychology students have been suffering through the semester in order to approach the topics in this section. The list of suggested topics are by no means exhaustive and it is entirely possible that the individual instructor will feel it necessary to add one or two topics in this section. Whether or not this is the case, I repeat an earlier warning that the syllabus must be carefully prepared in order not to give this last section only cursory treatment because of limited time remaining in the course.

References

(i) General

Quarton, G. C., Melnechuk, I., and Schmitt, T. O. (eds) (1967). *The Neurosciences: A Study Program.* New York: Rockfeller University Press. This volume deserves separate listing as it is unusually applicable to all of Section VII.

(ii) Motivation and emotion

Ax, A. F. (1953). The Physiological Differentiation Between Fear and Anger in Humans. *Psychosomatic Medicine,* **15**, 433–442.
Delgado, J. (1972). *Physical Control of the Mind.* New York and London: Macmillan.
Dement, W. C. (1972). *Some Must Watch While Some Must Sleep.* New York and London: Macmillan.
Heath, R. G. (1963). Electrical Self-stimulation of the Brain in Man. *American Journal of Psychiatry,* **120**, 571–577.
Nauta, W. S. H., Koella, W. P., and Quarton, G. C. (1966). Sleep, Wakefulness, Dreams and Memory. *Neurosciences Research Program Bulletin,* **4**(1).

Olds. J., and Milner, P. (1954). Positive Reinforcement Produced by Electrical Stimulation of the Septal Area and Other Regions of the Rat Brain. *Journal of Comparative and Physiological Psychology*, **1954**, 419–427.

Selye, H. (1950). *The Physiology and Pathology of Exposure to Stress*. Montreal: Acta.

Teyler, T. J. (1972). Altered States of Awareness. In: *Readings from Scientific American*. San Francisco: W. H. Freeman.

Valenstein, E. S. (1968). Biology of Drives. *Neurosciences Research Program Bulletin*, **6**(1).

(ii) Learning–memory

Bullock, T. H. (1966). Simple Systems for the Study of Learning. *Neurosciences Research Program Bulletin*, **4**(2).

Eccles, J. C. (1953). *The Neurophysiological Basis of Mind*. Baltimore: Johns Hopkins Press.

Livingston, R. B. (1966). Brain Mechanisms in Conditioning and Learning. *Neurosciences Research Program Bulletin*, **4**(3).

Nauta, W. S. H. (1964). Some Brain Structures and Functions Related to Memory. *Neurosciences Research Program Bulletin*, **2**(5).

Penfield, W., and Roberts, L. (1959). *Speech and Brain Mechanisms*. Princeton, Princeton University Press.

Pribram, K. H. (ed.) (1969). *On the Biology of Learning*. New York: Harcourt.

CLASSROOM MATERIAL

As indicated previously, the selection of the textbook is vital to the eventual success of any class. In the role of both producer and consumer, I have observed an interesting trend in the instructor's selection procedures for a textbook. Typically, the instructor looks at the Table of Contents and locates the chapters which deal with his or her areas of greatest expertise. This chapter is then sampled for its content and treatment as a representative of the strength of the entire book. If significant flaws are found in the sample, the book is usually rejected in favour of one with fewer flaws in the special area. The net effect of this is that the profile of strengths and weaknesses of the book (and the textbook author) tends to match closely the profile of strengths and weaknesses of the instructor. Thus, the course will show an uneven treatment throughout the semester depending upon the interest and knowledge profile of the instructor–author team. A case could and should be made for a selection procedure by which the weaknesses of the instructor are compensated for by the strengths of the author. I would suggest, then, that an instructor be aware of this consumer characteristic and try to compensate for it in the selection of the most appropriate textbook for the class. The other important criterion for selecting a textbook is the date of publication. With the rapid advances found in this area of research, a good textbook is rendered obsolete very rapidly.

Textbooks

Biological psychology textbooks tend to loosely categorize into two levels which can be summarized as freshman–sophomore introductory courses, or upper division–graduate comprehensive courses. Thus, the two categories in the references listed below.

References

(i) Introductory physiological psychology texts

Beatty J. (1975). *Introduction to Physiological Psychology*. Monterey, Calif.: Brooks/ Cole.

Bruce, R. L., (1977). *Fundamentals of Physiological Psychology*. New York: Holt, Rinehart & Winston.

Deagle, J. (1973). *Study Guide and Workbook—Physiological Psychology*. Englewood Cliffs: Prentice-Hall.

Isaacson, R. L., Douglas, R. J., Lubar, J. F., and Schmaltz, L. W. (1971). *A Primer of Physiological Psychology*. New York: Harper & Row.

Leukel, F. (1976). *Introduction to Physiological Psychology*. St. Louis: Mosby.

Plotnick, R., and Mollenauer, S. (1978). *Brain and Behaviour. An Introduction to Physiological Psychology*. San Francisco: Harper & Row.

Schwartz, M. (1977). *Physiological Psychology*. Englewood Cliffs, N.J.: Prentice-Hall.

Thompson, R. F. (1975). *Introduction to Physiological Psychology*. New York; Harper & Row.

(ii) Advanced physiological texts

Altman, J. (1966). *Organic Foundations of Animal Behavior*. New York: Holt, Rinehart & Winston.

Carlson, N. R. (1977). *Physiology of Behaviour*. New York: Allyn & Bacon.

Deutsch, J. A., and Deutsch, D. (1966). *Physiological Psychology*. Homewood, Ill.: Dorsey.

Grossman, S. P. (1967). *A Textbook of Physiological Psychology*. New York: Wiley.

Grossman, S. P. (1973). *Essentials of Physiological Psychology*. New York: Wiley.

Milner, P. (1970). *Physiological Psychology*. New York: Holt, Rinehart & Winston.

Morgan, C. T. (1965). *Physiological Psychology*. New York: McGraw-Hill, third edition.

Smith, C. U. M. (1970). *The Brain: Towards an Understanding*. New York: Putnam.

Thompson, R. F. (1967). *Foundations of Physiological Psychology*. New York: Harper & Row.

Laboratory Manuals

It is almost a travesty to teach a biological psychology course without associated laboratory experience. Unfortunately, not every institution has the resources to be able to provide a laboratory setting or laboratory material. The following references are potential supplementary textbooks for those programmes that have a laboratory and are also possible replacements for real 'hands-on' laboratory experience.

References

Brown, P. B., Maxfield, B. W., and Moruff, H. (1973). *Electronics for Neurobiologists.* Cambridge, Mass.: MIT Press.

Hart, B. J. (1969). *Experimental Neuropsychology.* San Francisco: Freeman.

Sidowski, J. B. (1966). *Experimental Methods and Instrumentation in Psychology.* New York: McGraw-Hill.

Skinner, J. E. (1971). *Neuroscience: A Laboratory Manual.* Philadelphia: Saunders.

Webster, W. G. (1975). *Principles of Research Methodology in Physiological Psychology.* New York: Harper & Row.

Zucker, M. H. (1969). *Electronic Circuits for the Behavioral and Biomedical Sciences.* San Francisco: W. H. Freeman.

Edited Readings

The use of original references is somewhat difficult in this area because of the widely scattered distribution of articles among many separate journals. The following texts provide a carefully selected compendium of landmark articles important to the understanding of biological psychology. These are useful resources in more completely understanding the phenomena described in the textbook as well as an efficient way to introduce the student to reading professional articles in the area.

References

Landaur, T. K. (ed.) (1967). *Readings in Physiological Psychology.* New York: McGraw-Hill.

Lubar, J. F., (ed.) (1972). *A First Reader in Physiological Psychology.* New York: Harper & Row.

McGaugh, J. L., Weinberger, N. M., and Whalen, R. E. (eds) (1966). *Psychobiology.* San Francisco: W. H. Freeman.

Scientific American (1979). The Brain. **241**, No. 3.

Strange, J. R., and Foster, R. (eds) (1966). *Readings in Physiological Psychology.* Belmont, Calif.: Wadsworth.

Thompson, R. F. (ed.) (1971). *Physiological Psychology.* San Francisco: W. H. Freeman.

The Teaching of Psychology
Edited by J. Radford and D. Rose
© 1980 John Wiley & Sons Ltd.

6

Cognitive Psychology

DAVID LEGGE

BEGINNINGS ...

One clear lesson from history is that it would be inordinately stupid to try to establish a definition of either psychology or any part of it, and to expect that definition to have indefinite validity. The same lesson applies to divisions of the discipline. Seventy years ago a discussion of psychology in terms of 'schools' would have been customary. Though, half a century ago, a single view, perspective or school could claim unique validity in psychology, such a monolithic view cannot be seriously maintained now. Different perspectives relate to different sorts of problem area.

By 1924 Boring (1941) had already identified a new branch of psychology dubbed 'experimental'. It stressed the prevailing goals of its exponents to examine behaviour empirically and to formulate hypotheses about its rules and component processes. This positivist approach did not deny phenomenal evidence. It treated phenomenal representations as intervening variables, which may, on occasion, be directly related to overt behaviour, and which offer valuable bases for developing new hypotheses. Boring (1941) lists his set of topics that qualified as the components of experimental psychology. With some reservation these same topics are recognizable today. They include sensation, perception, feeling, emotion, learning, memory, attention, action and thought. Many of these topics comprise what is now known as 'cognitive psychology'.

The classical analysis of the contents of psychological knowledge used the words cognitive and cognition to refer to various aspects of the acquisition of knowledge. In contrast was 'conation' which was concerned with 'willing' and 'action'. Tolman was criticized for leaving his 'cognitive' rat sitting in the maze lost in thought—a conative component is necessary in any theory to bridge the gap between knowledge and action. Modern terminology has retained 'cognitive' but 'conative' has all but disappeared in the intervening years. Perhaps the current conception of the experimental subject as a strategy-exercising, independently motivated actor rather than a mechanistic, enslaved agent of the experimenter, signals that conative psychology is about to reclaim its earlier position in ᵗhe psychological firmament.

The variety of approaches to a diverse set of questions which characterized psychology at the beginning of this century was severely reduced by the behaviourist revolution provoked by Watson's (1919) insistence on data open to public inspection. Spoken evidence suddenly became unacceptable. The advantages of using animal subjects instead of humans were quickly established. The degree of control that could be imposed was so much greater, and their lack of language, a deficiency that would have made them useless subjects for the Wurzburg School, was suddenly of no consequence at all. The fundamental reflex units posited by Sechenov (1863) and the essential continuity of the species proposed by Darwin (1871) combined in the new psychology of the white and hooded, if not blinkered, rat.

LANDMARKS OF CHANGE

The eventual overthrow of the S-R yoke and the development of alternative questions in the context of different theoretical perspectives is marked by three landmarks spanning a 30-year period from World War II.

S-R theory made a lasting impact on just about every part of experimental psychology. But the effect, though widespread, was not uniform. Some aspects of psychological enquiry, perhaps because they were not at the time enjoying a wave of popularity, survived almost untinged. Human performance theory, the analysis of perceptual-motor skills, was one such area that can be identified as a major component of the revival of an almost Jamesian view of psychology 50 years after his definitive text (James, 1890).

Skills psychology has an honoured place in history. Its central importance derives principally from the fact that most behaviour occurs in the context of an individual seeking to adjust to a set of circumstances in order adaptively to achieve some pre-defined end result. The minute analysis that characterized S-R theory is not particularly apposite in this context, a larger unit of analysis is preferable. The essential importance of skills theory was highlighted by Bartlett's (1958) claim that human performance offers a basic model for all adaptive behaviour including the operation of higher mental processes. Fencing is sometimes described as playing chess at lightning speed. In Bartlett's view, a truer analogy could not be drawn.

World War II suddenly highlighted the need to know how humans operate machines. The form of the questions brought into the limelight an approach to psychological processes that derives most obviously from engineering. The same urgency that motivated psychologists to understand human beings encouraged the invention and development of new and ever more sophisticated machines. In turn, these advances in engineering offered more sophisticated models for processes with which to describe the functional nature of human behaviour. In short, the first major landmark in the development of cognitive psychology was World War II and the consequential need to understand human behaviour at a practical level.

The second landmark was the development of language research. Virtually all psychological research on language for 10 years after 1959 has been related, either directly or indirectly, to the merciless attack that Chomsky (1959) made on Skinner's (1957) *Verbal Behaviour*. His influence was revolutionary in two important respects. It established the fundamental importance of underlying processes, in contrast with the Skinnerian 'empty organism' approach, and it championed the so-called 'rationalist' approach to research, in which theory sits squarely in the driving-seat and data-collecting empiricism plays an important but subordinate role.

It was predictable that eventually psychologists would turn to study that most human of the attributes of human beings, language. An essential problem, however, was the difficulty of conducting clear-cut, tightly controlled studies of complex behaviour so that experiments could lead to unequivocal conclusions. However, the rationalism offered by Chomsky was so extreme that almost any data had to be preferred to offering no defence against his criticisms. Unless psychologists developed a data base in language, others would proceed with only intuition putting constraints on the plausibility of their theoretical developments.

The third landmark was the 'flower–peace–freedom' movement that flowed around the Western hemisphere during the 1960s focusing on freedom, hedonism, humanism and people in preference to processes and procedures. Science was systematically scrutinized and challenged as the new religion. The old order could hardly survive. As never before an age was ushered in with the old certainties absent. In psychology two main trends emerged. The 'mind' returned and the subordinate, reactive role of the 'subject'/'patient' was rejected.

This change in interests in psychology was signposted by Miller, Galanter and Pribram (1960). Their book would have had much less influence at a different time. It sought to make wide-ranging general statements and its ideas had not been fully worked out. But it threw down the gauntlet that heralded the return of cognitive psychology which was to be confirmed by Neisser's eponymous text in 1967.

The watchword was relevance. Psychophysics gave way to psycholinguistics, human learning and memory overtook fundamental studies of learning in animals in terms of popularity. And at the same time 'freewill in the context of societal influences' replaced the notion of man mechanistically responding in terms of a set of personal attributes many of which he had inherited along with his genes. Areas of psychology, traditionally concerned with persons in their own right or in interaction with others, flourished with a new vigour.

At present, there is no sign that psychology has matured and achieved stability. Until it does, the syllabus that is claimed to be representative of cognitive psychology will be tied to its own time. It will evolve and, at times, undergo convulsive change. These changes may not always represent progress towards a fuller understanding though, as always, only our successors are going to be in a position to evaluate any particular changes in those terms.

A SYLLABUS

These myriad influences have left a syllabus that is broadly recognizable as cognitive psychology but which does not have such strong internal cohesive forces as to suppose that it is stable in the long term. It contains a mixture of old questions, some enjoying their third or fourth incarnation, and new ones which may ultimately discover stronger cognate ties with other areas of psychology. Some questions have yet to develop sufficiently to demand study in their own right and, until they do, enjoy a fostering relationship with cognitive psychology proper. And there are probably some sets of questions that will turn out to be either unanswerable or tautologous and will transmute into more useful forms some time in the future.

Cognitive psychology, as its name implies, is mainly concerned with information and knowledge. It is also concerned with how an individual puts that knowledge to use and with influencing the environmental context to his advantage. At its present state of development, emphasis is greatest on the acquisition of information, somewhat less on retaining it and least on putting it to use. This pattern conforms roughly to the relative research investment that has been made in the past. As research continues, the balance should change to a more even handed emphasis.

It is convenient and conventional to impose upon the area a number of arbitrary divisions as follows.

Information Acquisition

This part comprises the classical areas of sensation or (perhaps better) sensory coding, perception and attention. It would be relevant to include some information about the physiological systems which subserve these functions—insofar as such information is available. However, it would not be appropriate to pre-empt a course in physiological psychology or of physiology of the special senses, topics which deserve study in depth in their own right.

It is the aim of this part of the syllabus to build a picture of the processes which take up information and how they work. That includes evaluating the limitations of sensory systems, their interrelationship, the coding systems that are used and their adaptability. The study of attention should range widely over topics as diverse as focused concentration on a task to selection of certain aspects of a situation to the virtual exclusion of others. Examination of these topics will reveal that they cannot be treated in isolation and that they involve processes that work in close harmony with other processes not only concerned with the acquisition of information. Various aspects of memory are implicated.

The role of conscious awareness is brought into question in this area of enquiry, though it features in other areas as well. The nineteenth-century interest in perception was, at least in part, based in the analysis of consciousness. The importance of conscious awareness and the attempt to submit it to objective scrutiny has re-emerged with the decline of behaviourist influence outside the field of learning.

This section of the syllabus might include the following topics:

(i) Sensation. Sensory processes, sensory coding systems. Transducers; limits to sensitivity. Sensory physiology. Signal detection, pattern recognition. Sequential effects; contextual effects. Colour vision. Gestalt phenomena. Sensory memory.

(ii) Perception. Perceptual organization. Cognitive interactions; motivational influences. Phenomenal representation. Object identification. Constancy phenomena. Imagery. Subception. Movement perception. Time perception. Reading.

(iii) Attention. Concentration, effort and selectivity in perceiving and responding. Limitations and division of attention. Span of apprehension. Multitask performance. Single channel theory. Automaticity. Stroop phenomena. Self-determined strategies in effort and selection.

Registration, Storage and Retrieval

This section is about memory of all kinds. Any mechanism which functions to bridge a temporal gap in the extrinsic availability of information qualifies for discussion. In practice, the area is usually divided up into three parts, although current developments are so rapid that it is quite likely that in only a few years time five or more parts might be conventionally defined.

It has been plausible to postulate buffer stores at both the input and output interfaces of the behaving system. Hard evidence leading inexorably to their identification has been more elusive. However, iconic (visual) and echoic (auditory) sensory register stores have been confidently proposed. Their contents are typically thought to have decayed or be overwritten between 0.25 and 4 s after initial entry. Response buffer systems are explicit in Morton's (1970) model of reading aloud, implicit in Sperling's (1967) 'translator' which is included to permit writing behaviour, and developed quite substantially by Crossman (1964) and Legge and Barber (1976) in their models of processes underlying perceptual-motor skill.

Although it has been fashionable to partition memory mechanisms according to the timescale of the experiments conducted to examine the problem, other bases of partition may turn out to be more fundamental. For example, a distinction could be based upon the nature of the remembered information. Most fundamental is the specification of neural firing patterns which define a motor act of a particular kind. A complex pattern extended in time could define an habitual response unit such as a body movement or the articulation of a word. This is a fundamental piece of knowledge—how to make a particular response.

Another memory system is also required as a fundamental basis for accounting for behaviour. This is an organized system of knowledge. Clark and Clark (1977) have called it a mental encyclopaedia.

Our growing understanding of encyclopaedic memory systems owes as much to experiments designed to study language and thinking as memory. Orthodox presentations of discussions in this area tend to be under the heading of 'representations of meaning' and 'semantic memory'.

Taking either an ecological view of memory, or an analogy based on an electronic computer, at least one more sort of memory system is required to provide the basic systems of behavioural organization. Baddeley and Hitch (1974) have called it 'working memory'. Its characteristics derive from the functional necessity of specifying a workspace in which various mental operations can be performed.

Variations in the retrievability of to-be-remembered items, and changes in the sorts of errors that are made, coupled with the particular memory defects that arise from some sorts of brain injury have led many researchers to postulate two kinds of memory store. The most flexibly organized scheme of this kind was described by Atkinson and Shiffin (1968). A wide range of control processes are available so the actual processing that takes place in a given situation can vary and be altered by the operation of deliberately chosen strategies.

A syllabus could be framed around the following topics: Memory and remembering. Iconic and echoic buffer stores. Primary and secondary memory. Working memory. Episodic and semantic memory. Mental encyclopaedia. Memory scanning. Recall phenomena. Recall and recognition. Non-verbal memory. Motor memory. Organization, rehearsal, retrieval. Neuropsychology of memory.

Motor Control Processes, and Human Performance

The history of psychology records a vigorous investment in the study of perceptual processes and learning, and rather less of memory, though recent fashions have moved to redress that imbalance. Interest in understanding the processes most immediately underlying behaviour, that is those that are responsible for the production of behavioural acts themselves, has been relatively scant. This poverty has been reflected in curricular patterns so that many degree courses have until recently completely omitted any but a passing reference to this sort of problem.

Some tasks require a presented stimulus to be incorporated with some prior information, knowledge or instruction, and a response to be produced that reflects, in a discriminating way, the relationship between them. The reaction time (RT) experiment is one like this. Response latency provides an obvious measure of the efficiency with which this fairly straightforward problem is solved, and may provide insights into how the necessary processing is carried out. Associated tasks entail matching responses in a more detailed way to stimulus conditions. Tracking tasks that offer laboratory analogues of skills like car driving are like this. The measure of performance is not just a simple measure of time, but instead a complex of both spatial and temporal accuracy.

Two sets of problems are addressed in this area of the syllabus. One concerns the acquisition, development and deterioration of skilled performance. The other is the description and analysis of the psychological processes which underlie behaviours of these kinds. In essence, the problem is to give an account of the organization and control of voluntary movements.

The following topics may be central to the syllabus: Motor control processes and human performance. Physiological mechanisms, cybernetic systems. Sensory feedback. Inter-sensory integration. Response selection and generation. Open and closed loop control. Motor programmes. Motor constancy. Performance limitations. Stress. Skill acquisition; training and practice. Fluctuations in performance capacity. Decision-making and choice.

Thinking and Language

Some years ago those performance attributes that seemed to be the peculiar and unique feature of human beings were termed the higher mental processes. In content they often included verbal memory along with concept formation and problem solving. Language was hardly represented, mainly because of the paucity of literature upon which to draw. The last 10 years have seen a revolution in the psychological research on language, much of it initiated in response (if not resistance) to the linguistic 'competence' notions popularized by Chomsky. Nowadays higher mental processes are not too often referred to while courses on thinking and language have become *de rigueur*. These two areas are closely connected but not inseparable.

Thinking is essentially concerned with the development of class concepts, manipulating them in a deductive way and in developing novel concepts and solutions to problems that cannot be interpreted in terms of applying rules of logical reasoning. Grouping and manipulation are clearly important processes. Likewise the use of an efficient coding system may be essential for success at these tasks.

Language interacts very powerfully with thinking as a cluster of processes.

In fact, one might even argue that language (as distinct from communication of a general kind) may have evolved as a tool to serve thinking. It so assists problem solving that the survival value of an individual possessing it would be very appreciably increased. However, this facilitation of thinking by language is partly discounted by errors, distortions and limitations that can be traced to the use of language as a mediator in thinking. The nature of the language can impose its own limitations. The study of language itself is based on a descriptive analysis of linguistic structure, but with an eye on what people actually say (performance) rather than just outlining what they ought to be able to say and understand (competence).

It is customary to treat the motor processes in speech as part of the psychology of language, mainly because interest in them has been in the organization of programmes as they reflect aspects of language itself.

The components of the syllabuses are as follows:

(i) Thinking. Concept formation, problem solving, deductive reasoning. Algorithms and heuristics. Computer simulations. Interactions with language, linguistic relativity. Thinking as a skill. Cognitive style, creativity, convergent and divergent thinking.

(ii) Language. Linguistic and non-linguistic communication. Words and speech. Speech perception, reading. Statistical structures. Surface and deep structure. Syntax and semantics. Comprehension, sentence verification. Polysemy, disambiguation. Integration of verbal and non-verbal forms of knowledge. Mental lexicon. Language acquisition.

INTERPRETING THE SYLLABUS

Objectives

While a syllabus provides a valuable guide to the contents of a course, it does not provide a definitive description of it. The course may itself be only an aspect of the student's learning process and then has to be seen as orientational rather than a prescriptive and comprehensive treatment of the syllabus.

It is commonplace that much the same syllabus could be offered for a course at pre-degree level, or for a general degree or for an honours degree. The courses will differ, so will the advice and encouragement given to students about the objective of their private study. Level and standard may also be implied by bibliographies attached to courses, but since it is not the custom to interpret a syllabus through a course text, that index may be an imperfect one. It also fails to reflect the fact that a substantial part of private study at degree level is expected to entail consultation of original articles in the periodicals literature.

It may be appropriate to make a selection from the total range of topics included in a comprehensive syllabus. Increasingly psychology is invited to play a small but important role in combined studies courses. It is sad to see that sometimes very little thought seems to have gone into deciding exactly what aspects of psychology would be best in a particular context. Though it is possible to include a basic introduction to psychological concepts in such a course, with some benefit to the students, a much greater benefit might result from exercising a more discerning choice. The psychological content should be chosen deliberately to subserve a clearly defined function within the overall degree course.

Methods

As an area of enquiry cognitive psychology offers the teacher an opportunity to exercise a very wide range of teaching methods. In fact only the most extreme intuitive and empathic methods are completely inappropriate.

In this area empirical approaches are brought into conjunction with theory-oriented approaches in many different topics. Close attention to empirical methodology is not just a relevant study, it is an essential part of the course. Similarly, the use of methods to analyse the characteristics of theories, and the development of theories through the medium of simulation are also intrinsically important skills. Since at least some of the 'phenomena' of cognition are inferred from behaviour considered in the light of experience and the plausibility of generalizing processes across individuals, teaching cognitive psychology is not quite the same as teaching about an inorganic system. It does, however, have sufficient in common with such an aim that similar teaching methods may be employed much of the time.

The formal lecture has been villified by some—perhaps justifiably if it is to be the only situation in which staff and students make contact. However, it is an efficient way of conveying enthusiasm, pattern and outline. It is not the place to learn detailed facts—they can be obtained from published literature, where they are likely to appear free of inadvertent mistakes. Nor is it the place for students to test out their dawning appreciation of theoretical complexity. Seminars or tutorials are essential to satisfy that objective.

Clearly the laboratory would be a suitable place in which to embark on teaching some aspects of cognitive psychology. The methods intrinsic to the area need to be understood and their limitations appreciated. It is difficult to see how to arrange for the acquisition of such sophistication outside of a practical course, at least part of which would demand the resources of an experimental laboratory. Likewise, familiarity with electronic computers, both as tools and as the source of models in investigating human cognition, is becoming increasingly important. This familiarity is undoubtedly best achieved with access to a computing system sufficiently large to be able to run behavioural simulations.

The motives which lead students to psychology do not necessarily generalize to all aspects of the discipline. The motives themselves are not uniform either.

Cognitive psychology comprises a substantial fraction of psychology but it is a minority interest amongst students. This arises because by far the most common manifest reason for choosing to read for a degree in psychology is an interest in the light it can throw on human behaviour construed in 'person' terms. Aspects of psychology which seek to understand the processes underlying behaviour may adopt an analytic posture which threatens the concept of a person as an indivisible entity. Social and developmental psychology which offer person-orientated branches of study are correspondingly attractive and popular for that reason. The full development of psychology needs both perspectives on man to be pursued vigorously.

As a consequence, it must be recognized that teaching cognitive psychology, particularly those aspects which have been analysed in information processing terms, is sometimes met with resistance from students. It may be necessary to give serious thought to finding ways of overcoming it.

Experimental and other forms of practical work can have a valuable motivating influence. Investigations can be chosen to relate to specific theoretical variables and demonstrate their validity or, at least, usefulness. This kind of involvement with ideas transmuted into data tends to remove the mystique from the theory as well as increasing the level of personal involvement that the student feels for the topic. To some extent the degree of investment of effort and time is reflected in the consequential commitment.

For these reasons there is a great deal to be said for having practical work as an essential part of the course or, if not, closely associated with it, through common teaching personnel and temporal proximity.

Many students in all branches of psychology despair of the incompleteness of psychological knowledge sometimes to the point of recommending a moratorium on teaching topics before they have been fully understood! This general irritation tends to be amplified in areas such as cognitive psychology which are more remote from everyday experience and less holistic in structure than some other, more person-oriented areas. It is as if a scientific, analytical approach is justified only when it is right and offers reliable variables that can be put to work with confidence in the context of behaviour in action.

It has been an unfortunate feature of our system of elementary mathematics teaching that most students professing an interest in social sciences in general, and in psychology in particular, seldom enjoy thinking in mathematical terms. They are more at home with arguments which are couched in the purely verbal terms characteristic of everyday conversation and the humanities. The jargon of mathematics strikes them with a considerable shock and, not surprisingly, they are tempted to prefer those aspects of psychology which least depend upon mathematical concepts and numerical operations.

Most teachers of statistical methods in psychology have made the point to their students that the arithmetic involved is no more complex than anybody uses to balance his domestic budget. In effect the main problem is to avoid or control the sheer panic that tends to drown so many students faced by numbers and algebra. Provided that that emotional reaction can be controlled, most students find that seemingly insuperable problems can be mastered after all. The same precepts apply to overcoming the 'number neurosis' which haunts some students in their approach to (or perhaps avoidance of) cognitive psychology.

Cognitive psychology is interesting in another respect too. It is such a wide area that the antithesis of number neurosis may also threaten some students. In the area of deductive reasoning some authors write as if their main objective is to demonstrate their intellectual superiority. It is less than rewarding repeatedly to fail to solve problems that, of course, the author shows to have self-evident solutions. Similarly many discussions of language and semantic memory are couched in linguistically complex sentences, written by authors who seem to be indulging in demonstrations of their linguistic prowess. It is not surprising, perhaps, that psychologists with a special skill in using words should be drawn to a professional study of that skill, but it is as important for them to make allowances for less skilful students as it is for the more mathematically sophisticated teacher.

Perspectives

Cognitive psychology is about a cluster of problems and topics and it is not uniquely defined by a characteristic approach to them. No one particular paradigm or perspective is appropriate, though not all the perspectives that have currency in contemporary psychology are represented in cognitive psychology.

Historically the dominant perspectives were mentalistic (with a strong phenomenological component), physiological and behaviouristic. Different aspects of the total area attracted different approaches. Sensory processes were distinguished by benefiting most from consideration of the underlying physiological functioning. In contrast, the study of thinking and reasoning offered little for the physiologist and a rich pasture for mentalistic analysis. An exclusive dependence upon introspection was, however, uncharacteristic. Wundt's group in Leipzig, for example, made extensive use of behaviouristic measures (recording reaction latencies) as well as introspection.

The information processing approach now characterizes many areas of investigation, as it has done for nearly 20 years. Initially it carried with it an image of the subject in a psychological experiment that was directly transferred from the physics or electronics laboratory. The subject was a passive reactor to the informational situation defined by instructions, training and the contemporary stimulus situation. This view is ultimately mechanistic, the subject's performance being wholly determined by external constraints, past or present, in a straightforward way. As a basis for many aspects of perception and of short-term memory such a conception appeared satisfactory.

More complex processes are served rather less well by the model. Subjects are not easily likened to a reactive model only—especially when they insist that they believe they are taking an active initiative. A model which stipulates an interactive rather than a reactive role for the subject is more attractive. Fortunately the essential features of an information processing perspective are not compromised by construing the subject in an interactive relationship with his organic and inorganic environment. It simply raises the question of whether a robot of sufficient complexity, equipped with a history, would not be as interactive in nature as man. The increased sophistication of our concept of man does not require any fundamental change in the concept of man as an information processing system.

CONTRIBUTIONS TO A BIBLIOGRAPHY

The last decade has witnessed an explosive increase in the publication of non-fiction books, and the whole field of psychology has been affected, the area of cognitive psychology more than most. Increased interest by publishers has coincided with increased numbers of researchers, teachers and students, and with the continuing impact of the 'publish or perish' strategy governing academic security and advancement. The trend continues apace and each year sees several important new texts to add to the library shelves and compete for one's attention. As a consequence, no attempt to compose a definitive bibliography will be valid in a couple of years, even if such a goal were to be achieved on publication day.

Overall Introductions

There are hardly any texts which attempt to introduce their readers to the whole of cognitive psychology, and none that succeed. One of the best attempts to reveal the broad outlines of much of this area is:

Lindsay, P. H., and Norman, D. A. (1977). *Human Information Processing: An Introduction to Psychology*. New York: Academic Press, second edition. This book ranges widely in those areas of psychology entailing handling information and adopts an essentially analytic stance. However, though strong on the input side of the system, the output side governing the initiative and control of action is woefully meagre. It would be as well to suppress the subtitle, as well, since there are many aspects and areas of psychology which go unintroduced, unremarked and unrecognized.

A considerably shorter book with a similarly broad but not comprehensive coverage is:

Rumelhart, D. E. (1977). *Introduction to Human Information Processing.* New York: Wiley.

Advanced Introductory Texts

Though there is no single slim volume to recommend as an overall introduction to cognitive psychology, there are several modestly priced texts and collections of readings which support courses in this area, and, if only an elementary level is sought, may be sufficient without other than optional augmentation.

(a) Sensory Processes, Perception and Attention

Six volumes can be recommended. They have varying emphases and could play complementary roles in supporting a course. The first three are texts:

Barber, P. J., and Legge, D. (1976). *Perception and Information.* London: Methuen.

Gregory, R. L. (1966). *Eye and Brain.* London: Weldenfeld & Nicholson.

Massaro, D. W. (1975). *Experimental Psychology and Information Processing.* Chicago: Rand McNally.

A fourth text with an unusual layout intermixes extracts from published papers with the author/editor's own commentary:

Norman, D. A. (1976). *Memory and Attention.* New York: Wiley, second edition.

The other two are collections of readings that both exemplify this area of enquiry and offer readily available papers on which to base seminar discussions:

Coltheart, M. (ed.) (1972). *Readings in Cognitive Psychology.* Toronto: Holt, Rinehart & Winston.

Held, R., and Richards, W. (eds) (1972). *Perception: Mechanisms and Models.* San Francisco: W.H. Freeman.

(b) Registration, Storage and Retrieval

This area overlaps significantly with the preceding one, and that overlap is reflected in the relevance of some texts. In particular, Coltheart's (1972) readings are relevant here as well.

Two fairly slim texts are:

Gregg, V. H. (1975). *Human Memory.* London: Methuen.

Herriot, P. (1974). *Attributes of Memory.* London: Methuen.

A useful collection of readings both for illustrating lectures and providing bases for seminar discussions is:

Gardiner, J. M. (ed.) (1976). *Readings in Human Memory.* London: Methuen.

(c) Motor Control Processes and Human Performance

There are now four reasonably short and moderately priced texts so that students and teachers have a degree of choice in recommendation:

Fitts, P. M., and Posner, M. I. (1967). *Human Performance*. Belmont, Calif.: Brooks-Cole.

Keele, S. W. (1973). *Attention and Human Performance*. Pacific Palisades, Calif.: Goodyear.

Legge, D., and Barber, P. J. (1976). *Information and Skill*. London: Methuen.

Welford, A. T. (1976). *Skilled Performance: Perceptual and Motor Skills*. Glenview, Illinois: Scott, Foresman.

A collection of readings is available which, though becoming somewhat dated, continues to make relevant seminar readings readily accessible to students:

Legge, D. (ed.) (1970). *Skills: Selected Readings*. Harmondsworth: Penguin.

(d) Thinking and Language

Three volumes are cheaply available in this area. One introduces both thinking and language as areas of investigation:

Greene, J. (1975). *Thinking and Language*. London: Methuen.

The other two are more circumscribed in their coverage:

Greene, J. (1972). *Psycholinguistics: Chomsky and Psychology*. Harmondsworth: Penguin.

Thomson, R. (1959). *The Psychology of Thinking*. Harmondsworth: Penguin.

Three collections of readings complement these texts and are also still valuable for some more advanced work as well:

Adams, P. (ed.) (1972). *Language in Thinking*. Harmondsworth: Penguin.

Oldfield, R. C., and Marshall, J. C. (eds) (1968). *Language*. Harmondsworth: Penguin.

Wason, D. C., and Johnson-Laird, P. N. (eds) (1968). *Thinking and Reasoning*. Harmondsworth: Penguin.

Specialist and More Advanced Texts

(a) Information Acquisition

The following texts represent more advanced treatments of selected aspects of this section of the field of cognitive psychology. One, in particular, stands out as the text that confirmed the emergence of cognitive psychology as an entity:

Neisser, U. (1967). *Cognitive Psychology*. New York: Appleton-Century-Crofts.

A complementary collection of readings is offered by:

Haber, R. N. (ed.) (1968). *Contemporary Theory and Research in Visual Perception*. New York: Holt, Rinehart & Winston.

Which can accompany:

Haber, R. N., and Hershenson, M. (1973). *The Psychology of Visual Perception*. New York: Holt, Rinehart & Winston.

Some of the contributions to the Loyola Symposia are important to the development of this area. They can be found in:

Solso, R. L. (ed.) (1973). *Contemporary Issues in Cognitive Psychology: The Loyola Symposium*. Washington DC: Winston.

Solso, R. L. (ed.) (1975). *Information Processing and Cognition: the Loyola Symposium*. Hillsdale, NJ: Lawrence Erlbaum Associates.

Two graded texts devoted to the psychology of reading are, in order of complexity:

Smith, F. (1971). *Understanding Reading*. New York: Holt, Rinehart & Winston.

Gibson, E. J., and Levin, H. (1975). *The Psychology of Reading*. Cambridge, Mass: MIT Press.

Also relevant to that issue is:

Massaro, D. W. (ed.) (1975). *Understanding Language: An Information-processing Analysis of Speech-perception, Reading and Psycholinguistics*. New York: Academic Press.

(b) Registration, Storage and Retrieval

As research develops, clear separation between subfields in the area of cognitive psychology becomes increasingly difficult and arbitrary. In particular, dividing memory off from representations of knowledge and both of them from language depends upon making organizational decisions that do not stand up to sustained examination. For the sake of tidiness, therefore, in this section various forms of memory will be included and texts devoted to language will be reserved for the fourth and last section of this annotated bibliography.

A valuable theoretical basis is offered by:

Norman, D. A. (ed.) (1970). *Models of Human Memory*. New York: Academic Press.

Six more recent texts both fill out some of the data and offer further advances in theory:

Baddeley, A. D. (1976). *The Psychology of Memory*. New York and London: Harper & Row.

Brown, J. (ed.) (1976). *Recall and Recognition*. London: Wiley.

Crowder, R. G. (1976). *Principles of Learning and Memory*. Hillsdale, NJ: Lawrence Erlbaum.

Kintsch, W. (1977). *Memory and Cognition*. New York: Wiley.

Melton, A. W., and Martin, E. (eds) (1972). *Coding Processes in Human Memory*. New York: Wiley.

Murdock, B. B. (1974). *Human Memory: Theory and Data*. New York: Wiley.

Two books which establish the orientation to semantic memory are:

Kintsch, W. (1974). *The Representation of Meaning in Memory*. Hillsdale, N. J.: Lawrence Erlbaum.

Tulving, E., and Donaldson, W. (eds) (1972). *Organisation of Memory*. New York: Academic Press.

(c) Motor Control Processes and Human Performance

It is a feature of the somewhat uneven development of psychological knowledge, reflecting the uneven investment of time and effort by researchers, that whereas some areas are well served by advanced texts and volumes of contributed papers, some are not. To keep up with advances in response initiation and control it is still necessary to go to original reports in the journals. There are very few advanced texts. However, a short, rather heterogeneous list may help in relation to some particular issues:

Edwards, W., and Tversky, A. (eds) (1967). *Decision-making*. Harmondsworth: Penguin.

Poulton, E. C. (1970). *Environment and Human Efficiency*. Springfield, Ill.: Charles C. Thomas.

Poulton, E. C. (1974). *Tracking Skill and Manual Control*. London: Academic Press.

Stelmach, G. E. (ed.) (1976). *Motor Control: Issues and Trends*. New York: Academic Press.

Welford, A. T. (1968). *Fundamentals of Skill*. London: Methuen.

(d) Thinking and Language

Though these two topics have been put together reflecting their proximity in classical treatments, the advanced literature is increasingly defining a major conceptual boundary between concept development and reasoning on the one hand and language structures on the other. The relation between them persists but now there are more interesting questions within each topic than there are linking the two together. Three texts which provide a basis in the 'thinking and reasoning' literature are:

Bolton, N. (1972). *The Psychology of Thinking*. London: Methuen.

Johnson, D. M. (1972). *A Systematic Introduction to the Psychology of Thinking*. New York: Harper & Row.

Radford, J., and Burton, A. (1974). *Thinking: Its Nature and Development.* London: Wiley.

A collection of readings records a variety of approaches to finding new solutions to problems; solutions that do not arise deductively from the application of a simple algorithm:

Vernon, P. E. (ed.) (1970). *Creativity: Selected Readings.* Harmondsworth: Penguin.

The psychological study of language before Chomsky's influence was mainly behaviouristic and very much a minority interest. In the last 15 years a respectable literature has developed and is fairly represented by the four texts which follow. The treatments vary in perspective and difficulty. Two texts, in order of level of treatment, seek to introduce the psychology of language:

Taylor, I. (1976). *Introduction to Psycholinguistics.* New York: Holt, Rinehart & Winston.

Clark, H. H., and Clark, E. V. (1977). *Psychology and Language: An introduction to Psycholinguistics.* New York: Harcourt, Brace, Jovanovich.

Two others with a different flavour try to relate language processes to other psychological events and processes:

Carroll, J. B., and Freedle, R. O. (eds) (1972). *Language Comprehension and the Acquisition of Knowledge.* Washington DC: Winston.

Miller, G. A., and Johnson-Laird, P. N. (1976). *Language and Perception.* Cambridge, Mass.: Harvard University Press.

Periodical Publications

A very substantial increase in interest in the issues which comprise cognitive psychology occurred at much the same time as there was a massive expansion in publishing journals. Many new journals appeared towards the end of the 1960s with a considerable representation of cognitive psychology amongst them.

A unique number of the *British Medical Bulletin* (published by the Medical Department of the British Council) was devoted to, and entitled, *Cognitive Psychology*:

Summerfield, A. (ed.) (1971). Cognitive Psychology. *British Medical Bulletin,* **27**, 191–290.

Otherwise the following journals are either devoted to cognitive psychology or regularly carry articles concerning it. This list is not an exclusive one:

Acta Psychologica
Annual Reviews
American Journal of Psychology
British Journal of Psychology
Canadian Journal of Psychology

Cognition
Cognitive Psychology
Journal of the Acoustical Society of America
Journal of Experimental Psychology (Four sections:
    Animal Behaviour Processes; General; Human Learning and Memory;
    Human Perception and Performance)
Journal of the Optical Society of America
Journal of Motor Behaviour
Journal of Verbal Learning and Verbal Behaviour
Memory and Cognition
Nature
Perception and Psychophysics
Perceptual and Motor Skills
Psychological Bulletin
Psychological Review
Quarterly Journal of Experimental Psychology
Science
Scientific American
Vision Research

As never before, some sort of guide to the literature is imperative. Browsing now has to be nearly as selective as the detailed examination of particular articles. The main 'guide books' are: *Psychological Abstracts* and *Current Contents: Social and Behavioural Sciences.*

ACKNOWLEDGEMENTS

I am indebted to my wife, Dr Hilary Klee, for a great deal of the modern orientation reflected in this chapter. She was also responsible for reducing the turgidity of my style. It might have read quite well had I resisted less.

REFERENCES

Atkinson, R. C., and Shiffrin, R. M. (1968). Human Memory: A Proposed System and its Control Processes. In: Spence, K. W., and Spence, O. T. (eds). *The Psychology of Learning and Motivation: Advances in Research and Theory, Vol. 2.* New York: Academic Press.
Baddeley, A. D., and Hitch G. (1974). Working Memory. In: Bower, G. H. (ed.). *The Psychology of Learning and Motivation, Vol. 8.* New York: Academic Press.
Bartlett, F. C. (1958). *Thinking.* London: Allen & Unwin.
Boring, E. G. (1941). *Sensation and Perception in the History of Experimental Psychology.* New York: Appleton-Century-Crofts.
Chomsky, N. (1959). Review of *Verbal Behaviour* by B. F. Skinner. *Language*, **35**, 26–58.
Clark, H. H., and Clark, E. V. (1977). *Psychology and Language: An Introduction to Psycholinguistics.* New York: Harcourt, Brace, Jovanovich.
Coltheart, M. (ed.) (1972). *Readings in Cognitive Psychology.* Toronto: Holt, Rinehart, & Winston.
Crossman, E. R. F. W. (1964). Information Processes in Human Skill. In: Summerfield, A. (ed.). *Experimental Psychology, British Medical Bulletin*, **20**, 32–37.

Darwin, C. (1871). *The Descent of Man*. London: John Murray.

James, W. (1890). *Principles of Psychology*. New York: Holt.

Legge, D., and Barber, P. (1976). *Information and Skill*. London: Methuen.

Miller, G. A., Galanter, E., and Pribram, K. H. (1960). *Plans and the Structure of Behaviour*. New York: Henry Holt.

Morton, J. (1970). A Functional Model for Memory. In: Norman, D. A. (ed.). *Models of Human Memory*. New York: Academic Press.

Neisser, U. (1967). *Cognitive Psychology*. New York: Appleton-Century-Crofts.

Skinner, B. F. (1957). *Verbal Behaviour*. New York: Appleton-Century-Crofts.

Sperling, G. (1967). Successive Approximations to a Model for Short-term Memory. *Acta Psychologica*, **27**, 285–292.

Sechenov, I. M. (1863). Reflexes of the Brain. See Boring, E. G. (1950). *History of Experimental Psychology*. New York: Appleton-Century-Crofts.

Watson, J. B. (1919). *Psychology from the Standpoint of a Behaviourist*. Philadelphia: Lippincott.

The Teaching of Psychology
Edited by J. Radford and D. Rose
© 1980 John Wiley & Sons Ltd.

7

Social Psychology

WILLIAM DEJONG AND TERESA AMABILE

Teaching social psychology is both easy and difficult. It is easy because students who take a course in social psychology are generally well motivated. They are curious about themselves and their social environment: How can people ignore screams for help and not intervene in an emergency? Why do groups enforce conformity? Can anything be done to rid a society of interracial hatred? What factors trigger schoolyard fights, urban riots and war? Most of your students will have taken an introductory course with the hope of learning answers to these questions. And many will have been surprised to learn that a researcher who studies the workings of the cochlea and has only a nodding acquaintance with the writings of Freud and Jung is a member of the university's psychology department. Many of them will enter a course in social psychology armed with these same questions, and they will expect you to give them the answers. And that is what makes teaching this course so difficult.

The fact is that the kinds of answers that you can provide to such questions are not the kinds of answers students expect to hear. No elixir for the ills of society can be prescribed. No sweeping generalizations can be proclaimed. No general theory of human social behaviour can be unveiled. Research articles in social psychology resound with the complexity of behaviour, the subtleties of time and place and thought that determine what we do. Most social psychologists may take the ultimate discovery of general principles as a matter of faith, but they now recognize that the way is arduous and that the wide-eyed optimism of social psychology's early years was unfounded.

What, then, is there to teach in a course in social psychology? First, there is method. Students should learn that human social behaviour can be studied in a rigorous, scientific way, that systematic laboratory and field research offers more hope of untangling the complexities of human action than mere introspection or casual observation. They can learn to observe behaviour with new skill, to see patterns and regularities in behaviour heretofore unnoticed. They can learn what kinds of questions are most useful to ask and how answers to them might be obtained.

Most important, your students will come to see themselves and their own behaviour from a new perspective. Social psychology tells us of the power of situational pressures, of the variability of our own behaviour from moment to moment and place to place. This message can profoundly affect your students' view of their own capacity for good or evil. For example, when students learn that the vast majority of Milgram's (1974) subjects followed the experimenter's command to deal lethal shock, they are confronted with the realization that they might have done the same. When they learn that subjects in Latane and Darley's (1970) studies on bystander intervention were less likely to help when other potential helpers were nearby, they must recognize that in certain emergency situations they also might have failed to intervene. In our view, there are no more important lessons than these to be learned from a course in social psychology.

In discussing specific syllabus content we will focus on a fairly exhaustive list of possible topics to be covered in an introductory social psychology course. This list has been organized under nine major topic headings. Within each of these sections we will itemize more specific topics and provide a description of what may be covered under each. Of course, we are not suggesting that you attempt to cover every topic we have listed. There are clearly too many of them to make this possible, and there is some overlap between them. Also, while the ordering of topics is one that we prefer, it is certainly not immutable.

For the instructors of general psychology courses, we have put an asterisk by those topics we believe to work best for such a course. These have been chosen not merely because of their interest value, but also because they can be used to demonstrate clearly the special methodology of social psychology and the use of social psychological theory in guiding research. Where should coverage of social psychology come in a general course? Most introductory psychology textbooks reserve discussion of social psychology for the end. This makes a certain amount of sense; it is perhaps easier to understand relations between individuals when we have learned how the mind and body function. Since so much of contemporary social psychology is based upon principals of perception and cognition, these areas should be viewed as a framework in which social psychological phenomena can later be placed. In order for this approach to work effectively, though, the instructor should be cognizant of the principles which will be applicable and should make the students aware that these principles will later be relevant to a consideration of social behaviour.

Courses in social psychology are taught in a range of contexts, from undergraduate colleges to psychology graduate schools, from business and medical schools to schools of social work. The syllabus offered here is one best suited to an introductory social psychology course taught under the auspices of an academic psychology department. But the listing of topics which follows is sufficiently detailed that instructors who teach other kinds of students with different needs will be able to intelligently choose among them. The key to any such course is the instructor's ability to generate examples from the students' specialization that tie in with the research social psychologists have done. For example, business students who learn of Asch's (1956) experiments on conformity may be concerned about how a business executive can create a climate which fosters creative thought and innovation in his or her employees and minimizes 'groupthink'.

We have included a brief list of review articles and books which we feel can be used successfully by an instructor to brush up on (or to learn about) the key issues, major theoretical perspectives and research methodology specific to a particular topic. These appear in the reference section. In addition, there are two other primary source books you should consult: (a) the *Advances in Experimental Social Psychology* series, which is edited by Leonard Berkowitz; (b) *The Handbook of Social Psychology*, published in 1968 and edited by Gardner Lindzey and Elliot Aronson. There is no point to listing specific chapters from these sources. Between them a good review of almost any topic in social psychology is likely to be found.

INTRODUCTORY TOPICS

The First Day

On the first day of class, students want to know what kind of course they can expect to have. Is the instructor a good lecturer, and does he or she seem to be concerned about students as individuals? Is the instructor excited about the subject matter? How will grades be determined? Is the reading load light or heavy? What kinds of examination questions can be expected? What topics will be covered? Too often teachers will make a bore of a first class by plodding through the syllabus with the students, mechanically reciting the rituals to be followed during the semester. Such a task is best left to a handout which, along with a syllabus, can be distributed at the end of class.

Why do you find social psychology worthwhile, even exciting? Tell the class about it. What place does a course in social psychology have in a liberal arts education? What do you expect your students to learn about themselves? Tell them. Try introducing your course with a discussion of a research question you find especially intriguing. How do social psychologists study such a question? What different approaches are possible? And what has this research shown that is important? What new insights into human action and motives does it provide? Demonstrate to your students immediately what kind of teacher you are and why you want them to take your course.

Methods

Before specific content areas can be discussed in detail, students must become familiar with the basics of sound research design, the logic of hypothesis testing, and the special concerns of social psychological research such as experimenter bias, the use of deception, and demand characteristics (Carlsmith, Ellsworth and Aronson, 1976). Archival methods and ethological approaches should also be introduced.

Views of Human Nature

What are the philosophical underpinnings of social psychological theory? In social psychological theorizing Man is variously viewed as an animal driven by instinctual urges and drives; as a 'hedonist' seeking to maximize gains and minimize losses, both physical and psychological; and as a thinking being, seeking understanding of the social world and motivated to maintain cognitive consistency and exert control over the environment. Are these models of mankind in conflict, or is some kind of integration possible?

Theoretical Perspectives in Social Psychology

Certain classic theories of behaviour have continued to influence social psychological thinking, despite awareness that an omnibus theory of social behaviour cannot yet be advanced. Serious students should become familiar with the assumptions and tenets of each theory and learn of its limitations and weaknesses (Deutsch and Krauss, 1965; Shaw and Costanzo, 1970). When a specific content area is being surveyed later in the course, students should be told what insights each theoretical perspective has offered. The following theories deserve such discussion: (a) psychoanalytic theory; (b) Gestalt theory; (c) field theory; (d) social exchange theory; and (e) social learning theory (which would include discussions of modelling processes as well as stimulus and reinforcement control of behaviour).

THE SELF

The Self-concept

What information is contained in our conception of self? How do we describe ourselves to others, and what situational variables influence our self-image? Discussions of self-concept should focus on body image (and disturbances in body image); the 'psychological' self—that is, our understanding of our personality traits, motives and intentions; the ideal self and our desire for 'self-actualization'. What variables influence self-esteem and our reactions to success and failure (Gergen, 1971)?

The Motive to Understand the Self

Self-perception (or self-attribution) theory is concerned with our attempt to analyse the causes of our own behaviour, an analysis which weighs the explanatory power of dispositional (internal) and situational (external) factors (Bem, 1972). Besides its concern with attitude formation and self-concept development, the theory has been applied toward an understanding of emotional experience, by Schachter and Singer (1962), and motivation, by de Charms (1968), Deci (1975), Lepper (Lepper, Greene and Nisbett, 1973) and others.

The Motive to be in Control

Human beings function better, both physically and psychologically, when they perceive themselves to be in control of their environment. When people perceive that they are not in control, they display a host of symptoms, including apathy, withdrawal, and sometimes even depression—a syndrome dubbed 'learned helplessness' by Seligman (1975). Though circumstances can induce helplessness in any individual, some people generally believe that they have no control over their fate, that there is no connection between what they do and the rewards and punishments they receive; individual differences in locus of control have been studied by Rotter (1966), Lefcourt (1976) and others. Brehm (1972) argues that much behaviour is motivated by peoples' need to see themselves as 'origins'—that is, as being in control and having the freedom to act that such control brings.

The Motive to be Consistent

The assumption that we strive to be consistent in our actions and beliefs has been the cornerstone of several social psychological theories, including Festinger's (1957) theory of cognitive dissonance and Heider's (1958) balance theory. Such theories argue that the recognition of inconsistency motivates change in behaviour or attitudes. Rokeach (1975) suggests that behavioural engineers can exploit this fact of human nature, inducing change by actively confronting people with inconsistencies between their values and their beliefs. More recently, researchers in impression management have pointed to how people attempt to sustain a consistent *public* image.

The Motive to Look Good

How we present ourselves to others, what role we play, is greatly influenced by both our own goals and what we presume the goals of our 'audience' to be. As mentioned before, we not only strive to achieve a consistent public image, but we are also motivated by a need for social approval. The tactics of ingratiation, in which we knowingly create a false public image, have been analysed by Jones (1964).

ATTITUDE FORMATION AND CHANGE

The Measurement of Attitudes

Discussion of this topic must begin, of course, with a workable definition of 'attitude'. The affective (or evaluative) component is typically measured using Thurstone scales, simple Likert scales, or the semantic differential. Problems with these types of measurement have been identified, and alternatives have been suggested, including the use of the so-called 'bogus pipeline' technique, physiological measures, and a more intense focus on the behavioural component of attitudes.

Predicting Behaviour from Attitudes

Beginning with the classic studies by LaPiere (1934) several researchers have discovered relatively weak correlations between paper-and-pencil measurements of attitudes and behaviour. Attempts to understand this surprising, though frequently found, outcome have centred around measurement problems and the development of more complex theoretical models, such as that proposed and tested by Fishbein and Ajzen (1975).

Theories of Attitude Change

The mechanism by which attitudes change was a primary concern of social psychological researchers during the 1950s and 1960s. Several theoretical frameworks, and the empirical investigations they have inspired, should be addressed: (a) behaviorism (classical and operant conditioning); (b) social learning theory (modelling and imitation); (c) consistency models, especially dissonance theory; (d) self-perception theory and the 'contact hypothesis' (Kiesler, Collins and Miller, 1969).

The Art of Persuasive Communication

Social psychologists have expended tremendous effort in trying to learn how a persuasive communication can best be packaged to produce the greatest impact. What can be done to increase the probability that an audience will attend to a message, comprehend it, and then accept it? Research has focused on, first, the communicator—his level of credibility; his style and attractiveness; and his apparent motives. Second, the communication itself—whether only one or both sides of an issue should be presented and, if both, their order of presentation; the extremity of the position argued; the use of fear appeals; and the influence of distractions during the communication. Third, the audience —their initial attitudes; their level of intelligence and their capacity to attend. Making recommendations on the best strategy to use in any specific case can be treacherous, since the research has revealed a snakepit of higher order interactions and qualifiers that would scare off any would-be advisor (Zimbardo, Ebbesen and Maslach, 1977).

Racism, Prejudice and Discrimination

The sterile laboratory research which has dominated social psychology's study of attitudes can be better appreciated by students when it is reviewed within the context of understanding racism (Jones, 1972). Do theories of attitude change help us understand how people come to harbour prejudice, or do perspectives brought by other disciplines such as sociology seem more useful? How can a programme to change racial attitudes be structured? In addition, of course, the psychological and material costs of racism have been a concern of social psychologists. And more recent work has focused on how processes of selective attention, perception, and memory work to sustain the stereotypes we hold of 'out-groups'.

OUR PERCEPTIONS OF OTHERS

Impression Formation

Person perception research has grappled with our complex use of information about another's appearance and behaviour as we attempt to learn what that person is like and what we can expect of him (Schneider, Hastorf and Ellsworth, 1979). Much of that work, of course, has served to demonstrate how badly we deviate from what would be expected of completely rational information-processors. For example, research has documented the importance of the perceiver's perceptual set, expectations, and needs. It has been learned that physical appearance powerfully affects our impressions of others and our behaviour, to an extent that has surprised and fascinated many social psychologists. Work by Rosenthal (Rosenthal and Jacobson, 1968), Snyder (Snyder, Tanke and Berscheid, 1977), and others shows us how our expectations about another person can lead us to behave in ways which make our 'prophecies' come true. Finally, of course, the work by Asch (1946) and Anderson (1965) on peoples' combinatorial analysis of trait information about others should be covered.

Attribution Theory

The attributional perspective seized hold of social psychology in the 1970s, and there are no signs that it will soon release its grasp. Attribution theory, first articulated by Heider (1958) and later expanded by Kelley, Jones, and others (Jones, Kanouse, Kelley, Nisbett, Valins and Weiner, 1972), is concerned with our attempts to explain others' behaviour, to understand their intentions, and to know their underlying dispositions. Discussion should focus on Kelley's (1973) 'causal schemata', including the principle of covariation and the discounting principle. Again, much research has shown the errors and biases to which the attributional analysis is prone—for example, the differences between other- and self-attribution; the tendency to blame innocent victims under certain circumstances; and the effect of our feelings about another person on our attributions about that person's behaviour.

Social Comparison

Judgement of the soundness of one's opinions or the extent of one's abilities usually requires social information. Festinger's (1954) theory of social comparison should be discussed in detail. As described by Walster and Berscheid (Walster, Berscheid, and Walster, 1973), social equity theory is a theory of social comparison. They argue that people are motivated to establish and maintain relationships with others, to maintain a balance of rewards and costs in a social exchange relationship.

OUR INTERACTIONS WITH OTHERS

Interpersonal Communication

A detailed analysis of the role of language in human life is clearly beyond the scope of this course. But some mention of research on forms of address, communication networks, and rumour transmission could be made. Of greater interest to students will be non-verbal communication or 'body language'. The 1970s have seen a wave of fascinating (and methodologically sophisticated) studies on: (a) facial expression and the communication of affect (Ekman, Friesen and Ellsworth, 1972); (b) eye contact (Ellsworth and Ludwig, 1972); and (c) the use of personal space, crowding, and territoriality.

Affiliation

Schachter's (1959) functional analysis of mankind's affiliative nature continues to generate empirical research. This area provides one of the better illustrations of sound and systematic research in social psychology.

Interpersonal Attraction and Love

Social psychologists have identified several factors which predict who will be attracted to whom, including proximity, physical attractiveness, personality and attitudinal similarity, and rewardingness (Rubin, 1973). Beyond that, discussion should centre on the process by which people become friends, a process addressed by social exchange theory and Altman and Taylor's (1973) social penetration theory. Recent research also has studied romantic relationships that go sour and the possible predictors of such break-ups. The insights gained from social psychological work can then be compared to those gleaned from marriage and divorce statistics. It should be noted that many instructors include a discussion of Zajonc's (1968) mere exposure hypothesis at this point in the course.

Self-disclosure

Early research by Jourard (1964) focused on the contents and contexts of self-disclosure, telling us who will talk about what to whom. Later work has been concerned with the role of disclosure in friendship formation and the norms which govern the gradual shift to increasing intimacy (Derlega and Chaikin, 1975).

Sexual Behaviour

In addition to the frequency data gathered by Kinsey and later investigators and a catalogue of human sexual behaviour, discussion can focus on the development of sexual identity, sexual myths and attitudes, and affective reactions to pornography.

OUR BEHAVIOUR IN GROUPS

Group Formation

The evolution of a cohesive group—the establishment of its status heirarchy, its lines of communication, and its norms—will be the primary focus of this section. What types of leaders do groups have, and what kinds of personality characteristics and abilities do they usually possess? How do leaders acquire their power, and what must they do (and not do) to hold on to it? How does the flow of outside events change a group's structure and cohesiveness (Cartwright and Zander, 1968)? What variables affect the productivity of groups? What tasks are best done by an individual and what tasks by a group (Davis, 1969)?

The Influence of Groups on Behaviour*

Any teacher of social psychology can attest to the incredulity shown by students when they first learn about Asch's (1956) classic studies on conformity and Milgram's (1974) controversial work on obedience to authority. No other studies in social psychology can prove as convincingly the power of situational forces on our behaviour and so shake up students' views of human nature. Of course, Milgram's work will provoke discussion of the ethics of deceptive laboratory research and the possible use of alternative methods such as role-playing. Other topics which can be covered under this section include: social facilitation effects, the risky shift phenomenon, panic, and de-individuation and mob behaviour.

Sensitivity Groups

An increasingly popular topic of discussion with students is the sensitivity or 'experiential' group—its goals, its rules, the benefits to participants, and its potential costs.

SOCIAL BEHAVIOUR

Aggression and Violence*

Aggression has been viewed variously as an instinct, a drive, and a learned response. Bandura (1973) presents a convincing case for social learning theory as the best vehicle by which to understand both the acquisition and performance of aggressive responses. Much of the discussion will enumerate the circumstances which instigate aggression (Baron, 1977): frustration, physical or verbal attack, exposure to violent models, competition, environmental stress due to heat or crowding, and the presence of 'aggressive cues'. With Schachter's (1964) work on emotional plasticity as its foundation, recent work has focused on the role of anger and general physiological arousal on aggression. The debate over the impact of television violence rages on, and students will be interested in learning what psychological research has to say about this issue.

Prosocial Behaviour*

A discussion of help-giving should begin with an account of Latane and Darley's (1970) work on bystander intervention. Such an introduction may seem shop-worn by now, but the fact is that the problem of non-intervention and social psychologists' efforts to understand it continues to capture student interest. Of course, psychologists have studied a wide range of altruistic behaviour, from simple acts of charity to donation of bone marrow. A great deal of time can be spent in delineating the characteristics of person and situation which affect the probability of such actions (Bar-Tal, 1976). A second major topic to be discussed here is the development of conscience and the capacity for moral decision-making (Mussen and Eisenberg-Berg, 1977). Typically, the focus will be on major theoretical perspectives: psychoanalytic theory and social learning theory, plus the models of Piaget (1965) and Kohlberg (1969). Finally, an instructor may wish to include the research on co-operation and competition, exemplified by the well-known Prisoners' Dilemma studies.

TYPES OF PEOPLE

Personality

The study of certain personality 'types' and their behaviour has had a long history in social psychology, for it has proven itself as an effective way to gain insight into the processes which mediate social behaviour. Which research programmes are chosen for discussion depends on the interests of the individual instructor, but we strongly recommend inclusion of work on both authoritarianism (Adorno, Frenkel-Brunswick, Levinson and Sanford, 1950) and need for achievement (McClelland, 1971). There is controversy about the ability of personality inventories to predict individual differences in behaviour, and this issue should probably be addressed.

Sex*

Are there real differences in behaviour and temperament between males and females? If so, why? How do sex roles restrict our behaviour?

Race and Social Class

Much research in social psychology has examined the impact race has on person perception and important social behaviours like aggression and altruism. But the major concern to be addressed here is intelligence testing and the storm of controversy surrounding the fact of racial differences in IQ scores. Two models of mankind are pitted against one another—one view stating that IQ differences reflect differences in inherited ability, the other stating that the arid social environment of lower class blacks is responsible. Of course, the 'nature–nurture' controversy has long been a major theme in psychology.

TOWARDS A BETTER SOCIETY

Applying Social Psychology

Basic theoretical work in social psychology has generated both methodological expertise and a wide range of ideas to guide investigators interested in so-called 'applied' or 'problem-oriented' research. The areas of interest (and concern) are wide in scope; education; environmental design (Sommer, 1969); jury decision-making (Gerbasi, Zuckerman, and Reis, 1977); prisons, mental hospitals and other 'total' institutions; industrial management; social work. It is not always an easy matter to apply laboratory work to an understanding of social problems, but the importance of social psychology as a foundation for work in the field should be stressed.

Evaluation Research

The 1970s have seen a large number of social psychologists become involved in evaluation research designed to assess the effectiveness of social intervention programmes (e.g. school desegregation, Head Start, etc.). Work of this type presents a host of methodological difficulties, not the least of which is public antagonism towards the running of no-treatment control groups (Riecken and Boruch, 1974).

It is clear that the course organization we have presented is arbitrary in many respects, but this is unavoidable. Social psychology is a field of study unlike physics or chemistry; a growing set of facts and insights is emerging, but there is no widely accepted theory for students to learn and apply. Students, of course, will expect to see a parade of facts and firm conclusions unfolding in a logical and inevitable progression. But that simply is not possible now.

There are aspects of the outline we have suggested which dissatisfy us. For example, we have separated the discussions of attribution and self-perception, but many of the most interesting studies have examined differences between the two. We have found the present organization to work well in our own courses, but we recognize that there are many reasonable ways to structure this course. You must decide, of course, what will work best for you.

TEACHING METHODS

At most universities, social psychology classes are large. As a result, most professors fill their class time with lectures, believing it to be the best way of giving students the most for their money. And certainly an argument can be made that for most of us, who possess teaching skills something less than those of Socrates, lecturing is the most effective way of communicating facts and ideas to students at an introductory level. But as with any course, to rely on a lecture format exclusively is a mistake; it can be an awful bore, for the instructor as well as the students.

Before describing alternative uses of class time available to the social psychology instructor, however, we need to make three points about lecturing. First, you should try to use examples which relate to student life at your college.

Your students are amateur social psychologists, daily puzzling over their own behaviour and that of their friends. Exploit this as much as possible.

Second, the material to be covered in a social psychology course often lends itself easily to use of a brief demonstration at the beginning of class which will capture the students' attention. For example, a lecture on legal research, which should focus in part on the reliability of eyewitness testimony, can be launched effectively with a 'crime' staged before a startled class, which is then required to describe the 'criminal'. Some film material can be used in the same way. *Candid Camera* film clips (write: DuArt Film Laboratories, Cornell Candid Camera Collection, 245 W. 55th Street, New York, NY 10019, USA) can be used to introduce lectures on conformity, obedience to authority, reactions to deviant behaviour, and so on. Another approach that can be considered is introduction of a topic through citation of a well-known work of fiction or an incident from a famous person's life (cf. Levin, 1978). The point we are making is not that you must 'trick' your students into attending to you, but that you should show them why what you have to say might be of some importance to them. This is not something they necessarily take for granted.

Third, of course, you must be sensitive to the needs, priorities, and abilities of your students. At many colleges only the brightest may be interested in the minutiae of procedure and results which qualify the conclusions that can be drawn from experiments you describe. The majority may be content to learn of the field's theories and special insights, having little tolerance for emphasis on the *process* of social psychology. You must assess this and make a decision about what to do, even if it is to convert the heathens to a belief in the importance of method and detail.

Guest Lecturers

The use of guest lecturers can be a valuable addition to a course. It not only breaks the monotony for the students, but it also serves to introduce them to perspectives other than your own. Experts from outside psychology can talk about their first-hand experiences, giving new meaning to the research about which the students have learned and perhaps provoking discussion of how to apply social psychological principles and methodology.

Many different types of speakers would be appropriate: be imaginative. Former prisoners can talk of life behind bars; advertising executives can demonstrate how they exploit psychological principles to sell dog food or political candidates; government officers can talk about social policy—for example, the welfare system and its effects on motivation, the effects of school desegregation on race relations. Your colleagues from other departments can provide the perspective of their disciplines on such topics as deviance, aggression and crime, altruism, and group behaviour. Many business, law, and medical schools now have psychologists on their staffs.

Also available now are 'guest lectures' of another sort—talks given by famous social psychologists and recorded on audio-cassette tape. Two companies which market such tapes are:

(a) Harper & Row (write: Harper & Row Media, Order Fulfillment/Customer Service, 2350 Virginia Avenue, Hagerstown, MD 21740, USA); and

(b) Jeffrey Norton Publishers (write: Tape Department, East 49th Street, New York, New York 10017, USA).

Several things must be done to make a guest lecture a successful part of your course. First, you should meet with the speakers far in advance of their scheduled visits, appraising them of the structure of your course, the size of the class, and your students' interests and background. Second, be sure that your class is well prepared for the guest lecture. Have you covered in class the basic material they will need to know to appreciate what the visitor has to say? Provide them with biographical information about the speaker and a list of possible questions to think about before the class. Finally, be attentive to details: double-check the loudspeaker system and the audio-visual equipment; verify the speaker's arrival time; plan out an alternative way of spending the class time in case something goes awry.

In-class Demonstrations

We have already mentioned how demonstrations can be used to introduce a topic and capture the students' interest in what you have to say. But demonstrations can also be the major focus of a class period, often being much more effective in communicating complex ideas than a lecture. When students can see a phenomenon happen, and not just hear about it, they are more likely to be involved in what you say about it. And the fact is that many of the phenomena which social psychologists study seem fantastic and astounding and have to be seen to be believed.

Perhaps nothing has the power to embarrass an instructor as much as a demonstration which is introduced with a flourish and then fails. Any demonstration involves the risk of failure, of course, but certain preventative steps can be taken. First, be sure the demonstration is simple and straightforward. If the staging is complicated and requires extraordinary co-ordination, beware. Second, if the impact of the demonstration hinges on a single outcome, it should be used with caution. What does an instructor do when the class is broken up into smaller groups to debate the merits of various recommendations, and none shows the 'risky shift' effect? The phenomenon you wish to illustrate must be robust. For example, the effect of set on the interpretation of ambiguous figures can always be demonstrated. Another alternative is to use demonstrations which are more open-ended, for which any of several possible outcomes can launch you into a discussion of the points you want to make. Third, and most important, you must rehearse. You must come to know the procedure intimately and completely.

Films

Today almost every instructor of social psychology will use films to break the monotony of a steady (and sometimes bland) diet of lectures. The reasons for this are obvious. Films afford the same advantages as in-class demonstrations, but without the risks of failure (assuming the projection equipment is sound and a fresh bulb is handy). Films can show things and take your students places that no lecture or demonstration can. The range of topics for which films can be used effectively is unlimited. They are available from three types of sources: film distributors, publishing houses, and university film libraries. We have included an Appendix at the end of the chapter which lists those sources whose holdings we find to be the best. Catalogues are available from each.

Two other kinds of films can be used as well. Many instructors will make films or videotapes of the experiments they run, and these, of course, can be used to teach the class about a specific experiment and experimentation in general. In addition, you should keep your eye on popular films being shown; occasionally, one will be released that you will recommend the class to see. Some universities have film libraries which often contain older films no longer shown at movie houses.

Remember that 'movie day' is not your day off. For your students to get the most out of the film, you must introduce it properly. What questions do you want them to have in mind as they view it? To what do you want them to pay attention? How does the film tie in to material covered in earlier lectures or in the textbook? Discuss the film at its end; if you do not, your students will fail to learn from it as much as they could, and they may come to think of the films as mere entertainment.

Field Experiments

When reading about experiments in a social psychology textbook, students frequently conclude such experimentation to be a simple thing. Ideas seem to be translated easily into testable hypotheses. Operationalization of independent variables seems to pose no problems, nor does devising a valid dependent measure. The results may strike many students as unsurprising; indeed, some will say that social psychology is a fraud, that expensive experiments are being designed to confirm 'common sense'. Our experience has been that this illusion cannot easily be burst until students are given the opportunity to devise and run their own experiment. It is sobering for them to discover how many variables they need to control, how many different outcomes might reasonably be expected and how ambiguous and complicated data can be. Involvement in such a project is perhaps the best way for students to learn the principles of good experimental design and the proper procedures to follow in data collection. Presentation of their projects in class will also give them practice in communicating their ideas clearly. If your class is small (say, thirty or less), we recommend that you give this a try.

Given the heavy demand on space, equipment, and the subject pool at most universities, it will probably be impossible for your students to conduct laboratory studies. But that is not an obstacle. Many of the most interesting studies in social psychology are field studies. You will have to be armed with suggestions; for inspiration, we suggest that you consult an edited volume by Bickman and Henchy (1972), *Beyond the Laboratory: Field Research in Social Psychology*.

Term Papers

No professor enjoys trundling home after a busy day with a briefcase full of term papers and then wading through pages of broken English and disarrayed thoughts after supper. A few papers are well written and insightful, of course. But they are few.

It is not uncommon now for us to meet with juniors or seniors who are panicked about a term paper that is due soon and to be stunned by their inability to organize their thoughts and set them down on paper. What stuns us more is the too-frequent announcement that they have never before had to submit a term paper for a college course! They are whizzes at multiple choice examinations, but they simply cannot write a coherent paragraph. For too long, instructors have passed along the responsibility of our students' education to other professors.

There are three types of papers we have assigned in the past, the one we choose depending mostly on the abilities of our students:

(a) An important world event, a social problem, a play or a novel is chosen, and the student is asked to interpret it using social psychological principles.

(b) The student evaluates the evidence on a social psychological theory.

(c) The student proposes an experiment.

The first is the riskiest; writing such a paper well requires a level of creativity and writing flair beyond most students. The second two, of course, are more relevant to the everyday work of social psychologists and can stimulate students to think like scientists.

We have several recommendations to make regarding the assignment and grading of term papers.

1 It is best for you to provide a list of suggested topics to your students. Many of them will otherwise not know what is appropriate.

2 You must make yourself (and your teaching assistant) available for con-

sultation. Your students will need help ranging from getting a few key references to discussing at length the ideas they are planning to include in their papers.

3 In class it is important for you to introduce the students to the use of reference works like the *Social Science Citation Index* and *Psychological Abstracts*. Elliot (1971) lists and explains the organization of other reference books that may be helpful.

4 It is immensely helpful to your students if you collect and comment upon their first drafts well before the final product must be submitted. (This may be unmanageable for a large class, however.)

5 An alternative is to give students a chance to submit a new version of their papers after grades have been given. The students must understand that their grades will not necessarily go up when the revision is considered, but the experience of doing the revision will be a useful one for them nonetheless.

6 Students with professional ambitions are under tremendous pressure for near-perfect grades. The competition for graduate or professional school admissions is fierce. And, understandably, some students will be displeased with the grades they have received, and they will want to talk about it with you. We have adopted the policy of avoiding such face-to-face discussions if possible. Some students are inconsolable, and they will not listen to your explanations or to your listing of imperfections in their work. As an alternative, we suggest that you have students submit a written request for grade changes, requiring them to state coherently (and unemotionally) the basis of their complaints. You will then have the time to carefully and unhurriedly reconsider your decision before you write a reply.

7 Make photocopies of the better papers from former students and make them available (with the authors' permission) to the class. Seeing examples of good work will help them considerably.

Textbooks

It is of no use for us to pass along our personal list of best-loved social psychology textbooks. New entries into the textbook sweepstakes are published each year. Instead, we offer the following suggestions for choosing a book that is best for you and your students.

It is impossible to judge the adequacy of a text merely by scanning its table of contents and flipping through the pages, glancing at the boxes and *New Yorker* cartoons. You do need to check the breadth of topics covered and judge whether the book's overlap with your lectures and other class activities is about right. But you have to read a book to know it. Pick the chapter which talks about research you know well and read it. Does it read well without sacrificing attention to detail? Is it written at a level commensurate with your students' abilities? Is its treatment of controversies complete and even-handed? A text should also be judged on its length and density; books which work well for a semester-long course may be poor choices for classes that last only a quarter or are held during summer session. Many textbooks are accompanied by test booklets and an instructor's manual. Are the test items well constructed? Is the manual helpful with suggestions for lecture topics, discussion questions, and demonstrations? It is important to check them; they seem especially valuable when you are a few weeks into the class and battle-weary.

A fair number of books of readings are available, many of which are linked to best-selling textbooks. Some are quite good. But you should judge whether your students, hearing your perspective on social psychology, might be better served by a tailor-made list of readings which you put on reserve at the university library. You should also consider assigning monographs which focus on content areas of special interest; many of the sources we listed with the course syllabus would be good volumes for introductory students to read. Many of your brighter students will tire of the superficial treatment some textbooks provide and welcome the deeper level of analysis to be found in such books.

We have presented an annotated listing of topics which might be covered in an introductory course on social psychology, along with suggestions for supplementing lectures, choosing texts, and evaluating student performance. It is hoped that the range of suggestions has been wide enough to provide a useful starting point for most instructors. You should remember, however, that any suggestions must be adapted to your own style of teaching and your personal approach to social psychology.

APPENDIX

Some of the major distributors of social psychological films in the USA:

Macmillan Films.
34 MacQuesten Parkway South,
Mt. Vernon, New York   10550.

McGraw-Hill Films,
1221 Avenue of the Americas,
New York, New York   10020.

Prentice-Hall Film Library,
Englewood Cliffs, NJ   07632.

John Wiley & Sons, Inc.,
Educational Services Department,
605 Third Avenue,
New York, NY   10016.

Association Instruction Materials,
600 Madison Avenue,
New York, NY   10022.

Psychological Cinema Register,
Pennsylvania State University,
University Park, PA 16802.

Time-Life Films,
43 W. 16th Street,
New York, NY 10011.

CRM Educational Films,
Del Mar, CA 92014.

Psychological Films,
189 N. Wheeler Street,
Orange, CA 92669.

University of California,
Extension Media Center,
Berkeley, CA 94720.

REFERENCES

Adorno, T. W., Frenkel-Brunswick, D., Levinson, D., and Sanford, N. (1950). *The Authoritarian Personality*. New York: Harper & Row.

Altman, I., and Taylor, D. (1973). *Social Penetration: The Development of Interpersonal Relations*. New York: Holt, Rinehart & Winston.

Anderson, N. (1965). Averaging versus Adding as a Stimulus-combination Rule in Impression Formation. *Journal of Experimental Psychology*, **70**, 394–400.

Asch, S. (1946). Forming Impressions of Personality. *Journal of Abnormal and Social Psychology*, 1946, **41**, 258–290.

Asch, S. (1956). Studies of Independence and Conformity: A Minority of One Against a Unanimous Majority. *Psychological Monographs*, **70** (9, Whole No. 416).

Bandura, A. (1973). *Aggression: A Social Learning Analysis*. Englewood Cliffs: Prentice-Hall.

Baron, R. A. (1977), *Human Aggression*. New York: Plenum.

Bar-Tal, D. (1976). *Prosocial Behavior: Theory and Research*. New York: Wiley.

Bem, D. J. (1972). Self-perception Theory. In Berkowitz, L. (ed.). *Advances in Experimental Social Psychology*, *Vol. 6*. New York: Academic Press, pp. 1–62.

Berkowitz, L. (ed.) (1964–1977). *Advance in Experimental Social Psychology*, *Vols. 1–10*. New York: Academic Press.

Bickman, L., and Henchy T. (eds) (1972). *Beyond the Laboratory: Field Research in Social Psychology*. New York: McGraw-Hill.

Brehm, J. (1972). *Responses to Loss of Freedom: A Theory of Psychological Reactance*. Morristown, NJ: General Learning Press.

Carlsmith, J. N., Ellsworth, P. C., and Aronson, E. (1976). *Methods of Research in Social Psychology*. Reading, Mass.: Addison-Wesley.

Cartwright, D., and Zander, A. (eds) (1968). *Group Dynamics*. New York: Harper & Row, third edition.

Davis, J. H. (1969). *Group Performance*. Reading, Mass.: Addison-Wesley.

Deci, E. (1975). *Intrinsic Motivation*. New York: Plenum.

deCharms, R. (1968). *Personal Causation: The Internal Affective Determinants of Behavior*. New York: Academic Press.

Derlega, V. J., and Chaikin, A. L. (1975). *Sharing Intimacy: What We Reveal To Others and Why*. Englewood Cliffs: Prentice-Hall.

Deutsch, M., and Krauss, R. (1965). *Theories in Social Psychology*. New York: Basic Books.

Ekman, P., Friesen, W. V., and Ellsworth, P. (1972). *Emotion in the Human Face: Guidelines for Research and an Integration of Findings*. Oxford: Pergamon Press.

Elliott, C. K. (1971). *A Guide to the Documentation of Psychology*. Handen, CT: Linnet.

Ellsworth, P., and Ludwig, L. (1972). Visual Behavior in Social Interaction. *Journal of Communication*, **22**, 375–403.

Festinger, L. (1954). A Theory of Social Comparison Processes. *Human Relations*, **7**, 117–140.

Festinger, L. (1957). *A Theory of Cognitive Dissonance*. Stanford: Stanford University Press.

Fishbein, M., and Ajzen, I. (1975). *Belief, Attitude, Intention and Behavior*. Reading, Mass.: Addison-Wesley.

Gerbasi, K. C., Zuckerman, M., and Reis, H. T. (1977). Justice Needs a New Blindfold: A Review of Mock Jury Research. *Psychological Bulletin*, **84**, 323–345.

Gergen, K. H. (1971). *The Concept of Self*. New York: Holt, Rinehart & Winston.

Heider, F. (1958). *The Psychology of Interpersonal Relations*. New York: Wiley.

Jones, E. E. (1964). *Ingratiation*. New York: Appleton-Century-Crofts.

Jones, E. E., Kanouse, D., Kelley, H. H., Nisbett, R., Valins, S., and Weiner, B. (1972). *Attribution: Perceiving the Causes of Behavior*. Morristown, NJ: General Learning Press.

Jones, J. N. (1972). *Prejudice and Racism*. Reading, Mass.: Addison-Wesley.

Jourard, S. (1964). *The Transparent Self*. Princeton: Van Nostrand.

Kelley, H. H. (1973). The Processes of Causal Attribution. *American Psychologist*, **28**, 107–127.

Kiesler, C. A., Collins, B. E., and Miller, N. (1969). *Attitude Change: A Critical Analysis of Theoretical Approaches*. New York: Wiley.

Kohlberg, L. (1969). The Cognitive-Developmental Approach to Socialization. In: Goslin, D. A. (ed.). *Handbook of Socialization Theory and Research*. Chicago: Rand-McNally, pp. 347–480.

LaPiere, R. (1934). Attitudes and Actions. *Social Forces*, **13**, 230–237.

Latane, B., and Darley, J. M. (1970). *The Unresponsive Bystander: Why Doesn't He Help?* New York: Appleton-Century-Crofts.

Lefcourt, H. M. (1976). *Locus of Control: Current Trends in Theory and Research*. New York: Erlbaum.

Lepper, M., Greene, D., and Nisbett, R. (1973). Undermining Children's Intrinsic Interest with Extrinsic Reward: A Test of the 'Overjustification' Hypothesis. *Journal of Personality and Social Psychology*, **28**, 129–137.

Levin, M. (1978). *Psychology: A Biographical Approach*. New York: McGraw-Hill.

Lindzey, G., and Aronson, E. (eds) (1968, 1969). *The Handbook of Social Psychology*, *Vols. 1–5*. Reading, Mass.: Addison-Wesley, second edition.

McClelland, D. (1971). *Motivational Trends in Society*. Morristown, NJ: General Learning Press.

Milgram, S. (1974). *Obedience to Authority: An Experimental View*. New York: Harper & Row.

Mussen, P., and Eisenberg-Berg, N. (1977). *Roots of Caring, Sharing, and Helping: The Development of Prosocial Behaviour in Children*. San Francisco: Freeman.

Piaget, J. (1965). *The Moral Judgment of the Child.* New York: The Free Press.

Riecken, H. W., and Boruch, R. F. (eds) (1974). *Social Experimentation: A Method for Planning and Evaluating Social Intervention.* New York: Academic Press.

Rokeach, M. (1975). Long-term Value Change Initiated by Computer Feedback. *Journal of Personality and Social Psychology,* **32**, 467–476.

Rosenthal, R., and Jacobson, L. (1968). *Pygmalion in the Classroom: Teacher Expectation and Pupils' Intellectual Development.* New York: Holt, Rinehart & Winston.

Rotter, J. (1966). Generalized Expectancies for Internal Versus External Control of Reinforcement. *Psychological Monographs,* **80** (1, Whole No. 609).

Rubin, Z. (1973). *Liking and Loving: An Invitation to Social Psychology.* New York: Holt, Rinehart & Winston.

Schachter, S. (1959). *The Psychology of Affiliation.* Stanford: Stanford University Press.

Schachter, S. (1964). The Interaction of Cognitive and Physiological Determinants of Emotional State. In Berkowitz, L. (ed.). *Advances in Experimental Social Psychology,* *Vol. 1.* New York: Academic Press, pp. 49–80.

Schachter, S., and Singer, J. (1962). Cognitive, Social, and Physiological Determinants of Emotional States. *Psychological Review,* **69**, 379–399.

Schneider, D., Hastorf, A., and Ellsworth, P. (1979). *Person Perception.* Reading, Mass.: Addison-Wesley, second edition.

Seligman, M. E. P. (1975). *Helplessness: On Depression, Development, and Death.* San Francisco: W. H. Freeman.

Shaw, M., and Costanzo, P. (1970). *Theories of Social Psychology.* New York: McGraw-Hill.

Snyder, M., Tanke, E., and Berscheid, E. (1977). Social Perception and Interpersonal Behavior: On the Self-fulfilling Nature of Social Stereotypes. *Journal of Personality and Social Psychology,* **35**, 656–666.

Sommer, R. (1969). *Personal Space: The Behaviourial Basis of Design.* Englewood Cliffs: Prentice-Hall.

Walster, E., Berscheid, E., and Walster, G. (1972). New Directions in Equity Research. *Journal of Personality and Social Psychology,* **25**, 151–176.

Zajonc, R. (1968). Attitudinal Effects of Mere Exposure. *Journal of Personality and Social Psychology Monograph Supplement,* **9**(2, part 2), 2–27.

Zimbardo, P. G., Ebbesen, E. B., and Maslach, C. (1977). *Influencing Attitudes and Changing Behaviour* (2nd Ed.). Reading, Mass.: Addison-Wesley.

8

Developmental Psychology

JOHANNA TURNER

INTRODUCTION

Three questions are fundamental when considering teaching any subject:

1 What, as teachers, are we trying to achieve?
2 By what means can we realize our aims?
3 How can we assess the extent to which we have succeeded?

This paper will consider these questions with reference to the teaching of developmental psychology. It will, therefore, cover aims and objectives, course content, teaching methods and the question of evaluation. The transmission of knowledge is, perhaps unfortunately, not a linear process whereby the learner moves from ignorance to understanding. Rather it requires the teacher to present the subject, in this case developmental psychology, in such a way that learners are able both to understand contemporary theories and then go beyond their teachers by evaluating findings for themselves perhaps even contributing discoveries of their own. Such cognitive changes are not discrete entities; in learning to think like a developmental psychologist the student may find that his view of other subjects will change. He is thus personally experiencing an aspect of the process of growth and change that, more generally, forms the content of his subject of study. This dual perception, necessarily present in the learner when studying developmental psychology, can, if ignored, impede learning, if recognized, facilitate it.

AIMS

When formulating his aims the teacher needs to reflect upon three aspects of his task:

1 The distinguishing characteristics of the subject matter which he will teach.

2 The general and specific skills which the learner needs to develop.

3 The context in which a particular piece of teaching/learning will take place.

The third aspect is dependent on the other two. Once the teacher has determined the key concepts of his subject matter and the range of skills to be developed, he can choose to teach an appropriate sample of each, depending on the previous experience of the students and the type of course they are following.

Subject Matter

For the developmental psychologist the task of determining the distinguishing characteristics of the subject matter poses particular problems. A definition of developmental psychology is dependent on a prior definition of psychology in general. If psychology is thought to be the study of human behaviour and experience then developmental psychology is the study of changes in that behaviour over time. If, however, psychology is seen as the study of behaviour in humans and other species, then developmental psychology could cover changes in behaviour within the species (e.g. the development of attachment behaviour between parents and young) or, the development of behaviour patterns—in the sense of evolutionary development—between species (e.g. the length and function of immaturity) or, compare the developmental process of similar behaviours in different species (e.g. play or sexual behaviour). Developmental psychology can thus be broadly or narrowly conceived depending on whether it is confined to human behaviour or extended to include the behaviour of other species, the one common element being that it defines and considers the process of behavioural change. It would, however, be difficult to conceive of changeless behaviour unless one limits behaviour to simple reflexes or tropisms, and even these will change if the physiological condition of the organism improves or deteriorates. If the study of behaviour is closely linked to the study of change then developmental psychology and psychology appear almost synonymous. Clearly the teacher will have to make some distinctions at the outset or he will be overwhelmed by the diffuse nature of his subject matter. An attractive solution is to limit developmental psychology to the study of human growth and change but this rules out too much since both the evolutionary and the comparative perspectives exist and are necessary, but not sufficient, for understanding human development. A compromise can be reached by stating that developmental psychology focuses on growth and change in human behaviour whilst taking account of studies involving other species and of Man's evolution.

Developmental psychology is concerned with both describing and explaining change. Studies of the forms of behaviour exhibited at discrete points in the life cycle (e.g. the appearance of smiling in the human infant or the development of infant object permanence) are important but the explanation of why a particular behaviour changes over time in a particular way is both fundamental and complex. A theory of development may have to take into account the *interaction* of the individual's existing behaviour and external influences on that behaviour which cause the existing behaviour to adapt (e.g. Piaget's notion of equilibration whereby a child's cognitive schemes are thought to change if they are found to be inadequate when forced to cope with a new environmental stimuli). Alternatively a *holistic* approach may be adopted which argues that 'phylogeny ... has fashioned a balance between organism and environment so that all the human animal does is based on a marriage of cultural practice and biological predispostion' (Freedman, 1974, p. 6). It could be argued, however, that a comprehensive theory would need to take account of interactionism and holism.

In seeking to explain change the developmental psychologist has to decide when development can be said to begin. Is Freedman (1974, p. 18) correct when he argues that:

> Any item of behaviour takes on meaning only when examined in the light of the total species adaptation ... thus, an item of infant behaviour, e.g., the smile or cry, must be considered in terms of total hominid adaptation including the total life span ... it is no more logical to start with the baby in a description of human behaviour than in any other stage of life, for species survival and the evolution of adaptations involve all phases of the life span.

He also has to decide whether, within the life span, there are critical periods for change and, finally, whether development is complete at maturity or death.

Therefore the teacher when considering the distinguishing characteristics of the subject has in any particular instance to determine the limits of the relevant unit of behaviour, to describe changes in that behaviour and to explain such changes. A careful selection of content is essential otherwise the learner will become overburdened by a mass of material all of which could legitimately be included. The teacher needs to select key aspects of human development (e.g. the growth of cognitive competence or sociability) through which he can introduce the students to ideas of growth and change which, necessarily, go beyond the human species. At the end of three years of study the students should have developed an interest in, and capacity to see, broad conceptual issues in developmental psychology and be equipped to consider the evidence for or against them. Examples of such issues are: critical periods in human development and the evidence for reversibility; processes such as sex role identity; arguments about sociocultural factors, e.g. child-rearing practices and cross-cultural studies; 'norms' of behaviour; and the interrelationship of key variables, e.g. physical, cognitive, social and emotional development.

Skills

The teacher's second aim is concerned with the general and specific skills which learners need to develop. Generally, if learners are to understand human behavioural change they must know, when presented with a statement, how to judge what evidence is acceptable for determining the truth or falsehood of that statement. It is necessary to distinguish between evidence which is limited to observable behaviour (e.g. Piaget's description of a child's behaviour when faced with the three mountain problem) and evidence based on theorizing which goes beyond the observable behaviour (e.g. Piaget's theory of egocentrism). Current observations (crying infants will quieten when picked up by their mothers) must be separated from retrospective studies which attempt to link adolescent or adult behaviour with infant experience. Developmental psychologists commonly quote evidence from non-human studies and here a decision has to be made concerning the relevance of such evidence. The skill of interpreting the relevance of the evidence adduced by a researcher in support of his hypothesis is perhaps the most general skill to be acquired.

There are, however, more specific skills which are equally necessary and which relate to discrete approaches to the study of human behavioural change. The student needs to learn how to observe, how to behave in a professional/clinical setting, and how to analyse experiments.

Observational skills are essential for this subject matter and the students must:

1 know the various forms of observation (e.g. interaction analysis, time sampling, participant observation, and naturalistic studies);
2 learn to observe with the minimum of pre-conceptions, or at the very least to be aware of his own pre-conceptions; and
3 to be aware of what he has seen.

An observer has to be in touch with his own behaviour and values before he can view the behaviour of another with even a minimal degree of objectivity. Thus the students need an opportunity to learn about particular aspects of their own behaviour (e.g. situations in which they become anxious or defensive) while attempting to understand the behaviour of others.

Skills related to behaviour in a professional/clinical context are required when the student is either interacting with others whose behaviour he wishes to observe or influence, or when he is reading studies based on face-to-face interaction. He has to be made aware of:

1 how he, as perceiver, can influence what he sees;
2 how his behaviour can influence the behaviour of the other; and
3 how the behaviour of the other can influence him.

A psychologist interacting with other human beings has a more difficult task than researchers studying non-human phenomena since he is both an observer and the subject of another's observation.

Probably the best way for the student to learn to devise and analyse experiments is by becoming thoroughly conversant with the strengths and limitations of existing methodologies and by undertaking regular practical work as part of his course. The teaching of statistics can in this way be integrated with the analysis of data generated in practicals.

Context

The aims discussed so far will need to be modified by the teacher according to the context in which he is teaching. Courses in developmental psychology can be divided into four types:

1 Short courses, which are intended to inform but do not lead to any formal qualification.

2 Service courses which are provided when the students are preparing for a non-psychological qualification (e.g. Postgraduate Certificate in Education or Master of Social Work) but require a psychological component.

3 Part courses which occur when the students are studying for a general psychological qualification (e.g. B.A. or M.Ed. Psych.) and are required to study developmental psychology for a part of their time.

4 Full length specialized degree courses.

In short courses the teacher has three aims: to provide the students with information directly relevant to their area of interest; to give sufficient information to the students concerning the methods of developmental psychology for them to be able to put the information they are given in perspective; to give the students the opportunity for some practical experience, if only in observation. The main danger on an eight- or ten-week course is that the teacher be seen as an 'expert' with the result that his views will be accepted uncritically by the student. Inevitably the areas covered on such a course will have to be limited to one or, at most, two (e.g. 'cognitive development', 'social development', or 'moral development') with a careful selection of topics within each area. A whole course could, however, be spent considering one issue (e.g. adolescent development) with other topics raised as subsidiary issues. Service courses differ from short courses in that students taking these courses are most concerned with the qualifications they are seeking with the result that the psychological element of the course is seen as a means to an end rather than as an end in itself, whereas the short-course students, necessarily, have an intrinsic interest in the topic. The distinction here is perhaps between: (a) pursuing knowledge which is well founded on generally accepted evidence; and

(b) being prepared to apply what is known in answer to a practical problem. The teacher here has to ask himself, 'What aspects of developmental psychology would be most useful for a future X?' In these courses the students have no wish to become developmental psychologists but nor can they expect to receive pre-packaged and instant expertise. The teacher needs to know, in detail, what the students have covered in other parts of the course and aid them to develop understanding and practical skills which will complement their other areas of proficiency. Part courses and full length degree courses give the teacher more scope for achieving the aims discussed above (see p. 150). In part courses the teacher must aim to make clear to the students the concepts and methods which are peculiar to developmental psychology in contrast to those illustrated in other parts of the course whereas in the full length course the problem is reversed; here the teacher needs to ensure that, despite the course's developmental orientation, the student does have an adequate understanding of other areas of psychology with their own particular characteristics and practical skills.

COURSE CONTENT

This section will consider possible syllabuses and materials with reference to the four contexts outlined above.

Short Courses

It has been argued that in these courses the topic has an intrinsic interest for the students and the teacher can assume fairly high motivation but he cannot assume that the students have any background in the subject. An initial period of introduction or orientation is thus essential. At this stage students should read a selection of specifically introductory books (see Appendix 8.2). Students can also be encouraged to undertake some practical work. For example primary teachers or parents could be given a schedule of questions as an introduction to Piaget's work (see Appendix 8.1). Films can also be used and some useful catalogues to consult are:

  (i) *British National Film Catalogue* (British Film Institute);
 (ii) *Audio Visual Aids for Higher Education* (British Universities Film Council);
(iii) *Contemporary Education Library* (McGraw-Hill);
 (iv) *Open University* (Open University Educational Enterprises);
  (v) *Guild of Sound and Vision* (Guild of Sound and Vision).

After the introductory period more specific topics can be covered in detail and the reading can become more technical. Possible topics are play (Appendix

8.4h), language development (Appendix 8.4g) and adolescence (Appendix 8.4a).

Throughout the course each student could observe a child or adolescent regularly and produce a case study for group discussion. The student could also be presented with practical problems (e.g. a behaviour problem in class) and consider what questions could be asked, what solutions could be offered and how the questions and the answers could be formulated within the rules of psychology as a social science, thus exploring the limitations of psychology for the practitioner. At the end of the course time should be spent considering aspects which have not been covered and students given some direction on how to continue with their learning after the course has ended.

Service Courses

These courses have particular difficulties since the students often view them instrumentally (see p. 153). On these, as in the short courses, the teacher cannot aim to produce developmental psychologists as such and, therefore, need not seek to achieve all the aims mentioned in the introduction to this chapter. When planning such a course the teacher has a choice, either he can consider growth and change in the people with whom the students will have to deal and offer courses on, for example, the growth of competence (Appendix 8.4e) or cognitive development (Appendix 8.4d) for teachers, or adolescence (Appendix 8.4a) for social workers, or he can concentrate on growth and change in the students themselves, so that the experience of the students present becomes the content of the course. This second approach involves such notions as development to date and the students' changing sense of identity as they become aware of the demands of the professional role for which they are preparing. This approach can be extremely successful but relies upon introspection by the students, the possibility of teaching in small groups, and the teacher's ability to provide theoretical back-up as a concomitant rather than providing formal reading lists or showing films at a set time. The teacher also needs to have the skill to handle possible disturbances in his students if student change becomes an aim of the course.

Part Courses

As students on these courses are concurrently receiving instruction in other aspects of psychology these courses are potentially the most specialized developmental courses available. The aims which the teacher needs to bear in mind are conveying what is characteristic of developmental psychology and the significance of observational and interactional skills (assuming that statistics and experimental design are covered elsewhere). A decision that has to be made at the outset is whether the course will be structured around stages in the life cycle (infancy, middle childhood, adolescence, maturity and old age) or around topics (e.g. cognitive development, social development, or emotional development). The first way can become very fragmented requiring, for example, cognitive development to appear in each stage. It also plays down the developmental aspect of behaviour as students have to wait until the next stage to find out how any particular aspect of behaviour changes. However, by the end, the nature of developmental changes should have become apparent. Its strength is that topics such as infancy form discrete units and are more easily dealt with in this way. The second method of structuring the course around topics is conceptually easier particularly as classic writers such as Piaget, Erikson and Schaffer do concentrate primarily on aspects of development (e.g. cognitive, emotional, social) and only secondarily on age-related descriptions of behaviour. Its drawbacks are that the whole person may disappear amid his aspects. This can result in students, having divided development into aspects, experiencing considerable difficulty in synthesizing their understanding. They may, therefore, when faced with a client in a professional setting, fail to treat him as a whole but rather concentrate on discrete aspects of his behaviour. A compromise is required and, accepting that well-documented topics are always preferable on any course, possible topics for a part course could be: capacities of the neonate; infancy; attachment, separation and deprivation; language development; moral development; social development; culture and development; adolescence. Different theories or models should be presented and students given the opportunity to be aware of the frontiers of knowledge in specific areas of research.

Full Length Degree Courses

In these courses time constraints are lessened and the teacher can attempt to achieve all the aims set out above even though the students do have to become familiar with general psychology in addition to specializing in developmental psychology. The teacher, however, does need to offer topics which are well grounded in research. He is under no obligation to teach a topic if it is not well researched no matter how important it may be in human behaviour. Developmental psychology requires the tutor to relate the jobs of 'scientist', 'applied scientist' and 'practitioner' (Davidson, 1977). How they are related differs in academic and professional courses but the developmental psychologist cannot be a 'scientist' only. The role of practical work is particularly important and should, ideally, be related to the theoretical content in each section of the course. The whole range of teaching methods should also be employed (see p. 159). There are, obviously, many different ways of organizing such a course. Whether individual parts of the course should last for one, two or three terms will be determined by the convention in a particular institution.

The following is a description of the course followed by students studying developmental psychology in the School of Cultural and Community Studies at the University of Sussex. The students' time in their three years at Sussex is divided between Preliminary courses, Contextual courses and Major courses (Table 8.1). Only major courses are described here and it should be remembered that on the majority of courses the teaching aims to emphasize the developmental aspects of the topics. All courses are accompanied by one, two or three lectures a week, plus films when necessary, but the main course teaching takes place in tutorials (one tutor with two or three students for 1 hour) or, less often, seminars (one tutor with eight students for 2 hours).

Table 8.1. *B.A. in Developmental Psychology in the School of Cultural and Community Studies, University of Sussex*

		Year 1	
Autumn Term	1	School Preliminary Course—Critical Reading	
	2	Optional Preliminary Course (popular options are *Human Evolution, The Biological Basis of Sex Differences, Linguistics*)	
Spring Term	1	Introduction to Developmental Psychology	
	2	Second Optional Preliminary Course	
Summer Term	1	Cognition I	
	2	Statistics	
	3	Practicals	

		Year 2	
		Major Courses	*Contextual Courses*
Autumn Term	1	Cognition II	1st Contextual course
	2	Practicals	
Spring Term	1	Personality	2nd Contextual course
	2	Research Projects	
Summer Term	1	Human Growth and Development I	3rd Contextual course
	2	Naturalistic Observation Project	

		Year 3	
Autumn Term	1	Option I	4th Contextual course
Spring Term	1	Option II	
Summer Term		FINALS	FINALS

Course Rubrics

Introduction to Developmental Psychology

The aim of this course is to provide an introduction to the study of human behaviour within a developmental context. It is not intended that it should cover a range of developmental concepts but rather that it shall, by considering a few basic topics in some depth, provide an introduction to the content and methods of developmental psychology. The course is initially focused on the neonate, and introduces ideas concerning brain behaviour and development through studying the phylogeny and ontogeny of the neonate, its 'innate' capacities and the subsequent interactions of physiological and social development. Topics covered are: the capacities of the neonate, their evolutionary history, and their adaptive significance, the development of the brain in man and other species; post-natal development—learning, perception, and motor skills; aspects of mother–infant interaction. The questions considered are, 'What can the infant do?' and 'How did he get that way?' or 'What are the infant's capacities?' and 'How did they develop?'

Cognition I and II

This course is taken over two terms and covers those topics basic to psychology as a scientific subject. These include in Term 1: instinct, learning and motivation, arousal and emotion, perception, and attention. In Term 2: memory, imagery and lateralization, language, concept formation, reasoning and intelligence.

Personality

Here varying approaches to the study of personality are considered together with recent research findings related to the different approaches. Among the topics covered are psychoanalysis, factor analytic studies, personal construct theory, physique and personality and personality change (psychotherapy).

Human Growth and Development I

In this course the topics are studied as a general approach to the developmental psychology of childhood. They include infant social behaviour, cognitive growth, the acquisition of language, the development of sex differences, competence and achievement, moral development, adolescence.

Optional Courses

Two courses are to be chosen from the following list:

(i) Human Growth and Development II: A more advanced study of selected aspects of development in infancy, childhood and adolescence.

(ii) History of Psychology: The origins of, and influences on, modern psychological thinking. A study of the development of the principal schools of psychology together with an assessment of the individual contributions of some of their outstanding proponents.

(iii) Humanistic Psychology: Human experience as the focus for psychological enquiry. Western and Eastern ways of psychological growth, altered states of consciousness and humanistic theories of personality. Research methodology appropriate to these topics.

(iv) Psychopathology: The clinical and experimental study of abnormal psychology are considered in relation to classification, the neuroses and psychoses, organic disorders, personality disorders and psychopathic states.

(v) Psycholinguistics: Basic properties of language. Perception and comprehension of spoken and written language. Structure of the lexicon development of language in the child. Comparative studies of animal communication. Speech disorders. Social aspects of verbal communication.

(vi) Primate Behaviour and Human Ethology: Basic concepts in ethology, comparative social structures, reproductive behaviour, mother–infant behaviour, primate and human socialization, non-verbal communication, human ethology (particularly behavioural studies of pre-school children), ecological psychology, aggression.

The students may choose a special topic from either the social or experimental psychology major in place of one of the developmental psychology options.

Practical Classes

These last for four terms. The first two involve laboratory experiments together with a course in statistical methods. These are followed by an individual experimental research project and a naturalistic observation project in the following two terms.

TEACHING METHODS

Once the teacher has clarified his aims and syllabus he then has to determine the most appropriate teaching methods. In the case of developmental psychology the twin areas of concepts and skills will be found to require different methods but, firstly, the teacher needs to consider possible methods and their various uses. Broadly, methods can be divided into two groups, in the first both the teacher and the learners are present and in the second the learner/ learners work alone. The first group includes lectures/films, seminars, and tutorials. The second includes syndicates, programmed learning and project work. Laboratory work comes between the two in that the teacher is sometimes present and sometimes absent. Lectures have a role in conveying information in a systematic manner to large groups of students and may also have inspirational value but they have their limitations (McLeish, 1968). However in teaching developmental psychology large groups can be used when the teacher wishes to show a film or videotape. In any course a certain amount of time will be spent on infancy and students need to be familiar with the behaviour of infants. Many students, however, do not have access to an infant and films are a most convenient way of demonstrating infant behaviour and development. Animal studies are also more meaningful when viewed on film rather than described.

Videotapes are particularly valuable when introducing students to observational skills as they can be easily stopped and rerun or edited to suit the teacher's purpose. The teacher can also make his own videotapes of children interacting socially or performing cognitive tasks which can be shown to a large group and then discussed in small groups when they can be rerun. Videotapes are often essential when working with children since, understandably, a child will not wish to work with an experimenter on, say, a series of Piagetian tasks when being watched by a group of students but will accept a camera, particularly if the child has had several meetings with the experimenter with the camera running. Audiotapes are helpful for demonstrating child language or mother/child dialogue but they are not suitable for use with large groups unless the group is in a language laboratory when each student will have his own head set. A language laboratory should be used in this way if it is available.

Seminar groups of six to twelve students can be used for discussing certain set issues and are most appropriate for achieving the first aim of demonstrating the key concepts of the subject. A two hour, or two and a half hour, seminar could be devoted to attachment, conservation or adolescent self-image. In this situation each of the participants could prepare a short paper on different approaches to the subject and the aim would be to compare the approaches, their methods, findings, assumptions and evidence. A seminar is, essentially, a forum for the exchange of views and the teacher's main task is to ensure that all the students do participate and that the discussion does not become too diffuse. Direct instruction by the teacher should be kept to a minimum. Some practice in observational skills can be given in seminars by showing the groups videotapes and asking them to discuss what they saw or by letting them observe in a naturalistic setting (playground or playgroup) whilst filming the same sequence. The group can then compare their accounts of the naturalistic observation with the taped sequence firstly to judge the accuracy of their observations and secondly to see how a tape differs from a field observation. Seminars can also be used as reporting back sessions when students can share the results of their observations or discuss their research projects.

Tutorials of one, two or three students plus a tutor can combine the intensive study of a topic with individual instruction. Here the tutor is attempting to assess an individual student's grasp of a topic or concept as well as giving more instruction on particular details of the course that may not be clear to the student or that he may wish to take further than is possible in the larger seminar group. Tutorials can enable students to pursue their particular interests. This is important for morale in an areas as wide as developmental psychology when, necessarily, student interests will differ and yet, if only large groups are seen, coverage of several discrete areas in depth is impossible. In individual tutorials the tutor can help a student become aware of particular difficulties which he may be encountering in professional situations. He may play back videotapes of the student's performance. This can cause anxiety and is best done in a small group or individual setting initially. At this stage it can be helpful for the tutors to offer tapes of their own performance for student comment and criticism.

A combination of lecture, seminar and tutorial methods is highly desirable for instruction in developmental psychology which requires the student to develop both understanding of the subject matter and a range of practical skills. The second group of methods, in which the teacher is absent (i.e. syndicates, programmed learning and project work) also have an important function. In syndicates the students form smaller groups to discuss a topic, or carry out a task which can be followed by a plenary session to which the individual groups report. This method can be particularly useful for more experienced students who are ready to organize their work for themselves and yet can benefit from pooled observations. For this the tutor can suggest a general topic (e.g. 'curiosity, exploration and play in young children' or 'moral development') and leave the syndicates to organize their own approach, having previously outlined possible approaches. Programmed learning is, obviously, strictly for the individual and has most relevance for helping students to study a particular aspect of the course with which they are having difficulty (e.g. statistics or relevant aspects of physiological psychology). Its role in a developmental psychology course seems rather to give extra help with topics which developmental psychologists need to know but which are not part of the major course. Project work is essential for an empirically based subject. It is here that students will get experience in formulating hypotheses, testing them, and analysing their results using the appropriate statistical techniques. Both individual and group projects are possible, but individual projects should be able to be combined, as one-off studies with limited samples have little validity despite having instructional value for the student.

Practical classes in the laboratory are likewise essential for more controlled experiments. They are, however, often unpopular and require careful preparation by the teacher. It is frustrating for students to be continually writing up experiments with non-significant results even if they had a value in familiarizing students with the use of equipment. Children, and indeed adults, often will not agree to take part in experiments before a large group and therefore laboratory classes have to rely on one half of the class testing the other which can seem to have little relevance for the study of growth and change. One way round this is to occasionally replicate studies done on similar age groups (e.g. Kohlberg's moral dilemmas) and to compare the responses of the particular class group with the published findings.

EVALUATION

When a teacher has clarified his aims and decided on his course content and teaching methods he has to evaluate his course and, in the light of this evaluation, either modify the methods and content, if the aims are not being achieved, or change the aims. One form of evaluation is formal assessment, the aim of which is to test student learning. However this will give an inaccurate picture if the instrument is inadequate. Even with reasonably accurate instruments the teacher still has to consider why those who succeeded did so and what caused others to fail. Could the cause of success and failure be found in the students, the teacher, the topic or in their interaction? A course, however, can be evaluated by informal as well as formal methods. Developmental psychology was seen (see p. 149) to have a dual aspect in that the student is both learning about growth and change in human behaviour and growing and changing himself through his learning. Therefore one method of evaluation would be to see if the students—when working in a practical, clinical or professional setting—have, in fact, changed in their behaviour as a result of their learning on the course. This could be done by direct observation, videotaping, reports from supervisors/colleagues and self-reports. In many ways this would be an acid test since theoretical understanding which does not affect actual behaviour seems a very limited gain from a course unless it is valued as learning for the sake of learning. Likewise the student's ability to go beyond the teacher towards gaining new knowledge as well as demonstrate expertise in experimental design and statistics can be simply evaluated by a formal research element but can also be assessed by follow-up studies of what students actually do after completing a course. Follow-up evaluation would be particularly useful for short and service course students.

Theoretical understanding is conventionally assessed by written work but how best to do this is still in dispute. An alternative to the conventional unseen papers, extended essays and dissertations would be to present the student with several pieces of evidence or observations and ask him to comment fully on them. This would have the advantage of enabling the teacher to evaluate the success of his first aim but only with respect to certain topics. Once again a compromise seems to be required whereby there could be in-course evaluation by both short tests and group discussion, formal assessment exercises in a variety of modes, reports on practical behaviour change and follow-up studies. This last element is rare and would be most useful for the teacher in evaluating his course.

CONCLUSION

This paper has considered the teaching of developmental psychology in terms of the teacher's aims, course content, teaching methods and evaluation. Aims were seen to require the consideration of three relevant aspects, first, the distinguishing characteristics of the subject matter, second, skills to be developed, and third, the context of the course. Courses were divided into four types; short, service, part and full length with content and materials being suggested for each. Teaching methods were divided into those with the teacher present and those with the teacher absent. Finally evaluation was found to require three stages; in-course assessment, formal assessment, and post-course follow-up studies. Since developmental psychology, being the study of growth and change in human behaviour, is a large topic and its teaching can take place in many contexts it is almost inevitable that any course will prove inadequate for its subject matter. The teacher, and indeed the students, may well feel with T. S. Eliot in *East Coker* that

> ... every attempt
> Is a wholly new start, and a different kind of failure.

ACKNOWLEDGEMENT

I would like to thank Dr May Eppel, Dr Peter Mayo, Mr John Sants and Mr Nick Tucker for their detailed comments and additions to the content of this paper and also for their contributions to the reading lists. Also Miss Jan Collings for her advice on selecting films.

APPENDIX 8.1: PGCE PSYCHOLOGY—PRACTICAL ASSIGNMENTS

Piaget

As part of your normal work in schools please ask the children some or all of the following questions, or let them try some of the tasks. Try to be relaxed and casual and ask the questions in any way that seems natural to you. Follow up your first questions with others if this will help you to understand what the child is saying.

Classification

(a) Have prepared:
   One black square
   Three black circles
   Three white squares
Then show the child the black square, and ask him to put with it the ones that 'are the same' or 'go with it'.
   (b) Have prepared counters of *three* colours and *four* shapes. Then ask the

child to put together the ones that 'are the same' or 'go together'. If he does this, using colour or shape, ask him if he can 'put them together' in a *different* way.

(c) Have prepared four red flowers and two yellow flowers. Make sure the child names the colours or names the flowers and then say 'Are there more red flowers or more yellow flowers?'.

(You can add further questions if you like.)

Conservation of Amount

Show the child two balls of Plasticine. Ask him if he thinks they have the same amount in each and change them until he is satisfied that they do have the same amount. You can word this any way you like, e.g. 'Does one have more?' Ask him to watch carefully while you roll one ball into a sausage shape. Then repeat your original questions.

Number

Lay out a row of counters. Match them with another row of counters, or coins, in one-to-one correspondence. Ask the child if there are the same number in each row. Ask the child to watch carefully and bring together all the counters or coins in one of the rows so that they are in a pile or close together and ask again if there are still the same number in each row.

Causality

Ask the child:

(a) What is a shadow? or What makes a shadow? or Where does a shadow come from?

(b) Ask the child why clouds move.

(c) Ask the child why the Sun and Moon stay in the sky.

APPENDIX 8.2: INTRODUCTORY READING

Relevant titles from *Essential Psychology* series, edited by Peter Herriot, London: Methuen.

Relevant titles from *The Developing Child* series, edited by Jerome Bruner, Michael Cole, Barbara Lloyd, London: Fontana/Open Books.

Bower, T. G. R. (1977). *A Primer of Infant Development*. San Franciso: W. H. Freeman.

Foss, B. M. (ed.) (1974). *New Perspectives in Child Development*. Harmondsworth: Penguin.

Lee, L. C. (1976). *Personality Development in Childhood.* Monterey, California: Brooks/Cole.

Lewin, R. (1975). *Child Alive.* London: Temple Smith.

Richards, M. P. (ed.) (1974). *The Integration of a Child into a Social World.* Cambridge: Cambridge University Press.

Sants, J., and Butcher, H. J. (eds) (1975). *Developmental Psychology.* Harmondsworth: Penguin.

APPENDIX 8.3: SELECTED GENERAL READING

Bateson, P. D. G., and Hinde, R. A. (1976). *Growing Points in Ethology.* Cambridge: Cambridge University Press.

Bower, T. G. R. (1974). *Development in Infancy.* San Francisco: W. H. Freeman.

Clarke, A., and Clarke, A. D. B. (1976). *Early Experience: Myth and Evidence.* London: Open Books.

Connolly, K. J., and Bruner, J. S. (1974). *The Growth of Competence.* London: Academic Press.

Erikson, Erik H. (1950). *Childhood and Society.* Harmondsworth: Penguin.

Flavell, J. H., (1977). *Cognitive Development.* Englewood Cliffs: Prentice Hall.

Hetherington, E. M., and Parks, R. D. (eds) (1975). *Child Psychology: A Contemporary Viewpoint.* New York: McGraw-Hill.

Hinde, R. A. (1974). *Biological Bases of Human Social Behaviour.* New York: McGraw-Hill.

Lipsitt, L. P. (ed.) (1976). *Developmental Psychobiology: The Significance of Infancy.* Hillsdale, New Jersey: Erlbaum.

Munroe, R. L., and R. H. (1975). *Cross-Cultural Human Development.* Monterey, California: Brooks/Cole.

Mussen, P. H. (ed.) (1970). *Carmichael's Manual of Child Psychology, Vols 1 and 2.* New York and London: Wiley, third edition.

Stone, L., Smith, H. T., and Murphy, L. B. (eds) (1974). *The Competent Infant.* London: Tavistock.

APPENDIX 8.4: SPECIFIC REFERENCES

(a) Adolescence

Alexander, T. (1974). *Children and Adolescents, A Biocultural Approach.* London: Aldine.

Coleman, J. C. (1974). *Relationships in Adolescence.* London: Routledge & Kegan Paul.

Conger, J. J. (1977). *Adolescence and Youth.* New York: Harper & Row.

Fogelman, K. (1976). *Britain's 16 Year Olds.* London: National Children's Bureau.

Mayerson, S. (ed.) (1975). *Adolescence, Vols 1 and 2*. London: Allen & Unwin.
Rutter, M., Graham, P., Chadwick, O. F. D., and Yule, W. (1976). Adolescent Turmoil. Fact or Fiction? *Journal of Child Psychology and Psychiatry*, **17**.
Thomae, H., and Erdo, T. (1974). *The Adolescent and his Environment*. Basle, New York: Karger.

(b) Attachment

Bowlby, J. (1969). *Attachment and Loss, Vol. 1, Attachment*. Harmondsworth: Penguin.
Gewirtz, J. L. (ed.) (1972). *Attachment and Dependency*. New York and London: Wiley.

(c) Culture and Development

Bronfenbrenner, U., and Mahoney, E. (1975). *Influences on Human Development*. New York: Holt, Rinehart & Winston.
Benny, J. W., and Dasen, P. R. (1974). *Culture and Cognition: Readings in Cross Cultural Psychology*. London: Methuen.
Campbell, B. G. (1974). *Human Evolution*. London: Aldine, Chapter 10.
Cole, M., and Scribner, S. (1974). *Culture and Thought*. New York and London: Wiley.
Leiderman, P. H., Tulkin, S. R., and Rosenfeld, A. (eds) (1977). *Culture and Infancy: Variations in Human Experience*. London: Academic Press.

(d) Cognitive Development

Bruner, J. S. (1975). *Beyond the Information Given*. London: Allen & Unwin.
Bryant, P. (1974). *Perception and Understanding in Young Children*. London: Methuen.
Elkind, D. (1970). *Children and Adolescents, Interpretative Essays on Jean Piaget*. Oxford: Oxford University Press.
Elkind, D., and Flavell, J. H. (eds) (1969). *Studies in Cognitive Development*. Oxford: Oxford University Press.

(e) The Growth of Competence

Bruner, J. S. (1973). *The Relevance of Education*. New York: Norton.
Nardine, F. E. (1971). The Development of Competence. In: Lesser, G. S. (ed.). *Psychology and Educational Practice*. Foreman.
White, R. W. (1960). Competence and the Psychosexual Stages of Development. In: Jones, M. R. (ed.). *Nebraska Symposium on Motivation*.

(f) Infancy

Bower, T. G. R. (1974). *Development in Infancy*. San Francisco: W. H. Freeman.

Freeman, D. G. (1974). *Human Infancy: An Evolutionary Perspective*. New York and London: Wiley.

Lewis, M. (1976). *Origins of Intelligence: Infancy and Early Childhood*. New York: Plenum.

(g) Language Development

Brown, R. (1973). *A First Language*. London: Allen & Unwin.

Ferguson, C. A., and Slobin, D. I. (eds) (1973). *Studies of Child Language Development*. New York: Holt, Rinehart & Winston.

Halliday, M. A. K. (1977). *Learning how to Mean. Explorations in the Development of Language*. Amsterdam: Elsevier.

Moore, T. E. (ed.) (1973). *Cognitive Development and the Acquisition of Language*. London: Academic Press.

Slobin, D. I. (1972). London: Seven Questions about Language Development. In: Dodwell, P. C. (ed.). *New Horizons in Psychology, Vol. 2*. Harmondsworth: Penguin.

(h) Play

Bruner, J. S., Jolly, A., and Sylva, K. (eds) (1976). *Play: Its Role in Development and Evolution*. Harmondsworth: Penguin.

Herron, R. E., and Smith, S. (eds) (1971). *Child's Play*. New York and London: Wiley.

(i) Separation and Deprivation

Bowlby, J. (1973). *Attachment and Loss, Vol. 2, Separation*, Harmondsworth: Penguin.

Clark, A., and Clark, A. D. B. (1976). *Early Experience Myth and Evidence*. London: Open Books.

Morgan, P. (1975). *Child Care: Sense and Fable*. London: Temple Smith.

Rutter, M. (1972). *Maternal Deprivation Reassessed*. Harmondsworth: Penguin.

REFERENCES

Davidson, N. (1977). The Scientific/Applied Debate in Psychology: A Contribution. *Bulletin of the British Psychology Society*, **30**, 273–278.

Freeman, D. G. (1974). *Human Infancy: An Evolutionary Perspective*. New York and London: Wiley.

McLeish, J. (1968). *The Lecture Method*. Cambridge: Cambridge Institute of Education.

The Teaching of Psychology
Edited by J. Radford and D. Rose
© 1980 John Wiley & Sons Ltd.

9

Practical Psychology and Statistics

COLIN ROBSON

In 1877 James Ward proposed that a laboratory should be established in Cambridge to study psychophysics. This was rejected by the University Senate on the grounds that it would 'Insult religion by putting the human soul in a pair of scales'. However things have now changed so that 'It goes without saying that a training in psychology must include experimental work, both human and animal, and an increasing mathematical, statistical, computing component' (Hearnshaw, 1973).

Thus Hearnshaw, in giving a historical background to the teaching of psychology in Great Britain, indicates a conviction shared by many teachers of psychology.

Similar views have been expressed in relation to school-level courses. Radford (1975), for instance, in reporting on the deliberations of a Working Party on the revision of 'A' level psychology courses refers to their unanimous view that ' ... psychology at this level must include practical work'. Underlying this conclusion is his belief that the practical part of the syllabus ' ... is not only that most enjoyed by students, but the part that is potentially of greatest value ... students must really get to grips with the nature of scientific method and its application to human behaviour.'

The high enjoyment rating for practical work claimed by Radford appears to be in accord with the impressions gained by many experienced teachers of psychology. However, when one turns to the statistical techniques needed to support this practical work, Evans' (1976) claim that 'The teaching of statistics to psychology students is probably the biggest area of failure and frustration in most psychology departments' will also strike an answering chord.

I will take it as self-evident that the analysis of most practical work in psychology requires the use of statistical techniques. My basic proposal in this chapter is that, in order to teach psychological statistics effectively, it must be closely and clearly related to the practical work in psychology. It is perhaps not too fanciful to see this as an application of Premack's principle (Premack, 1959) where the low preference activity of work in statistics is placed in contingent relationship to the high preference activity of carrying out practical work, such that learning a technique in statistics then enables the student to carry out some appropriate experiment or other practical work.

This is an oversimplification as there are students who find statistics and the underlying ideas of considerable intrinsic interest. Conversely, there are ways of setting up practical sessions so that they possess such aridity and predictability that they become definitely aversive.

It must be stressed that consideration here is limited to the role of statistics in supporting practical work in psychology. Teaching statistics per se, as a separate academic discipline, for example as a part of a joint course or a subsidiary element within a course which is predominantly psychology, while obviously both feasible and defensible, raises different issues and will not be considered here. We will concern ourselves with that core of statistics which appears to be a necessary part of the psychology course.

SYLLABUS: TOPICS AND SEQUENCE

Collating the stated aims of the practical element in a selection of psychology courses, there appear to be three major themes:

(a) Training students in a range of techniques of inquiry in psychology.

(b) Helping students to learn to observe and understand psychological phenomena.

(c) Stimulating the development of the students' motivation for carrying out investigations in psychology.

Regula (1971) points out that aims such as those quoted above are those generally recognized in other disciplines as being served by the traditional science laboratory experience. However, taking into account the wide variety of forms of psychological enquiry, it would be an unfortunate restriction to equate practical psychology with laboratory work, and hence exclude field studies of all kinds.

The practical psychology course must provide coverage both of types of investigation and of methods of data collection. The practical studies will perforce also cover substantive content areas of psychology. Finally, those statistical techniques needed to analyse and interpret the practical work must be included.

Types of Investigation

Practical work in psychology courses has tended to concentrate on the laboratory experiment. This emphasis probably reflects both the perceived importance of the laboratory experiment itself and also the degree of control over the situation, the probability of getting replicable and analysable results afforded by laboratory experimentation.

Covering these experiments provides a setting for the considerations of issues of experimental design including:

(a) hypotheses and hypothesis testing including null hypotheses;
(b) subjects and sampling;
(c) random samples, biased and unbiased samples, sampling error;
(d) variables including independent and dependent variables;
(e) response measures and their selection;
(f) confounding;
(g) methods of control; randomization, matching and counterbalancing;
(h) particular designs (e.g. simple randomized, matched samples, repeated measures, single subject, factorial designs, mixed designs—within subject and between subject variables).

Measurement aspects might usefully be considered here and could include:

(i) levels of measurement and scaling;
(ii) reliability;
(iii) validity—content, criterion-related, and construct validity.

Texts which emphasize these considerations include Anderson (1966), Edwards (1972), Borkowski and Anderson (1977), Kerlinger (1973), Winer (1971) and Kirk (1968)—here listed in roughly ascending order of depth and extent of treatment.

While the study of experimental design might be isolated both from carrying out experiments and statistical analysis, it should be possible to devise a sequence of experiments which can serve to interrelate all three. Admittedly, carrying out any experiment requires consideration of virtually all the items in the list given above but by starting with simple studies, usually quite heavily 'pre-designed' by the tutor, it is possible to gloss over many of the points in the earlier studies and gradually introduce them in later ones.

Experimental work need not be confined to the laboratory. Practical psychology need not be experimental. The extent to which the practical psychology course can be broadened depends on 'practical' considerations as well as on the range of substantive areas of psychology to which the practical course is to relate. At a simple level it is difficult to carry out studies in the field if anything less than an afternoon is available—particularly when the 'field' is some distance away. An important aspect concerns the potentially dangerous and disruptive effects of keen but inexperienced experimenters in the field. Apart from direct effects on subjects (where the provisions of a 'Code of Practice' must be strictly adhered to—see the tips on teaching practical psychology below) there may be serious repercussions from any 'gaffes'. However, the increased naturalness and applicability of the studies and the enthusiasm of students for these activities outweigh both the disadvantages given above and the reduced experimental control possible in the field.

Both field experiments and non-experimental field work of an *ex post facto* type where there is no direct manipulation of an independent variable are possible. Useful references include Bickman and Hendy (1972), Evans and Rozelle (1970), Snordowskey (1972), Willems and Rausch (1969), Rossan and Levine (1974).

The use of 'unobtrusive measures' as advocated by Webb *et al.* (1966) is valuable in its own right and also reduces the risks arising from student inexperience. A representative range of studies is provided by Silverman (1977).

Methods of Data Collection

Practical work in psychology, whether in or out of the laboratory, requires expertise in a range of techniques of data collection. Clearly training in these techniques should be a definite part of the course. It is worth noting that one of the most important skills is in the general handling of and relationships with subjects. Role-playing can play a useful part here as well as modelling where the tutor provides examples for the students and, of course, detailed and explicit instructions. Techniques of data collection which merit inclusion are:

(a) *Behavioural Observation.*   Weick (1968) provides general reference to systematic observation schedules. For the indirect observation approach of content analysis see Holsti (1968).

(b) *Interviewing and Questionnaire Construction.*   Many references available including Cannell and Kahn (1968) and Kornhauser and Sheatsley (1959).

(c) *Objective Test and Scale Construction.*   Includes intelligence, aptitude, achievement, personality, attitude and value tests and scales. Kerlinger (1973) concentrates on research uses and lists references.

More specific techniques which might be considered include sociometry (Lindzey and Byrne, 1968), semantic differential (Snider and Osgood, 1969) and *Q*-sorts (Kerlinger, 1973).

Statistical Techniques

Edgington (1974) argues that frequency of use of statistical procedures in recently published papers should dictate course content. His argument is that frequently used statistical procedures are not only those that the student needs to understand in order to interpret psychological publications, but are also those that the student is likely to find useful for data analysis. While this type of relevance is clearly important, there are problems in this approach.

If we let current practices play the major role in deciding which topics to include in statistics courses, this is likely to have a stultifying effect on the development and dissemination of new statistical techniques (Hodge, 1974).

Such preservation of the status quo would be more defensible where there was a clear consensus about the adequacy and appropriateness of the presently popular approaches. However, there is no such consensus, for example Kerlinger and Pedhazur (1973) among others make a strong case for the replacement of analysis of variance by multiple regression analysis.

A researcher will naturally tend to set his studies in such a form that they are analysable in terms of techniques with which he is familiar, these techniques being based on what he learned as a student, with this in turn being influenced in no small measure by the content of widely used texts. Take, as an example, the relative weighting given to an analysis of qualitative and quantitative data in psychological statistics texts. The influential and very widely used text by Winer (1971) gives less than 10 per cent of its space to questions of how to treat data based on counts of the number of times a particular event has occurred rather than on some quantitative aspect of the data.

As Smith (1976) points out 'The main reason for this wildly disproportionate emphasis on measurement statistics has not been insensitivity on the part of the text-book writer but rather the lack of well-documented and convenient qualitative methods.' He goes on to review the 'very rich set of tools now available in the statistical literature for analysing qualitative data as qualitative data in terms of parameters natural to that data.'

Similar considerations apply in the analysis of single subject experimental designs. Here a combination of the Skinnerian's superstitious fear of anything other than the intuitive approach of 'eyeballing' the data and the admittedly suspect nature of some suggested analyses inhibited the use of statistics. More recent developments now provide a range of possible tests (Hersen and Barlow, 1976).

In deciding on the syllabus for 'psychological statistics', we need to consider the likely usefulness to the psychologist of available tests and techniques, whether this is indexed by present use or projected value. There are further considerations. It is clearly desirable that the course should be internally coherent, should progress from simple to complex with appropriate but not undue repetition and redundancy; that it should relate to—give support to and be supported by—the practical work in psychology, and more generally to the rest of the student's course.

It is, of course, not possible to produce a universal syllabus for psychological statistics. Content will depend on level—school or college; first, second year, etc. It also depends on the time available, and on whether or not a separate mathematical statistics course is being followed.

I will distinguish two levels of psychological statistics courses which I will term 'basic' and 'advanced'.

Basic Psychological Statistics

This is probably the most important of the statistical courses and, paradoxically, the one which is most difficult to teach, or at least to teach well. A basic objective is to enable students to design, carry out, analyse and interpret simple psychological investigations. For this, students need an introduction to statistical inference as exemplified in at least one statistical test, together with coverage of a range of descriptive statistics. Anderson (1966) provides a particularly clear example of an approach that might be taken. Here the only form of investigation covered is the experiment—the text being essentially an introduction to scientific method as applied to psychology. The logic of statistical inference is developed leading up to the sign test, which is the only test of statistical inference covered. Clearly the range of tests covered could easily be extended and in fact is in the second edition of the same text.

The traditional approach, still adopted in many texts, is to start with descriptive statistics. While this has the merit that the material is conceptually simple, it can easily become boring, especially if one feels the need to cover more detailed aspects such as calculating the median from frequency data. The utility of descriptive statistics in summarizing data does become clear to students when they are in a position to work on their own data but it is difficult to generate studies which rely solely on descriptive statistics without them appearing to be data-generating exercises. Again, a consideration of standard deviation, if it is to give any indication of why it is used, must cover the normal distribution. While this is not necessarily difficult it does take time.

An alternative approach is to start by getting the students to carry out an experiment of some form almost immediately. This can be prefaced, as in Anderson (1966) and in Robson (1973), by some consideration of scientific method and simple principles of experimental design. If at all possible this experiment should be keyed into other parts of the psychology course so that we now have the student with data of some relevance. It is not unknown, especially in the introductory course, for the tutor to now disappear with the data, carry out some unexplained mumbo-jumbo and then return with the message that the results are 'significant' (or even 'not significant'). While this does give the tutor the opportunity to select from a wide range of tests from the start and perhaps (from his point of view) to be doing more interesting experiments, it is surely to be condemned. A little ingenuity and some compromise can produce a graduated set of experiments appropriately keyed in to the rest of the course which put the student in the position of analysing data according to the test(s) currently under consideration.

Although many different sequences are possible, an easy introduction to statistical inference is afforded through counting outcomes when only chance operates. This naturally involves discussion of probability and easily leads on to a discussion of significance level, type I and type II errors and to the 'sign-test' tabulation of probabilities. The beauty of the sign test from a teaching point of view is that, poor as it is in power-efficiency terms, beginning students can handle it easily without getting involved with the computational hassles which for some obliterate all other considerations.

The data from this first experiment can also provide a clear justification for the use of descriptive statistics. Following this there are several possible alternative sequences (e.g. the normal distribution, standard deviation, standard error, t-test route). As a good understanding of this material is crucially important for more advanced statistics, there is a lot to be said for including one or more further experiments using the sign test to gain student confidence in the logic of hypothesis testing and significance.

There is also a case for including a discussion of correlation as a part of the initial consideration of descriptive statistics. This is perhaps best restricted to one or other of the rank order correlation coefficients at this stage of the course. Product-moment correlation, if it is to be taught, fits happily with a consideration of regression analysis which would probably be seen as a part of the advanced course. In choosing between Spearman's Rho and Kendall's Tau the latter has the advantage of being calculable directly from the scattergram (and hence the heuristic value of forcing the student to actually draw the scattergram, which is useful in its own right) and of being preferred by statisticians, largely because of peculiarities in the sampling distribution of Spearman's Rho. However, the computational simplicity of Rho, particularly when compared with the procedure for computing Tau when there are ties, should be taken into account. More generally, there is much to be said for seeking approaches which simplify procedures so that the chance of computational error is decreased (Darlington, 1972; Wilcoxon and Wilcox, 1964).

There would not appear to be strong arguments for the particular sequencing of the remaining parts (if any) of the introductory course. The variance ratio or F-test follows on naturally from the t-test. Chi-squared, both as test of association and of goodness of fit, is probably best dealt with later when the students are relatively sophisticated, rather than earlier, if only because of the high rate of misuse of the statistic. In this connection Lewis and Burke's (1949) classic review is still relevant and together with the rejoinders from Peters (1950), Pastore (1950) and Edwards (1950) with riposte from Lewis and Burke (1950) forms useful background for the teacher of psychological statistics. Additional non-parametric statistics such as the Mann-Whitney and Wilcoxon tests could be seen as fitting in at virtually any point of the course—alongside or in replacement of the sign test; immediately following the independent samples and correlated samples t-tests respectively; or at the end of the course as a separate section when the issue of non-parametric versus parametric tests can be brought up. A case can also be made for the inclusion of the so-called 'non-parametric analysis of variance' tests (e.g. Friedman, Kruskal-Wallis, Page's L'etc.), particularly in connection with their computational simplicity, although it is more usual to restrict the basic course to two-sample tests. A definitive judgement on the relative merits of parametric and non-parametric tests is not easy to make. These arguments have been rehearsed in other places (e.g. Meredith *et al.*, 1974, especially pp. 464–466). Insofar as textbook availability is one factor to be taken into account, it is worth pointing out that Siegel's (1956) well-known book which is disliked by some instructors as being too much of a cook-book, is now supplemented by the excellent work by Mosteller and Rourke (1973).

Advanced Psychological Statistics

The advanced course in psychological statistics is usually seen as primarily concerned with analysis of variance. For those impressed by the arguments in favour of a move to multiple regression analysis, Kerlinger and Pedhazar (1973) provide a readable account (see also Cooley and Lohnes, 1971, and Bennett and Bowers, 1976). Staying with current practices and concentrating on analysis of variance the progression appears to be a straightforward one. It is essential to establish very clearly the meaning of sums of squares and the partitioning of the total sums of squares into within groups and between groups components. This aspect is treated competently in many texts, particularly so in *Information and Error* (Diamond, 1959).

The sequence of development followed by Winer (1971) is typical:

(a) single factor designs;
(b) single factor repeated-measures designs;
(c) factorial designs;
(d) multi-factor experiments with repeated measures on one or more factors;
(e) balanced lattice and incomplete-block designs;
(f) Latin square designs.

Alternatively there is a case for covering factorial designs immediately after single factor designs and then moving on to repeated measures. This latter may be preferable if it is proposed to cover arguments about the appropriateness of repeated measures analyses (Greenwald, 1976; Poor, 1973; Poulton, 1973; Namboodiri, 1970).

The total range of designs covered is naturally dependent on the time available, it being advisable to cover each design fully, preferably in the context of analysis of an actual experiment. Once the principles for calculation of mean squares of variance ratios and of degrees of freedom is understood, this can be generalized to more complex designs. Access to a handbook (such as Kirk, 1968) with a wealth of designs and worked examples is a useful protection for the student.

Related issues such as multiple comparisons (see Edwards, 1972, for a particularly clear review of different multiple comparison tests); non-normality and heterogeneity of variance—and possible scale transformations; trend analysis; expected mean squares in random effect and mixed models, etc., are probably best introduced in conjunction with the first design for which they are appropriate.

Further topics which claim inclusion in the advanced course include:

(a) Non-parametric 'equivalents' of analysis of variance (e.g. Kruskal-Wallis, Friedman); and of trend tests (e.g. Pages' L test, Jonckheere's Trend test);

(b) Linear regression;

(c) Product-moment correlation.

Other areas, which are of importance but which it is difficult to see sufficient time being available to cover in detail, include:

(a) multiple regression and multivariate analysis (e.g. Kerlinger and Pedhazar, 1973);

(b) multiple and partial correlation (e.g. Hays, 1973);

(c) factor analysis (e.g. Child, 1976);

(d) time series analysis (e.g. Glass, Willson, and Gottman, 1975);

(e) Bayesian methods (Edwards, Lindman and Savage, 1963; Novick and Jackson, 1974).

It should be made clear that this chapter covers suggestions for content and sequencing and that other approaches are possible. Diamond (1959) in an idiosyncratic and entertaining text argues plausibly for a development where the student starts with Eta-square before standard deviation, analysis of variance and Chi-square come before correlation, with Factor Analysis following on.

In teaching statistics, the psychologist has to come to terms with a number of areas of controversy between statisticians. In this context it is of considerable help that many of these issues have been debated in relatively non-technical terms in psychological journals. Mention has already been made in the chapter of three such areas: first, the relative merits of parametric and non-parametric tests; second, the appropriate situations when Chi-square can be used; third, the analysis of repeated measure designs. Other areas include:

(a) Significance testing (Bakan, 1969; Morrison, 1970; Lykken, 1968).

(b) One-tail versus two-tail tests (Burke, 1950; Kimmel, 1957).

Useful books of readings on these and other controversial areas include Lieberman (1974), Steger (1971) and Heerman and Braskamp (1970).

PRACTICAL PSYCHOLOGY AND STATISTICS IN RELATION TO OTHER AREAS

In considering the timing of work in practical psychology relative to other areas, the main feature appears to be the sequencing of the subject matter of the practical work so that it fits in closely with work done in other courses. This can be difficult to arrange if there is a single practical course which is attempting to make simultaneous contact to several different 'theory' courses. However, the problems are not insurmountable, particularly when it is borne in mind that strict simultaneity is seldom essential and sometimes undesirable. There is often positive value in setting the scene for the consideration of an area by carrying out prior practical work; conversely a practical follow-up of material covered in theory can further understanding and enable a particular aspect to be followed up in detail.

There are, of course, no difficulties of this kind if practical training is carried out in the context of specific content courses, such as learning or cognition, with more narrowly focused experimental work. Hence this latter approach does merit consideration in comparison with the more traditional course where practical work, methodology, design and statistical analysis come together. However, practical work split according to content areas then poses problems in relation to the teaching of statistics. The tendency is to revert to a 'theoretical' statistics course, which, in my view as indicated earlier, tends to work against the learning of statistics.

A compromise approach is to retain the overall practical course, viewing the experimental work there as of help in developing points of design, methodology and analysis. The psychology-content courses on the other hand include some practical work primarily of a 'demonstration' type using the experiments to illuminate the content areas.

ORGANIZATION OF THE PRACTICAL COURSE

When running practical sessions, several different arrangements are possible, including:

(a) Class Study.   All (or some) of the students act as subjects with the tutor deciding on the study and acting as experimenter. This is useful to demonstrate a phenomenon or generate data rapidly. The main disadvantage is that all the students take on the 'passive' role and hence none get experience of actually carrying out the study.

(b) Class Study.   Students in groups of two or more, carrying out a series of replications of a study laid down by the tutor. One or more student in each group acts as experimenter, one or more as subject. This is a common model. Here some means has to be found whereby the experimenters get the information needed to run the study while keeping appropriate details away from the subjects. This can be handled either by detailed handouts giving instructions to subjects, etc., or by getting rid of the subjects for a period of time. If the results are to be handled on a class basis, it is important that all experimenters do the same thing.

(c) Group Study.   Students in groups of two or more carrying out different studies as laid down by the tutor. This is usually arranged in a circus fashion where groups rotate from one study to another. This tends to be used where there are a limited number of sets of apparatus and it is felt that all students have to be involved with all the pieces of equipment.

(d) Group Study.   Students in small groups carrying out variants of the same study which has been designed by group members from general suggestions made by the tutor. This is an intermediate stage between tutor and student designed experiments. It is valuable to insist that the detailed design, procedure and analysis is discussed and agreed with the tutor (or other members involved in running the course) prior to the actual carrying out of the study. As the intention is that all students have been involved with the design it will usually be necessary to recruit subjects from outside the group. It is sometimes possible for one group to act as subjects for another group.

(e) Group Study.   Students in small groups carrying out different studies designed by group members.

(f) Individual Study. Students individually carrying out different studies designed by themselves. This approach and the previous one probably require that students first get a general problem or topic approved as appropriate to the context. They then go away and design the study and come back for further discussion when they have done this. Again subjects will come from outside the group.

This list is not exhaustive. Hybrids are possible and one can conceive of widely different models, but the above probably cover the main approaches.

Moving from approach (a) through to (f) represents a general transfer of control and decision-making from tutor to student. Hence it is appropriate that, as a course progresses in time, one moves from the earlier approaches to the later ones as the student gains in experience and knowledge. This is only a rough progression and one would expect, for instance, to introduce a considerable degree of student decision-making within the context of a simple study at a quite early stage of the course, interspersing this between sessions with more tutor control. Conversely, at a later stage, the main priority might be to introduce students to a particular range of apparatus and in so doing revert to a more tutor-defined set of studies.

A system where the tutor is initially largely in control of design of the studies not only enables him to develop points of design but also permits the parallel development of the statistics course. With a little ingenuity it can be so arranged that the analysis of that particular study now undertaken requires the use of the statistical technique just completed. As the course progresses, some aspects of the experiment requiring analysis by techniques covered at an earlier stage can be included, so that the risk of a particular test being viewed as useful only within the context of the analysis of a particular experiment is reduced.

When the course progresses further, the tight relationships between a particular statistical technique and contiguous practical study is relaxed because the decision about design of a study will be increasingly a student matter. However, it is both possible and desirable to revert to a closer relationship and more control by the tutor when there is a need to exemplify the use of a particular new statistical technique or a new aspect of experimental design.

Another reasonable progression is in terms of the length of time spent on each investigation or study. A common pattern in three-year degree courses is to have short first-year studies taking an hour or two to complete, together with a similar amount of preparatory time. Typically, there would be interpolated sessions covering points of design, introduction to statistical tests, and analysis of previous results. In the second year the tendency is towards longer studies, each perhaps up to half a term in length. However, alternative models are possible. I have, for example, taught for some years a highly structured analysis of variance course with interspersed and relaxed experiments.

The final year practical work is commonly a lengthy project, usually on an individual basis. Support for this is likely to be on an ad hoc tutorial basis.

As far as the teaching of statistics is concerned there are some studies which advocate, on more or less theoretical grounds, the teaching of statistics in one way rather than another. Thus Lovie and Lovie (1973) inveigh against a 'cookbook' approach and Levy (1973) advocates a guided discovery approach. Evans (1976) presents an interesting attempt to relate findings from studies of complex thought processes to the teaching of statistics. His analysis supports Levy's advocacy of a guided discovery approach. While the unanimity of conclusion is encouraging it must be pointed that there is no directly supporting evidence.

The statistics tutor has to face up to the fact that while psychology courses continue to attract and accept students without an advanced mathmatical background, his task will be difficult. It is a truism that what is required is good teaching and it may be that this can take on many forms, ranging from an essentially cook-book approach so enriched by examples and analysis that a working intuitive understanding is developed, to a strictly mathematical stance which compels by its lucidity and elegance. My impression is that Diamond (1959) is right when he says that his main aim is 'to keep the student's intelligence from "freezing" in a way that is all too common in statistics courses for the social sciences.' However, whatever approach one takes it is inevitable that some students will be 'lost'. It is worthwhile considering a range of back-up facilities and approaches which might be made available to assist students, particularly those in difficulties. These include tape-slide sequences, videotaped material, programmed material (e.g. Ellzey, 1976; Young and Veldman, 1977), 'Keller Plan' approaches (e.g. Myers, 1970) and computer-aided instruction (e.g. Main, 1972).

'TIPS' IN TEACHING PRACTICAL PSYCHOLOGY

Apparatus and Equipment

Make sure for yourself that the equipment is in working order and that you, together with anybody who is assisting, know both how to use it and anything that is likely to go wrong. Your attitude to equipment is likely to colour your student's attitude. Fumbling amateurism in relation to equipment and audio-visual aids may confirm your stereotype as the academic who is above all this, but helps neither your teaching nor the students' approach to practical work.

If you are working with sets of equipment it is useful to keep at least one in reserve. It is better to start with slightly larger groups knowing that if anything goes wrong one can switch apparatus and continue.

Reporting Practical Work

It is important to stress that an experiment or other investigation is not concluded when the practical work is finished but only when the report of that work has been produced. Contingencies which encourage both rapid writing-up of the work when it is completed, and swift feedback on the adequacy of the report, are highly desirable. Several texts on practical work devote space to report writing (Borkowski and Anderson, 1977, is a particularly clear example). While students benefit from clear and well-written models of 'good' reports it is easy to be over-prescriptive and insist on a particular style or use of sub-headings which it would be difficult to justify as being the definitive approach. For instance, is the passive essential as the voice of science? It certainly puts off some students and it is interesting to note that an active presentation is now permitted by the APA publication manual. Graduate students acting as demonstrators for practical classes need to be kept firmly to heel on such matters or they are likely to savage deviant reports.

Subjects

Convenience usually dictates that the subjects for practical psychology sessions are drawn from the course members themselves. In doing this the practical course mimics published research where it appears that the majority of subjects used are psychology students (cf. Jung, 1969, who finds 80 per cent in a survey). The resulting problems of generalizability of results and generally in-bred nature of the enterprise can be reduced by gathering subjects from outside the class. If this is done, a greater care and application from students is likely both in preparation and actually running the experiment.

Recent work which studies the psychological experiment itself and some of the factors affecting subject behaviour in this special situation should be of interest to those running practical classes (Silverman, 1977; Pepusky and Patton, 1971; Wuebben, Straits and Schuman, 1974).

Ethical Principles for Practical Psychology

In carrying out experiments or other forms of practical work with human subjects it may be that what is proposed involves some form of deception, stress for the subject, or encroachment on his privacy. While it may be unnecessarily restricting to impose a blanket ban on such studies they clearly have to be undertaken with the utmost care and the tutor concerned must take direct responsibility for what is taking place. There is much to be said for an explicit set of ethical principles governing any practical work (cf. the principles proposed by the Scientific Affairs Board of the British Psychological Society printed in the *Bulletin* of the Society, February 1978, pp. 48–49).

Ideas for Experiments

It is no easy matter to find novel, interesting, and relevant studies which illustrate the required statistical and experimental design points—and which work. Sources include:

(a) Colleagues running theory courses. This is the most important source if you are to achieve maximum integration.

(b) Your own interests, and those of any demonstrators. Beware of hogging things and using the class as subject-fodder.

(c) Journal articles. Particularly recent ones which may be suitable for extension, modification, or simplification.

(d) Published experimental manuals. See the section on information sources, below.

(e) Experiments you did as a student. A not uncommon phenomenon which while demonstrating continuity in psychology has stultifying effects—Muller-Lyer illusions unto the fourth and fifth generations!

(f) Students.

Use of Random Number Tables

Left to themselves few students appear to be able to appreciate the variety of ways in which random number tables can be used. However, a short discussion on the meaning of the tables and the principles on which they are established is usually all that is called for. Discussion on their use can be found in several texts (Meddis, 1975; Robson, 1973).

Working with Animals

The most common practical work with animals is probably the operant conditioning laboratory conducted with rats, or sometimes pigeons. Although there is some confusion in interpretation it appears necessary for anyone running such a class in the UK to hold a Home Office Licence. It is also necessary for the animals to be housed in a licenced animal-house.

Work with fish and invertebrates (earthworms, snails, woodlice, mealworms, etc.) is relatively easy to implement and can be used to investigate simple learning processes, conditioning, habituation, turn alternation, etc. Again there are references in the manuals mentioned in the section on information sources, below.

'TIPS' IN TEACHING STATISTICS

Initial Fears

A minority of students, either because of fear or ignorance, or usually a mixture of the two, fail to make contact with the work in statistics presented in the early weeks of the introductory course. Clearly this can have very serious consequences because of the essentially cumulative nature of what is done.

It is helpful to require an experimental report including appropriate statistical analysis, within at the most two weeks of the start of the course. Supportive tutoring can then be fed in before the problem becomes intractable. Useful material can be found in Meddis (1975) (e.g. on index and subscript notation, probability—including permutations and combinations, logarithms, squares and square-roots).

Statistical Symbols

One of the first major obstacles for students in learning to use statistics is the symbolic language. Confusion often arises when the lecturer is inconsistent from week to week (moment to moment in some cases) in the use of symbols. Similarly inconsistencies between lecturers' usage and that in the recommended text(s) can cause unnecessary confusion. Hanson (1977) in a review of the use of statistical symbols makes useful suggestions.

Step-by-Step Procedure and Worked Examples Sheets

The use of detailed step-by-step procedure sheets supplemented by worked examples which are exactly keyed in to the procedure sheets can be very helpful to students using statistical tests. Both procedure and worked example sheets are necessary: the former because worked examples by themselves can be ambiguous; the latter because the worked examples can provide useful models for layout and reminders about interpretation of instructions and symbols. It is, of course, essential that they are both clear and free of mistakes.

Some tutors object to the use of such sheets, maintaining that they spoon-feed students to such an extent that the students do not attempt to work out for themselves what is involved. To the best of my knowledge, there is no empirical evidence on this issue although it is worth pointing out that the sheets are primarily concerned with helping the student to carry out the computation correctly.

Layout of Computations

I have noted a strong positive correlation between the neatness of layout and correctness of answer. The message to get over is that a carefully presented systematic layout saves time as it greatly reduces the chance of an error occurring—and of finding the error if one has occurred. Exhortation and example are clearly important (and the use of pre-prepared transparencies with the overhead projector helps you to set a good example). Requiring students to present full details of their analyses, as an appendix to their practical reports, means that the student has at least got to think about it being seen by another person and also gives you the opportunity of presenting feedback on presentation.

Workshop Sessions

Regular workshop sessions where students work problem examples illustrating techniques recently covered can do much to develop skills and confidence. Interest can be maintained if there is a clearly perceived need for the technique, preferably in relation to practical work.

Use of Electronic Calculators

With the increasing availability of electronic calculators and their decreasing price it becomes feasible to ask each student to purchase a personal calculator. New (1977) provides a useful review of those currently available. It is advisable to provide encouragement for the student's use of the calculator in the early stages of the course, and explicit tuition. This latter is obviously simplified if all students have been asked to get hold of the same machine, which is also useful if there is any intention of restricting the type of calculator students can use in examinations (e.g. possibly ruling out programmable calculators).

At least one recent text is designed for use with pocket calculators (Downie and Starry, 1977).

Use of Computer Packages

The comments here are restricted to the use of computer packages to carry out statistical analyses in relation to practical work. Several sets of packages are now available; one or more of which may already be available on the institution's computer. The disadvantage of using a package is that this becomes very much a 'black-box' operation. Unless special steps are taken there is no necessity for any student involvement between programme selection and data input on the one hand and reading the print-out on the other.

Coping with a Mathematical Statistics Elective

While this is an excellent feature in itself, which provides the students concerned with a greater background and understanding, it sets some teaching problems. Almost inevitably the students with greater mathematical expertise opt for the statistics, producing a markedly biomodal distribution of statistical knowledge in the psychological statistical course. The danger here is of essaying a middle ground between the two groups which ends up by being appropriate to neither. The only solution is to ensure that the material in the psychological statistics course is accessible to those students not doing further statistics, giving additional tutorial support when possible, and making the statistics directly and obviously related to specific psychological investigations. Incidentally, a 'pseudo-solution' is not uncommon where students do not perceive any relationship between the two courses; where the mathematical statistics course appears to have no relevance to psychological concerns. Here it is your responsibility to discuss this situation with the statistics lecturer. While there may be excellent reasons for his course being as it is, it could at the least take note of the fact that the students, or some of them, are studying psychology and draw examples, perhaps with your help, from the psychological literature.

INFORMATION SOURCES

Journals

Psychology Teaching, Teaching of Psychology, Bulletin of the British Psychological Society and *American Psychologist* appeai to be the main sources of comment on approaches to teaching practical psychology and statistics. *Contemporary Psychology* provides reviews, often comparing statistics texts. *Psychological Bulletin* provides a useful check on developments in experimental design and discussion on different statistics. Articles in the *Annual Review of Psychology* on 'Statistics and data processing' provide a rapid review of recent developments.

Experimental Handbooks

A fairly random selection is given. They seem to go out of print rapidly, but may be available in libraries.

Jung, J., and Bailey, J. (1976). *Contemporary Psychology Experiments*. New York and London: Wiley. Adaptations of experiments from contemporary journals. Successful breakaway from the traditional set of experiments.

Marrone, R. L., and Rasor, R. A. (1972). *Behavioural Observation and Analysis*. New York: Rinehart. Experimental manual covering human and animal work (includes invertebrates). Sections on care of animals, report writing, statistical analysis and tables.

Humphrey, G. (1963). *Psychology Through Experiment*. London: Methuen; and Humphrey, G., and Argyle, M. (1962). *Social Psychology*. London: Methuen. Somewhat dated but interesting set of studies, well presented with good introduction.

Carron, A. V. (1972). *Laboratory Experiments in Motor Learning*. Englewood Cliffs: Prentice-Hall; and Lockhart, A. S., and Johnson, J. M. (1970). *Laboratory Experiments in Motor Learning*. New York: Wm. C. Brown. Aimed at PE students; some interesting suggestions.

Brown, G., Charrington, D. J., and Cohen, L. (1975). *Experiments in the Social Sciences*. London: Harper & Row. Attractively presented set of experiments; wider than psychology, includes statistics.

Notterman, J. M. (1971). *Laboratory Manual for Experiments in Behaviour*. New York: Random House. Includes both human and animal work; lot of apparatus required.

Gardner, J. M., and Kaminska, Z. (1975). *First Experiments in Psychology*. London: Methuen. Unimaginative but 'safe' collection of well-tried experiments.

Hart, B. L. (1976). *Experimental Psychology: A Laboratory Manual*. San Francisco: W. H. Freeman. Covers the more common psychobiological techniques. A useful addition to the range of manuals.

DeBold, R. C. (1968). *Manual of Contemporary Experiments in Psychology*. Englewood Cliffs: Prentice-Hall. Very detailed instructions. Standard experiments.

Tables

Wilkenning, H. E. (1973). *The Psychology Almanac: A Handbook for Students*.

Belmont, California: Brooks/Cole. Primarily a dictionary of psychological terms but does include an extensive set of statistical tables.

Lindley, D. B., and Miller, J. C. P. (1968). *Cambridge Elementary Statistical Tables*. Cambridge: Cambridge University Press. Standard set of 10 useful tables.

Neave, H. R. (1978). *Statistics Tables*. London: George Allen & Unwin. Comprehensive range of tests, including common non-parametric tests.

Fisher, G. H. (1976). *The New Form Statistical Tables*. London: University of London Press, second edition. Graphical presentation.

STATISTICS BOOKS

The number and range of statistics books aimed at psychology students precludes any attempt at exhaustive listing. Your choice will have to depend on statistical tests covered, notation used, and how the style and general approach accords with your own preferences.

Those listed below are selected on the basis of some particular feature of note:

Edwards, A. L. (1972). *Experimental Design in Psychological Research*. New York: Holt, Rinehart & Winston, fourth edition.

Edwards, A. L. (1974). *Statistical Analysis*. New York: Holt, Rinehart & Winston, fourth edition.

Ferguson, G. A. (1976). *Statistical Analysis in Psychology and Education*. New York: McGraw-Hill, fourth edition.

Guilford, J. P. (1973). *Fundamental Statistics in Psychology and Education*. New York: McGraw-Hill, fifth edition. Texts which have stood the test of time. Little to choose between them—they are all pretty extensive, cover the usual range of tests and are well provided with examples.

Hays, W. L. (1973). *Statistics for the Social Sciences*. New York: Holt, Rinehart & Winston, second edition. A brilliant exposition of the reasoning behind the use of statistics. Not easy but ideal for the bright non-mathematical student who wants to know why.

Minium, E. W. (1970). *Statistical Reasoning in Psychology and Education*. New York and London: Wiley. Similar approach to Hays (see above).

Mosteller, F., and Rourke, R. E. K. (1973). *Sturdy Statistics*. New York: Addison-Wesley. Deserves to take over from Siegel's *Non-parametric Statistics* as the definitive text in this area—excellently written.

Ellzey, F. F. (1976). *An Introduction to Statistical Method in the Behavioural Sciences*. Belmont, California: Brooks/Cole. There is a programmed version of this text which may be useful for non-mathematical students.

Young, R. K., and Veldman, D. J. (1977). *Introductory Statistics for Behavioural Sciences*. New York: Holt, Rinehart & Winston, third edition. Included for its exercises and reviews in the form of linear programme sequences.

White, D. (1973). *Statistics for Education with Data Processing*. New York: Harper & Row. Included as being closely keyed in to the use of computer packages for statistical analysis. Also gives remedial help for students with inadequate basic mathematics.

Downie, N. M., and Starry, A. R. (1977). *Descriptive and Inferential Statistics*. New York: Harper & Row. Designed for use with pocket calculators.

Schulte, J. G. (1977). *Everything You Always Wanted to Know About Elementary Statistics (but were afraid to ask)*. Englewood Cliffs: Prentice-Hall.

Runyon, R. P. (1977). *Winning with Statistics*. New York: Addison-Wesley.

Lovejoy, E. P. (1975). *Statistics for Maths Haters*. New York: Harper & Row. Three creditable attempts to break through the 'frightened of statistics' barrier.

Diamond, S. (1959). *Information and Error*. New York: Basic Books. Idiosyncratic but inspiring introductory text. Somewhat difficult to get hold of but valuable alternative route through statistics. Advocates using the slide rule!

Sinclair, J. D., and Senter, R. J. (1970). *Analysing Data—Workbook*. Glenview, Illinois: Scott Foresman. Excellent set of exercises keyed in to the latter author's book of the same title.

Morris, P. (1974). *The Statistical Tests Handbook*. Milton Keynes: Open University. An unashamed cook-book.

Anderson, B. F. (1971). *The Psychology Experiment*. Belmont, California: Brooks/Cole, second edition. Introductory. Clearly and simply written.

Robson, C. (1973). *Experiment, Design and Statistics in Psychology*. Harmondsworth: Penguin. Introductory level. Aims to provide clear step-by-step procedures and worked examples for tests with some rationale.

Child, D. (1976). *The Essentials of Factor Analysis*. New York: Holt. Clear exposition; basically non-mathematical.

Miscellaneous

New, P. (1977). Calculators for the Psychologist. *Psychology Teaching*, **5**, 193–196. Reviews pocket calculators currently available in UK.

Prismatron Productions Ltd., 9 Gloucester Crescent, London, NW1 7DS. Useful set of tape-slide programmes on statistics.

Addresses of equipment suppliers can be found from advertisements in psychological journals.

REFERENCES

Anderson, B. F. (1966). *The Psychology Experiment*. Belmont, Calif,: Wadsworth.
Bakan, D. (1969). *On Method*. Josey-Bass.
Bennett, S., and Bowers, D. (1976). *An Introduction to Multivariate Techniques for Social and Behavioural Sciences*. Halsted.

Bickman, L., and Hendy, T. (eds) (1972). *Beyond the Laboratory: Field Research in Social Psychology*. New York: McGraw-Hill.

Borkowski, J. G., and Anderson, D. C. (1977). *Experimental Psychology: Tactics of Behavioural Research*. Glenview, Ill.: Scott Foresman.

Brown, G., Cherrington, D. H., and Cohen, L. (1975). *Experiments in the Social Sciences*. New York: Harper & Row.

Burke, C. J. (1950). Further Remarks on 1-tailed Tests. *Psychological Bulletin*, **51**, 587–590.

Cannell, C., and Kahn, R. (1968). Interviewing. In: Lindzey, G., and Aronson, E. (eds). *The Handbook of Social Psychology*. New York: Addison-Wesley, second edition.

Child, D. (1976). *The Essentials of Factor Analysis*. New York: Holt.

Cooley, W. W., and Lohnes, D. R. (1971). *Multivariate Data Analysis*. New York: Wiley.

Darlington, R. B. (1972). Comparing Two Groups by Simple Graphs. *Psychological Bulletin*, **79**, 110–116.

Diamond, S. (1959). *Information and Error*. New York: Basic Books.

Downie, N. M., and Starry, A. R. (1977). *Descriptive and Inferential Statistics*. New York: Harper & Row.

Edgington, E. S. (1974). A New Tabulation of Statistical Procedures Used in APA Journals. *American Psychologist*, **29**, 25–26.

Edwards, A. L. (1950). On 'The Use and Misuse of the Chi-squared Test'. The Case of the 2 × 2 Contingency Table. *Psychological Bulletin*, **47**, 341–346.

Edwards, A. L. (1972). *Experimental Design in Psychological Research*. New York: Holt, Rinehart & Winston.

Edwards, W., Lindman, H, and Savage, L. J. (1963). Bayesian Statistical Inference for Psychological Research. *Psychol. Rev*, **70**, 193–242.

Ellzey, F.F. (1976). *A Programmed Introduction to Statistics*. Belmont, Calif.: Brooks/Cole.

Evans, J. St. B. T. (1976). Teaching Statistics: Some Theoretical Considerations. *Bulletin of the British Psychological Society*, **29**, 172–174.

Evans, R. I., and Rozelle, R. M. (eds) (1970). *Social Psychology in Life*. NY: Allyn & Bacon.

Glass, G. V., Willson, V. K., and Gottman, J. M. (1975). *The Design and Analysis of Time-series Experiments*. Colarado Associated University Press.

Greenwald, A. G. (1976). Within-*S* Designs: To Use or Not to Use. *Psychological Bulletin*, **83**, 314–320.

Hanson, R. (1977). Review of Statistics Books. *Contemporary Psychology*, **22**, 498–501.

Hays, W. L. (1973). *Statistics for the Social Sciences*. New York: Holt, Rinehart & Winston, second edition.

Hearnshaw, L. S. (1973). The Teaching of Psychology in Great Britain. Historical Background and General Problems. *Psychology Teaching*, **1**, 2–13.

Heerman, E. F., and Braskamp, L. A. (eds) (1970). *Readings in Statistics for the Behavioural Sciences*. Englewood Cliffs: Prentice-Hall.

Hersen, M., and Barlow, D. H. (1976). *Single Case Experimental Designs: Strategies for Studying Behaviour Change*. Oxford: Pergamon Press.

Hodge, M. H. (1974). Edgington's Tabulation of Statistical Procedures. *American Psychologist*, **29**, 781–782.

von Holstein, G. A. S. S. (1974). *The Concept of Probability in Psychological Experiments*. Dordrecht, Holland: Reidel.

Holsti, O. (1968). Content Analysis. In: Lindzey, G., and Aronson, E. (eds). *The Handbook of Social Psychology*. New York: Addison-Wesley, second edition.

Humphrey, G., and Argyle, M. (1962). *Social Psychology through Experiment*. London: Methuen.

Jung, J. (1969). Current Practices and Problems in the Use of College Students for Psychological Research. *Canadian Psychologist*, **10**, 280–290.

Kerlinger, F. N. (1973). *Foundations of Behavioural Research*. New York: Holt, Rinehart & Winston, second edition.

Kerlinger, F. N., and Pedhazur, E. J. (1973). *Multiple Regression in Behavioural Research*. New York: Holt, Rinehart & Winston.

Kimmel, H. D. (1957). Three Criteria for the Use of One-tailed Tests. *Psychological Bulletin*, **54**, 351–353.

Kirk, R. E. (1968). *Experimental Design: Procedures for the Behavioural Sciences*. Belmont, Calif.: Brooks/Cole.

Kornhauser, A., and Sheatsley, P. (1959). Questionnaire Construction and Interview Procedure. In Selltiz, C., *et al.* (eds). *Research Methods in Social Relations*. New York: Holt, Rinehart & Winston.

Levy, P. (1973). Psychological Statistics: A Teaching Paradigm. *Bull. Brit. Psychol. Soc.*, **26**, 9–12.

Lewis, D., and Burke, C. J. (1949). The Use and Misuse of the Chi-squared Test. *Psychological Bulletin*, **46**, 433–489.

Lewis, D., and Burke, C. J. (1950). Further Discussion of the Use and Misuse of the Chi-squared Test. *Psychological Bulletin*, **47**, 347–355.

Lieberman, B. (ed.) (1971). *Contemporary Problems in Statistics*. Oxford: Oxford University Press.

Lindzey, G., and Byrne, D. (1968). Measurement of Social Choice and Interpersonal Attractiveness. In: Lindzey, G., and Aronson, E. (eds). *The Handbook of Social Psychology*. New York: Addison-Wesley, second edition.

Lovie, A. D., and Lovie, P. (1973). Is Your Cookbook Really Necessary? *Bull. Br. Psychol. Soc.*, **26**, 13–16.

Lykken, D. T. (1968). Statistical Significance in Psychological Research. *Psychological Bulletin*, **70**, 151–159.

Main, D. B. (1972). Toward a Future-orientated Curriculum. *American Psychologist*, **27**, 245–248.

Meddis, R. (1975). *Statistical Handbook for Non-statisticians*. New York: McGraw-Hill.

Meredith, W. M., Frederiksen, C. H., and McLaughlin, D. H. (1974). Statistics and Data Analysis. In *Annual Review of Psychology*, **25**.

Morrison, D. E. (ed.) (1970). *The Significance Test Controversy*. London: Butterworths.

Mosteller, F., and Rourke, R. E. K. (1973). *Sturdy Statistics*. New York: Addison-Wesley.

Myers, J. L. (1966). *Fundamentals of Experimental Design*. New York: Allyn & Bacon.

Myers, W. A. (1970). Operant Learning Principles Applied to Teaching Introductory Statistics. *J. Appl. Beh. Anal.*, **3**, 191–197.

Namboodiri, N. K. (1970). Experimental Designs in Which Each Subject is Used Repeatedly. *Psychological Bulletin*, **77**, 54–64.

New, P. (1977). Calculators for the Psychologist. *Psychology Teaching*, **5**, 193–196.

Novick, M. R., and Jackson, P. H. (1974). *Statistical Methods for Educational and Psychological Research*. New York: McGraw-Hill.

Pastore, N. (1950). Some Comments on the Use and Misuse of the Chi-squared Test. *Psychological Bulletin*, **47**, 338–340.

Pepusky, H. B., and Patton, M. J. (1971). *The Psychological Experiment: A Practical Accomplishment*. Oxford: Pergamon.

Peters, C. C. (1950). The Misuse of Chi-squared. *Psychological Bulletin*, **47**, 331–337.

Poor, D. D. S. (1973). ANOVA Repeated Measures. *Psychological Bulletin*, **80**, 204–210.

Poulton, E. C. (1973). Unwanted Range Effects from Using Within—*S* Experimental Designs. *Psychological Bulletin*, **80**, 113–121.

Premack, D. (1959). Toward Empirical Behaviour Laws: I. Positive Reinforcement. *Psych. Rec.*, **60**, 219–233.

Radford, J. (1975). GCE 'A' Level in Psychology. Past, Present and Future. *Psychology Teaching*, **3**, 2–4.

Regula, C. R. (1971). Some Suggestions for Improving the Psychology Laboratory Course Experience. *American Psychologist*, **26**, 1020–1021.

Robson, C. (1973). *Experiment, Design and Statistics in Psychology*. Harmondsworth: Penguin.

Rosenthal, R., and Gaito, J. (1963). The Interpretation of Levels of Significance by Psychological Researchers. *Journal of Psychology*, **55**, 33–38.

Rossan, S., and Levine, M. (1974). Field Methods: A Course for Teaching Non-laboratory Research Methods. *Bull. Brit. Psych. Soc.*, **27**, 123–128.

Siegel, S. (1956). *Non-parametric Statistics*. New York: McGraw-Hill.

Silverman, I. (1977). *The Human Subject in the Psychological Laboratory*. Oxford: Pergamon.

Smith, J. E. K. (1976). Analysis of Qualitative Data. *Annual Review of Psychology*, **27**.

Snider, J., and Osgood, C. (eds) (1969). *Semantic Differential Technique: A Source-book*. London: Aldine.

Snordowskey, A. (ed.) (1972). *Social Psychology Research: Laboratory–Field Relationships*. New York: Free Press.

Steger, J. A. (ed.) (1971). *Readings in Statistics for the Behavioural Scientist*. New York: Holt, Rinehart & Winston.

Webb, E. J., Campbell, D. T., Schwartz, R. D., and Sechrest, L. B. (1966). *Unobtrusive Measures: Non-reactive Research in the Social Sciences*. Rand McNally.

Weick, K. (1968). Systematic Observational Methods. In: Lindzey, G., and Aronson, E. (eds). *The Handbook of Social Psychology*. New York: Addison-Wesley, second edition.

Wertheimer, M. (1961). *Productive Thinking*. London: Tavistock.

Wilcoxon, F., and Wilcox, R. A. (1964). *Some Rapid Approximate Statistical Procedures*. Laderle Laboratories.

Willems, E. P., and Rausch, H. L. (eds) (1969). *Naturalistic Viewpoints in Psychological Research*. New York: Holt, Rinehart & Winston.

Winer, B. J. (1971). *Statistical Principles in Experimental Design*. New York: McGraw-Hill, second edition.

Wuebben, P. L., Straits, B. C., and Schulman, C. I. (1974). *The Experiment as a Social Occasion*. Glendessary Press.

Young, R. K., and Veldman, D. J. (1977). *Introductory Statistics for Behavioural Sciences*. New York: Holt, Rinehart & Winston.

10

Contextual, Integrative, and Ethical Issues

RICHARD J. ANDERSON

INTRODUCTION

Arising out of an amorphous area of interest and casual concern, psychology, in the 100 years of its existence, has become a vast complex of related scientific specialties, academic disciplines, and myriad professional and practical applications. Some of this rather rapid topsy-turvy development did lack rigour, both in content and in systematic organization. Popular appeal, human interest, the fascination of looking into one's own self, and the excitement of probing the psyches of others often pre-empted topics of fundamental importance without much attention to well-articulated research.

Such a situation poses enormous problems for the teacher of psychology. Even in the most elementary of introductory courses, students do tend to over-reify, and to apply naively, oversimplified, initial versions of intricate psychological concepts. Some may see such threats within themselves that they seek to alter fifteen to over thirty years of past orientation in response to a slogan, cliché, or novel motion. New and elaborate reperceptions are more often projected into relationships with friends, siblings, professors, fellow students, co-workers, spouses, parents and other significant persons with consequent strain on these very close involvements. The teacher of psychology needs to keep this sort of thing under control and in proper perspective. Pontificating, or forbidding unauthorized application by amateurs, even merely suggesting that we may but they cannot, alienates students and loses both control and credibility. Frank, open discussion in class concerning the attempts to apply course insights and understandings is always helpful. It is more constructive if conducted on a class-wide, mutual basis of interaction among all parties.

Proper perspective in general education or the liberal arts tradition regards all teaching as enhancing the total enlightenment of the student. Within all disciplines it seems that all knowledge is equally esteemed within this context. How then, can we restrain; how do we control or direct the use of what is learned? Are confusion, conflict, confounding and corruption inevitable? A chemistry student learns to make black powder, a simple mixture, which can be used to clear stumps or rocks from idle, unusable land, to bring it into productive use—or the same explosive can be used to blast open safes, derail trains, etc., or to wreck any similar sort of destruction. All fields can offer numerous examples of misuse or improper application and religion, law, philosophy, political science, economics, medicine, sociology, etc., are confounded, as is psychology, by closeness, intimacy, self-concepts, social judgements and personal values, all due to human interactions. Thus, the constraints placed upon psychology raise integrative, contextual and ethical issues of tremendous importance which need to be communicated within the field and to our students.

Our small samples and micro-statistical orientation lead us to deal with vague data and unreliable measures, often reduced to a universe of *ONE*, the unique patient, client or subject. Scientists from other fields with large sample, macro-statistical orientations, especially those whose traditions or even pretentions are of a rigorous and absolute nature, tend to depreciate psychological data and the conclusions based thereupon. Students influenced by such thinking in earlier science subjects, or ones imbued with the harsh absolutism of the value systems of the young and inexperienced may need to be made more aware of the relativistic approach of psychology. Those who demand or presume sterner models, goals and objectives, to be pursued by unequivocal procedures and direct methods need to be taught that our probabilistic, statistically sophisticated designs, in which we settle on some occasions for α probabilities of $p = 0.05$, or in more rigorous cases for $p = 0.01$, are not necessarily the 'certainties' which are fully and completely adequate for all of our purposes. Often they are the best we can command at this moment. Moreover, even the naive absolutism of the classical physicist and other early scientists has given way to a modern sophistication in the Uncertainty Principle, which comes over to the view that acceptance of results as accurate within carefully stated limits of precision may be very much more useful and trustworthy than holding a result to be unquestionable. Too frequently, some residual doubt is still held, leading to reservations or insecurities. Indeed, in our varied psychological pursuits, often it is necessary to observe the realities of 'Situational Ethics' and accept pragmatic realities as to what must be dealt with in this instance, or that application.

Taking a course in psychology leads—more often than long-term teachers may still continue to recognize—to jokes, anecdotes and jibes about the private use of 'tricks of the trade' or the public exhibition of adroit strategems. Public opinion in general is quite hostile to the idea of 'brain washing', and there are hosts of complaints and protests over the ethical aspects of conditioning or reinforcing people to do things against their wills, even when it may well be for the good of the individual so controlled. Some of the present barratry in the name of consumerism even demands that people be kept from experiencing the consequences of their own folly, especially with respect to unwise purchases or investments or the improper or abusive use of commercial products.

Professional intentions escaped critical scrutiny and the real objectives of experimenters were accepted to be as announced. Personal and professional integrity and competence were taken for granted and not questioned, even though there were disagreements and conflicts within the field of psychology. Today, however, uncritical acceptance, or merely respectful tolerance cannot be presumed. Testing of school children by proper authorities, personnel procedures for the selection and evaluation of employees, civil service or merit system examinations to determine the fitness of public employees and protect the public from spoils system payroll padding, all and any such objective and soundly based traditional psychological procedures may be challenged in the press, at open meetings, in the courts, or in the vague rumour mills and areas of innuendo. Any hostile report on the utilization of psychology today may gain as much instant support and become as popular as the smearing of a politician or the castigation of an industrial corporation. Without defensiveness and in all candour, the teacher of psychology must maintain the position that the protection of subjects in research is a serious professional responsibility so that both human and animal subjects are treated with individual care and concern not afforded an abstract symbol in a mathematical equation. The academic and governmental agencies which presume and exercise their jurisdictions over psychological research may sometimes be poorly aware and uninformed watchdogs who obtrude non-constructive delays and even prohibitions into research plans. The teaching of our discipline, maybe more than most, should be grounded in responsible awareness of the sensitivity of the public to the possibilities of exploitation, abuse, intrusion or manipulation which exist within psychology itself and in the peripheral areas of student application and involvement, or in the marginally informed general interpretations of the nature of psychology.

BACKGROUND CONSIDERATIONS

Considerations within the purview of this chapter were among the perplexing factors which delayed the clear delineation of a science of psychology until a scant 100 years ago. Ambivalence, confusion and contradiction between empiricism – nativism, association – apperception, as positions and procedures tended to isolate insights within philosophy from other philosophical positions, and scientific observations from systematic organization or reconciliation to philosophical concepts. Precursors existed before Wundt performed the masterful systematic synthesis which established an integrated psychology with clear context in relation to earlier sciences, their subject matter, theories, and experimental evidence as well as assimilating philosophical work in the field into a new scientific approach. More than 300 years ago, Descartes, in his Mind–Body Interactionism, sought to put mental and conscious interpretations into cross-connected bodily aspects taken together as the total response or reaction of a dualistic person integrating two realms of existence into one individual pattern. Over 200 years ago, David Hartley, enlightened by almost twenty years of practice as a physician, advanced a psychophysiological parallelism which integrated mind and body with an updated knowledge and understanding of the medical awareness of bodily processes, and Cabanis, by the start of the nineteenth century, sought to continue the blending of empirical associationism with physiological understandings of bodily processes. Herbart provided psychology with some systematic amalgamation of the once-competing concepts of association and apperception and he did extend the use of mathematical models, but he ruled out the use of experimental investigation and did not see the physiological basis for the processes we call psychological.

So the task remained undone until the second half of the nineteenth century when Wilhelm Wundt placed into its present contexts a vibrant and systematically well-integrated new science—Psychology! By the time of the publication of the first of the six editions of his *Grundzüge der Physiologischen Psychologie* in 1873–4 he had integrated a science which was experimental, analytical, and based upon the tremendous advances made by Sir Charles Bell, Magendie, Flourens and Johannes Müller, and in a broad context which made it compatible with the existing sciences. At the same time he incorporated both association and the philosophical continuities from empiricists such as Locke and Hume, along with the principles of apperceptive organization from Leibnitz, Kant, and other philosophers who were nativistic in persuasion. His belief in the continued use of the method of *Geschichte* as an ecological approach to the understanding of mankind, and human psychological processes by investigation of the social and political institutions within which people operate, kept open innumerable avenues for the investigation of the city, state, nation, family, totem, tribe, law, world culture, religions, economic activities and world trade as arenas within which the activities of individuals portrayed the parameters of psychological realities. Observation and the statistical analysis of demographic data were used to supplement experiment and to advance into areas where experiment would be resisted, improper, or impossible. His *Völkerpsychologie* was in fact a far broader and more meaningful approach than any contemporary social or community psychology. His religious background acquired from his father's assistant as well as from the old pastor himself, his personal knowledge of government and politics gained as a member of the legislature in the sovereign kingdom of Baden, where he was the outstanding exponent of the liberal cause, and grounded in his early years when he lived with grandparents while attending Gymnasium and attended carefully to the events in the life of an Inspector for the Royal government, and the seriousness with which he approached his duties as Professor of Philosophy, with a Medical doctorate, add his diligence as Rektor, heading the University of Leipsig, all of these qualities and the continued combining and recombining of the experiences generated in such activities were swept up into a comprehensive specialization with psychology as the common denominator. Wundt's artless tendency to apply all of this psychology to any problem, wherever encountered, had many avenues for expression. Even his critics had to recognize that he could place any new experimental finding into context and integrate it into his system. He could also tie in with expansive technical discourse the most abstract metaphysical concerns and preserve the integrity of psychology.

This benign, eclectic, almost osmotic ingathering of all facets of a once unstructured field, produced such a model of total integration and harmony of contexts, that no follower, contemporary, successor or revisionist has ventured to grasp the whole of the approach. In a book such as Edna Heidbreder's (1933) *Seven Psychologies* or the similar *Contemporary Schools of Psychology* by Woodworth, we observe that the doctrinaire builders of systems all in some degree are narrowers of the scope and context of original psychology and in some cases, extremely rigid and exclusive proponents of one limited view and rejecters of all of the rest of a tremendously extensive field. Seldom does a teacher of psychology clarify this problem of parochial loyalties and dogmatically restricted viewpoints for the student.

Not only should students be made aware of the divisions and dichotomies which exist, have existed, or will come to be, they deserve to be told the effects of narrowness of scope or partisan editorial position on the kind of research published in our journals and consequent circumscription of the field of psychology as that publication contributes to its development. The earliest journal to begin publication, *Mind*, founded by Bain in 1875, has always had an almost choatic openness. The versatile orientation of Sir Francis Galton and his lack of constraints as an independent researcher along with Bain's non-experimental, traditional associationism, and the discursive, encyclopedic approach in British universities during the days of Sully, Ward and Stout all fit with this policy. *Anné Psychologique* founded by Binet and Beaunis in 1895 has the eclectic orientation to be expected of these two well-grounded experimental psychologists, who did follow the typical French integration of academic and clinical or applied psychology, and it is not only very broad in scope, it has in their days, and under Pieron for 52 years longer, offered to the world a forum for publication, in a widely used language, of the outpourings of laboratories all over the world, with tremendous advantage for those psychologists whose own languages and home countries do not afford this visible and prestigous avenue for publication. From Ribot this view, combining academic with clinical outlooks and integrating the work done in other countries, carried on under Charcot and Janet provided this outlook. However, both in the USA and in Germany, the numerous journals tend to be polemic, exclusivist, or highly topical in orientation. The 1978 list of journals to be ordered through the American Psychological Association contains 115 titles and it is not at all complete. A quick look at the list will indicate that there is no place in any of them for most thesis and dissertation research, nor for much sponsored or grant supported research. Agencies controlling journals typically do, and must, restrict publication to that for which the journal exists and all else is extraneous.

Similarly, the programmes in many teaching departments are, or have been, notoriously narrow, elitist, exclusive, or polarized theoretically. This constitutes a part of the total presentation of psychology and it should be put into perspective.

CONTEXT AS INTERRELATION

Psychology has to be taught in cohesive individual courses or training programmes assimilated into a total and harmonious whole and reconciled to sciences generally. Instructional programmes should make this clear and if implicit awareness does not attain this clarity, it should be made explicit, intrusively if necessary. As a nascent psychology emerged in Wundt's burgeoning system there was no question about its host of interrelationships, and the acute sense of where it had ties to other fields was manifest. Of course psychology was based upon the centuries of philosophical speculations and theoretical explanations! Wundt's awareness of the importance of the rapidly growing science of chemistry and his admiration of the work of Bunsen while he was a student at Heidelberg led to the recognition of the 'Chemistry Model' as a foundation for Wundt's system, analysing the complex processes of the mind into elemental content processes; just as the chemist finds metals and non-metals, combining and interacting in oxidations and reductions. Wundt found sensations and feelings joining together in associations and being organized into apperceptive masses. Physics constituted the basis for the study of the sound and light which are the forces evoking sensation as stimuli. For the physiological core of Wundt's work there were solid and fundamental biological foundations. The Völkerpsychologie dealt with the continual interplay of psychological variables within the realms of sociology, religion, political science and economics. Within what contexts, then, does psychology fit?

Decades ago when psychology as a newer science was seeking to make firm a place within the academic scene, there was a tendency to put forth a host of requirements to insure the broad preparation for interrelation with cognate fields. Hence it became typical that majors in psychology would be required to take biology, physics, chemistry, philosophy, mathematics, sociology, all of the above, four of these six, or some N out of X year courses as cognate requirements to supplement the major. Statistics would usually be incorporated within the psychology courses, but now that is more often an outside cognate with computer studies of some sort in similar adjunct status. Recent indications in the older universities, polytechnics, state colleges, community colleges, lycees, junior colleges, liberal arts colleges, and the whole gamut of institutions would seem to show a trend away from tight specification of curriculum and considerable lessening of demands for background cognate work in the related academic disciplines. Under newer orientations we are more likely to find area courses and interdisciplinary programmes of instruction. These serve both to bolster psychology programmes with the equivalent of a broad body of information from other subject matter sources, and also to incorporate psychology within behavioral science survey type courses or other basically psychological cross-departmental conglomerate courses.

Fundamentally, psychology is and always has been a biological science, at least, obviously so in contrast to being physical science. This usually means that administrative organization may put psychological course work in a division of the life sciences, in a medical centre or in some intermediate level administrative unit of a biological sort. Sometimes it also means that psychology courses may be used to satisfy group or area requirements for biological components in general education programmes or in any specification of distributed background courses. From such situations we derive much non-major enrollment and marginal involvement in psychology courses at the general introductory level, or in sensation, motivation, learning and maturation as factors in the organization of stimulus–response behaviour, human growth and development, personality dynamics and much similar specialized first-course level areas of the field.

On the other hand, there is a strong, and probably growing, tendency to put psychology into a conglomeration of social sciences for purposes of administration. Lumping our concern with the single subject as an individual unit for study and investigation, with these other fields dealing with institutions as such and humankind in the aggregate, does create a few problems but it is our needs for laboratory space and highly technical equipment, more similar to physics for our experimental work, and akin to biology for animal research and physiological experimentation, which typically cause the misunderstandings and inability to foster common objectives within such programmes. The virtue of being in a social science connection is that the natural affinity for course work in such areas as sociology and economics provides very valuable background for professional careers in psychology or for the understanding of areas of overlapping context. Many psychologists work for local, regional, national, federal, or other levels of government and within the very wide diversity of conditions with respect to law, constitutions, and regulations. Adequate understanding of the operation of various levels of governmental activity and a recognition of the sources of power, its limitations and safeguards, as it is used within public bodies, is the necessary background to operate effectively in such employment areas. The awareness of funding by legislative appropriation or governmental agency budget, approved by political bodies, is also an area in which psychology students should not remain ignorant at the academic levels, only to encounter these problems as overwhelming in professional jobs, when viewed by inexperienced and naive newcomers to governmental employment.

Whether psychology is free-standing as a department within a college, or tied to some sub-unit in behavioral sciences, which it may well dominate, in social science where it may be less focal, in life sciences where it may be a newer and growing area, or indeed still kept in an administrative relationship with philosophy as it was in earlier days, there is obvious need to keep close contact with hosts of other disciplines. Wundt and many early psychologists had medical degrees and were products of this approach to physiology. Such ties are still needed and must be maintained. Indeed, in clinical, sensory, and basic physiological aspects of psychology there is present evidence of growing integration with such combined or co-operating programmes. The field of education or pedagogy from its beginnings had close ties to psychology and some individual pioneers such as Herbart had key roles in the emergence of both. Perhaps today there is more tendency for the schools and colleges of education to internalize their teaching of psychological subject matter rather than to require the background in psychology courses but this remains an obvious area of mutual concern.

Our basic concern with counselling, and the sources of the areas of disturbance for counsellees, leads us into co-operation and mutual interest with law, religion and the outgrowths of these early professions which do, as does psychology, continually exchange insights and understandings, and the fields of criminal justice, parole, pre-trial investigation, and the full roster of rehabilitation, delinquency, retardation, and the various areas of treatment and concern with the incapacities of people, all of which tie-in psychology along with law and the total concerns in spiritual, medical and related contexts. Just as psychology and psychologists cannot take full responsibility for all counselling applications of our core of subject matter, we are ineffectual in any attempts to cover application of the by-products of our theories and research in social, economic or business specializations. Social work and the dealing with social pathologies, or agency programmes of social intervention and amelioration need basic insights from psychology and must incorporate understandings of our principles, but except for general background from introductory psychology, courses, the details of these applications are under their own professional auspices. Some psychologists are directly concerned in marriage counselling, family relations, child-rearing problems, etc., and also in the areas for the business world, government and industry—which require testing, personnel evaluation and training—advertising, consumer orientation, attitude or aptitude surveys. Corporations, the military and government bureaux employ thousands of psychologists for such specializations. However, jurisdiction over these applications is moving into specialized programmes of instruction, and regulation of training, and certification or licensing, by bodies constituted within these areas of professional application.

The field of speech and communication has abundant and varied ties to psychology. Psycholinguistics and the concern for putting language and communication in psychological terms is basic, but relations between the forensic, dramatic and other individual characterizations and our psychological variables, and the connections between pathology in both speech and psychology, including the mutual support given by simultaneous speech therapy and psychotherapy, serve to add greater depth to this overlap of considerations and clientele. Similar collaboration and mutual concern can be found with physical education, athletic and health programmes which use vitally important psychological aspects of these modes of dealing with people as fundamental parts of their approach.

The teaching of psychology must then be organized and conducted to embrace all of these interrelationships and the incorporation of background from related fields to bolster our psychological training is necessary to achieve our objectives. Likewise, the co-operative extension of our data, expertise and knowledge to aid professional workers, academicians and scientists in other disciplines is a major focus for the teaching of psychology.

CONTEXT WITHIN PSYCHOLOGY

Goals established for any course or programme of psychological instruction should be clear and unequivocal. Faculty members teaching such courses can be assumed to be deeply dedicated to careers in psychology and involved in a core activity around which all else is structured. This may not be the case for many students. Many may be there unwillingly, apathetically or frivolously. Psychology is a popular human interest area and sometimes the study of psychology is elected more by default or on the basis of convenience rather than more serious interest. To establish an effective context for the course it is necessary to get the student involved. Consequently, the students should be well informed concerning course content and objectives at the time of the first class meeting and this should be confirmed rather than taken for granted. Written as well as verbal presentation is advisable with respect to all class meetings, research participation, tests, requirements and other student obligations which are being accepted, and the use of textbooks, references, audiovisual aids, reading lists and other materials should be detailed, so should the grading and evaluation practices to be followed. Students ask seemingly unnecessary questions, such as, 'Is the final examination to be given at the time and place already announced in the printed schedule?', and some of the questions may appear inane, but all such inquiries should be answered directly and used as an opportunity to open a discourse to see what else the student wishes to know or what opening gambit is being used to explore some further topics for discussion. Many students are slow to accept a course, the instructor, or the fellow student peers, who may all be strangers. Some courses may not fit congruently into some student's conception of what his or her programme is, or ought to be. Catalogue descriptions, rumours, feedback from other students, reputation based on past incidents or conditions that do not now pertain, and general confusion which frequently exists at the start of an academic term, all may raise explicit questions or evoke vague anxiety for the student. Participation and interaction will be the basis for making the course meaningful and putting it into context for the involved student.

In recent years it is more common that students will doubt, contest or object to established course procedures and customary requirements, or seek to define personal objectives and fulfil their own goal orientations. Frequently these idiosyncratic intrusions are not as realistic or reasonable as they appear to the student proposing such revisions. The earliest opportunity is probably the best time to allay these possible disturbances and all clarification of mutual commitments should be an open presentation before the entire group with revisions of written materials distributed as soon as possible, also in writing. Some courses do have narrow goals and fit into specific niches in programmes. Additions or modifications in the interest of any student should be entertained and assimilated openly, unless there is some matter which really requires confidentiality.

Lectures and class discussions, with much interaction and feedback possible, even in large classes, may well remain the major mode of class presentation for the long-term future as it has proven to be effective over the long-term past. It can be more involving and stimulating to the student and fit personal objectives better if there is opportunity for discussion, questioning, or clarification. In psychology we do not use work sessions, small group discussions, problem solving centres or 'talk back' reviews as much as they are used in some fields. For the students who have seen these procedures work in other fields or who desire to introduce them it could be an excellent way to quicken the interest and intensify commitment. A brief session with another person can often bring out a tremendous amount of further understanding and capitalize very well on the original exposure to material that needed further confirmation or elaboration.

Traditionally, term papers, position papers, and individual reports are often tremendously effective in producing involvement. This is more true if student interest determines the topic of the paper and if the details of the writing and style of the paper are fairly open. When exacting training for a particular task is demanded this must be compromised but freedom to be innovative often encourages more ego involvement and evokes more effort. Even more than a term paper, the presentation of a topic to the class by a student as an essential part of the course can be very conducive to involvement. This internalizes the student's approach to the course and brings forth new personal ideas and viewpoints. Role playing, encounter groups and such similar therapy techniques capitalize on this same stance of producing activity, personal expression and exposition to the group.

In many institutions today there is concern over erosion of grading standards and student performance. This may be due to the broadening of the base of college attendance, the rapid expansion of new programmes, a greater dependence on television instead of reading, etc., for entertainment, information, such as news, and the whole process of packaging or merchandising end results, or so-called bottom line conclusions. Members of a class may want quick, easy and superficial operations leading to guaranteed and successful outcomes. Preparation for tests is more of a students' problem than the teacher's problem. Presentation of the material and preparation of valid and reliable tests is the teacher's job. Teaching the answers to test questions depreciates the present and future intrinsic values of psychological material being presented and over-emphasizes a few chosen items. Teachers should make students aware that any test contains but a small sample of the thousands of questions which could be asked to cover the material. Hopefully, the small sample is representative and reliable but specific test items are trivial means to an end and never the end result or the ultimate objective of teaching. However, students ought to know the nature of the examination they will have to take, its length, the coverage, the types of item, what is or is not to be told in advance about scoring procedures and the policy established for appraisal of the students' performance. Sample questions may be helpful, especially if there are types of question or different sorts of test materials than the students are accustomed to taking. From the standpoint of student orientation and personal responsibility, it might be helpful to encourage the student to seek to decide which materials and topics are most important, more likely to be tested, and what types of items or specific wordings of questions could best be used with the specific material. Viewing the testing situation from both sides in this fashion promotes sounder organization of the course content by the student and puts the information in the proper context to prepare for examination.

Using dons, dozents, peer advisers, even ombudsmen may be of great value to the individual who needs added perspective and a more rounded view than the limited personal perspective. This should never be a counsellor who takes responsibility or initiative from the student but someone who will bring more coherent organization to the material and better understanding of the content of the course and appreciation of the people involved and their roles. Such aid can augment the student's resources.

With regard to concerns in these areas of context, integration and ethics the teacher of psychology not only has the duty and obligation of imparting a body of academic subject matter, but also of placing the view of psychology which is presented into perspective in its relationships with other academic fields—so that the course work will fit harmoniously—and at the same time put it more in comfortable juxtaposition with the other aspects of the total programme of psychology. Placing these with other classroom and administrative matters of logistics and organization is frequently a matter of integration as well as context. The discussion of integrative issues will include some aspects of context with regard to the polemics and cross-currents within psychology.

INTEGRATION AS BASIC SYNTHESIS

Wilhelm Wundt fulfilled a tremendous role for the new science of psychology with the publication of the *Grundzüge der Physiologischen Psychologie* in 1873–4 by uniting the empiricism and associationism of Locke, Hartley, Hume, James Mill and John Stuart Mill with the philosophical psychologies of a different order advanced by Leibnitz, Kant and Herbart stressing apperception and taking psychology out of the rational and speculative domain of philosophy, into science. This science of psychology of Wundt's was analytical, experimental, and based upon the nineteenth century advances in physiology made by Flourens, Johannes Müller and Helmholtz. His total system of psychology went far beyond the mere combining of all these tracks of the past and took off into a wide advance across a front adding the method of geschichte and experiment as two proven and productive techniques for the unfolding of psychological knowledge. As a natural history, or ecological method the geschichte approach used observation of human institutions and the clear inferences which could be drawn to provide information different from and additional to that which could be obtained in the laboratory by means of experiment. His earlier works portrayed the full scope of the system intact but in later years the *Völkerpsychologie* dealt mainly with the geschichte study of social institutions, forces and interactions, with experiments rarely cited as such, and the contributions from experimental psychology integrated in by presumption, at the same time his *Grundriss der Psychologie*, which began a few years earlier and went through an equal number of editions between 1896 and 1911 as the *Völkerpsychologie* with its ten from 1900 to 1920, held to the opposite tack more succinctly. Little but direct citation of experimental research and revision of theory or hypothesis based upon laboratory evidence filled the *Grundriss*. During these years the total system as revealed in the *Grundzüge* was not again revised. Since there was such scattering of Wundt's students into so many areas of specialization and no one psychologist, not a traditional group at Leipzig, ever sought to preserve and maintain the total scope and keep the initiative of building along all fronts, the totality of his synthesis is usually lost, even in the understandings of historical reviewers. His early dozent Emil Kraeplin went on the become 'the Father of Psychiatry' and contribute the foundations of the system of classification which continues in use today. Külpe, who was a student with Wundt only one year before completing his degree, was perhaps the best known during his dozent days, pursued experimental psychology quite narrowly and then at Wurzburg developed the School of Imageless Thought, only to turn in later years back toward the philosophical roots which underlay Wundt's original system but had not intrigued the early Külpe. In England Ward and Stout, following upon Bain's work as well as Wundt's, assimilated psychology broadly without being embroiled in experimental controversy and Stout's books cover the field in an eclectic and comprehensive but not systematically doctrinaire way. Hall and James McKeen Cattell returned from Leipzig as the same sort of broad eclectic and comprehensive contributers to psychology after their years with Wundt. However, Titchener after early study at Manchester and Oxford, when he completed his studies with Wundt, and Külpe, at Leipzig, went on to Cornell in upstate New York and advanced the view that his structuralism was the essence of Wundt's system, while Judd who studied closely with Wundt returned to America, and at Yale and Chicago proclaimed his interpretation that Wundt was plainly and clearly a functionalist.

COUNTER INTEGRATIVE INFLUENCES

Although major forces have been at work to preserve the intact field and system of psychology, the prominent and publicized movements or schools which capture the public's attention and usually make disciples out of students have been divisive. The gestalt movement in Germany was a reversal from Wundt, nurtured by Stumpf at Berlin, which went away from associationism and empiricism and back to the more traditional germanic thinking embracing apperceptive organization, nativism and phenomonology. Adding experiment to the tools of the gestalt group put Wertheimer, Koffka and Köhler within an experimental tradition of science but counter to Wundt on many fundamental positions.

Within the USA there have been very strong and dogmatic schools or movements with fixed mutual opposition and even rejection of basic premises. American psychology must accommodate to a scrambled heritage of a nation founded upon thirteen states which united in spite of the fact that they had been a cluster of hostile, warring, mutually distrustful colonies, some Dutch or Swedish before becoming English, and the English colonies founded by religious or social groups who left their motherland due to fanatical beliefs or social rejection. Often adjacent colonies were populated by those who left England to escape from one another. Add to this a terrible Civil War and an expansion which now embraces several areas which were early French colonies, thousands of miles apart from one another, and equally dispersed Spanish domains, during the colonial wars of past centuries, and it is understandable that this is a land of diversity. Much that is culturally pluralistic typifies American thinking and this pervades American approaches to psychology. So which forces promote integration and which do not is a matter of great concern. An omnivorous appetite for anything called psychology characterized G.

Stanley Hall, and the American Psychological Association, which he founded and dominated, is broad, open and eclectic. However, on closer examination it has taken on the character of the federal government, as prototype, and presently consists of thirty-five divisions based upon interests, professional specialization, polemic position, or activist concern. These vary greatly in size, power, age and relationship to their members. They and the numerous state groups, which grew up as separate psychological bodies concerned more directly with the legal regulation of the practice of psychology, since this is constitutionally a state function and not a federal one, vie for seats on the governing council.

With that as the most potent integrative force in American psychology, some attention to what were referred to as movements or schools on page 197 will clarify these divisive forces. Structuralism under E. B. Titchener repudiated everything but the analysis of the conscious content of the mind as studied by introspection, done in the laboratory by a trained observer, and restricted to a standard terminology of terms which described the elemental attributes of the content processes. Americans who did not concern themselves with the analysis of conscious content and talked about stimuli, responses and the teleological ends served by psychological activities, were labelled functionalists by Titchener. Some of them welcomed his opposition. A group centred at the University of Chicago, including James R. Angell, John Dewey, G. H. Mead and A. W. Moore took the position of functionalism and proclaimed it as the solid, middle-of-the-road mainstream of the field of psychology. They included animal research, social and educational applications of many sorts, and they talked of holistic units of S-R patterns as arcs with no dichotomies tolerated. This unified the older mind–body distinction and advanced a system not at all in keeping with Titchener's. However, John B. Watson, who received the first Ph.D. degree from Chicago in this tradition, went even further in opposition to structuralism. Taking the term behaviourism from the context in which it had been used by William McDougall in a tradition which emphasized adaptive use of instinctive responses and tied behaviour to social and physiological interpretations, Watson redefined behaviourism to contradict the structuralist definitions of psychology according to Titchener, and at the same time reverse McDougall's use of the terminology and all related concepts. Watson threw out consciousness, introspection as a method of investigation, all references to anything mental, and the use of physiological interpretations for psychological acts. He said that all behaviour is learned, by a simple process of stimulus substitution, and that conditioning and reconditioning account for all higher psychological processes as well. This emphasis on animal research and objective methods is seen in the work of neobehaviourists, including Lashley, who did reintroduce physiology, Hull, Tolman and Skinner.

Various psychoanalytic movements have had some difficulty in becoming part of psychology. Freud's three levels of conscious, foreconscious (or preconscious) and unconscious and the later description of Ego, Superego and Id were long resisted as mystical and unverifiable by scientific psychologists and their organizations. Individual Psychology of Adler, stressing the personal life style and the overcoming of initial inferiority by developing within a social mileau and the Analytic Psychology of Jung with its emphasis on present dynamics instead of fixations and regressions, and the use of systems of classification of modes of functioning, both seemed to be more in keeping with psychological approaches and gained favour for psychoanalytic viewpoints. Integration into the clinical practice of the 1940s and 1950s has helped to incorporate these notions.

When we turn to the synthesis of a programme of instruction in general psychology we must think in terms of the strenuous *tour de force* required to place these divergent vectors into an integrated context. How different to have been studying under Titchener at Cornell, where the firm indoctrination of the trained observer to report in the technical terms of a specific vocabulary, the content revealed by introspective analysis of the structure of consciousness in the form of elemental content processes, and that alone ... or—with the Chicago Functionalists to learn new adaptive responses as an intact, whole organism, adjusting to the environment, aware of teleological objectives and conscious of unfilled needs ... or—at Johns Hopkins under Watson merely observing an animal in a piece of apparatus under experimental controls, reporting behaviour objectively, but nothing concerning anything of physiology, consciousness, experience, purposes, goals, etc., and interpreting nothing except that behaviour itself, stated impersonally and reported objectively without anthropomorphizing ... or—at Frankfurt-am-Main with the gestaltists, experimenting with principles of figure-ground perceptual integration, and the rules of perceptual organization using nativistic and phenomenological constructs...or—at Vienna seeking hidden dynamics of personality within the theoretical frameworks of either Freud or Adler.

These were, still are, vastly different integrative contexts for psychology. Values held by adherents of these positions are powerful cross-currents within our field. Judgements of a dogmatic sort, based upon strong convictions, can be seen as restricting the form of psychological research, narrowing its focus, thus forcing hypotheses and theories into axiomatic bounds set by the position. As with the learning of a language, the law, medicine, religion, or a non-Euclidian geometry, there are definitions, rules, orders and delimitations to be learned along with factual subject matter. The teacher of psychology must be clear in imparting awareness of the variety of views within the field, to that degree appropriate to the backgrounds and orientations of the students. Inappropriate use of controversial concepts would readily become chaotic and overwhelming were it not properly integrated.

This book itself is a synthesizing and integrating force within psychology and all such similar ventures serve to keep the cohesion of the discipline intact.

National and international associations are tremendous integrating forces. Since application of psychological subject matter, especially by people marginal or peripheral to the field, has a tendency to fragment topics and remove specific usages of ideas and understandings from the jurisdiction of psychologists, a a force such as the International Association for Applied Psychology is a good example of this type of influence, in the best interest of an intact field.

True integration of the entire field of psychology has rarely ever been the goal, much less the accomplished result, of any school or movement, and seldom has any individual theorist attempted this. However, Egon Brunswik (1952), in a brief monograph amounting to less than 100 pages, in contrast to the over 1500 in the later editions of the Wundt *Grundzüge*, has attempted a masterful synthesis in his terse but exhaustive work, and has had amazing success in reconciling and assimilating theoretical viewpoints. The scope and concentration of such a work demands too much background and tremendous effort to grasp its packed content. Obviously it is an ultimate ideal that the student be kept informed and enlightened at all levels as progress is being made in mastering the field. Having a system which is quite complete and fully integrated is not assurance that all things can always be taught in the unique context and ultimate position. Balancing the polemic, scientific, humanistic, academic and applied factors which intrude into the areas of concern of a psychology course is a principal task for the teacher and must be approached as a stated objective within reasonable limits, as each student develops an appropriate personal integration of psychology.

SOURCES OF ETHICAL CONCERNS

Back as far in time as Hippocrates, 460–377 BC, mankind has had the problem of determining the relationship which should exist between any practitioner and the recipient of professional services. Consideration for the patient, client, subject, or student as the primary, or sole objective of such service was stated as an ideal in a oath which has inspired medical practitioners down through the ages and now serves to orient our attempts to convey the essentials of our ethical values. The public today is inclined to challenge and even to distrust scientists, doctors, teachers, professors and others whose titles and positions might have been presumed to convey high regard, trust and public confidence. Debunking, barratry and consumerism have taken a heavy toll. Psychologists are ready to protect the public from possible abuse through misapplication of procedures, incompetent or fraudulent quacks, or manipulation and exploitation. We even seek laws, regulations, certification, licenses, etc., to protect the public from THEM, but we are often unaware of the public's desire to be protected from US.

Within the cultural tradition which we acknowledge as Western civilization there are two ethical roots. One from the Ancient Greeks is humanistic and negotiates compacts or agreements among parties on the basis of mutual interests or compromise. Aristotle did not place moral connotations upon the term ethics. He regarded as ethical that which was excellent, brought happiness, or was done with elegant style. On the other hand the Biblical Hebrews did hold moralistic convictions and their laws, rules, rituals and commandments were accepted as revelations from an omnipotent God; thus, they were obeyed. We still hold both kinds of ethical philosophies but today there is more reliance upon laws and rules and regulations to enforce those positions deemed to be ethical.

Where psychology itself does not impose ethical safeguards on application and practice the professional areas of applied jurisdiction are taking over and legislating or regulating. At his presidential address to the APA in New York in 1961, Neal Miller talked of 'giving psychology away', that is making our knowledge and the results of research within our purview, available to all the world for open usage to meet whatever needs exist. He pointed out that we cannot determine or control such use any more than mathematicians are able to patent or copyright arithmetic. Teachers of psychology should seek to establish with all students the opinion that sharing of our information entails keeping some concern for the use to which it is put and imposes a responsibility upon the learner to internalize our ethical standards, individually and corporately.

Within a climate of academic freedom we are prone to grant the right of all persons to information and knowledge with no constraints and no restriction of access. Yet the public is all too aware of the potential for abuse in the use of attitude manipulation, thought control, hypnosis, behavioural modification, or the feared 'brain washing' by any and all who acquire a bit of psychological expertise.

Physicians often assume that a patient, or those responsible for the patient, should not know some aspects of diagnosis, prognosis, or things thought not to be in the interest of the health of the patient. In the confidentiality of the confessional and in other religious contexts, clergymen frequently do not convey information to interested parties or to the public, on the conviction that here are things not to be divulged. Lawyer–client relationships not only grant much latitude to legal counsel in concealing matters, facts or information on behalf of defendants vulnerable to prosecution, they also permit the professional determination of what should be the client's information and knowledge and what the client ought not know. Where do we as psychologists and teachers of psychology stand in such matters?

IMPLEMENTATION OF ETHICAL STANDARDS

Teachers have great latitude in class. Many permit even wider freedom for students to express ideas or seek to influence others. Presentations in class which evoke hostilities, encourage attacks on targeted 'enemies', call for uprisings against entrenched and well-defended governments, or openly defy the laws of the locality are not unknown. Students engage in violent demonstrations against industrial plants, foreign legations, the symbolic centres of the domestic government, and even in reckless attack upon armed troops, which may be occupation troops, but which are frequently local police or the military of the home country. Teachers who provoke these acts for political, economic, social or personal goals of their own, are exploiting the vulnerable and gullible students who accept these skilful exhortations and place themselves in jeopardy. Self-imposed restraints and proper concern for professional conduct should prevent this abuse and the teacher should seek to avoid any such effect produced by students or colleagues. The extreme case of exploitation and control over enslaved followers seen in the incident in Guyana in 1978, which took over 800 lives, is but one excessive example which strains credulity. On a lesser scale this is going on in some degree in places where teachers of psychology can stop such manipulation.

The US Government, an employer of millions of people, put forth guidelines on 30 December 1977 expressing values and making demands with massive effect on testing and other psychological procedures to be used by federal agencies, but proclaiming that these policies would be enforced against states, unions or trade associations, and all companies doing any business with the government. Any selection or advancement of an employee can be questioned on the grounds of possible discrimination. The APA has produced a code of ethics concerning the use of subjects in research which seeks to protect human and animal participants from being victimized. As President of the American Society for Value Inquiry, William T. Blackstone (1975) has made an appraisal of this code concluding that it may and does protect the rights, dignity and safety of human subjects, but experimenters may be in a position of seeking alternatives to procedures which are possibly threatening, and, from the costs–benefits position large amounts of compensation might have to be paid for harm which might be done. These value determinations may be made in retrospect and could be retroactive. The *APA Monitor* (1976) has above its masthead, in the most prominent position possible, an attack on Sir Cyril Burt, quoting *The Sunday Times* and not merely questioning the procedure of determining IQ correlations for degrees of kinship on one set of data and assuming it later, but calling his work fake and expressing strong negative ethical value judgements. No chemist would be exposed to failing to take into account the difference between atomic weights of samples of the same element, based upon varying ratios of the isotopes, as an ethical concern, if his work preceded the awareness of isotopes.

Ethical concerns are so vital to the proper teaching, practice or study of psychology that they must be observed at all costs and in all instances. However, exaggerated concern with trivia must not be permitted to stultify our science or to blockade progress.

SUMMARY

To place the teaching of psychology into proper context as a totally integrated field with ethical as well as systematic integrity is a complex objective. It entails using more of the modern video and electronic techniques, student involvement in roles and projects and richer presentation of our materials. The basic scientific foundations of psychology within physiology and the biological sciences generally, and our tie-in with physics for the study of stimuli, or with mathematics and statistics for data treatment and analysis, need stressing and our students must be made more aware of needed background in all of these areas as well as the present focus of mutual concern with social and behavioural common interests with law, religion, sociology, anthropology, economics, political science and a wide array of collaborating areas. Students must be taught about the sources of controversy within the field and assisted in bringing about reconciliation of contending views and contesting interpretations. Personal attitudes and specialized interests ought to be acknowledged and put into perspective for the student's own evaluative decision. The coercion of ethical viewpoints, practices, and classroom procedures, as well as professional applications of psychology, needs to become so internalized that the guidelines and regulations will exist to reify the attitudes professed and the principles followed.

REFERENCES

APA Monitor (1976). December Lead Article. Washington DC: American Psychological Association.

Blackstone, W. T. (1975). The American Psychological Association Code of Ethics for Research Involving Human Participation: An Appraisal. *The Southern Journal of Philosophy*, **XIII**, No. 4.

Brunswik, E. (1952). The Conceptual Framework of Psychology. In: *The International Encyclopedia of Unified Science, Vol. 1, N. 10.* Chicago: University of Chicago Press.

Heidbreder, E. (1933). *Seven Psychologies.* New York: D. Appleton-Century.

Woodworth, R. S. (1931). *Contemporary Schools of Psychology.* New York: Ronald Press.

SECTION III

Teaching Psychology in Different Contexts

Psychology finds itself in such various contexts that it is impossible to be comprehensive. Most academic psychologists have probably been called on to give one lecture on tests or attitudes to policemen or personnel managers. Nevertheless we think our authors cover the most frequent and numerically largest areas, and ones moreover which have distinct needs and problems.

One particular problem here is that context varies considerably between countries. Most of the book, we hope, is generally applicable at least within the confines of 'Western' psychology. Much of this selection is so too; but one cannot ignore the differences that exist, for example, in patterns of academic work even between the UK and the USA. Indeed Robert Daniel has specifically disavowed crossing national boundaries in his chapter. He is too modest, for at least much of what he says has wider application. Partly for these reasons we felt that the Third World must be at least represented. Here too the authors do not claim to generalize; but for many psychologists trained essentially in British/American methods such Third World countries constitute a very new context in which to offer what they have learned.

The Teaching of Psychology
Edited by J. Radford and D. Rose
© 1980 John Wiley & Sons Ltd.

11

The Academic Context in the USA

ROBERT S. DANIEL

The full range of formal academic contexts extends from kindergarten through the doctoral or even post-doctoral years. Thus, in a longitudinal view of the teaching of psychology, theoretically we could touch a student's life through two decades. Psychology has been taught in the early school years, at least in the sense of assisting youngsters in problems of human relations, and to some degree in a broader range of topics (e.g. Long, 1972–3).

At the secondary school level, the teaching of psychology has been growing rapidly since the middle 1960s. In that context, the emphasis is mainly on personal adjustment, but in some high schools a course is offered with a more general, science-oriented approach. Either Fisher (1974) or Kasschau and Wertheimer (1974) may be consulted for a survey of the teaching of psychology in the secondary schools.

Our present concern is primarily with the teaching of psychology at the post-secondary level. The most striking feature of this endeavour is its tremendous diversity—in the nature of students taught, methods of teaching, theoretical approach, topics covered, and the setting in which the teaching takes place. The heterogeneity is evidenced elsewhere in this book for most of these variables. Academic setting or context will be the focus of the present chapter.

THE CONTEXTS

The 3000 institutions of higher education in the USA also include considerable diversity—in size of student body, primary purpose, academic standards, entrance requirements, faculty quality, and of course geographical locale. These factors contribute in no small way to the manner in which any subject is taught, but more so to a discipline like psychology than to mathematics or languages, for example. An analysis of the impact of each demographic input is beyond the scope of this chapter. Nevertheless, some attention must be given to the major types of academic institutions as a source of influence.

The Two-year College

Growth of the two-year college in the USA during the late 1960s was phenomenal. In one year, fifty-two new campuses opened their doors ('one new school each week') and it was estimated conservatively that one in every three students taking introduction to psychology did so at a two-year college.

These institutions comprise two types in terms of goals, although both may be represented on a single campus. The older ones, usually known as junior colleges, prepared students for the more rigorous last two years of a regular baccalaureate programme. Rapid expansion of late has been more pronounced in the type known as the community college. In the latter setting, emphasis is upon service to (usually) an urban area in terms of assisting the upward mobility of its citizens and providing an employable pool of people for intermediate level occupations. In many of these colleges, awareness and action programmes concerning community social problems are being fostered through training curricula.

Whereas the psychology offerings at a more traditional junior college differ little in kind from those available to a student at a four-year college or university in the underclass years, the community college concept calls for courses with a strong applied emphasis. Programmes leading to the Associate of Arts degree include training as mental health aides, social action managers, and child development specialists, among others. Field work, practicum, or supervised experience in some form is a mainstay of these programmes (Moses, Delaney and Rubin 1971; Sheanin, 1972).

Psychology teachers in two-year colleges typically report an isolation from the mainstream of their profession, frustration with the problem of the heterogeneity of the student body, and lack of opportunity to continue their own training (Daniel, 1970; Losak and Beal, 1970). Yet their task is challenging, their work is satisfying, and their role is firmly established (Norton, 1972). Preparation of these teachers, by and large, is less thorough than it ought to be (Fricke, 1975). Many of them were trained in a different discipline; a few were overtrained, and the majority hold the traditional masters degree with little or no prior teaching experience or training. A few universities are beginning to offer specialized masters programmes to provide for the two-year college job market. Perhaps because the community college is not encumbered in tradition, it has been the source of much innovation in the teaching of psychology. Hershey and Lugo (1969) have compiled source information on both innovations and problems.

The Four-year College

This is the traditional institution often idealized in American song and story. Many began, and some continue, under the aegis of one or another religious denomination (see Ellison, 1973), and more than a few 'grew up' to become large universities.

Psychology teaching in the four-year college is probably found in its most traditional form. Classes are small to moderate in size; teaching is by lecture, discussion, or seminar format; faculty members are devoted to teaching and are rarely distracted by extensive research efforts; students are capable and accepting of a rigorous programme. Among several surveys (Miller, 1953; Bartlett, Finger and Williams, 1957; Very, 1966; Viney and Titley, 1972), the most recent, by Cole and Van Krevelen (1977), shows that in the four-year college there is a low student–faculty ratio (about 13 : 1), a median of forty-five upperclass majors, and a median of 4.2 psychology faculty members. Programmes are primarily designed for those students who plan to continue in graduate school; and it is tacitly assumed that those who do not will also profit from the same curriculum. Many teachers question the validity of that assumption (see Blum, 1968). Quite a few of these college psychology departments have excellent records of placing graduates into post-baccalaureate programmes.

An interesting sketch of the activities of a faculty member in a typical small liberal arts college (Ray, 1972) gives insights into the nature of that context. Ray's account of the joys and satisfactions in his work make his article especially helpful to a graduate student looking to that setting for possible employment. He makes the teachers role seem idyllic, yet busy and rewarding.

The State University

Another recent trend in US higher education is the transformation of former teacher's colleges into state universities. Typically, psychology departments in these institutions offer a limited graduate programme, and an undergraduate programme not greatly different from that found in the four-year college. The influence of traditions from the education field still may be found in psychology offerings, or in terms of what is not offered. But here, as elsewhere, much variability is the rule, so that generalizations can be misleading.

Little has been reported on teaching problems unique to the state university context. Thornton (1974) described a survey study of graduates from six state colleges in Pennsylvania and drew some implications for curriculum emphasis: 'preparation for a well informed life as parent and citizen ... and experiences that employers demand of our graduates'.

The Professional School

Psychology is taught in various professional schools within a context requiring a very different management and structure than one finds in any of the other higher education settings. A comprehensive programme leading to a degree in psychology is not usually offered, although colleges of education may do so in educational psychology, school psychology, or counselling, and some seminaries offer degrees in pastoral counselling. Psychologists also teach extensively in medical schools (Matarazzo, Lubin and Nathan, 1978), colleges of business administration (Nixon, 1970), child and family development departments of home economics schools, and to a lesser extent in schools of journalism, library science, dentistry and occasionally in others.

As one would expect, the work of the psychologist is tailored to the needs of the professional training goal in these specialized settings. Here psychology teachers must bridge the gap between that part of their own field most pertinent to the goal of the host school and the mainstream of that subject. They confront strong competition for student's time and attention and often are not fully accepted as a part of the faculty team, although these identity problems are fading as psychology gradually proves itself useful (Witkin, Mensh and Cates, 1972).

Collins and Spiers (1973) have made a case for psychology being taught in the seminary, based upon data showing that a large proportion of people who need help in personal problems consult a clergyman.

Four teaching problems of the psychologist in a medical school are discussed by Stone, Gentry, Matarazzo, Carlton, Pattishall and Wakeley (1977), and it is probable that one could change a few words here and there to make their paper applicable to other professional school contexts. Those questions (and condensed answers) are:

(a) Why do our students not learn more about psychology? (We expect more than we should.)

(b) What parts of psychology are relevant? (Emphasize data and facts; only that part of theory which permits generalization.)

(c) What teaching strategies are most effective? (Move from case reports to general principles.)

(d) What are the best organizational settings? (No clear advantage to several types in use, but they should permit close interaction with the mainstream of psychology and give the teacher full status within the professional school faculty.)

The Large University

In contrast to all of the above described settings, the psychology department of a large university is dominated by research endeavours of faculty members and graduate students. Teaching at the underclass level, more often than not, is delegated to the younger faculty members or graduate assistants. A few departments have held to a custom of some kind of quota of lower division teaching for every member of the faculty, but these cases are the exception.

A university psychology department will have a larger faculty and more variety in course offerings than do other institution types, but it usually has a much less favourable teacher–student ratio. Its service courses for other departments and divisions on campus will be extensive, and it usually shows considerable interdisciplinary activity in other respects. In addition, the university psychology department is frequently involved in considerable outreach activity within the community, state or region.

The university teaching of psychology has been disturbed by the ongoing controversy and conflict between the basic research-teaching mission and the various applied-service missions of the field. When Harvard was facing the splintering of its department President Conant appointed a blue-ribbon commission to advise him on the future of psychology in the university context. The report of that group was widely circulated under the title *The Place of Psychology in the Ideal University* (Gregg, 1947). It set forth prospects for a prosperous psychology era in which we would have 'freedom for change and development' with all psychologists on campus interacting, and centred in a large department staff with a wide variety of specialities represented. That prediction had materialized, more or less, for many universities in the 1960s, with rapidly increasing enrollments, graduate programmes expanding through federal support in both research and training, and the increasing opportunities for psychologists in all of its traditional roles—teaching, research and service.

But the uneasiness between the academic and the applied interests was not quieted. 'Ideal U' was revisited by a special issue of the *American Psychologist* (Appley, guest editor, 1970) containing both a look at the recommendations in retrospect and a review of the current scene. Alternate models for psychology's place in the university were described by McQuitty, Webb, Sears, and Coffey (see Appley, 1970). A central theme running through these articles and others in the set was a plea to maintain the unity of all of psychology—a defence of the interdependence of the basic and the applied—for the structure of the discipline and the context in which it is taught.

The Harvard report had included a recommendation for the Doctor of Psychology degree for those going into practice, but expected it to be kept in the hands of the arts and sciences department faculty. (There is some question about a majority of the Commission group favouring that proposal; see Appley, 1970, p. 418. Indeed, the retrospective comments by five of the original members, pp. 411–420, are all of considerable interest.) Whereas the great majority of service-oriented psychologists are still trained in the university context, in the late 1970s we saw the emergence and quickening spread of the professional school of psychology, sometimes affiliated with a university but sometimes not.

The impact of this recent trend cannot be fully assessed, yet it is clear that psychology in the USA is suffering appreciable trauma as a result of fundamental differences in the incentives, needs, and interests of the scientifically oriented versus the practice oriented groups of psychologists. In addition, and more recently, the social-action orientation is emerging, apparently not clearly in alignment with either of the other two groups. A study by Lipsey (1973) suggests that there are four ideologically separable groups in psychology: (a) pro-social action, anti-experimental; (b) pro-social action, pro-experimental; (c) anti-social action; anti-experimental; and (d) anti-social action, pro-experimental. Because faculty and graduate students studied differed in their distributions across these four classes, the authors draw implications that 'psychology tomorrow' will be more socially concerned and more humanist in orientation.

The importance of these issues for our present consideration is clear. Shall the academic context in which psychology is taught remain centralized in the traditional arts and sciences department, as envisioned in the Harvard report, or shall it become divided into two or more separate and independent enterprises (like physics–engineering or biology–medicine)? Many departments, ideologically committed to unity, have greatly expanded teaching efforts (graduate and undergraduate) into the applied areas, but the issue is not thereby resolved. In any case, the contexts for the teaching of psychology are currently in a state of flux.

ORIGIN OF ACADEMIC PSYCHOLOGY IN THE USA

In the early period of psychology teaching in higher education, courses were taught within the department of philosophy ('mental philosophy'). By the 1880s, courses under the title psychology were being offered at Cornell, Amherst and Brown, but some historians credit James's laboratory at Harvard in 1875 as marking the first true recognition of the discipline in the USA (Daniel and Louttit, 1953, pp. 15–16). I shall not develop the history or the growth of academic psychology thereafter, except to point out that academic organizational and course patterns emerged and changed slowly, being 'handed down' from mentor to student who carried them into the next generation.

CURRICULUM RECOMMENDATIONS

The first significant attempt to influence the pattern of undergraduate programmes was apparently the report of a conference at Cornell in 1951 (Wolfle, 1952). A group of six distinguished teachers of psychology met for eight weeks to exercise their collective judgement 'to develop a better undergraduate curriculum' than was typical at that time.

The recommended curriculum plan consisted of a broad, science-based introductory course leading laterally to special interest and applied courses, and vertically to a set of intermediate core courses, thence to upper level specialized and integrative courses. Considerable detail was provided for each course to be included, as well as a defence of the exclusion of some other courses. The programme was science-based throughout, and avoided the vocational or self-help type of course.

Whatever direct impact this report may have had on programmes was never assessed systematically, but if one allows some variations in detail, it does seem to characterize a great many departments in the period that followed.

A second, and similar, conference was held at Michigan nearly ten years later (McKeachie and Milholland, 1961). As in the Wolfle report, the emphasis was on designing the curriculum for liberal education and avoiding different tracks for different goals. However, instead of a single structure, the Michigan report offered three acceptable designs: the inverted pyramid, the hourglass, and the flexible. In any case, the suggestion was made that a department define a core of courses (or topics) required for every major. As this summary suggests, the Michigan report favoured more flexibility and innovation than had the Wolfle report.

Recent Curriculum Information

Again after about a decade, the report of a project of the American Psychological Association (APA) appeared (Kulik, 1973) following a three-year study funded by the National Science Foundation. This time, it was a data-based investigation 'to describe undergraduate education in psychology nationwide and to report on innovative approaches that may point the way to the future' (p. 3). The task was accomplished by extensive mailed survey and case study, interview methods.

I shall cite here only a selected few of the impressive number of demographic quantifications which were made from the survey; these data are based upon a sampling and overall 31 per cent representation of all institutions in the USA. Surprisingly, more than 500,000 students were in attendance at schools which did not offer a major in psychology, not counting two-year colleges (although some psychology courses were available to them), but nearly 4,000,000 students did have the psychology major option available. Such data would seem to suggest that the development of a full curriculum in many institutions is still a frontier for the teaching of psychology.

Only about one fourth of the total psychology enrollment was filled by psychology majors, but 25 to 35 per cent of those majors entered graduate school in psychology. This figure has been obtained in a number of other studies over a period of years, but one might expect it to decrease as employment opportunities for psychologists have become tighter in the late 1970s. The mean faculty size ranged from 4.36 in two-year colleges to 24.44 in public universities, and the 4.81 mean given for four-year colleges compares favourably with the previously cited figure of 4.2 (median) from the Cole and Van Krevelen study (1977).

The mix of courses offered provides an interesting contrast with patterns found twenty-two years earlier. Where the major was offered, 6 per cent of the courses were introductory, 11 per cent methodology, 19 per cent natural science, 32 per cent social science oriented, 7 per cent history and systems, 15 per cent applied and 10 per cent other, according to the authors classification scheme. This,distribution differs from that for 1947 (derived from Sanford and Fleishman, 1950) in that there is heavier emphasis on natural science processes and less on applied work in 1969.

More detailed, and more recent data on course offerings are available from a report by Lux and Daniel (1978). From a total sample of 178 college catalogues for 1975–76 or 1976–77, 1356 different psychology course titles were found, whereas only 261 titles were reported by Sanford and Fleischman (1950) from 180 catalogues twenty-five years earlier. The 'inflation' was believed to be determined by emerging fields, subject matter fragmentation, experimentation with a greater variety of topic combinations within courses, specialized and experiential course popularity, and overt efforts to make courses more appealing. The top thirty courses, in terms of incidence in three types of colleges combined is shown in Table 11.1.

The order of rankings in each of the three types of colleges (university, four-year, and two-year) is, of course, somewhat different than the collapsed data shown. Four additional courses were needed to complete the university list, four different.ones to complete the four-year college list, and seven more (three in common with the college list) to complete the two-year college list. In general, incidence of particular courses declined across the three types in the order just mentioned. The authors made historical comparison based upon three previous studies and examined shifts to verify Kulik's finding for colleges and universities of: (a) an increase in field work experience and human services courses; (b) an increase in natural science type courses; (c) a less, but still pronounced, increase in social science oriented courses; and (d) decrease in the traditional applied course. Two-year colleges showed the greatest increase in categories (a) and (c).

Kulik reports that the variety of plans to satisfy the major requirements was so great as to defy reduction to a summary quantification or description. This observation suggests that the fairly tight plans recommended in the earlier conference reports had little impact by 1969. He goes on to describe a host of innovations that have been integrated into requirements by a significant portion of his respondents. These innovations (most of which are discussed elsewhere in this book) include: (a) student participation in curriculum planning, teaching, or research; (b) field experience; (c) independent study; (d) extensive use of teaching instruments (including computers); (e) programmed

Table 11.1. The incidence of courses being offered in a sample of 178 universities, four-year colleges and two-year colleges.

Rank	Courses	%*	Rank	Courses	%*
1	Introductory	96	16	Industrial	32
2	Social	73	17	Independent Study	31
3	Abnormal	65	18	Seminar	30
4	Personality	59	19	Comparative	30
5	Child	59	20	Field Work	28
6	Learning	57	21	Educational	28
7	Physiological	57	22	Motivation	26
8	Tests/Measures	51	23	Perception	25
9	Statistics	46	24	Exceptional Child	25
10	Adjustment	42	25	Sensation/Perception	24
11	Experimental	39	26	Research	24
12	Developmental	38	27	Human Sexuality	23
13	History/Systems	35	28	Counselling	22
14	Adolescent	33	29	Research Methods	21
15	Special Topics	33	30	Applied	21

*Of institutions in the sample.

approaches (including PSI); (f) encounter groups; (g) team teaching; (h) grading innovations; (i) interdisciplinary, social issues, or humanistic courses; and (j) multi-track programmes for students with different goals. These ten innovations were found in from 4 per cent (grading innovations) to 28 per cent (teaching instruments) of the schools.

Following the questionnaire study, site visits were made to seventeen of the colleges and universities selected on the basis of some unique feature, and descriptions of ten of them comprise Chapters 6 to 13 of the report. They make interesting reading and contain a great many ideas for teachers or staff considering modification of the academic context where they work.

Thus we find that the typical undergraduate electing to major in psychology has an academic smorgasbord to choose from, will probably encounter modern techniques of teaching in one or more of his courses, has an opportunity for some exposure to human services training, but still gets a strong natural science base in his education. Students who transfer from one institution to another are likely to encounter a new set of requirements and curriculum structure, with the exception of junior college transfers where the programme is coordinated with a college or university.

CURRENT PROBLEMS IN UNDERGRADUATE PSYCHOLOGY EDUCATION

Departmental faculties must continuously monitor themselves and their programmes and they must maintain flexibility in order to respond to shifting needs of students and society. Although academia is notoriously slow to respond to change, information culled from the literature and summarized in the previous section of this chapter would suggest that psychology is a rather fluid discipline, with many of its problems being tackled if not resolved. I shall not discuss current problems which psychologists share with other faculties (e.g., shifting or declining enrollment, budgets, declining local and federal funding, and the like). But I do believe there are a few critical within-the-field problems deserving of more attention and investigation—problems which, in part, establish the context of teaching psychology.

Problems of Identity

Students are bewildered with the variety of material, roles, and models they encounter in courses. Some are turned away by the confusion. Psychology is variously classified in academic organization charts (Natural Science, Biological Science, Behavioural Science, and even in the Humanities at different schools), and our courses may be used to satisfy many different college requirements. We relate to biology, sociology, anthropology, physics, philosophy, education, medicine, law, child development, speech and other disciplines—who are we? How do we clarify our identity to the student?

Unfortunately, we are often confused ourselves. The identity of psychology is clearly shifting at the professional and national association level and we would be less than honest to represent ourselves otherwise to students. The traditional three role functions: (a) generation of knowledge; (b) communication of knowledge; and (c) application of knowledge, is shifting from emphasis on (a) and (b) to (c), and (c) seems to be expanding from service to people and institutions into the social action arena. McKeachie (1972) has analysed the problem of the emerging social action concern, and made proposals for embracing it with minimal trauma. Unless and until these shifts stabilize, or we become fragmented and separately identified at a professional level, we must be prepared to tolerate ambiguity ourselves and avoid the excessive foisting of confusion on our students.

The problem of multiple role representation to the student is more intense in the large-faculty situation of the university department. Few such departments have escaped the emergence at some time of intrafaculty conflicts. When these are known by students, and especially when a teacher exposes students to stabs at other specialties, the department has an identity problem at best and a problem of ethics at worst.

One promising arrangement for a proper representation of psychology's identity is the 'fields of psychology' course, described most recently by Gottleib (1975) and Bluestein (1977). Introductory texts include at least a brief introduction to the topic, but that exposure requires extension and clarification by the teacher. After all, the mass of one-course-in-psychology students (reported to be more than in any other subject after English and mathematics) represent a tremendously important segment of educated citizens. They deserve to have as clear an image of the discipline as is possible to give them. The public image of psychology is not as accurate or fair as it ought to be—the first course offers a splendid opportunity to improve it.

Problems of Mission

What is the psychology department mission within the college and campus of which it is a part? I have an uneasy feeling about our tendency to become too insular, especially in the university—exactly where there are multiple opportunities to interact profitably. Expansion of psychology's base through broader campus involvement could add stability to the context of teaching.

Interdisciplinary courses appear to be a barely tapped means of counter-acting parochialism. Recent literature includes descriptions of such courses for introductory psychology (Levine, 1977), experimental psychology with physics (Douglass and D'Arruda, 1973), a course in creativity (Domino and Wechter, 1976), and psycho-biology (Thompson, 1972). Even greater co-operation and cross fertilization can be had from joint programmes such as one at the University of Washington to produce AB level para-professional psychologists (Lunneborg and Kanda, 1970) or one for social psychology (Solomon, 1972).

A second mission problem is one teachers are not discussing much in recent years—should we mount a major's programme to produce psychologists or to produce scholarly educated citizens in the liberal arts tradition? There are sometimes subtle, but very real differences between the two, and the second alternative has greater compatibility with the objective of embedding psychology more deeply in the college programme.

Harper (1954), in reporting a conference on this subject, conveys the words of Dashiell that a well-educated person has the ability to generalize soundly, to insist upon evidence, and to judge objectively. If these are prime goals, then our academic context should feature sampling over a wide range of content material, be directed to needs of the individual, develop and exercise intellectual processes, and use a problem solving approach. For the most part, our psychology courses fall short of these characteristics. In contrast, they put undue emphasis upon learning facts and methods; or at least many of us so believe.

In a fictional 'annual report to the president', Lichtenstein (1960) developed nicely how a psychology department might mount a science-oriented programme within the liberal arts tradition. Stress was to be placed upon values, problems, and issues rather than on facts, vocational techniques, or mere knowledge. Psychology, like some other disciplines, has moved away from the liberal arts tradition or simply assumed that the student will be able to bridge the gap. Did we really intend to redesign our context in that fashion? I suspect not.

A third mission problem is a corollary of the second: do we design programmes for all of our majors or primarily for the graduate-school bound? It has become trite to point out that if N students on campus take general psychology, $0.25N$ will take additional courses, $0.04N$ will become majors, and $0.008N$ will go on to graduate school. (Multipliers are subject to some leeway, but not much.) Yet we ask ourselves, are we not usually addressing that small 0.8 per cent in our teaching? The issue has been with us for many years, it is resolved in some departments, but certainly not in all of them.

This problem *has* been subjected to considerable examination and action in recent years, at least in terms of some thought for the employability of bachelor graduates. In fact there is a growing literature on the placement of graduates (Erdwins and Olivetti, 1978). An increasing number of departments are adding field work experience for credit in an effort to give graduates marketable skills (Derner, 1976; Korn, 1974; Korn and Nodine, 1975; Kuppersmith, Blair and Slotnick, 1977; Thomas, 1975; Pinkus and Korn, 1973); others have introduced field work without expressly planning for vocational preparation (Bry, Marshall, West and Zollo, 1975); or as expressly intending only educational enrichment (Smith and Spatz, 1974); and some have attempted to integrate practical training into a liberal arts programme (Caffrey, Berger, Cole, Marx and Senn, 1977).

To what extent can practical experience or technical course work be added to the liberal arts curriculum without degrading or redirecting its intent? Should we be planning an *under*graduate professional school as an alternative? Should we give up the general education tradition altogether? Before we move too far and too fast toward professionalization of the AB degree, perhaps we should consider some alternatives, at least as transition measures. A strategy not yet tried is the utilization of intersessions and summer periods to build up (say 15–20) credit hours in applied work beyond the traditional 120, then award an appropriate certificate along with the AB degree.

The fourth mission problem to be discussed involves the distinction between courses for the major student and service courses offered to others. I believe this area provides another opportunity for a psychology department to strengthen its role on the campus in contributing to the education of a wider range of students than most of us do now.

Individual faculty members too often treat service courses as a necessary evil, to be tolerated only because it helps hold up enrollment (and thereby supports the budget). This attitude is incompatible with Miller's now famous 'giving psychology away' concept. Unless or until a sister department builds up enough of a need to justify appointing its own psychologist, we have responsibility to teach other students just as we send our own majors to other departments for support courses. Unless psychology takes pains to integrate itself into the collegiate mainstream, it will stagnate.

Finally, I want to support a position Brown (1973) clarified in his discussion of the Kulik book. A mission of the psychology department should be to structure its programme in terms of the needs of its own campus—perhaps even at the expense of emulating an admired department in another school, or a hypothetical norm. There is no *standard* department programme, nor is there any standardization board for establishing one. Much of the literature in this subject speaks to the need for innovation, exploration, and adaptation. As Professor Brown put it, each department 'must make a concentrated effort to determine the place of our science within the context of [its own] institutional goals, strengths, resources and the current needs of [its] students.'

Problems of Responsibility

Simon (1974) has made an earnest and convincing plea for teachers not only to listen to students, but to actively seek their concerns; then to pay attention to them by modifying our curricula to satisfy those needs. Many departments have added graduate and undergraduate students to important committees. Others have conducted opinion surveys of graduates, some of which have been published (e.g. Carrier, 1962; Daniel, 1974; Harris 1969) and have specifically influenced the modification of programmes.

There are, of course, two sides to this responsibility coin. The general practice of admitting students to faculty committees, an outcome of the activist 1960s, has not always worked out as well as had been hoped. Faculty members may take the position that students cannot be expected to know what is best for their intellectual diet. Yet the practice of student evaluations of teachers and classes as input for assessing quality and relevance is now widespread. No doubt, the wisest posture is effected through close and frequent interaction of faculty and students on the issues.

The ethical and liability implications of innovations we introduce must also be accepted as a responsibility. A current example of this problem evolves from the rapid introduction of field work courses. Van de Creek and Thompson (1977) have most clearly stated the 'concerns ... about guaranteeing proper management of undergraduate ... intern programs ....'

First, there are the academic concerns—will the *academic* programme be enhanced? Will the student make a contribution to the agency? How should assessment and grading be handled? How much and what kind of student selection is proper? Second, there are supervision concerns. A department embarking on field work opportunities for the first time is likely to underestimate the faculty time requirements for a programme of acceptable quality. Lastly, and most often overlooked, is the question of who is responsible if there is a malpractice claim against a student intern.

We must accept the responsibility of assessing our innovations. Do they improve the level of achievement, ease or speed of learning, or the attitudinal aspects of the teaching/learning process? Classroom research, in common with other research outside of the laboratory, is difficult to manage with rigour, but it can be done. A 1973 APA convention symposium (Wright, 1973) was devoted to strategies applicable to the assessment of teaching innovations. Unfortunately, teachers often plan a new approach with care, but fail to follow through with a demonstration of its value.

As we move into a greater concern for the employability of our graduates, we must recognize that there are adjunct responsibilities which cannot be separated from employment preparation: advisement and placement. Academic advisement is very familiar to psychologists, but many of us worry that it is too often not done with the thoroughness it deserves, and it is the subject of frequent complaint of students. We tend to toss off the problem by noting that the administration does not credit faculty for advisement time or quality. Clearly, if we undertake training for AB careers, we must also assume responsibility for *more* (not less) advisement of students into career types, career ladders, and planning for shifting job demands.

I suspect that psychologists are even less well prepared to become involved in placement activities at the AB level. At a large university, placement offices for the professional schools are commonplace, but those institutions are just recently beginning to accept responsibility for students from liberal arts programmes. On many campuses, it may be that the department does it or it does not get done.

CONCLUSION

In 1971, McKeachie (1972) claimed it was 'a time of crisis for departments of psychology' and he went on to list some of the almost continuous crises he has faced. Some years later Nazzaro (1976), from his vantage point as Educational Affairs Officer of the APA, wrote a brief summary piece entitled 'Identity Crisis in Psychology'. Crises are commonplace in the rapidly shifting world of higher education, so the above account of teaching psychology in an academic context should be considered no exception. Crises are the instigators of change; the challenge to ingenuity.

Whither psychology in the academic scene? One can be sure it will continue to play a vital role in higher education. But it will probably become even more scattered across the campus, serving students at the point of need with teachers who are specialists in psychology *and* in the field they service. Students will continue to press for course work in applied fields, humanistic psychology, and even the more exotic fringes of psychology. Some of these pressures are clearly anti-scientific, even at the level of the graduate school and the profession. May we hope that those future psychologists who engineer restructuring and the evolution of the field are wise enough to protect the empirical research base from which all branches must continue to draw new knowledge.

REFERENCES

Appley, M. H. (guest ed.) (1970). Special Issue: The Place of Psychology in the University. *American Psychologist*, **25**, 387–468.

Bartlett, N., Finger, F. W., and Williams, S. B. (1957). Survey of Some Matters in the Organization of Undergraduate Instruction in Psychology. Unpublished Report, American Psychological Association Committee on Undergraduate Education.

Bluestein, V. (1977). Variations on the Fields of Psychology Course. *Teaching of Psychology*, **4**, 132–134.

Blum, F. (1968). A Note on the Neglected Middle in Teaching Undergraduate Psychology. *Canadian Psychologist*, **9**, 20–21.

Brown, D. (1973). The Undergraduate Major: A Look at Alternative Strategies, Present and Future. *Teaching of Psychology Newsletter*, May 1973, 3–7.

Bry, B. H., Marshall, J. S., West, L. M., and Zollo, J. S. (1975). A Pilot Course for the Training of Peer Counselors for Educationally Disadvantaged Students. *Teaching of Psychology*, **2**, 51–55.

Caffrey, B., Berger, L., Cole, S., Marx, D., and Senn, D. (1977). Integrating Professional Programs in a Traditional Undergraduate Psychology Program. *Teaching of Psychology*, **4**, 7–13.

Carrier, N. A. (1962). Feedback Study of Psychology Graduates. *American Psychologist*, **17**, 47–48.

Cole, D., and Van Krevelen, A. (1977). Psychology Departments in Small Liberal Arts Colleges. *Teaching of Psychology*, **4**, 163–167.

Collins, G. R., and Spiers, D. E. (1973). Psychology in Professional Schools: A New Challenge. *Teaching of Psychology Newsletter*, May 1973, 7–8.

Daniel, R. S. (1970). Teaching Psychology in the Community and Junior College. *American Psychologist*, **25**, 537–543.

Daniel, R. S. (1974). Surveys of Psychology Baccalaureate Graduates. *Teaching of Psychology Newsletter*, February 1974, 8–10.

Daniel, R. S., and Louttit, C. M. (1953). *Professional Problems in Psychology*. New York: Prentice-Hall.

Derner, G. I. (1976). The Education for the Profession of Clinical Psychology and Psychology Technician. *Clinical Psychologist*, **29**, 1–2; 13.

Domino, G., and Wechter, V. T. (1976). Joint Teaching of Undergraduate Courses in Creativity. *Teaching of Psychology*, **3**, 123–127.

Douglass, F. M., and D'Arruda, J. J. (1973). Experimental Psychology in the Physics Lab. *Teaching of Psychology Newsletter*, October 1973, 7–8.

Ellison, E. W. (1973). Profile: Psychology Faculty in Christian Colleges. *Journal of Psychology and Theology*, **1**, 51–63.

Erdwins, C., and Olivetti, L. J. (1978). Psychology Related Employment Settings for Graduates of Submasters Programs in Psychology: A Bibliography. *Teaching of Psychology*, **5**, 38–39.

Fisher, H. (ed.) (1974). *Developments in High School Psychology*. New York: Behavioral Publications.

Fricke, L. R. (1975). A Study of the Perception of Three Groups Regarding the Preparation of Community College Psychology Teachers in Florida and Texas. *Dissertation Abstracts International*, **35B**, 3554 (Microfilm no. 75–1579).

Gottlieb, M. C. (1975). Introduction to the Fields of Psychology: A Course Proposal. *Teaching of Psychology*, **2**, 159–161.

Gregg, A. (1947). *The Place of Psychology in an Ideal University: Report of the University Commission to Advise on the Future of Psychology at Harvard*. Cambridge, Mass.: Harvard University Press.

Harper, R. S. (1954). The Knox Conference on the Relation of Psychology to General Education. *American Psychologist*, **9**, 803–804.

Harris, T. M. (1969). *A Follow-up of Psychology Majors Graduated from the LaCrosse State University, 1965–1968*. Wisconsin: Wisconsin State Universities Consortium of Research Development.

Hershey, G. L., and Lugo, J. O. (eds) (1969). *Teaching Psychology at the Two-year College: Innovations and Problems*. New York: Macmillan.

Kasschau, R. A., and Wertheimer, M. (1974). *Teaching Psychology in Secondary Schools*. Washington DC: American Psychological Association.

Korn, J. H. (1974). Training and Employment of BA Psychologists: Report of a Symposium. *Teaching of Psychology Newsletter*, February 1974, 10–12.

Korn, J. H., and Nodine, B. F. (1975). Facts and Questions Concerning Career Training of the Psychology Major. *Teaching of Psychology*, **2**, 117–119.

Kulik, J. A. (1973). *Undergraduate Education in Psychology*. Washington DC: American Psychological Association.

Kuppersmith, J., Blair, R., and Slotnick, R. (1977). Training Undergraduates as Co-Leaders in Multifamily Counseling Groups. *Teaching of Psychology*, **4**, 3–6.

Levine, R. V. (1977). An Interdisciplinary Approach to the Introductory Psychology Course. *Teaching of Psychology*, **4**, 132–134.

Lichtenstein, P. E. (1960). Perspectives in Psychology: XIV. Psychology in the Liberal Arts Curriculum. *Psychological Record*, **10**, 131–139.

Lipsey, M. W. (1973). Psychology Tomorrow: A Survey of Graduate Students and Faculty in Psychology. *JSAS Catalog of Selected Documents in Psychology*, **3**, 3 (Ms no. 334).

Long, B. (ed.) (1972/3). *People Watching.*, 2 vols. New York: Behavioral Publications.

Losak, J. G., and Beal, R. (1970). A Survey of Psychology in the Junior College. *Junior College Journal*, **40**, 62, 66–72.

Lunneborg, P. W., and Kanda, C. N. (1970). Interdepartmental Programs to Produce Bachelors Psychologists. Unpublished Report, University of Washington.

Lux, D., and Daniel, R. S. (1978). Which Courses are Most Frequently Taught by Psychology Departments? *Teaching of Psychology*, **5**, 13–16.

Matarazzo, J. E., Lubin, B., and Nathan, R. G. (1978). Psychologists' Membership on the Medical Staffs of University Teaching Hospitals. *American Psychologist*, **33**, 23–29.

McKeachie, W. J. (1972). The Psychology Department and Society. *American Psychologist*, **27**, 643–646.

McKeachie, W. J., and Milholland, J. E. (eds) (1961). *Undergraduate Curricula in Psychology*. Chicago: Scott, Foresman.

Miller, E. O. (1953). Teaching Psychology in the Small Liberal Arts College. *American Psychologist*, **8**, 475–478.

Moser, H. A., Delaney, D. J., and Rubin, S. E. (1971). Psychology and the Junior College. *Improving College and University Teaching*, **19**, 291–292.

Nazzaro, J. R. (1976). Identity Crisis in Psychology. *Change Magazine* (Special issue, Report on Teaching no. 1), **8**(2), 44–45.

Nixon, G. (1970). University Instruction in Behavioral Science: Development and Testing of an Evaluation Model. *Dissertation Abstracts International*, **31A**, 2619.

Norton, F.-T. (1972). Two-year College Instruction: Opportunities for Psychology. *American Psychologist*, **27**. 445–450.

Pinkus, R. B., and Korn, J. H. (1973). The Professional Option: An Alternative to Graduate Work in Psychology. *American Psychologist*, **28**, 710–718.

Ray, W. S. (1972). The Psychology Professor in the Liberal Arts College. *American Psychologist*, **27**, 441–444.

Sanford, T. H., and Fleishman, E. A. (1950). A Survey of Undergraduate Psychology Course in American Colleges and Universities. *American Psychologist*, **5**, 33–37.

Sheanin, M. (1972): Adventures in Developing a Psychological Services Curriculum in a Two-year Community College. *American Psychologist*, **27**, 584–587.

Simon, G. C. (1974). Some Important Suggestions Regarding the Future of Undergraduate Education in Psychology. *Teaching of Psychology Newsletter*, April 1974, 5–6.

Smith, R. G., and Spatz, B. (1974). A Review of Mental Health Practice for Undergraduates. *Teaching of Psychology Newsletter*, April 1974, 7–8.

Solomon, W. E. (1972). An Undergraduate Program in Social Psychology. *Improving College and University Teaching*, **20**, 137–138.

Stone, G. C., Gentry, W. D., Matarazzo, J. D., Carlton, P. L., Pattishall, E. G., and Wakeley, J. H. (1977). Teaching Psychology to Medical Students. *Teaching of Psychology*, **4**, 111–115.

Thomas, E. R. (1975). An Alternative Approach to Undergraduate Training in Psychology. *Teaching of Psychology*, **2**, 80–81.

Thompson, N. S. (1972). Psychology as a Form of General Education. *American Psychologist*, **27**, 580–582.

Thornton, G.L. (1974). The BA Degree in Psychology in State Colleges: Where Do Graduates Go? What Do They Do? *Teaching of Psychology Newsletter*, February 1974, 5–6.

Van de Creek, L., and Thompson, G. (1977). Management of Undergraduate Psychology Internships. *Teaching of Psychology*, **4**, 177–180.

Very, P. S. (1966). The Place of Psychology in Some Finer Liberal Arts Colleges. *Psychological Reports*, **19**, 1231–1238.

Viney, W., and Titley, R. W. (1972). Support Levels of Undergraduate Departments in Four-year Colleges and Universities. *American Psychologist*, **27**, 1070–1072.

Witkin, H. A., Mensh, I. N., and Cates, J. (1972). Psychologists in Medical Schools. *American Psychologist*, **27**, 434–440.

Wolfle, D. (1952). *Improving Undergraduate Instruction in Psychology: Report of a Study Group at Cornell University*. New York: Macmillan.

Wright, J. C. (1973). Symposium: Instructional Research in Psychology (papers by Hohn, R. L., McKnight, P. C., Semb, G., Trefinger, D. J., and Feldhusen, J.). *Teaching of Psychology Newsletter*, October 1973, 3–17.

Note Added in Proof

An important addition to the literature of academic psychology in the USA has just appeared:

Woods, P. J. (ed.) (1979). *The Psychology Major: Training and Employment Strategies*. Washington DC: American Psychological Association.

12

The Liberal Studies Context

PETER SHEA

THE CONTEXT

The borders of the liberal studies context are blurred indeed. In teaching one might cross them either way without noticing. It has become habitual among educational administrators and theorists to distinguish liberal studies classes from those devoted to vocational training or instruction. The theoretical view is that training or instruction predetermines the responses of the student, who is thereby bereft of choice and self-determination. Liberal studies on the other hand encourage one to pursue one's own curiosity, to experiment, to take decisions and to grow in one's own way. For similar reasons liberal educationists would tend to exclude from their camp courses for which the syllabuses are controlled by external examining bodies, and where success is assessed by the extent to which examinees give conformist answers. But the critical question is whether a course of study releases the individual in some way from the confines of ignorance or incompetence, from emotional inhibitions or a lack of confidence, or from the lethargy of non-commitment. To take the non-vocational–vocational dichotomy too seriously is to believe that formal preparation for careers or examinations never encouraged anyone towards practical experimentation or the exploration of new ideas quite outside the syllabus. It is also to believe that the effects of liberal studies cannot flow over into practical, working lives. Common experience denies these propositions. The effects of even the most authoritarian instruction cannot be contained. Any piece of learning might be a catalyst in some mind, bringing unplanned revelation, creating unintended structures and unexpectedly changing attitudes.

Having said that, it can reasonably be argued that even if common experience shows that vocational or examination centred studies can have genuinely liberal side-effects, these are usually fortuitous and are not the primary aim of the teaching. The objectives of these courses can normally be more precisely defined than those falling clearly within the liberal studies context.

From this viewpoint it may be claimed that school children, whose development, particularly in the later stages, might be confined by examination schedules, would gain much from programmes of liberal teaching designed primarily to give wings to latent talent and curiosity without predetermining the paths these should take.

In response to this view, as we shall see, liberal studies were often pressed upon students in higher education of a technical kind during the 1950s and 1960s, but less so now. They were not always appreciated.

Although some examining bodies are more liberal nowadays in allowing schools and colleges to suggest the contents of their syllabuses, the natural home of liberal studies is to be found in the context of non-vocational adult education, where men and women, paying their own fees, voluntarily take them up, and can as freely put them down, expressing their personal choice and wishes as they reach out towards higher levels of understanding and competence. This essay will be mainly about this field.

The ideas that cluster around the concept of liberal education elude precise definition, but generally they dance around the ideal of a free individual, unique in some respects, self-determining and precious, adjusting to the world in ways which allow him, or her, through application and creativity, to move towards higher and more desirable levels of adjustment usually described in terms of maturity, self-fulfilment or self-actualization. These ideas and values settle more easily within the political philosophy of individualism than that of collectivism, but neither of the two can entirely ignore the other, and liberal educationists normally include in their statements of aspiration some concern for the collective values of society. The self-actualizing individual ought also to be a responsible citizen.

PLEASURES AND PAINS IN LIBERAL ADULT EDUCATION

The challenges and satisfactions of teaching go together; the two are wedded. Teaching psychology to adults in the context of liberal education has its own distinctive pleasures and pains.

Not uncommonly, psychologists sign on as part-time tutors in evening institutes, with the Workers Education Association, or with university departments of extra-mural studies, not only for the leisure money (the fees are rarely regarded as life-savers other than by young graduates reading for higher degrees); but also as an agreeable means of keeping fresh the full range of their psychology, defeating the effects of specialization which keep one academic corner brilliantly polished while allowing the rest to rust. But rewards flow from successful classes and these are not achieved simply at the opening of a register. The adults who enroll, not seeking a diploma or degree, do so because it promises to meet some personal need or want. They may attend or not as they please. Insofar as the course satisfies their motives for enrolling, or gives some other, unanticipated pleasures, they will try each week to push competing commitments to one side so as to attend. The tutor then finds himself, or herself, an adult among adults, in mutually satisfying transactions, and friendships begin to root. If, however, the student finds that he or she—and it is more likely to be a 'she', for women students outnumber the men—is gaining little or nothing from the teaching, other pulls will claim his or her time, and falling attendances make the sensitive teacher uncomfortable. Some fall-off throughout voluntary non-vocational education is quite normal, but a growing host of noughts competing with the ticks on the register is something of a criticism as well as an embarrassment. One needs, quite continuously, to be reviewing one's teaching methods and attitudes as well as the contents of the course. Children learn to suffer a good deal of pointless teaching and, to a degree, carry the tolerance into adulthood, but they are then free to turn away when limits are reached. Sufficient of the psychology taught to adult students must be felt by them to be relevant to their concerns if they are to continue to attend, or it needs to be so intrinsically interesting as to generate their enthusiasm or curiosity.

The challenge, then, to the tutor is to maintain a positive teaching relationship with a group of adults of diverse experience, abilities and anticipations, through presenting psychology in ways that speak to their interests without robbing it of its integrity, its standards or its sense of scholarship. It is no mean challenge. Old hands assert that the satisfaction of meeting it, and of teaching one's peers, is of a special order.

THE PARTNERSHIP OF TUTORS AND STUDENTS

The relation of tutor and student in a University Tutorial Class— as indeed in any other class of adults—is entirely different from the relationship of teacher and pupil. The teacher is in real fact a fellow-student, and the fellow students are teachers. Humility of spirit and an appreciation of the vast, unexplored reaches of knowledge, are at once the inspiration and the vital force of such study, which is always pursued in accordance with the wills and desires of the students. For, unless they are vitally interested, no group of students will persist in studying a subject from which they receive no material reward and gain no recognition. The pursuit of knowledge for its own sake, or as a means of development of body, soul and spirit, can never be stimulated artificially: it must arise out of the very needs of the people.

This statement of proper tutor–student relationships among adults was written by Mansbridge (1913), one of the great pioneers of adult education.

He had founded the Workers Education Association as a consumers' organization of adult students and was the driving inspiration behind the growth of co-operation between the WEA and the universities through the development of the Tutorial Class movement. Three-year tutorial classes, with no examinations and no awards, are fewer in number nowadays but they remain an impressive pillar of liberal education. Commonly, in the spirit of Mansbridge's idea, the syllabuses are not written or printed until tutors and students have discussed together what they should cover.

Clearly, in shaping a common course of exploration, tutor and students should respect each other's areas of interest and knowledge. The tutor, whilst trying to meet those of the members of the group, has the right to keep within the orbit of his expertise for which he was contracted to exercise. The teaching will suffer if he is forced outside. Yet the students should not be expected to bend to the tutor's enthusiasms if they are bored by them. A teacher's enthusiasm is a powerful attribute in the classroom, but it must not run away with him.

Adults new to psychology sometimes hold flattering and naive beliefs that psychologists have insights of a mystical order into the nature of human behaviour. They know little of the pain of self-doubt of psychologists who think, from time to time, that their discipline has nothing useful at all to say about the human condition; who are embarrassed by the imaginative leaps that are made in making statements about people generally on the basis of evidence gathered from creatures great and small behaving in extraordinary conditions. But this is to take an unnecessarily pessimistic view of the theories and models that have accrued as a consequence of psychological experimentation and reportage. Certainly evidence is never complete, there is always a gap, always some risk when one applies a theory in a practical way to a human problem, but the same goes for medicine and other applied sciences where the individuality of people is involved. Psychologists can do no more than suggest, with a greater or lesser degree of confidence, that their theories and models offer insights. Telling is outside their range; but so is it foreign to liberal education, other than in the matter of simple, verifiable facts. Discussion is the essential adult educational method.

Liberal education flourishes in the liberal mind that can live with doubt and ambiguity, and where further curiosity is generated by both. Growth implies leaving the rut of one's present level of beliefs and adjustments to face unknowns, insecurity and the risk of failure. Some adults have not got the confidence for this. They seek for a certainty that is not to be had. Part of the teaching task is to encourage a realistic view of our discipline whilst holding to the belief that the search for insights continues to be worth while.

The psychology courses will have been advertised in the brochures and handbooks of the evening institute, the WEA or the university extra-mural department. A title will indicate the field within which the tutor is ready to work.

Everywhere in education student numbers are of administrative significance. A minimum number of enrollments, varying with the organization, but probably between ten and fifteen, will be necessary if the class is to open, and the fall-off in attendances must not be too great if it is to run its course. Specialist titles have narrower appeal and there is an understandable tendency to advertise titles that cast widely the net. Courses may offer, then, a consideration of a specific problem, Television and the Child, for instance, or reflect one of the university divisions of psychology and be concerned with, perhaps, child development or abnormal behaviour; or sometimes the course titles are those of large encyclopaedic textbooks and promise insights into the whole of human behaviour and experience. Tutors offering courses should be clear about how widely they are prepared to range.

Similarly, the men and women who respond to the advertisements may be prompted by motives that are general or specific. They may have a broad, academic interest in discovering what psychology is all about, but usually the initial concern is more localized. Those who join are likely to include professionals—teachers, nurses, salesmen, ministers of religion, journalists—who believe that psychology is saying something that bears upon their work. Mothers, too, of course, will come for the same reason. Some may have anxieties or interests of a non-vocational kind, reflecting concern with problems of a social, political, educational or religious nature. Not infrequently matters of a more personal kind prompt them to try and find out what psychology has to say about them: perhaps their teenage children are being troublesome, or mental sickness has cropped up somewhere in the family, or their own marital relationships have crumbled and they are seeking for themselves a clearer explanation. It might seem at first sight that no educational course could meet the diverse interests of fifteen or so such students without the tutor abandoning his teacher's role for that of therapist or counsellor, but in fact this difficulty is more apparent than real. Usually the initial interests of individuals expand to embrace at least most of the syllabus shaped by the tutor and the concensus of students. Just down the corridor from the psychology class other adults may be studying another corner of the non-vocational field—motor maintenance. Individually they may have enrolled because of concern with particular faults which their cars are prone to, but they see the sense of acquiring an overall view.

However, it is not uncommon for a class to attract somebody who has personal difficulties that require the professional one-to-one help of a clinical practitioner. The new tutor of psychology would do well to ponder his role as teacher and to decide what the limits of his responsibility are before he sets foot in a classroom. He is not contracted to treat the personal complaints of his students and should be ready to explain this gently as soon as the matter arises.

AGENCIES OF LIBERAL EDUCATION

Enlightenment may dawn anywhere, and many and diverse are the informal places where face-to-face teaching of a kind is pursued and, on occasions no doubt, psychological understanding advanced. But 'liberal studies' suggests the acceptance of role relationships by teacher and taught. Even so, they are furthered in Britain by an extraordinary variety of organizations, clubs, guilds, governmental establishments, movements, adult colleges and universities. The main stream is channelled through LEA adult institutes, the WEA and university extra-mural departments.

Our LEA institutes evolved from the night schools of the nineteenth century which, for 1 penny a week upwards, offered the workers a basic education in school subjects. School teachers and school premises were often used. They still are. Adult education is rarely furthered in premises designed and built for the purpose. But despite much second- or third-class accommodation as many as 1,800,000 students were enrolled for LEA adult courses in 1976.

The WEA, founded in 1903 by Albert Mansbridge, has a nationwide network of local branches, and is controlled democratically by its membership through unpaid committees. It employs full-time district and national officers. It offers the public programmes of courses on academic subjects which on the whole reflect university teaching.

The extra-mural movement was initiated in this country by the University of Cambridge in 1873. By 1976 some thirty-three universities in Britain were participating in it and were members of the Universities Council for Adult Education. The typical extra-mural course, open to all adults without reference to their educational attainments, or lack of them, meets twenty-four times during the academic year for two hours weekly. Students are often given access to university libraries and are expected to study sufficiently seriously to produce pieces of written work. Extra-mural departments do offer examinable, award-bearing courses, but much of their work is free of such constraints. In this latter context the tutorial class might be regarded as the peak of the mountain of liberal education. Here tutors and students commit themselves to three years of study together for whatever intrinsic personal satisfactions it might bring. It is not surprising that the number of such courses is declining, but the UCAE report for 1975/6 shows that there were in that year over 14,000 enrollments for them.

For many, 'liberal studies' is associated with the burgeoning concern for the liberalizing of technical education during the late 1950s and 1960s. A White Paper, *Technical Education*, was presented to Parliament in 1956. It was a call, supported by Sir Anthony Eden, the Prime Minister, for an immense increase in the numbers of qualified scientists, engineers and technicians, since Britain was far behind America and the USSR in this respect. The White Paper also asserted that a place must always be found in technical studies for liberal education. This was essential if students, destined for responsible positions in industry, were to emerge from their technical education with a broad outlook. Spiritual and human values could not be neglected.

So it was that liberal studies departments were developed in polytechnics, technical colleges and colleges of art. Not infrequently the students, and indeed their teachers of technology, could not see the point of it all. The liberal studies teachers had a cause to win. Many joined together in the Association for Liberal Education inaugurated in 1961. Reading through its journal, *Liberal Education*, for the 1960s and early 1970s, one feels the fires of contention, bright and hot during the early years, gradually die down. This was due not so much to the battle having been won as to changes in the work of liberal studies departments. There was a great expansion in the work of the colleges with young people not particularly interested in technical careers, but seeking a diversity of 'O' and 'A' levels. This work was well suited to liberal studies teachers, and their departments tended to be transmuted into General Studies Departments, providing them with acceptance, respectability and a much more favourable career structure.

HOW LARGE A SHARE HAS PSYCHOLOGY HAD IN LIBERAL STUDIES?

Subjects that contribute to the diversity of liberal education wax and wane in popularity as this subject or that catches the interest of adults with a disposition to study, promising perhaps to offer insights related to some current of anxiety or curiosity running through public awareness. So interest might bubble up, and then die away, in international affairs, astronomy, sociology or Eastern religions. In the few figures available I have been unable to detect great swings in public interest in psychology as a whole, although there are fluctuations of interest in the various concerns that make up the discipline.

In wondering how much psychology is taught in the liberal studies context, a cardinal fact to remember is that the number of persons qualified to teach the subject has, in this country, been very small indeed. British Psychological Society statistics show that its total membership in 1941 was only 811. Very roughly it grew by 1000 members a decade until 1970 when its membership was 3811. Then there was a dramatic increase and in the six years to 1976 there were more new members than the total roll twenty-five years before, and a total of 5896 was reached (British Psychological Society, 1976/7). Although not all graduates in psychology join their learned society, it is clear that there have not been more than a sprinkling of graduates around Britain, and only a small proportion wishing to contribute to liberal education. Yet some eminent psychologists have done their share.

About 88 per cent of mainstream adult courses are put on by LEA institutes. They embrace an immense number of subjects from Macrame to Yoga, from architecture to navigation. There are no figures to tell us how many classes there are in psychology, but among the thousands of classes they would be sprinkled very thinly indeed.

We know more about the strength of psychology in the other 12 per cent of mainstream adult education organized by extra-mural departments, the WEA and one or two other minor organizations which collectively are known as 'responsible bodies' for government grant purposes. The annual report of the Universities Council for Adult Education for 1975/6 shows that of the 9665 extra-mural courses given in nineteen subjects, 396, or 4.1 per cent were psychology. In a rank order of the nineteen subjects, dominated by social studies (10.95 per cent) and history (10.72 per cent), psychology is placed tenth and is the median subject.

Russell (1973) adds a little to these figures. The 'responsible bodies' enrolled 10,448 students to study psychology in 1969/70, 32 per cent being men and 68 per cent women. They made up 4.19 per cent of the total student body. In 1960/61 the percentage was 3.67; so psychology has gained a little ground in its popularity, or perhaps in its ability to provide sufficient, effective part-time teachers in the subject.

A significant step forward that is likely in the long run to strengthen the public's regard for psychology, to rob it of some of its fringe nonsense and the anxiety with which some regard its study, is the introduction of 'A' and 'O' level courses into secondary schools.

In 1967 an investigation by the British Psychological Society revealed that psychology was already taught in the schools of a number of countries, but particularly in Scandinavia and the USA. As a consequence of some pioneering work by a group of British psychologists 'A' level examinations were initiated here in 1970. In 1977 some 2150 candidates sat the examination.

In 1977 an 'O' level syllabus was introduced to meet the needs of sixth form students for whom higher level examinations were not appropriate and also the needs of students in Colleges of Further Education, and mature students. The first examinations were held in 1978. One of the aims of the syllabus, 'To give the student an overall perspective of the direction of human development, with general reference to childhood, adolescence and old age', is a promising vehicle for liberal education.

As students leave schools having studied psychology, there will be a strengthening of demand for continuing courses in it. Parents, too, are likely to view it more warm heartedly, and some will be prompted to study it for themselves.

THOSE WHO JOIN CLASSES

Pieces of research within the context of liberal education are very thin on the ground, and those focusing upon the teaching of psychology within it are for practical purposes non-existent; a few tiny grains. Charnley's (1974) review of master and doctoral theses presented since 1945, notes but a handful directly related to psychology. Kelly's (1974) survey has three references to the teaching of psychology, and none after 1951. But there have been two notable pieces of research that tell teachers something of those who join classes and why a quarter or more are unlikely to stay their courses.

Adult Education—Adequacy of Provision (Chataway, 1970) was the report of an enquiry committee set up by the DES. 'The most substantial study of its kind in the field of adult education in Britain' was a fair description of it by Christopher Chataway, the committee's chairman. It researched the organized provision of educational opportunities for mature people in five areas of the country, selected and ranked according to socioeconomic data. The study excluded technical and vocational courses. Joining a class reflected personal decision and voluntary participation.

The degree of confidence and initiative required of adults to reach the situation where they are completing enrollment forms, is not possessed by considerable numbers of the population. The report found that reasons given for never having enrolled on a course suggested that something like half of the adult population was inhibited by attitudes that are probably deeply rooted in social circumstances and earlier education. Those who had had an extended school or higher education were more likely to join classes. Those who left school at the minimum legal age were under-represented. The extension of school life and higher education is likely to expand the demand for adult classes.

Extra-mural classes are more academically oriented than the LEA courses and the class bias of the student body is probably greater. The 1972 statistics of London University's Department of Extra-mural Studies show that only 5 per cent of their students belonged to social classes IIIM, IV and V.

The Adequacy of Provision researchers interviewed a sample of over 3500 persons. They asked them why they joined classes. Their report commented, 'Motives are multiple, uncertain and fluctuating. They are affected by general attitudes not easily identified and categorized.' Although their classes were classified as being 'non-vocational', 'work' was one of the main reasons for attending. Self-development, family and personal interests, recreational needs, the social contacts of the class and the desire for community service were prominent among the reasons given.

Having paid their fees, why do so many students drop out? The study found that half the reasons given by those not completing their courses could be classified as being due to domestic and external circumstances. These, as might be expected, were also the reasons given for not enrolling at all. It is likely that many students, on joining, are too optimistic about their ability to fit classes into their everyday pattern of commitments. Only small numbers cited the learning situation as the reason for leaving: 10 per cent disliked the tutor or the atmosphere of the class, 6 per cent found the work too advanced, 2 per cent found it not sufficiently advanced and 5 per cent found it of little interest.

Significantly, perhaps, there was a stronger tendency for those of the higher social classes to admit that the standard of work was too high: possibly the less articulate were less prepared to declare that the work was above their heads.

The City Literary Institute is one of the most prestigious of Britain's adult education centres. Glynn and Jones (1967) investigated the reasons for student drop-out there from non-vocational courses during the 1965/6 session. Questionnaires were despatched to 1049 students who had ceased attendance by six weeks before the end of their courses. 43 per cent responded. As many as 73 per cent said that they had left for reasons unconnected with their courses or the Institute. 33 per cent admitted disappointment with their courses. Of these 12 per cent were disappointed in the subject itself, 17 per cent said it was presented too uninterestingly, 9 per cent claimed there was too little discussion, 8 per cent did not like the tutor, 5 per cent complained that there had been no opportunity to get to know other students and 4 per cent who had, did not like them. 6 per cent found the standard of work too high and 9 per cent found it too low.

Nicholle (1976) researching into class drop-outs in the Haywards Heath area found that the wastage varied from one subject to another and was greater from those requiring homework. There were some 30 per cent drop-outs from GCE courses and only 12 per cent from those devoted to dressmaking. Another interesting finding, indicating the complexity of variables at work in the teaching situation, was that one tutor with a number of classes in the same subject had wastage rates ranging from nothing to 40 per cent. Nicholle also found that the tutors did not know why 28 per cent of the drop-outs had left. Feedback of some value was being neglected.

Glynn and Jones commented that where classroom doors are opened to all, more wastage than among the highly selected students of universities is almost certain to occur and should be accepted without disquiet. They called for varied and flexible approaches to the teaching tasks and in the length and intensity of the courses.

It is clear that the teacher of psychology, facing his students at the beginning of a course, cannot tell just how strong is the motivation that draws them to his class, or how powerful are the forces that have to be overcome by them if they are to attend without neglecting other responsibilities or attractions. Circumstances may be stacked against the teacher, but he must treat every absence as a possible criticism of his teaching if complacency with his methods is to be avoided. He, better than most, should be aware of the defences adopted by adults, and the social skills which they may use, in hiding their real reasons for dropping out. The writer has written on his conscience the polite note sent to him by one quiet, elderly woman student saying that domestic circumstances prevented her attending his class any more, and thanking him for his interesting evenings. Only then did it dawn on him with great certainty that he had been teaching far above her head. Sometimes, however, even in the full knowledge of the situation, there is little one can do. If, for instance, a student joins a class believing that Jung is God and Skinner the devil, experience has shown that even gently dissenting from this theology will lose the student for ever.

ASPECTS OF THE TEACHING TASK

Every teacher has his, or her, own style and ought to be left to develop it in their own way; in liberal education, perhaps, more so than elsewhere. The following ideas are offered as suggestions only, as a kind of check-list against one's own practices.

Good liberal teaching, and not only with adults, has much in common with the ways and values of common courtesy. Everyone is valued. One should know people's names. At the first meeting invest 10 minutes in getting students to make name plates of folded paper showing how they like to be called. Do the same yourself. Be interested in personal data but do not press for it; allow individuals to reveal themselves at their own pace. Round-the-class introductions, often recommended, can be embarrassing for some. Chairs, or school desks, should be placed as nearly as possible in a circle, facilitating eye holding and giving students and tutor equal access to each other. Test, as an hypothesis, that the more of each other's bodies can be seen, the more fluent the verbal interactions, and that clear sight lines to knees, where possible, are particularly helpful. Consider the possibility that the model for good teaching of adults is nearer to that of a modern infants' classroom than that of a university lecture hall. Sometimes the students sit in a ring that includes the teacher, sometimes they break into smaller groups, occasionally there is one-to-one tuition, though this probably happens before or after the class or during the breaks. Accept that the breaks for refreshment half-way through the period are not an indulgence, but an essential opportunity for the students and tutor to discover each other and to strengthen relationships.

The first meeting of a class is both the most critical for a tutor and the most difficult. He must aim to send each student home with a sense of, at least, modest excitement at the prospect of things to come. Better still if this is accompanied by a feeling of some new understanding. Don't take chances: get to the centre early. Settle yourself down, with the room arranged as you want it, before the students arrive. One may condition them to arrive punctually later, simply by starting each week on time, but the first evening there should be a few minutes grace: students may well be new to the building and the way to the classroom may be badly signposted. The tutor may find, happily, that the conditions within which he will teach are both elegant and comfortable, or he might quickly realize that he must fight their influence from the beginning. Adults classes are not often found in rooms designed and built for the purpose. More often they are housed in primary, or scratched and inkstained secondary class rooms, in church halls, public libraries and youth centres, and occasionally in the sitting rooms of private houses. Remember that enthusiasm is contagious. To catch more interests, cover more surface area of psychology the first evening. If the teaching is attractive, after a few weeks, through a spread of effect, even the less comfortable and elegant of conditions will begin to feel a little like home.

Ruddock (1972), psychologist and experienced teacher of adults, wrote a helpful article for tyros called, 'All Right On The Night—A Survival Kit for Absolute Beginners'. His tips for survival include: acknowledge people as they come in but try to avoid being taken over by the class leader or in-group. Observe seating choices and apparent friendships. A modest display of scholarship is not inappropriate. Speak briefly about recommended books and techniques of study. Talk 10 to 15 minutes, introducing subject, stopping two or three times for feedback and to check comprehension. Invite discussion. If there is a silence, present one or two questions to the group, prepared in advance. Present a summary review in the last 8 minutes. Rearrange chairs and tables in original positions if so requested by the principal or caretaker.

The lecturing tradition emphasizes the importance of content but minimizes consideration of the receptivity of the audience. In poor lecturing there is a 'take it or leave it' implication. This, in the liberal studies context, would be to invite dissociation. Travelling home from a class, begin your assessment of the period, trying to see and hear it through the eyes and ears of each of the group. Has each been stimulated by the teaching and discussion and likely to have been in touch with what was going on?

Recommending suitable reading in psychology to adults who have done no serious study for years, if ever, is often a problem, although with the growth of introductory paperback series and the availability of Open University publications it is much easier than it was. The use of the easier reading of fiction and of biographical descriptions of personality development may well be useful in establishing the confidence of non-studious adults in their ability to abstract ideas from books. *Psychology Teaching*, the Bulletin of the Association for the Teaching of Psychology, has published a number of valuable articles listing fictional and biographical accounts.

To get adult students to face the discipline and the anxiety of putting their ideas down on paper for the scrutiny of a tutor, presents the greatest problems, but it can be done, and the gradual improvement in the standard of the written work is a most satisfying form of feedback. It may be necessary to begin with the two kinds of writing the average adult is familiar with, letter writing and form filling. To get the students to write a personal letter to the tutor explaining why they have joined the class, whether they have had any kind of contact with psychology before and what they hope to get from the course, is a well-tried method of reintroducing adults to the discipline of communicating ideas to a teacher through writing. The correct response is for the tutor to write a note back to each. Familiarity with form filling may be used in the early stages of the course by duplicating questionnaires based upon previous meetings of the class. Leave spaces for the answers which should require anything from a 'yes' or 'no' to three or four sentences. Some experienced tutors get students to keep a class log book. Reportage is less testing than essay writing and the members of the class take it in turns to write an account of the previous week's meeting. This is read at the beginning of the next period. Although time consuming it does reveal to the tutor how well his material is being assimilated.

The ages of the members of an adult class in psychology might range over as many as fifty years. The teacher should be alert to the possible variations in the facility for learning of the men and women sitting with him. Knowing a student's age does not allow one to make any certain predictions about their mental abilities but the study of adult learning and aging usefully points to probabilities.

A student's capacity for grasping abstract material from middle age onwards is likely to rest upon the quality of his early education and the nature of the mental exercise provided by his occupation. A mind that has been well and continuously exercised through to its sixties may present the tutor with an exciting challenge and opportunity, but the middle aged man of basic early education and with a non-demanding job may need sensitive encouragement.

Older students tend to be at a disadvantage to the degree that the input is diverse, rapid and continuous. They need more time to codify the information. Holding it in the mind and needing to cogitate upon it before translating the ideas into activity tends to be difficult. The older the students the more likely it is to be necessary to present them with an input that is uncomplicated and unhurried. Teaching methods should allow them to share the control, of the pace of teaching: to cry 'Whoa!'.

It is commonplace to find with older people trouble in the retrieval of information from the memory. They know that 'What's his name' put forward a theory called...but the nouns escape them. Be patient: avoid embarrassment. It may well happen to you.

The older person will have acquired a vast repertory of practical schemas, ways of doing things, heavily reinforced throughout the years. Give a group of them some practical instructions and somebody will ask, 'Can I do it this way?'. As far as is possible let them use old habits. Not to do so is to waste previous learning.

Psychology tries to make sense of, to find structure within and behind human behaviour and experience. Adults varying in age by forty or fifty years bring with them a collective experience of life of great diversity and richness. They may recognize in their own personalities the consequences of that experience. Living through their childhood at the time of World War I, or after World War II, or between them, they will have enjoyed or suffered the critical experiences of family, education, work and play in differing social and historical settings. The challenge to the young graduate teaching such a class is to be able to spot the harmonies and discords between his ordered academic psychology and the beliefs and attitudes of the students, often so much older than he is, arising from their own experiences of life and death. It can be met. I once enjoyed watching the sensitivity of a young, graduate bachelor who was teaching the psychology of child-rearing methods to a class almost entirely of mothers and grandmothers. He gathered in their experiences, listened to them, found the common themes and related these to academic explorations. There was no dogmatic assertion, no certainty, but simply the liberal probing of ideas which helped the group to find more meaning in their own experiences.

Much of the attention and admiration of society is focused upon youth; they are the stuff of which winners are made. Coming to terms with an aging body and diminishing youthfulness is a major adjustment of the life cycle. For many women this must be made at a time when their sense of personal value is undermined by the departure into adulthood of their children. The self-esteem of aging adults may not be of a high order. They may be skilled at hiding their feelings about themselves, but do not underestimate their need for reassurance.

AIMS AND OBJECTIVES

The liberal studies teacher, anxious to avoid the charge of dogmatism, trying at all times to maintain a balanced view of the evidence, may overlook that, nevertheless, in his classroom methods and attitudes he positively reflects values and aims—or the lack of them. As the therapist will have a view of what constitutes sound mental health and will help the client to make his way towards that condition, so the teacher should know what he stands for and is aiming at. Psychologists are likely to have their own preferred descriptions of the adult personality, mature, ongoing, ever developing, which they regard as the best kind of adjustment that can be made in our society. These will provide useful frames of reference in class discussions about the changes which applied psychology seek to bring about, but they also give the teacher a starting point for considering the aims of his own classroom methods.

Teaching of a kind can be done without reference to ultimate aims or immediate objectives, but it is slapdash workmanship. A psychologist, with his well-developed concepts of cognitive growth, of attitude formation and change, and the nature of the acquisition of skills, is in a better position than many to define where he aims to take his class.

Aims are often regarded as ends, and objectives as the intermediate steps towards them. If one is not familiar with Bloom's taxonomy of educational objectives, the two volumes are worth reading as an admirable attempt by a group of examiners to define a classification of educational objectives based upon the psychological knowledge of the day (Bloom, 1956, 1964). The taxonomy is far too complex and time-consuming for most teachers to use, and psychologists are likely to find Professor Foss's simplified classification of human learning much more helpful in considering objectives, and in assessing achievements afterwards (Foss, 1975). He classifies nine sets of possible goals; learning descriptions of things and supposed facts—learning diagrams, pictures, maps, structures, etc.—learning categories and labels—learning skills and techniques—learning concepts—learning explanations—learning to solve problems—learning to innovate—and, finally, the learning of attitudes and beliefs.

MEANS TO ENDS

There are teachers who keep their psychology and their teaching methods in sealed compartments, not allowing the former to suggest modifications of their classroom practices. Some teach as if the whole body of learning theory and the study of remembering had no suggestions to offer, even to the extent of ignoring the value of structure, of engaging receptors other than the ears, and of discrete repetition. There should be an effort after consonance between the theory one expounds and the practices one utilizes.

One needs to seek for methods that are effective and yet economical with time. The typical adult liberal studies class meets for two hours only during the week, and normally in the evenings. The group and the teacher will need to shake off the fatigue of the day's work as they settle together. The tutor must plan to catch their interest from the start. There is a place for the occasional inspired lecture, but generally the value of long expositions is more apparent than real as courteous students politely listen. Guided discussion should be more productive. It requires care in seeing that all are mentally engaged, and in keeping it moving forwards among the sloughs of extended personal anecdote and of hogging by the over-articulate. Discussion should end with a summary of the path travelled and the conclusions reached.

Experiments of a simple kind often catch the interest of students and get them interacting, though they may be very time-consuming. There is unlikely to be available any of the hardware of the psychological laboratory, but pencils and paper, playing cards and lists of words and nonsense syllables can carry one quite a long way. If one is to test long-term memory, launch the experiment early in the course.

Role playing and simulation techniques are worth studying. Without it they can be both embarrassing and a waste of time. The group will need to have generated enough confidence in each other before risking loss of face in adopting dramatic roles. Occasionally these exercises allow the non-academic to step forward and shine.

The experiential methods of humanistic psychology range from the slightly playful and the pleasantly communicative to those exciting emotions of intensity. There is plenty of scope for selecting exercises which will develop group cohesiveness as well as illustrating personality themes.

Studies of the qualities that make for successful and popular teaching indicate that one needs to be of a divine order: savant, saint and warm-hearted comedian. Most of us struggle on with our imperfections, but in the classroom find ourselves among others of similar humanity. This makes the total effort worth while.

BIBLIOGRAPHY

On Adult Education

Rogers, J., and Groombridge, B. (1976). *Right To Learn*. Arrow Books.
Kelly, T. (1970). *A History of Adult Education in Gt Britain: from the Middle Ages to the Twentieth Century*. Liverpool University Press.
Lowe, J. (1970). *Adult Education in England and Wales—A Critical Survey*. Michael Joseph.
Lawson, K. H. (1975). *Philosophical Concepts and Values in Adult Education*. University of Nottingham Department of Adult Education.
Journals:
Adult Education. Studies in Adult Education.

Teaching

Rogers, J. (1977). *Adults Learning*. Open University Press, second edition.
Cleugh, M. F. (1962). *Educating Older People*. Tavistock.
Rogers, J. (ed.) (1972). *Adults in Education*. BBC Publications.
Stephens, M. D. and Roderick, W. (eds) (1971). *Teaching Techniques in Adult Education*. David & Charles.
Beard, R. (1972). *Teaching and Learning in Higher Education*. Penguin.
Elsdon, K. T. (1975). *Training for Adult Education*. University of Nottingham.
Journal.
Psychology Teaching.

Psychology and Adult Education

Dave, R. H. (1976). *Foundations of Lifelong Learning*. Pergamon, especially Chapter 5: Cropley, A. J. Some Psychological Reflections on Lifelong Education.
Kidd, J. R. (1973). *How Adults Learn*. NY Association Press.
Jessup, F. W. (ed.) (1969). *Lifelong Learning: A Symposium on Continuing Education*. Pergamon.
Kuhlen, R. G. (1970). *Psychological Backgrounds of Adult Education*. Center for Study of Liberal Education, Syracuse, New York.
Howe, M. J. A. (ed.) (1977). *Adult Learning: Psychological Research and Applications*. Wiley.
Bromley, D. B. (1974). *The Psychology of Human Ageing*. Penguin.
Bischof, L. J. (1976). *Adult Psychology*. Harper & Row.
Kimmel, D. C. (1974). *Adulthood and Aging*. Wiley.
Botwinick, J. (1973). *Aging and Behaviour*. Springer.

REFERENCES

Bloom, B. S. (ed.) (1956). *Taxonomy of Educational Objectives I—The Cognitive Domain.* Harlow: Longmans.

Bloom, B. S. (1964). *Taxonomy of Educational Objectives II—The Affective Domain.* Harlow: Longmans.

British Psychological Society (1976/7). *Annual Report, Appendix II.* London: British Psychological Society.

Charnley, A. H (1974). *Research in Adult Education in The British Isles.* London: National Institute of Adult Education.

Chataway, C. (1970). *Adult Education—Adequacy of Provision.* London: National Institute of Adult Education.

Committee of the Association for the Teaching of Psychology and the Standing Advisory Committee on Education in Psychology of the British Psychological Society (1977). Joint Statement: The Teaching of Psychology in Schools. *Teaching Of Psychology,* **5,** No. 2.

Foss, B. M. (1975). Classification of Human Learning. *Psychology Teaching,* **3,** No. 2.

Glynn, D. R., and Jones, H. A. (1967). Student Wastage. *Adult Education,* **40,** 139–149.

Kelly, T. (ed.) (1974). *A Select Bibliography of Adult Education in Great Britain, Including Works Published to the End of the Year 1972.* London: National Institute of Adult Education.

Mansbridge, A. (1913). *University Tutorial Classes.* Harlow: Longman, p. 1.

Nicholle, D. J. (1976). Student Wastage in Adult Education. Dissertation, University of London.

Ruddock, R. (1972). All Right on the Night—A Survival Kit for Absolute Beginners. *Adult Education,* **5,** No. 3, p. 143.

Russell, L. (1973). *Adult Education: A Plan for Development.* London: HMSO, Table 14.

The Teaching of Psychology
Edited by J. Radford and D. Rose
© 1980 John Wiley & Sons Ltd.

13

The Medical Context

DOUGAL MACKAY

In recent years, the amount of time devoted to the teaching of psychology in medical and para-medical courses has risen steadily. Although nurses, occupational therapists and physiotherapists now receive quite substantial tuition on human behaviour, this trend has been particularly marked in the medical schools. Fifteen years ago, very few of them offered any formal teaching in psychology, except in relation to psychiatry. At the present time, only one of the thirty-four British medical schools which have pre-clinical departments does not run a course in psychology. Considering the competition for teaching time, the fact that, on average, 72 hours are set aside for behavioural science courses (General Medical Council, 1977) indicates that the inclusion of psychology and sociology is no mere token gesture on the part of the medical schools.

Similarly, those responsible for the organization of medical education in most other countries are now appreciative of the role psychology can play in the training of future doctors. In Australia and New Zealand, for instance, behavioural science teaching is at least as well advanced as it is in Britain (Winefield, in press). In the USA psychology is a well-established subject in the curriculum of most medical schools, although there is currently a move towards the humanities (e.g. anthropology) at the expense of the social sciences (Banks, 1974).

Most of the pressure for teaching in psychology and sociology came orginally from general practitioners who were concerned that their medical training did not equip them to deal effectively with a significant proportion of their patients. Teaching-hospital medicine, with its emphasis on acute, severe illnesses is very different from that practised by the family doctor. A much higher percentage of patients seen in the primary health care setting present with chronic health problems of a relatively minor sort. In many of these cases, an understanding of the ways in which psychological factors relate to illness behaviour, combined with some expertise in patient management, is of more value than knowledge of basic medical principles. Consequently, in an attempt to eliminate this deficiency, the General Medical Council (1967) included the following statement in its list of recommendations: 'The Council considers that instruction should be given in those aspects of the behavioural sciences which are relevant to the study of man as an organism adapting to his social and psychological, no less than to his physical, environment' (p. 104). With the publication of the *Todd Report* (Royal Commission on Medical Education, 1968) a year later, behavioural science became firmly established in the medical curriculum.

Despite the demand for behavioural science teaching from the medical schools, and the enthusiasm of psychologists and sociologists to provide it, student response to these courses (e.g. Sheldrake, 1974) does not provide grounds for complacency. However, as Pritchard (1970) points out, 'Student opinion is surely irrelevant to the main issue. The proper question is whether the practising doctor needs to be familiar with the subject matter and concepts of these particular disciplines or not.' In order to be able to answer this question properly, it is necessary to be able to specify the objectives of these courses and to demonstrate that the content and teaching methods are consistent with these aims. The purpose of this chapter is to examine some of the views which have been expressed on these and other matters, and to offer some practical suggestions as to how this teaching might most effectively be carried out. Inevitably, the emphasis throughout will be on the teaching of psychology to medical students, since progress has been more rapid in this area than in any other connected with health care personnel. However, most of the points raised are very relevant to the education of student nurses, occupational therapists, physiotherapists and health visitors.

OBJECTIVES

The following objectives have been put forward by the various contributors to this field although, as will be seen, not all have received universal acceptance:

1 To demonstrate the importance of psychological factors in illness. All those concerned with behavioural science teaching are in agreement that one of the principal aims of these courses should be to help the student to appreciate the involvement of psychosocial factors at all stages of the illness process. As Pritchard (1970) points out, psychology teaching should 'serve as a corrective to the reductionism of the cell biologist with his worship of DNA and the tertiary structure of protein'. In other words, it is believed to be important to get across the concept of the patient as a 'whole person', whose behaviour is

influenced at all times by a combination of psychological, social and physiological factors.

While this would appear to be a perfectly laudable aim, difficulties arise when attempting to relate it to the subject matter normally covered in introductory psychology courses. A series of lectures on such standard topics as size constancy, the bar-pressing responses of pigeons, and maze learning in the laboratory rat, interspersed with occasional speculations about the social reinforcement of illness behaviour, is obviously an unsatisfactory arrangement. Yet the link between 'mainstream psychology' and general medicine is, for the most part, a tenuous one. This issue will be raised again in the next section.

2 As a foundation for psychiatry. The rationale for covering most of the material in the pre-clinical programme is that it provides a sound basis for the teaching of clinical medicine. Thus neurologists can take it for granted that their students are familiar with the fields of neuroanatomy and neurophysiology, while those concerned with the teaching of therapeutics can proceed on the basis that the students have had a thorough grounding in pharmacology. It is not surprising to find therefore that many medical personnel consider psychology to be simply an introduction to psychiatry. Those who are not familiar with either discipline distinguish between them on the basis that psychology is concerned with the normal whereas psychiatry deals with the abnormal. Since psychiatric symptoms involve disorders of thinking, emotion, motivation, perception and memory, it is assumed that a general understanding of these processes is required before studying psychopathology.

Such a view is deceptively simple. It assumes that psychologists are not interested in the abnormal except in those instances when they assist psychiatrists. However there are currently a wide range of psychological models of both normal and abnormal behaviour in existence and, as Mackay (1975) points out, most or these are antithetical to the 'medical model' utilized by the majority of psychiatrists. Thus it could be argued that, far from providing a foundation for psychiatry, psychology, with its emphasis on the person, will make the students as critical of disorder-based psychiatry as, say, disorder-based dermatology.

However, although there may be ideological differences between psychology and psychiatry, most contributors (e.g. Royal Commission on Medical Education, 1968; Coleman and Mackay, 1975; Bennett, 1976) feel that the behavioural science course should, at least, make students aware of the special sorts of problems psychiatrists have to deal with. Nevertheless there is general agreement that this should not be the sole, or even primary, objective of the course. As Griffiths (1976) points out, 'such an aim places unrealistic and undesirable limits on the potential contribution of psychology to the health service'.

3 To teach students about the doctor–patient relationship. The Todd report (Royal Commission on Medical Education, 1968) places a great deal of empha-

sis on making students aware of the effect of their social behaviour on others, so that they might become more effective in their interactions with patients at a later stage. Many psychology teachers attempt to achieve this by carrying out demonstrations and practical sessions on various aspects of the communication process between doctors and patients. These sessions are, not surprisingly, among the most popular with the students (Sheldrake, 1974) because they can immediately see the relevance of this material to their future careers. Todd, however, is less convinced that it is appropriate to concentrate on clinical situations before the students have had any experience of interacting with patients. This report advocates that students should be given 'some understanding of social skills' (para. 254) in the behavioural science course, but that teaching on 'doctor–patient relationships can best be given at the clinical stage when the student can see for himself what it is all about' (para. 255).

This is one of the Todd recommendations which has been ignored by many psychology lecturers. After all this topic is one of the most obvious bridges between academic psychology and clinical medicine. It can be argued that most medical students will have thought carefully about what being a doctor involves, and the sorts of difficulties they might encounter when adopting this role, long before they come to medical school. In any case, it would seem to be important to orient the students towards the importance of clinical, as opposed to medical, skills from the outset, otherwise they are likely to become over-committed to the disease-centred approach and therefore resistant to input, at a later stage, which is not consistent with it. Another important point here is that, since many clinicians are reluctant to discuss the less tangible aspects of patient care with the students, the 'art of medicine' (Tait, 1974) may never be raised in a coherent and structured fashion. It would therefore seem preferable to expose the students to this material prematurely rather than not at all.

4 To show students that behaviour can be studied scientifically. According to the *Todd Report*, one of the aims of behavioural science courses should be to demonstrate that psychology is concerned with data 'whose reliability and validity can be systematically appraised and that concepts and theories about human behaviour can be and must be submitted to experimental verification' (Royal Commission on Medical Education, 1968, para. 246). Griffiths (1976) agrees that it is important for students to appreciate that 'behaviour and experience can be investigated in an objective and meaningful manner'. The main difficulty here is that those areas of psychology which have been researched into with the scientific rigour advocated by Todd are, for the most part, of little relevance to the needs of medical students. If 'soft' data were to be excluded entirely, then a course unit on, say, psychosocial factors affecting illness would be a very brief one indeed. Many medically qualified writers on this subject have professed little patience with the over-concern with scientific respectability demonstrated by some psychologists: 'Exaggerated claims for an exclusively traditional scientific approach to the study of behaviour should not be made; rather the

contributions of the humanities should be acknowledged and respected' (Bloch, 1973).

Thus although it is important to get across the notion that contemporary psychological notions do not emerge from armchair musings, a course which restricts itself to well-established scientific 'truths', and which places a great deal of emphasis on the ways in which psychologists study their subject matter, is likely to be perceived as boring and irrelevant by a large proportion of the students. As Davis (1970) points out, 'There is no point in giving medical students a cursory elementary coverage of the middle chapters of a standard introductory book on psychology. They do not want to be psychologists at all.'

5 To augment the teaching of other pre-clinical subjects. Many contributors (e.g. Coleman and Mackay, 1975) argue that many topics in psychology, which have a high factual content and which are related in some way to the subject matter covered in other pre-clinical courses, should be included as part of the general education of the medical student. Ideally, the teaching of these topics should be carried out in conjunction with the relevant lectures from physiologists, anatomists and biochemists so that the ways in which psychology complements the basic medical sciences will be apparent. Thus, for example, if basic principles of perception are to be dealt with in any depth, the most appropriate time to do this would seem to be when physiologists are carrying out their teaching on the sense organs. Todd, in fact, strongly recommends that 'Psychologists should participate in some aspects of the physiology course' (Royal Commission on Medical Education, 1968, para. 253).

There are two problems here. The first is that the policy of introducing new material into an overcrowded programme, on the grounds that it is connected in some way to certain core topics, is open to question. Such a practice could clearly be carried out indefinitely. As Pritchard (1970) points out, 'There are many other fascinating subjects from philosophy to history which would have an equal right to be included if the sole criterion is that the subject should form part of the mental armamentarium of every educated person. However there is undoubtedly a place for such topics as operant conditioning of cardiovascular responses in any pre-clinical curriculum.'

The second difficulty concerns the more general issue of 'topic teaching'. There is little point in implementing integrated teaching programmes if the lecturers themselves have not made the necessary links, and if the relevant boards of studies are unable to contemplate the possibility of hybrid examination questions. Thus, although there are a number of psychological topics which link up neatly with physiology, biochemistry and pharmacology, this fact alone does not justify their inclusion in the pre-clinical programme, particularly when the points of contact have not been dealt with in the other courses.

6 To help students to be more empathic. In addition to making students aware of the relevance of psychological factors to illness and teaching them inter-

viewing techniques, some writers on this subject feel that the behavioural science course should attempt to render future doctors more sensitive to the needs of their patients. It has been argued that one way of achieving this is to help students to understand more about their own behaviour. Bloch (1973), for example, states that one of the objectives of the course should be to promote 'the continuing development of the student as a human being, so making him sensitive to human problems and enabling him to deal with sick human beings rather than with organs or diseases'.

There are a number of assumptions here which need to be examined before discussing this issue further. (a) A course in psychology will lead to an increase in self-awareness. (b) Increased self-awareness will make an individual more sensitive to the needs of others. (c) Greater sensitivity will be reflected in an increase in empathic behaviour. (d) The greater the degree of empathy, the more effective the clinician will be.

As Griffiths (1976) points out, there is no empirical evidence to support any of the first three assumptions. So far as the fourth is concerned, positive results have been achieved in the field of psychotherapy (e.g. Truax and Cark-huff, 1964), but it is not clear as to what extent these findings are relevant to more orthodox medical treatments. In any case, since most lecturers in psychology find themselves teaching 100 or more exam-oriented medical students, fresh from a dissecting practical, in a multi-tiered auditorium designed for anatomy demonstrations, it is difficult to envisage how such an objective could be achieved in any case. Thus, although many psychologists feel it to be important to give medical students some 'insight' into their own feelings and behaviour, there is some question as to the feasibility of such a goal.

Rather than attempt to achieve all of these goals simultaneously, it is advisable to divide the material into separate units, each of which is linked to one particular objective. In this way, both the lecturer and the students will be clear as to why a particular topic is being considered at any one point in time. Anecdotal evidence would suggest that medical students find it difficult to tolerate ambiguity, presumably because of the tight discipline and structure of the basic medical sciences. Since many find the relatively nebulous nature of psychology a problem in itself, it is essential that the organization of the course should be as clear-cut as possible.

CONTENT

Decisions as to course content are very difficult to make, particularly for the new lecturer with a 'pure' academic background, who has been trained to support every statement with a string of references. He is more likely to concentrate on 'safe' topics which have been well researched, rather than on areas which have proved more difficult to study objectively and are therefore easier to criticize. The problem here is that since, for example, skin conductance responses to 75 dB tones have been found to be more susceptible to experimental investigation than attitude changes during illness, such a strategy is unlikely to lead to a course which will stimulate the majority of students and meet the major objectives. On the other hand, the lecturer who decides to ignore formal psychology completely and provide a series of unsupported generalizations about doctors and patients is unlikely to prove any more successful. Medical students are as intolerant of 'waffle' as they are of irrelevant, esoteric research summaries.

The most logical procedure would seem to be to carry out a 'job analysis of the doctor's job' (Graham White, 1970) and use this as a basis for deciding what sort of information medical students need to know. The difficulty here is that the medical profession constitutes an extremely heterogeneous body, with cell biologists at one pole and Kleinian psychoanalysts at the other. However, the fact that general practitioners account for about half of the number (Tuckett, 1976) and a significant proportion of the remainder are involved in clinical medicine of one kind or another makes the task a little less daunting. Nevertheless a comprehensive job analysis of the work of the general practitioner has not even been carried out as yet and so, under the circumstances, the next course of action would seem to be to base the course on some of the objectives described above.

What is proposed here is that instead of delivering a series of lectures on such standard topics as learning, perception, memory and personality, with the occasional reference to the clinical situation, the whole process should be reversed. In other words, the actual framework should be directly related to the requirements of the medical students and the subject matter of psychology should be adapted to fit this particular structure. In practical terms, this means that a topic such as 'learning' will have to be broken down into smaller units (e.g. skills acquisition; operant conditioning of autonomic responses) which can then be dealt with in different parts of the course. Although there is always the possibility that, by doing this, students may not fully grasp the holistic nature of the concept, this should not constitute a deterrent. After all, the main purpose in introducing this subject into the pre-clinical curriculum is to produce better doctors, not semi-trained psychologists. The advantage of dividing up the material in this way is that the theme of the course, at any particular point in time, will be apparent to all. It follows from this that the lecturer will be put under more pressure to justify the inclusion of every topic he chooses to present under this system than under a more traditional one. He will therefore have to think out carefully the links between psychology and medicine by himself, rather than deliver an orthodox series of lectures and expect the students to do this by themselves.

One possible way of designing a course, based on the principles described above, is outlined in Table 13.1. Here, each unit is linked to one of the objectives isolated earlier. Selected 'core' topics in psychology can then be related to the

Table 13.1. Proposed framework for courses on psychology as applied to medicine.

Core topics	*"Bridging" topics*
Unit A Psychological factors affecting illness Theories of child development, adolescence, adulthood and old age; maternal deprivation; intellectual deterioration; patterns of aging; experimental approaches to personality; heredity and environment; unconscious motivation and defence mechanisms; theories of emotion; cognitive labelling; anxiety and performance.	Children in hospital; psychosomatic disorders in adolescence; anorexia nervosa; psychological effects of physical deterioration; caring for the elderly; pain tolerance and complaining behaviour; sensory deprivation and the effects of hospitalization; suggestibility and placebos; coping with the psychological effects of illness.
Unit B Doctor–patient communication Motivated perception; perceptual defence; verbal and non-verbal behaviour in social situations; cognitive set; stereotypes and prejudice; styles of leadership; attitude change; intelligence and its measurement; short-term and long-term memory; self-control; serial position curves; arousal and retention; group processes and factors affecting cohesiveness and morale.	Factors influencing the patient's perception of symptoms; the roles of the doctor and patient; interviewing techniques; doctor–patient communication and recovery from illness; patient satisfaction and compliance; uses of placebos; helping patients to remember what their doctor tells them; preparing patients for hospital admission; the hospital ward as a primary group.
Unit C Normal and abnormal behaviour The disease concept in medicine; principles of classical and operant conditioning; personal construct theory and the repertory grid technique; validity and reliability of questionnaires, inventories and projective techniques.	The disease concept approach in psychiatry; psychosocial models of abnormal behaviour; learning theory formulations of psychiatric disorders; psychological theories of cognitive disturbance; conflict and neurosis; assessment in clinical psychology.
Unit D Psychology and general medicine The concept of arousal; sleep and wakefulness; sleep deprivation and its consequences; diurnal rhythms; menstrual cycle stages and performance; hypothalamus and eating behaviour; pain as behaviour; the nature of stress; operant conditioning of visceral responses.	Pharmacological influence on arousal; sleep disturbances in psychiatric disorders; factors affecting obesity; the effects of physiological changes on performance; stress, personality and psychosomatic disorders; biofeedback techniques for tension headaches, cardiac arrhythmias; essential hypertension and epilepsy.

theme of a particular unit through certain 'bridging' topics. In this way, both the academic respectability and medical relevance requirements can be met. A similar scheme, for linking basic psychological concepts to course objectives is described elsewhere (Winefield, in press).

WHEN SHOULD IT BE TAUGHT?

In its recent survey of behavioural science teaching in British medical schools, the General Medical Council (1977) found that psychology and sociology are included in the pre-clinical curricula of all those schools which offer such courses. However, many psychologists (e.g. Griffiths, 1976) have questioned whether this is the most appropriate stage to introduce this material.

Some of the advantages of teaching psychology pre-clinically are as follows. Students tend to be much more enthusiastic and open-minded on entering the medical school, and are therefore more likely to absorb the material and discuss its implications at this stage than if it were to be presented to them for the first time in their clinical years. Furthermore, while many students regard psychology as a welcome relief from the medical sciences, it is doubtful whether they would turn to it with the same zest if clinical medicine was available to them. Finally, it would presumably be easier to put across the notion of psychology as a science, if this is considered to be an important objective, if it is taught alongside physiology and biochemistry.

However there are advantages too in teaching psychology during the clinical years. As mentioned earlier, there is a danger that much of the material on doctor–patient communication and psychological aspects of illness, if taught in the first two years, will be forgotten by the time the student sees his first patient. Furthermore, the relevance of much of the subject matter will only become fully apparent once he has had some clinical experience. Finally, once the Second MB hurdle is out of the way, the majority of students become less exam-oriented for a while and are therefore better able to contemplate material which is not saturated with 'essential facts'.

The real issue here, of course, is not whether it is better to teach psychology pre-clinically or clinically. The vast majority of those involved in the teaching of this subject would like to see it included in both programmes. Some of the topics mentioned in Table 13.1 (e.g. Unit D) should ideally be taught in conjunction with physiology and pharmacology, whereas other areas (e.g. Unit B), as Todd points out, are most usefully dealt with when the students are involved themselves in interacting with patients. However the more traditional medical schools seem unable to contemplate the possibility of a subject which transcends the pre-clinical/clinical barrier. The rigid divisions between the medical sciences and clinical practice, and between the social sciences and somatic medicine reflects the uncertainty which underlies medical education. There

are many who share the belief of the respondent in the General Medicine
Council's (1977) survey that 'teaching of behavioural sciences cannot make
progress until the structure and ethos of the whole medical course is changed'
(p. 774).

WHO SHOULD TEACH IT?

The issue of who should teach psychology to medical students is a controversial
one. Todd is in no doubt that what is required is 'a body of teachers with both
a full academic training in the behavioural sciences and a qualification in
medicine' (para. 248). However there are relatively few people with dual
qualifications available to carry out this function. Moreover, it is unrealistic
to think that many people are going to spend the best part of a decade studying
both medicine and psychology in order to be able to lecture on a behavioural
science course. Consequently, different types of specialist have taken up the
challenge of organizing and teaching courses in psychology as applied to
medicine. The claims of some of the main contenders for the job will now be
considered briefly.

Psychiatrists

Until comparatively recently, the bulk of pre-clinical psychology teaching
was carried out by psychiatrists. At first glance they would appear to be the
candidates who approximate most closely to the Todd ideal of medically
qualified lecturers with a background in psychology. Having been through the
medical education system, they have a better understanding of the needs of
the student than psychologists. Their knowledge of physiology, biochemistry
and pharmacology should enable them to see many ways of integrating psychology more effectively with the other pre-clinical subjects. The very fact
that they are medically qualified means that their status, from the point of
view of students, colleagues and college administrators alike, is relatively high.
It is therefore not difficult to understand why psychiatrists were the obvious
first choice of most medical schools, particularly in the pre-Todd era.

However, although they are well equipped in some ways to carry out this
teaching, they are deficient in others. The psychology course which doctors
have to undertake in order to obtain the Diploma in Psychiatric Medicine or
Membership of the Royal College of Psychiatrists is far too brief and superficial to provide a basis for later teaching of this subject. Most psychiatrists
would readily agree that, not only is their knowledge of basic psychology extremely limited, but they have only a vague understanding of the experimental
approach as used by psychologists. It is not surprising to find, therefore, that
psychology courses organized by psychiatrists tend to be very clinical, both
in terms of the material covered and the approach to problem solving which

is advocated. Thus, although psychiatrists can make a very useful contribution to the pre-clinical teaching of psychology, they do not have a sufficient degree of understanding or knowledge of this subject to enable them to run courses effectively along the lines suggested here.

General Practitioners

The case for and against the family doctor as a teacher of psychology in relation to medicine is similar to that of the psychiatrist. The main advantage the non-specialist in the community has over his counterpart in the hospital is that he has a considerable amount of first-hand knowledge of the effects of psychological factors on illness behaviour, having treated complete families over a number of years. In addition, he can refer to a wider range of medical problems than the specialist. However his knowledge of psychology is likely to be even more rudimentry than that of his psychiatric colleague. Even Tait (1974) who strongly argues the case for general practitionery involvement in behavioural science teaching reaches the conclusion that they should 'work along with behavioural scientists to devise learning experiences that combine real life experience with a theoretical input from the basic behavioural sciences' (p. 159). Thus the role of the general practitioner in behavioural science teaching should be to augment the contributions of the more academic lecturers.

Academic Psychologists

There are undoubtedly a number of advantages in having the teaching carried out by academic psychologists from the social science faculty. They are often engaged in research work closely related to the topics they are asked to cover, and are therefore more intimate with the material than someone who has 'mugged it up' from an introductory textbook. Unlike the other contenders for the job, they are professional teachers and are therefore less likely to be overawed by the prospect of facing a group of 100 medical students. Finally, on a practical note, they have ready access to the equipment and materials which are required for laboratory practicals.

However, the evidence to date would suggest that the teaching provided by lecturers from the social science faculty has proved unsatisfactory on the whole. As Todd points out, 'In psychology particularly, the approach of many academic teachers to their subject has offered little of the practical interest which is essential if it is to be attractive and useful to the medical student' (Royal Commission on Medical Education, 1968, para. 248). One can speculate as to the reasons why the contributions of academic psychologists have not, on the whole, been well received by medical students. For instance, it can be argued that the last person to talk at an introductory level about perception, and draw some medically relevant inferences in the absence of hard data, is the university expert on perception. He is too close to the material to make the sorts of generalizations that are required. Another factor is that, since the academic psychologist is not a full-time employee of the medical school, he is perhaps less motivated than a clinician in the hospital to find out about, and try to meet, the needs of the consumer. In other words there is a tendency for the university lecturer to arrive, deliver a sophisticated lecture on his speciality and depart, leaving the students to relate this material to general medicine. The situation is often exacerbated by the fact that the students themselves are often antagonistic to outside speakers, particularly those who have no clinical involvement. Thus the low committal of many academic lecturers, combined with the negative set of the students towards visiting specialists, can lead to a very unsatisfactory learning situation.

Clinical Psychologists

According to the General Medical Council (1977) survey, clinical psychologists make a significant contribution to behavioural science teaching in twenty-three of the thirty-two schools which run courses and, in thirteen of these, no other psychologists are involved. There are a number of reasons why members of this group have been so much in demand as pre-clinical lecturers. In addition to having undergone a full training in psychology, they have had experience of treating patients, working closely with their medical colleagues, and participating in hospital life. Because they are actively involved in clinical work, their credibility, from the point of view of the students, is higher than that of academic specialists. Finally, in view of the fact that clinical psychologists generally participate in the teaching programme organized by psychiatric departments, the case for their involvement at the pre-clinical stage could be argued strongly on continuity grounds alone.

The major disadvantage of using clinical psychologists as pre-clinical lecturers is that they have a tendency to place too much emphasis on abnormal behaviour in their teaching. This after all is their particular field of interest and the fact that it tends to go down well with the students provides further encouragement for concentrating on this area. However, as mentioned above, the provision of a foundation for psychiatry is only one of the many possible objectives of a behavioural science course. The fulfilment of some of the other objectives can only be achieved by lecturers who have a sound knowledge of basic psychological principles. In view of the fact that the majority of clinical psychologists will not have studied many of these concepts since their undergraduate days, it could be argued that they are not familiar enough with the material to teach it effectively. Thus, although clinical psychologists have a valuable contribution to make here, it is arguable whether they should ever be given total responsibility for the organization and teaching of this subject.

Medical Psychologists

There is, as yet, no formally recognized equivalent of medical sociology in the field of psychology. However there is an ever-increasing number of academic and clinical psychologists, working in British hospitals, who have only a tenuous link with the department of psychiatry. Clinical trials research, paediatric assessment, the treatment of hypertension, and medical rehabilitation are just some of the non-psychiatric areas to which psychologists are currently contributing. In view of the scale of this work, Rachman (1977) has proposed that a new subject, called *medical psychology* should be established. He argues that, in addition to providing services such as these, 'Psychology can also expect to benefit medicine as a whole by contributing to theories of illness, concepts of sickness behaviour, doctor–patient relationships, the theory of pain and its alleviation, the behaviour and feelings of doctors, patients' expectations, fears and satisfactions, and many other critical subjects' (p. 7). Although he makes no specific reference to teaching, it would seem to follow that psychologists who are engaged in research of this kind would be strong candidates for the job of organizing and implementing behavioural science courses in conjunction with medical sociologists.

Todd (Royal Commission on Medical Education, 1968, para. 249), however, regards 'with considerable concern' the proposal of building up departments of medical psychology:

Medical schools cannot hope to provide within their own resources first-class departments in all the subjects which are now becoming recognized as desirable in the medical course; moreover, the establishment of rival departments, one teaching the general aspects of the subject and the other its medical applications, could seriously impede the general development of those subjects.

Nevertheless, with the establishment of academic posts of professorial status in several British medical schools, it would seem to follow that departments of medical psychology are becoming a reality. It would seem to follow that those who staff them should be primarily responsible for the teaching of psychology as applied to medicine. To conclude, it is the opinion of this author that the bulk of teaching should be carried out by psychologists who are working in the medical setting. Academic psychologists, working in the medical field, would seem to be the group best qualified to carry out this function, with clinical psychologists the next strongest contenders for the job. Psychiatrists, general practitioners and external academics can make a valuable contribution to the course but their role should be an ancillary one. Generalizations such as these must, of course, be treated cautiously since, in the final analysis, the success of the course depends as much on the lecturers' ability to put the material across in an imaginative and stimulating way as on their professional background.

ASSESSMENT

Twenty-three of the medical schools in the General Medical Council (1977) survey hold formal written examinations in behavioural science. In only five institutions do projects or fieldwork reports contribute to the overall assessment of the students. Since there should be a direct link between objectives and assessment, this is obviously an unsatisfactory state of affairs. It is not possible to gauge the extent to which the student has learned to regard an individual patient as a 'whole person', and developed the skills to put the patient at his ease and help him to understand and follow instructions, from his performance in a written examination. However, other possible procedures, such as providing dummy patient interviews for each student, are clearly impractical. In any case, most universities insist that the written examination should account for the major part of the course assessment. Under the circumstances, therefore, course organizers must attempt to produce an exam paper which will enable them to judge the extent to which each student has grasped the fundamentals of *medical* psychology. This will not be achieved by setting questions of the 'Compare and contrast two theories of personality' type. A more appropriate item might be 'Examine the factors responsible for individual differences in the tendency to report pain'. Thus, in the interests of consistency, it is important that the medical relevance theme should be as apparent in the assessment procedure as in the teaching.

TEACHING METHODS

So far as the traditional subjects are concerned, the importance of the material is usually so self-evident to the students that those who teach it do not have to work hard at trying to 'sell' it. By contrast, those involved in behavioural science courses have to employ a wide range of imaginative techniques in order to get the interest of the students and to help them appreciate the relevance of a subject which is less obviously useful to them. Since the other pre-clinical teachers are interested primarily in imparting facts and teaching skills, most of them see no reason to depart from the long-established format of lecture series combined with laboratory practicals. Psychology teachers, on the other hand, are attempting to produce changes in attitude in addition to achieving these goals, and consequently should be prepared to use less orthodox techniques as well. In recent years, many teachers have experimented with new ideas, and some of the more successful of these enterprises will be described in this section. In addition, the uses and limitations of the more traditional teaching methods will be examined.

Lectures

It is inevitable that with classes of 100 or more students, much of the course time has to be taken up with formal lectures. The inflexible nature of the teaching accommodation, the shortage of fully trained psychologists, and the lack of secretarial back-up services, which are features of most British medical schools, mean that plans for alternative teaching arrangements on a large scale are quite impractical. Consequently, decisions have to be made as to what material can be put across most effectively by this method. Most teachers would agree that those topics with a high factual content, and which are obviously related to medicine (e.g. Unit D, Table 13.1), are most suited to this vehicle. Attempts to get students to appreciate the subtle nuances of the doctor–patient relationship, through didactic teaching, are generally less successful. In other words, the lecture is a more appropriate technique for teaching psychology as a science rather than medicine as an art.

Forums

Much of the material covered in the pre-clinical psychology course is not sufficiently clear-cut to lend itself to the didactic teaching approach. It is included, in many cases, because it encourages the students to question their beliefs concerning a variety of issues which are relevant to medicine. Where diverse interpretations of data are possible, and where these reflect differences in ideological positions, then a panel of speakers can be more effective than a single lecturer in stimulating the students to think about and discuss the topic. One controversial area which lends itself to this mode of presentation is the applicability of the 'medical model' to psychiatry (Unit C, Table 13.1). In the experience of this author, debates between psychiatrists, psychoanalysts, behaviour therapists and personal construct therapists on the nature and causes of abnormal behaviour are particularly well received by the students.

Seminars

The medical education system is not geared to small-group teaching and, consequently, setting up a series of seminars in psychology can be more of an administrative chore here than in other teaching environments. Nevertheless, it is difficult to envisage how some of the course objectives can be achieved if the students are not provided with the opportunity to discuss the relevance of psychological concepts to medicine in an atmosphere conducive to self-disclosure. The seminar provides an ideal setting for enabling students to 'debrief' following visits to community facilities such as old peoples' homes (see Unit A, Table 13.1) and general practitioners' surgeries (see Unit B, Table 13.1). Thus, despite the organizational difficulties, some provision should be made for small-group teaching in every pre-clinical psychology course.

Laboratory Practicals

In their endeavour to break away from the monotony of the formal lecture, some teachers resort to standard psychology practicals (e.g. visual illusions) and attempt to get across the medically relevant message (e.g. symptoms and signs are not always what they appear to be) during the discussion. Such a strategy is rarely effective. As Hooper and Humphrey (1968) point out, 'if it is fair to describe the typical psychology practical as consisting of long periods of idleness interspersed with footling activity then the medical students wanted none of it'. The practical can be a useful teaching device in this setting, but it is essential that the point of the exercise should be always apparent and that the students should be fully occupied throughout. An example of a practical which is well received by medical students (Mulhall, 1978, personal communication) is as follows:

> *Attitudes to medical specialities*
> Students are given personal communication concepts such as 'myself', 'myself as I hope to be when qualified', 'physicians', 'surgeons', and 'general practitioners' and are asked to complete a semantic differential for each of them. They are then shown how to present the results diagrammatically on a three-dimensional graph. The subsequent discussion typically centres on such issues as the 'public image' of medical specialities, the presumed effects of medical education on the individual student, and personality factors in relation to career choice.

Demonstrations

In view of the practical difficulties involved in the organization of seminars and laboratory classes, many teachers choose to use demonstrations in order to clarify the relevance to medicine of material covered in the lectures. In the author's experience, it is advisable, when doing this, to give the non-participating students a clearly specified observation task to carry out in order to maintain their interest. Once again, the point of the exercise should always be apparent. A demonstration, which meets both of these requirements is as follows:

> *Recall of medical instructions*
> Three volunteers from the group are asked to seek an appointment with a particular clinician in the hospital, supposedly in order to get

some experience of being a patient. They are given identical detailed instructions concerning the symptoms they are to present with. The specialist, who has been primed beforehand, gives the same information on each occasion. The real aim of the experiment is to find out how much the students remember of what their doctor told them. Recall is tested immediately after the interview and a few days later in front of the whole group. On this second occasion, the observing students are asked to make a note of omissions, inclusions, and distortions, and also to isolate the types of message (e.g., advice statements) which are most likely to be forgotten. The implications of these findings for medical care are discussed.

Projects

In the majority of pre-clinical courses, students are required to carry out a piece of original research and present the results formally. This may take the form of a tightly structured experiment or, more usually, a survey of patients' attitudes and behaviour. The principal aim of the latter is to give the students the opportunity to visit institutions, general practitioners' surgeries, and patients in their homes in order to help them see illness in a different context to that of the hospital. The following example (Mitchell and Hillier, 1978, personal communication) serves to illustrate the type of project which medical students typically undertake:

Stress and locus of control

The reasons why patients decide to seek help from their doctors at a particular time are investigated by interviewing patients in general practice surgeries. Information about life events (Brown, 1976) is integrated with data from a personality inventory (Rotter, 1966) to determine whether there is any interaction between the two sets of results which can be related to the tendency to seek a consultation.

READING MATERIAL

There is, as yet, no volume which presents psychology as applied to medicine in the way suggested in this chapter, at a level which is suitable for an introductory course. The books fall into two groups. Some are based on the standard undergraduate textbook format (learning, memory, perception, etc.) and include case illustrations and clinical anecdotes to show that they have been written for medical readers.

However, despite the unimaginative way in which the material is presented, health care students prefer them to basic psychology texts. The ones most commonly used are as follows:

Coleman, J. C. (ed.) (1977). *Introductory Psychology: a Text Book for Health Students*. London: Routledge & Kegan Paul.

Hetherington, R. R., Miller, D. H., and Neville, J. G. (1964). *Introduction to Psychology for Medical Students*. London: Heinemann Medical.
McGhie, A. (1973). *Psychology as Applied to Nursing*. Edinburgh: Churchill Livingstone, sixth edition.
Mowbray, R. M., and Rodger, T. F. (1973). *Psychology in Relation to Medicine*. Edinburgh: Churchill Livingstone, fourth edition.

The other books in this area achieve a more successful integration between psychology and medicine but are of limited value to health care students because of their restricted content and relatively high level of sophistication. They are intended to be read primarily by psychologists with an interest in working within non-psychiatric medicine. However they serve as useful reference books, particularly so far as the special topics included in Unit D of Table 13.1 are concerned:

Rachman, S. J. (ed.) (1977). *Contributions to Medical Psychology, Vol. 1*. London: Pergamon.
Rachman, S. J., and Philips, C. (1975). *Psychology and Medicine*. London: Temple Smith.

CONCLUSIONS

As has been shown, there are a number of reasons why psychology courses, in the majority of medical schools, have not been altogether successful. The medical education authorities are unclear about the purpose of psychology teaching and its importance in relation to the basic medical sciences. Moreover, academic psychology has failed to provide a set of coherent guidelines as to how this subject should be taught. To date, the majority of teachers have had interests in other areas and have therefore not been committed to the development of this branch of psychology. The solution, in this author's opinion, is to appoint medical psychologists who will fulfil a consultancy role in the hospital setting, carry out research into the areas mentioned in this chapter, and use this material as the basis for the teaching of medical and para-medical students. Although it is unlikely that the course objectives, as outlined in this chapter, would alter significantly as a result of this, the development of the research and applied functions of the medical psychologist would provide this field with much needed factual content.

However, it has to be recognized that many of the problems of pre-clinical psychology are really the problems of medical education as a whole. The students are unlikely to develop a true psychosomatic approach to medicine so long as psychology teaching is kept isolated from the traditional clinical teaching provided by surgeons and physicians. The fact that these high-status figures typically concentrate on the disease at the expense of the person means that much of the impact of psychology teaching is lost by the time the students qualify. Many would agree with Harper's (1971) viewpoint that psychologists might be better advised to concentrate their efforts on attempting to change the attitudes of their colleagues rather than attempting to devise the perfect medical undergraduate course.

REFERENCES

Banks, S. A. (1974). The Newcomers: Humanities and Social Sciences in Medical Education. *Texas Reports on Biology and Medicine*, **32**, 19–30.

Bennet, G. (1976). Whole-person Medicine and Psychiatry for Medical Students. *Lancet*, **1960**, 623–626.

Bloch, S. (1973). Goals in the Teaching of Behavioural Sciences to Medical Students. *British Journal of Medical Education*, **7**, 239–243.

Brown, G. W. (1976). Social Causes of Disease. In: Tuckett, D. (ed.). *Medical Sociology*. London: Tavistock, pp. 291–333.

Colman, J. C., and Mackay, D. (1975). The Teaching of Psychology in Medical Schools. *Bulletin of the British Psychological Society*, **28**, 55–58.

Davis, D. R. (1970). Behavioural Science in the Pre-clinical Curriculum. *British Journal of Medical Education*, **4**, 194–197.

General Medical Council (1967). Recommendations as to Basic Medical Education.

General Medical Council (1977). Conference on the Objectives of Basic Medical Education.

Graham White, J. (1970). Synopsis of a Symposium. *British Journal of Medical Education*, **4**, 198–201.

Griffiths, R. D. P. (1976). The Teaching of Psychology in Medical Schools: A Pat on the Back or a Kick in the Pants? *Bulletin of the British Psychological Society*, **29**, 269–273.

Harper, A. C. (1971). The Social Scientist in Medical Education: The Specialist's Safeguard. *Social Science and Medicine*, **5**, 663–665.

Hooper, D., and Humphrey, N. (1968). Behavioural Science for Pre-clinical Students. *Lancet*, **ii**, 1293–1295.

Mackay, D. (1975). *Clinical Psychology: Theory and Therapy*. London: Methuen.

Mitchell, W. I., and Hillier, S. (1978). Personal Communication.

Mulhall, D. J. (1978). Personal Communication.

Pritchard, J. J. (1970). Soma Without Psyche. *British Journal of Medical Education*, **4**, 185–188.

Rachman, S. J. (1977). *Contributions to Medical Psychology Vol. 1*. Oxford: Pergamon.

Rotter, J. B. (1966). Generalised Expectancies for Internal versus External Control of Reinforcement. *Psychological Monographs*, **80**, No. 1 (Whole No. 609). Royal Commission on Medical Education (1968). *Report 1965–1968*. Cmnd. 3569. London: HMSO.

Sheldrake, P. (1974). Behavioural Science: Medical Students' Expectations and Reactions. *British Journal of Medical Education*, **8**, 31–48.

Tait, I. (1974). Person-centred Perspectives in Medicine. *Journal of the Royal College of General Practitioners*, **24**, 151–160.

Truax, C. B., and Carhhuff, R. R. (1964). Significant Developments in Psychotherapy Research. In: Abt, L.E., and Reiss, B. F. (eds). *Progress in Clinical Psychology*. New York: Grune & Stratton.

Tuckett, D. (1976). *An Introduction to Medical Sociology*. London: Tavistock.

Winefield, H. R. (in press). Behavioural Science in the Medical Curriculum: Why and How? In: Christie, M. J., and Mellett, P. G. (eds). *The Psychosomatic Approach in Medicine, Vol. 1*. London: Wiley.

The Teaching of Psychology
Edited by J. Radford and D. Rose
© 1980 John Wiley & Sons Ltd.

14

The Social Work Context

ELIZABETH P. MCWHIRTER

EXPECTATIONS?

This chapter endeavours to cater principally to the perceived needs of the
new or potential teacher of psychology within the broad context of social work;
that is, on courses such as social work itself but also to students of counselling
and guidance, youth work or community work. Some of the points may appear
obvious, even banal—in the sense of being unpretentious. If this is the case,
so much the better. What follows is derived from personal experience allied
to material which emerged from a brief survey of the teaching of psychology
within the context at the present time. However, undoubtedly due more to
the former than latter, the discussion at times will undoubtedly see-saw between
seemingly fixed alternatives; within psychology, alternatives such as pure
versus applied, scientific or experimental versus personal or humanistic.
Unfortunately space does not permit consideration of the relationships between, for example, the professions of social work, community work, youth
work and counselling, or between the practice, for example, of clinical psychology, counselling and guidance, psychotherapy or 'case-work'. (See Hughes,
1976; Daws, 1976; Vaughan, 1976; Watts, 1977; Hopson and Scally, 1977,
for brief but interesting discussions on these issues.)

How psychology within the context of social work might be developed is
of paramount importance. Some new and exciting approaches are considered
but clearly much depends on how the professional contexts and practices
themselves develop. This is particularly true of the newer professions within
the context but equally applies to social work itself. For example if the New
Careers Model for the disadvantaged (Hodgkin, 1973) becomes more widely
established, one can immediately see that if the student in his professional
principles and practice is considering methods of intervention which do not

reinforce the clients' dependency, supportive psychological substance would include core topics such as extrinsic and intrinsic reinforcement, self-esteem, achievement motivation, attribution theory, etc.

A central theme is that psychology merits more than an ancillary role; it must be one of the core curricular elements and must also be an integral part of the students' total experience. The chapter cannot consider separately different levels of student and it also tends to fluctuate between the separate professional roles within the social work areas in the assumption that the students have sufficient common needs with regard to psychology. The principal concern is with the application of psychological concepts, theories and research to the wide field of social work, but, of course, the approaches and material which any particular teacher will use must be tailored to the particular needs of a particular professional group working in a particular environment. Hopefully after reading this chapter the teacher of psychology will consciously avoid the common error of offering nothing more than what one correspondent called 'techniquery', and jargon to those who may be in a vacuum as to their identity and professional role, but instead will be able to offer some useful frameworks, approaches and content to effectively guide professional action.

WHERE?

The teaching of psychology in a social work context shares many of the characteristics of the teaching of psychology within any professional area, but it does have particular features which highlight some of the challenges, tensions and frustrations of teaching the discipline to professional students as well as some of the satisfactions. Preferred models of training, curricula and methods of teaching depend not only on the basic definitions of psychology which proponents of differing viewpoints presume but also on the characteristics of the context in which the psychology is being taught. The academic psychologist, in striving to offer a relevant curriculum might search for his base in requirements stipulated by 'The Profession' regarding the education and training of its students allied to an identification of skills based upon theoretical knowledge (McWhirter, 1974). The whole question of training is valid only to the extent that success might be determined by the conscious application of techniques, but the true professional, unlike the tradesman, is not a mechanical purveyor of techniques; his practice must be related to a systematic discipline base which he understands.

However, because definitions tend to be somewhat arbitrary and simplistic, many professionals find difficulty in providing criterial characteristics for their occupation or in precisely delineating their role. This is particularly the case in the field of social work: the context is ill defined and the role of the professional worker is both diverse and diffuse.

Socal work is concerned with the interaction between people and their social environment which affects the ability of people to accomplish their life tasks, alleviate distress and realise their aspirations and values. The purpose of social work, therefore, is to:
(1) enhance the problem-solving and coping capacities of people;
(2) link people with systems and provide them with resources, services and opportunities;
(3) promote the effective and human operation of these systems; and
(4) contribute to the development and improvement of social policy
(Pincus and Minahan, 1973).

This quotation, taken from a standard text in social work practice, is undoubtedly open to challenge. Nevertheless, by focusing on the relationships and interactions between people and resource systems and the problems to be faced in the functioning of both individuals and systems, it illustrates the immense breadth and complexity of the context of social work. Social work involves counselling or casework, in its dealing with the relationships of family life and social factors related to mental and emotional illness, subnormality and deviancy, but it also encompasses vast areas of social need as a legitimate concern. New methods are continually being explored in order to relieve suffering and poverty—statutory care provisions, citizens' rights, social action, community work. Thus the social work spectrum includes a wide band of 'helping professions' and 'caring organizations', both statutory and voluntary, which encompass the areas of *counselling, community* work and *youth* work.

There are many types of professional 'social worker' each characterized by the specialized context in which he works: social service departments, child care, residential work, probation services, prison welfare, education welfare, psychiatric setting, voluntary agencies, etc. Clearly the constellation of social work tasks are not inflexible; they are situational. The diverse institutional settings influence the precise job requirements and render some of the purposes of social work (such as those above itemized by Pincus and Minahan) more important or relevant than others, but permeating all of these specialized roles is the generic concept '*social work*'.

The remainder of the chapter will therefore focus on a range of component activities, skills and knowledge of common concern to various practitioners, irrespective of their specific professional roles. What follows is not fully exhaustive, of course, but it is a blend of personal observations and comment, and information obtained from a number of different departments and/or courses offering training in 'social work', or 'guidance' and/or 'counselling' or 'youth' and/or 'community' work. In these contexts consideration of aims, principles and approaches is of vital importance, and, in view of the immense range of content available, is undoubtedly of greater import than concentrating only on substance.

WHAT? AND WHY?

In the context of social work, counselling, youth and community work it is of vital importance to consider aims, principles and approaches before looking at the content in detail. Official publications from professional organizations and directories of training (e.g. Bolger, 1977) suggest that human development appears to be generally recognized as a prime psychological area of study for the social work student. However, McWhirter (1978) has argued forcibly against a discrete developmental course alone for professional students. This can serve as a useful exemplar of the tensions and frustrations existing between the discipline specialist and practitioner of that discipline, and also underlines the problems faced by the teacher of psychology who not only tries to cater for the needs of the social work student but who, as an academic, is also keen to work within the internal constraints of the discipline and to represent fairly the current state of psychology.

Contemporary developmental psychology has an ultimate concern for development of the whole person, but almost inevitably as the field has developed it has become molecular rather than molar. In consequence, it has diversified into a number of more or less discrete areas, each with its own theories, problems and techniques of investigation. The scientific psychologist may propound the philosophy that prediction and control necessitate 'good' theory and a sound basis in understanding; as a developmentalist he may admit to the inability of his emergent discipline to provide solutions to many problems of professional concern. Conversely, however, the question remains as to whether he can do justice to his discipline if he fails to consider the few existing sophisticated research methodologies used to uncover the 'facts' about development throughout the life-span.

Developmental psychology undoubtedly has the basic concepts, information and methodology for the observation. analysis and understanding of the behaviour of people of different ages and also of the psychological changes within individuals with age but, by itself, it lacks a basis for the understanding of problems as encountered in social work. Furthermore, also missing in a conventional developmental course is a means for bridging the gap between theory and practice. Developmental psychology for the social work student must be seen in a context wider than developmental processes. It must be merged with a study of *individuals* and *individual differences* and be supplemented with *abnormal* and *clinical psychology*. Social work is largely concerned with individuals and individuals who have social and/or psychological problems: differential psychology is now re-emerging as a respectable area worthy of academic study; clinical psychology has a very well developed technology for professional application regarding the analysis and change of individual behaviour. Such an integrated psychology course should facilitate a bridging between the psychological theory, concepts and knowledge necessary for the understanding of behaviour and the psychological techniques required for changing behaviour.

Furthermore such a course would espouse more than 'pure' psychology, application would emerge as of paramount interest. It would also inescapably challenge the scientific paradigm which typifies contemporary developmental psychology (and, of course, so much of psychology in general); humanistic approaches would feature large.

Much has been said of late about the similarities and differences between scholarly, scientific and professional pursuits and the debate is of particular relevance in discussing the modus operandi of the social work student. For the pure psychologist *understanding* is a guiding principle which is well served by the scientific paradigm. Behaviour *changes*, however, are the domain of most practictioners of psychology; the social worker in the generic sense views 'observation, analysis and understanding' as a context for change. He needs to be both 'reflective and effective' (Davidson, 1977). Method must therefore be supplemented with relevant substance, and a greater desire on the part of the psychologist to be concerned with the importance of his data; problems and products must take precedence over methodology (Azrin, 1977).

As Albee and Loeffler (1971) remind us, scientists are concerned with falsifiable statements; the scientific experimental training of the academic psychologist leads him to avoid errors of incautious assertion, particularly type I errors which assert relationships falsely at the expense of relatively frequent type II errors which deny relationships which do actually exist. As a scientist, he should maintain an open mind regarding the methods of enquiry and a healthy scepticism regarding the validity of his results. By contrast, the professional student in social work is mainly concerned with learning how to apply the best available knowledge to the solution or relief of human problems, and to matters of social concern. He must focus on his client and cannot luxuriate only in clearly definable questions.

Moreover, the social worker must often act on the basis of weakly supported propositions and thus risk type I errors since ignoring significant relationships may be as damaging to the client as presuming relationships which do not exist. Also, he may at times need to act with a confidence which available psychological knowledge does not justify. Thus public criteria of an open method plus conservatively formulated conclusions, hallmarks of scientific psychology today, might destroy effective professional action (Peterson, 1976).

If this persuasive argument is extrapolated to the teaching of a relevant curriculum for the social work student it would appear that data or 'facts' about behaviour should take precedence. Furthermore, the less scientific, the 'soft' personal aspects of psychology should also merit due consideration— perhaps these are of *more* relevance to professional practice.

Selection and organization of psychological material on any course is a formidable task but, for the individual teacher of psychology in the social work context, the job is less vast due not only to the nature of the social work context itself, but also the particular professional orientation of the course in which he is involved, its structure, the amount of time available, the level of student, the teacher's own academic and professional background and psychological biases, etc. It is obvious, for example, that a course of counselling within education which specializes in developmental counselling with clear educational objectives will manifest a very different scope, emphasis and purpose than one which espouses a clinical, psychotherapeutic orientation to counselling with mental health and prophylactic aims (see Daws, 1976, for further elaboration). Similarly a two-year certificate course for youth workers will probably be tailored for a less academically qualified or sophisticated group of students than a Masters degree in social work.

In outlining a range of topics within psychology deemed relevant to the student of social work, counselling or youth and community work, it is assumed that this material might be presented to the student in a variety of ways (see next section). He might also encounter it either in a course on psychology or as a component of professional practice and/or principles. However, if the two strands of psychology and professional training are not integrated, they must be intimately related and interdependent.

How this might be achieved permeates the remainder of this section although the next section, which considers appropriate teaching and learning methods, focuses particularly on this problematic area of teaching not only relevant but also influential psychology.

Rather than attempt to prescribe a certain substance, which would be undesirable, if not impossible, the key areas considered important and worthy of inclusion within psychology (on the basis of the foregoing deliberations) will be surveyed with the aid of selected references (Appendices 14.1 to 14.3). Although the lists are selective and not mutually exclusive, it is hoped that by directing attention, by and large, to some recent publications within a few general areas, the psychology teacher will find it easier to build a solid edifice, and one which will be tailor-made to suit the resources and needs of the particular occupants and also the particular builder.

Appendix 14.2 details some texts on *introductory* and *general psychology* which the teacher and student should find interesting, relevant and challenging. The selection of books was shaped by a belief that social work, community work and counselling all mean 'being something' as well as 'doing something' and that psychology in this context must be, first and foremost, about people. Psychology can be presented with both its practical and personal bases; to demystify people if not to dehumanize them. Empirical psychology can fruitfully be seen as a form of behaviour; a grounding in psychological methodologies can form the foundation for the later practice of the professional student in his relating and interacting with others and also in his problem-centred activities. A methodological approach to teaching empirical psychology should also facilitate the development in the student of a critical, evaluative attitude to professional practice and hence develop the profession. This approach is currently being developed in an exciting and imaginative way at one Youth and Community Department[1] in an attempt to make psychology more meaningful and more influential. The approach follows a 'psychological approach to psychology teaching' (Hobbs and Cornwell, 1977) within a 'behaviour influences' framework so that by studying what psychologists actually do and the context in which the action takes place, the student can learn how to behave more like a psychologist in his professional encounters with people. What these authors advocate is a focus on the similarity between the processes the psychologist describes in his subjects and the processes the professional engages in.

Psychology, introduced as a mode of exploration, rather than merely a body of specific knowledge to apply, with an emphasis on means and processes as well as outcome involves a vast range of approaches, empirical and theoretical, utilized by psychologists in order to articulate knowledge and experiences. These can be sampled successfully—from the very scientific pole of the psychological continuum, with its goal of objectivity and rigour in thought and empirical methods of investigation, hypothesis formulation and verification, to the opposite pole, humanistic psychology, with its concern for experience rather than behaviour and performance, and its involvement with the affective, most personal aspects of people. The content perhaps should be, for the social work student, emotionally as well as intellectually challenging.

Appendix 14.2 provides a selected, and of necessity, a brief list of recent books within areas of particular relevance viz: (a) *development throughout the life-span*; (b) *self* (personality in general could, of course, cover a wide range of theoretical approaches, e.g. psychodynamic, phenomenological, transactional, existential, self-actualization, construct, social learning); (c) *interpersonal behaviour* and *group work;* (d) *social skills training*; and (e) the application of these areas to the *changing of people's behaviour*.

The selected references on behaviour change span the general areas of *casework* and *counselling* and specific models and techniques, but focus particularly on relevant topics within *abnormal* and *clinical* psychology—including a whole fascinating panorama of the wonderful (and sometimes weird) varieties of psychotherapeutic techniques which exist and which are applicable within the social work context. The sample of recent references in no way constitutes an inclusive review of the current psychotherapeutic scene; such a review would be impossible in view of the recent explosion of interest and the many thousands of publications which have resulted. The aim of the teacher should therefore be, in sampling the range of techniques, to convey to the student a sense of the divergent goals, methods and ideologies underlying the different approaches—such as the traditional developmental–historical approach (e.g. classical psychoanalysis) and the more modern approaches such as the behaviourist approach (e.g. operant therapy, token economies, aversion therapy, desensitization therapy, modelling), humanistic and existential approaches (e.g. Roger's client-centred therapy, construct and repertory-grid techniques, transactional analysis, Gestalt therapy) or the rational problem solving approach (e.g. reality therapy, Ellis' rational-emotive therapy).

The teacher and student may well consider that some of these extravagant and putative therapies, like Primal therapy, belong (if anywhere) within the National Health Service rather than the social work context. However, by at least considering the immense range of special circumstances used in therapy for producing change; 'intimate disclosures from one person and interpretations from another over many years; disclosures about the self, unfailingly met with empathy and approval from another; groups devoted to studying their own group processes; rewards made absolutely contingent on desired actions; practice in relaxing while imagining things that ordinarily make you anxious; screaming and throwing fits either solo or in concert' (Brown and Hernstein, 1975, p. 622), the professional worker who is constantly critical of his practice and of its theoretical bases should come to the realization that the problems of psychotherapy are the problems of psychology—personal, affective characteristics and cognitive processes such as perception, attention, discrimination, learning, transfer and cognitive structure, as well as group processes; in other words, psychology as a whole.

HOW?

Conventional Teaching Methods

Traditional teaching methods used in tertiary education, including the more passive methods, used judiciously and by a psychology teacher consciously aware of the student's professional needs, can serve a valuable training function in social work in addition to their usual didactic purpose. For instance, the lecture in its conventional form provides a good training for the potential social worker who will be required to attend closely to and perhaps record accurately, but in brief form, the meaning of words spoken by his client. Directed reading can serve as a welcome alternative to lectures especially for the social work student who is also able to benefit from small-group seminars and/or individual tutorials which are more akin to the interpersonal encounters he will meet professionally. In this way the potential professional worker is able to develop a variety of effective communication skills which he will need for interviewing, etc., in the field. When the student is required to present a paper prepared by him on a predetermined topic it is useful professional practice for him to 'talk it' rather than read it verbatim, as he might be required to do at a case conference. The individual tutorial also allows the social work student close contact on a contractual basis, somewhat analogous to the professional–client relationship. Programmed learning and learning packages are also useful in this context especially with students from widely different educational backgrounds, and with students on different lengths and levels of course. Self-paced learning is also extremely suitable for restoring the intellectual self-confidence of the mature student (perhaps seconded in order to obtain a professional qualification) who has not engaged in academic pursuits for many years. A useful model which the teacher may follow is that adopted in many Open University course units for professional students learning at a distance (see, for example, *P252, An Ageing Population* and *P251, The Handicapped Person in the Community*).

The above teaching methods are commonly used, of course, in tertiary education in academic courses where the emphasis is on the acquisition of knowledge but the student of social work is more concerned with application—doing and being: the practitioner of psychology will be required to employ a well-developed repertoire of skills and, as the essential instrument through which his professional practice is mediated, he must also be helped explicity to gain self-insight. Therefore, alternative modes of teaching and learning are desirable.

Learning in the Field: Practical Placements

A deep-seated conviction in the value of learning through experience underlies the concept of practical placements (or learning in the field) which is a hallmark of professional training in many different contexts. Rather than learning by academic methods only about the nature of professional practice—impressions, beliefs about current practice, or practice 'in theory'—the student experiences practice as it actually occurs and, with a judicious choice of placements, he has the opportunity to sample a variety of situations, agencies, problems,etc. While this may be seen as a vital component of professional principles and practice it also provides an arena for experimenting with and testing of psychological concepts, methods and theories at work. A dilemma for all professional educators concerns the theories espoused by the worker and those which can be deduced from his actual behaviour in the field. This paradox of training, so well aired by Argyris and Schon (1974), clearly suggests the need for college-based learning and activity to anticipate and follow-up professional placement so that theory and practice may be merged.

A number of different approaches to this are possible within the framework of psychology teaching. One is to have a graduated programme of skills training (see below) prior to each placement, and perhaps concurrently with it, allied to a concentration by the student on special aspects, or certain facets, of practice on each placement.

One school which follows a skills-based approach[2] also utilizes joint placement visits by both the professional tutor and the academic specialist. By giving psychology tutorials on placement it is hoped that the student may be aided to apply psychological insights to problems he is engaged in at that moment, and that the psychology teacher will gain a greater understanding of professional practice which should illuminate his teaching. Thus the benefit is two-fold.

One may also adopt a problem-centred approach to the psychology teaching which relates explicitly to fieldwork practice. On one course,[3] for example, the tutors believe that while there are few generally agreed facts or theories for the social or community worker to rely on, and no agreed framework of formal learning for the newer helping professions, something is known about the sorts of problems a worker is likely to face. Thus students are, to a large extent, responsible for their own learning and increasingly involve themselves in professional situations of their own choice. Information derived from psychological investigation is included, as and when it is relevant, in discussions with students, separately and in groups (e.g. a lecture series on adolescence and on deviance) and also in specific projects in the field work. However, the students' major resource is considered to be 'a capacity to get on with a wide variety of people, to understand and learn from them' and it is thought that he needs to develop 'sensitivity, courage and flexibility'.

Skills Training

Training in the specialized skills of the profession for which students are being prepared is now recognized by many to hold a central position particularily in pre-service training. Formerly the training of social work students consisted largely of a lot of theoretical input with little practical links but it is now widely believed that the trainee should be more equipped on a more practical level to face the realities and actual problems of field work. Placing the student in the field is one way for him to gain some experience of the job, as considered above, and until lately supervised placements were the only form of practical training used within the social work context. It is now being increasingly recognized, however, particularly within the sub-area of counselling, that the training offered by placements is more effective if preceded by a graduated programme of activities related to the component skills of professional practice. Clearly it is advantageous if students have the opportunity to acquire their basic skills in the 'safe' atmosphere of the college department rather than risking the mis-handling of a 'real' social work situation. Immediate and accurate feedback (e.g. through CCTV replay), coupled with an encouragement to evaluate critically the simulated interaction which has just occurred in the give and take of small-group discussion, involving tutor and peers, helps foster an objective self-awareness and enables the student to become more sensitive and perceptive in social situations (Hargie and Caul, 1977; Hargie, Tittmar and Dickson, 1977). A well-planned programme of skills training also facilitates the development of a commitment to the profession and to the attitudes and values upon which it is based (Fulton, 1978).

The effectiveness of the practical skills programme will be increased if it occurs across a number of practical placements so that cases and problems the student has encountered in the field can be further analysed, discussed and rehearsed (anonymously, of course) in college. In this way, a link is made between theory and practice and also between simulated and real practice. At one department,[4] for example, teachers underwent training in guidance and counselling progress through four stages in their skills training programme: structured exercises; micro-situations (involving closed-circuit television recordings and role plays); longer simulations (examples drawn from placement); video and/or audiotapes made on placement. In another course,[5] a similar attempt is made to shift from the micro to the macro situation in training undergraduate social work students with a move from 'microcounselling' to 'thematic' analysis of professional practice. Students devise role-play situations on the basis of recent practical experience in the field in order to facilitate the analysis of such themes as confidentiality; self-determination; explanation of agency function; the family as a social system; ongoing assessment with the individual family or groups; settings for decision making, e.g. juvenile court.

Specific counselling skills which have been identified range from the specifically behavioural to the more global type of communication or social skill, and involve both individual and group skills, verbal and non-verbal aspects of communication. Hargie and Caul (1977), for example, identify the following skills: set induction, closure, variation, minimal encouragers, paraphasers, reflection of feeling, questioning.

Experiential Learning Methods

To the uninitiated the phrase 'experiential learning' may conjure up images of students indulging in psychologically adventurous, and at times perhaps psychologically dangerous, games. The assumption, however, among those who advocate learning through personal experience is that self-knowledge is correlated with one's ability to help others. Therefore, the prime intent is to involve the student in a real-life disciplined study of himself as a person and to enable him to have a deeper and more accurate understanding of who and what he is. This approach should help integrate theory and practice since it provides the means for transferring psychological concepts and theories into action. In dealing with the here and now experiences as they occur, it represents the reflexive nature of psychology—the scientist studying himself at work.

Of course, the area of personal growth can be approached indirectly by traditional academic teaching methods, as indicated above, by providing a psychological climate conducive to self-exploration, but, more formally, self-knowledge can be acquired by the student in regular and continuing experiences which involve interpersonal-dynamics and interactive skills. Few would argue that in introducing students to therapy, the teacher must go beyond the ideas which lie behind the different therapies and what goes on in the different types of therapeutic sessions; the professional student must also consider their benefits, limits and risks. Some would go further and argue that he must also experience at least some of them himself—the 'becoming' referred to earlier as opposed to the 'knowing' and 'doing'. As Lieberman, Yalom and Miles (1973, p. 4) have noted, the general aim of group work is to attempt to provide an intensive, high-contact group experience. Groups are generally small enough (six to twenty members) to permit a lot of face-to-face interaction so that self and social awareness are increased and behaviour change is possible. As a means to these ends group members are usually encouraged towards openness, honesty, self-disclosure, strong emotional expression and interpersonal confrontation.

Clearly, however, not everyone would have the skill, let alone the desire, to use as a starting point people's immediate experience of each other in a small-group setting and to work back from this by examining concepts and information from different research areas as and when appropriate. The aim, however, is simply to encourage the fusion of the didactic aspect of training with the experiential. One department,[6] which aims to demystify and to deprofessionalize counselling, professes a skills approach but experiential methods of learning play an important role in developing in the student an awareness of the appropriate personal and interpersonal skills. As Hobson and Scally (1977) state 'the main mode of developing individual counselling skills is experiential, with participants having an opportunity to discover their own counselling strength and areas for development, and to practice new techniques'. Attendance at such a course is a prerequisite and the student is also given 'an experiential introduction to group dynamics, including the topics of leadership, power, decision-making, group norms and climate, with an opportunity to practise group discussion, leading and co-leadership'.

Experiential learning is only one way to help develop in the student an ability to be able to articulate his own implicit psychological theories and to compare these with formal psychological theories so that he can permit his work to be influenced by psychological teaching on reasoned and real terms rather than on authority or textbook grounds. Thus the theories which he actually follows in his practice should more closely mirror those which he professes, and his increasing effectiveness in practice should also be accompanied by increasing psychological sophistication—one hallmark of a successful student from a successful course of psychology in the social work context.

Thus in concluding, one might say that for those who wish to become professional workers within the broad context of social work, psychology in its broadest and deepest sense provides one vital source of knowledge, but experience (practical and personal) plus self-knowledge provide others which enable the former to be translated into effective practice.

ACKNOWLEDGEMENTS

The author wishes to think the many psychology lecturers and professional tutors who so kindly provided information with regard to their own experience of the teaching of psychology in the general field of social work. It is very difficult to give an adequate account within a single chapter and without their help the picture would undoubtedly have been biased and unrepresentative of the current scene. Responsibility for the generalizations, advice and suggestions which emerged rests, of course, firmly with the author. Thanks are also due to the typist who so patiently struggled with untidy scribbles, changes of mind and corrections on top of corrections.

NOTES

The author wishes to thank the following people for the relevant information:
1 David Cornwell of Jordanhill College of Education, Scotland.
2 Eilean Wornock of Ulster College, Northern Ireland Polytechnic.
3 Harold Marchant of Goldsmiths' College, University of London.
4 Professor Sean Fulton of Queen's University, Belfast.
5 Brian Caul of Ulster College, Northern Ireland Polytechnic.
6 Peter Heaviside of the North East London Polytechnic.

APPENDIX 14.1: SOME RECENT BOOKS PARTICULARLY APPROPRIATE WITHIN THE SOCIAL WORK CONTEXT TO THE TEACHING OF *INTRODUCTORY* AND *GENERAL PSYCHOLOGY*

Dempsey, D., and Zimbardo, P. G. (1977). *Psychology and You: A Student's Introduction*. London: Scott, Foresman.

Deriega, V. J., and Janda, L. (1978). *Personal Adjustment: The Psychology of Everyday Life*. London: General Learning Press.

Eysenck, H. J. (1977). *Psychology is About People*. Harmondsworth: Allen Lane Press.

McNeill, E. B., and Rubin, Z. (1977). *The Psychology of Being Human*. London: Harper and Row, second edition.

Pollack, O. (1976). *Human Behaviour and the Helping Professions*. New York: Wiley.

Wertheimer, M., and Rappoport, L. (1978). *Psychology and the Problems of Today*. London: Scott, Foresman.

Zimbardo, P. G., and Ruch, F. L. (1977). *Psychology and Life*. London: Scott, Foresman.

APPENDIX 14.2: SOME SELECTED REFERENCES TO RECENT BOOKS ON AREAS WITHIN PSYCHOLOGY OF PARTICULAR RELEVANCE

The Developing Child Series (dates from 1977). London: Open Books.

Life-span Human Development Series (dates from 1978). California: Brooks/Cole.

Maier, H. W. (1978). *Three Theories of Child Development* (Revised edition). New York: Harper & Row, third edition.

Shaw, J. (1978). *The Self in Social Work*. London: Routledge & Kegan Paul.

Calhoun, D. W. (1976). *Persons-In-Groups: A Humanistic Social Psychology*. New York: Harper & Row.

Priestly, P., Mcguire, J., Hemsley, V., Flegg, D., and Williams, D. (1978). *Social Skills and Personal Problem Solving. A Handbook*. London: Tavistock.

Trower, P., Bryant, B., and Argyle, M. (1978). *Social Skills and Mental Health*. London: Methuen.

Adams-Webber, J. (1979). *Personal Construct Theory: Concepts and Applications*. Chichester: Wiley.

Bolger, A. W. (ed.) (1977). *Training in Counselling: A Directory* (revised edition). London: The British Association for Counselling.

Fischer, J. (1978). *Effective Casework Practice. An Eclectic Approach*. New York: McGraw-Hill.

Fix, A. J., and Haffke, E. H. (1976). *Basic Psychological Therapies: Comparative Effectiveness*. London: Human Sciences Press.

Fransella, F., and Bannister, D. (1977). *A Manual for Repertory Grid Techniques*. New York: Academic Press.

Gambrill, E. D. (1977). *Behaviour Modification: Handbook of Assessment, Intervention and Evaluation*. London: Josey-Bass.

Grayson, H., and Loew, C. (1978). *Changing Approaches to the Psychotherapies*. Chichester: Wiley.

Herbert, M. (1978). *Conduct Disorders of Childhood and Adolescence: A Behavioural Approach to Assessment and Treatment*. London: Wiley.

Lewis, J., and Lewis, M. (1977). *Community Counselling: A Human Services Approach*. New York: Wiley.

Sinick, D. (1978). *Counselling Older Persons: Careers, Retirement, Dying*. London: Human Sciences Press.

APPENDIX 14.3: VALUABLE SOURCES OF INFORMATION FOR THE PSYCHOLOGIST TEACHING WITHIN THE SOCIAL WORK CONTEXT

British Association for Counselling (BAC) (formerly Standing Conference for the Advancement of Counselling), la Little Church Street, Rugby, CV21 3AT. This organization, a registered charity, acts as a facilitating and co-ordinating body for a variety of organizations and individual members. It is concerned with education and training, standards of counselling, exchange of information, courses, conferences and occasional publications, and has different divisions covering counselling work in different fields.

Careers Research and Advisory Centre (CRAC), Bateman Street, Cambridge. This centre is an important source of literature on the whole field of careers work.

The Psychology and Psychotherapy Association (PPA). The PPA was started in 1973 and is now 'a multidisciplinary organization for people who are professionally or academically involved in trying to understand and offer therapeutic or educational assistance to others and who recognize the importance of their own personal involvement in the work they do'. Local area groups provide contexts for learning, training and mutual support. Workshops and training meetings are organized annually and the journal *PPA Forum* is published quarterly. Current Secretary is W. S. Barnes, Psychology Department, Rainhill Hospital, Prescot, Merseyside, L35 4PQ.

Central Council for the Education and Training of Social Workers (CCETSW), Central Office, Derbyshire House, St Chad's Street, London, WC1 H8AE. This body is concerned, among other things, with the validation of social work courses in Great Britain and the social work qualifications of individuals wishing to work in Great Britain who have been trained elsewhere.

American Personnel and Guidance Association (APGA), 1607 New Hampshire Avenue NW, Washington DC, 20009 USA.

Also in Washington:

The American Psychological Association (APA) has a Counselling Division and the National Training Laboratories run courses on group work.

REFERENCES

Albee, G. W., and Loeffler, E. (1971). Role Conflicts in Psychology and Their Implications for a Re-evaluation of Training Models. *Canadian Psychologist*, 4, 465–481.

Argyris, C., and Schon, D. (1974). *Theories in Practice: Increasing Professional Effectiveness*. San Francisco: Josey-Bass.

Azrin, N. H. (1977). A Strategy for Applied Research Learning Based but Outcome Oriented. *American Psychologist*, February 1977, 140–149.

Bolger, A. W. (ed.) (1977). *Training in Counselling: A Directory*. London: British Association for Counselling.

Brown, R., and Hernstein, R. J. (1975). *Psychology*. London: Methuen.

Davidson, M. A. (1977). The Scientific/Applied Debate in Psychology: A Contribution. Presidential Address to the British Psychological Society. Exeter, April 1977. Reproduced in *Bulletin of the British Psychological Society*, **30**, 273–278.

Daws, P. P. (1976). *Early Days. A Personal Review of the Beginnings of Counselling in English Education during the Decade 1964–1974*. Cambridge: Careers Research and Advising Centre.

Fulton, S. (1978). *Training in Counselling Skills*. Paper given at the Annual Conference of the Northern Ireland Section of the British Psychological Society. Virginia, Co. Cavan, Eire, May 1978.

Hargie, O. D. W., and Caul, B. (1977). The Role of Microcounselling in Relation to Social Work Training. *Quest: Journal of Social Work and Welfare Law in Ulster*, October, 1977, No. 7.

Hargie, O. D. W., Tittmar, H. G., and Dickson, D. A. (1977). Social Skills Training: Applying the Concept on a Careers Guidance Course. *Bulletin of the British Psychological Society*, **30**, 214–216.

Hargie, O. D. W., Tittmar, H. G., and Dickson, D. A. (1978). Microtraining: A Systematic Approach to Social Work Practice. *Social Work Today*, **9** (31), 14–16.

Hobbs, S., and Cornwell, D. (1977). A Psychological Approach to Psychology Teaching. *Further Education*, **2**, 21–25.

Hodgkin, N. (1973). *New Careers for the Disadvantaged: NACRO Papers and Reprints No. 8*. London: National Assoc. for the Care and Resettlement of Offenders.

Hopson, B., and Scally, M. (1977). Demystifying and Deprofessionalising Counselling: The CCDU Approach. *The Counsellor*, **2** (2), 32–35.

Hughes, P. M. (1976). The Place of Psychology in Counsellor Education. *Psychology Teaching*, **4**, 33–27.

Lieberman, M. A., Yalom, I. D., and Miles, M. B. (1973). *Encounter Groups: First Facts*. New York: Harper & Row.

McWhirter, E. P. (1974). The Psychology Syllabus in Interpersonal Professional Courses. *Bulletin of the British Psychological Society*, **27**, 493–496.

McWhirter, E. P. (1978). Expectation and Frustration: Developmental Psychology for Professional Courses. *Psychology Teaching*, **6**, 12–19.

Peterson, D. R. (1976). Is Psychology a Profession? *American Psychologist*, August 1976, 572–581.

Pincus, A., and Minahan, A. (1973). *Social Work Practice: Model and Method*. Atasca, Illinois: F. E. Peacock.

Vaughan, T. D. (ed.) (1976). *Concepts of Counselling*. London: Bedford Square Press.

Watts, A. G. (ed.) (1977). *Counselling at Work*. London: Bedford Square Press.

The Teaching of Psychology
Edited by J. Radford and D. Rose
© 1980 John Wiley & Sons Ltd.

15

The Educational Context

DENNIS CHILD

HISTORICAL PERSPECTIVE

Of all the conceivable ways in which psychology has been applied, undoubtedly the most frequent in terms of the number of students being taught is in educational contexts. Not only is every student-teacher in this country likely to have some part of the syllabus devoted to psychology in one form or another, but in-service diplomas, Bachelor's and higher degrees, qualifying courses for educational psychologists and many short courses for serving teachers have usually an educational psychology component on offer. The justification is a *prima facie* one. If psychology includes the study of human behaviour, involving such concepts as learning, perceiving, remembering, etc., then the case is strong for its inclusion in the introductory and continuing education of teachers both for the personal and professional importance of the concepts.

The history of the systematic and deliberate application of psychology in an educational context goes well back into the last century. The influence of Herbart (1824) or Froebel, for instance, takes us back a century and a half. Examination of the texts used gives a fair guide to the importance placed on various aspects of psychology. By the turn of this century, textbooks on the subject were in regular use in teacher training colleges (Compayré, 1893; Sully, 1886). Frequently, these texts were used in much the same way as they are today. Basic principles were enunciated, lecturers were encouraged to fill out the principles with practical illustrations and references to original sources (although clearly these were nowhere near as numerous as they are today). Compayré's book contains intriguing lists of 'facts', 'do's and don'ts' such as 'Memory is a habit, and, like all other habits, grows strong with repetition; hence the importance of summaries, recapitulations, and reviews' or 'Written exercises are the most important of all' (exercises that is).

In fact, one could not fail to marvel at the certainty apparent in the uncompromising presentation of these early texts. This had its origins in the belief that there were essentially two ways in which knowledge could be gathered—*experientially*, that is knowledge based on an individual's experiences, and *scientifically*, that is knowledge based on a wide survey of 'facts' and their subsequent generalization. Sully (1886) summarizes this by saying that 'the conclusions deduced from empirical knowledge are precarious, whereas the conclusions properly drawn from scientific principles are *perfectly trustworthy*' (my italics). Such faith in the infallibility of findings in the neo-science of psychology is not quite so evident nowadays.

The drift in emphasis, and subsequent modifications in the syllabuses and methods of presentation between these early days and now, makes a fascinating study in itself. For our present purposes, it is instructive to know just how psychology crept into the study of educational contexts. At first, the *subject matter* being taught was all important. A teacher arranged the subject matter in a sequence (based partly on trial and error and partly on word of mouth advice) and hammered it home relentlessly. The possibility of individual differences between teachers or pupils had either to be ignored or disbelieved, although every generation of teachers must have had those who were sensitive to the individual needs of youngsters. Nevertheless, study was essentially of a cerebral kind with Latin or Euclidean primers heading the list of texts.

It is only quite recently, within the last 150 years, that questions about the how and why of learning began to be asked. In other words, teachers were becoming more overtly concerned about *pupils* and their differences. My classics colleagues tell me that verbs of teaching govern two accusatives—one of the person, the other of the object, and this highlights quite effectively the shift in attitude from a concentration on the subject alone to a consideration of both the subject and the taught. The views of Froebel and his followers did much to focus attention on the child. The 'nurturing of the delicate plant' metaphor owes much to Froebel's influence on such people as Pestalozzi. One weakness was that whilst Froebelians rightly alerted teachers to the importance of *knowing* the child, they said little or nothing about *why* the child might be what he or she was.

At the turn of the century, most texts for student-teachers referred to above dwelt on three major factors—the physical, intellectual and moral education of children. Chapters were given over to hygiene, fitness, the sense organs and the physiology of the nervous system in the belief that a healthy body was a prerequisite for a healthy mind. Intellectual studies for student-teachers dealt with inductive and deductive reasoning, memory, imagination, judgement, and so forth. Moral education dwelt on feeling, the will, emotion, character, rewards and punishments. Emphasis was clearly upon *effects* through associationism.

As psychologists began to look for causes, the work of McDougall (instincts and sentiments particularly), the psychometricians (exploring intelligence), the biologists (Galton and the quest for an inherited component in behaviour) and the psychoanalysts starting with Freud's work, gradually had an influence on what was being regarded as important for students in teacher training colleges. Syllabuses in the years between 1910 and the 1930s began to contain such topics as instincts, inheritance and variation, individual differences in physical, mental and personal characteristics, interests and attitudes. At the same time, largely by way of the associationist schools of thinking, research on the 'laws of learning' were beginning to penetrate into the syllabus. Examples of textbooks extant about this time, which make enlightening reading, if only as historical records of trends in the topics thought to be relevant in educational contexts, were written by Kennedy-Frazer (1923), Fox (1925), Sandiford (1928) and Catty (1934).

In the years from the mid-1930s three further factors have appeared. These are a greater regard for the place of physical, mental and social growth and development, the nature of the teacher and teaching, and the setting (social and intellectual milieu) inside and outside the classroom. Texts which began the growth and development trend were written by such authors as Ross (1931) and Griffith (1939). Inevitably, because of the time lag between the appearance of the theory and its adoption, the hypotheses expounded by Piaget did not permeate into the 'system' until after World War II. I know from my own experience that the work of Piaget was still not on the syllabus of some training colleges in the mid-1950s.

The 'qualities of the good teacher' were only just being investigated in the early 1940s (Tudhope, 1942, 43). Social psychology, still struggling for a place in the curriculum of those in initial training, began to make a contribution in the 1950s. In these post war years, the balance swung from intellectual to affective influences (motivation, personality, attitudes) on performance.

This gradual accumulation of psychological topics thought to be crucial to those in training or in service as teachers—the subject, the pupil, the teacher, the setting—is neatly illustrated in Fig. 15.1 taken from a chart prepared by Semeonoff (1976). The rise and fall of fashions in psychology shown in the figure are reflected in the syllabuses found in educational courses over the years and alluded to above.

PSYCHOLOGY APPLIED TO EDUCATION TODAY

This section is based on the educational system of the UK but the issues have, of course, wider relevance. Within education courses, different expectations and demands have given rise to varied curriculae in terms of content, presentation and evaluation. For ease of description I shall consider five subdivisions which,

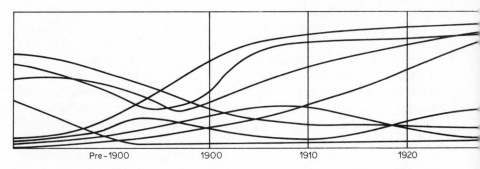

Figure 15.1 Relative activity and influence of the different approaches. Over the year different approaches to psychology rival each other in terms of research effort, importan discoveries and academic and popular influence and prestige. The vertical scale on thi

though they overlap, have recognizably different objectives. These are: (a) initial teacher training divided further into non-graduate (Certificate in Education), graduate (BEd, BA (Educ)) and postgraduate (Graduate Certificate in Education); (b) post-experience diplomas, first and higher taught degrees; (c) higher degrees by research; (d) professional training as an educational psychologist; and (e) non-qualifying, up-dating or general interest courses for serving teachers in adult education, short courses, teachers' centres, public lectures, etc.

Initial Training for Teaching (UK)

As indicated above, students who attend courses leading to qualified teacher (QT) status almost invariably cover some aspects of psychology and its application to education. There are two major groups. These are:

(i) the three-year course leading to the Teachers' Certificate in Education run essentially in colleges of education, institutes of higher education and polytechnics; and

(ii) the one-year Graduate Certificate in Education concentrated in university schools and departments of education and some of the institutions mentioned in (i).

These are divided intentionally in this way because the length of time involved and the pre-suppositions made about the entry make for differences in the courses on offer. Entrants to the three-year Certificate are most often school leavers of 18 + whilst graduate entrants will have spent three or four years in undergraduate studies. Thus, in the former case main and often subsidiary subjects are studied in depth. The latter are assumed to have sufficient knowledge of their degree subjects not to need further tuition in the qualifying year. In both cases subjects are studied in relation to their relevance in primary or secondary education.

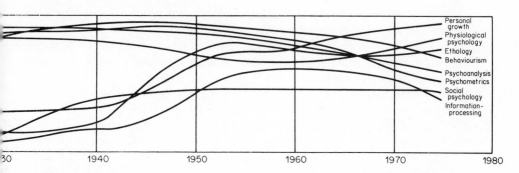

Personal growth
Physiological psychology
Ethology
Behaviourism
Psychoanalysis
Psychometrics
Social psychology
Information-processing

30   1940   1950   1960   1970   1980

hart is arbitrary; so, to some extent, is the placing of the lines when they are close. But
he general representation here is a fair one. (Chart prepared with the advice of Dr Boris
Semeonoff; taken from *Psychology Today*, **2**, No. 8, pp. 32–33, reproduced by permission
of Gemini Publishing Ltd.)

It is not easy to generalize about the psychological content of the above courses. However, two surveys of the three-year course have been carried out which give an indication of content during the 1960s and early 1970s. One, *Teaching Educational Psychology in Training Colleges*, was published by the British Psychological Society in 1962; the other was part of a research into curriculum design in educational psychology by Stones and Anderson (1972). No similar study of the Graduate Certificate course exists to my knowledge.

Stones and Anderson give a useful summary of requirements of a course in educational psychology: e.g. 'To enable the teacher to make use of psychological knowledge, not to be a second rate psychologist.' They also classify topics most frequently found in initial non-graduate teacher training courses (learning, developmental psychology, educational measurement, psychology and the teacher's job).

The teaching methods used vary extensively both between and within institutions. However, the time-honoured techniques of large and small group lectures, seminars and tutorials are still common to most. Years are most often divided down into groups with course tutors (divisions, tutorials) sometimes isolated and sometimes mixed according to the main subject or to the age range within which a student has opted to teach.

Practical experience has always been regarded as vital. In the early history of formal teacher-training, a monitorial system developed in which a student was attached to a teacher and class and learnt the skills by, in effect, 'sitting next to Nelly'. 'Demonstration Schools' also became attached to colleges where teachers in the school or the college lecturers would give 'model' lessons. This method has largely been replaced by a system of 'school observation' sessions where students early on in the course visit schools for a few weeks and observe teachers in action.

In addition to these initiation rites, all students are required to undertake 'school practice'. They go to prearranged placements in schools covering the subjects and/or age groups chosen by them for their professional careers. Some schools provide 'school practice tutors'; others have class teachers, particularly in the primary school where a student is generally attached to one class and the corresponding teacher. Other kinds of contact with children in which the psychology syllabus is involved include visits to special schools, voluntary work with youth clubs, assignments involving small-scale enquiries (for example Piagetian type concepts, trying out equipment such as cuisenaire rods or Nuffield science apparatus, attitude measurement) and the 'child study'. This latter usually requires the student to make a detailed observational examination of the intellectual, social and physical attributes and development of one child.

Many institutions are rapidly heading towards an all-graduate entry and there is little doubt that by the 1980s the Certificate in Education will have been replaced by the Bachelor's degree. The psychology component of the degree is undoubtedly more theoretical. Another growth area in the last ten or so years has been the introduction of courses dealing with the understanding and inter- pretation of educational research using, in the main, psychological findings. An increasing number of colleges now offer psychology as a main study.

Much less is available, in general terms, about the courses considered below.

Post-experience Taught Courses for Serving Teachers

In-service taught courses divide roughly into three: diplomas (Diploma in Educational Studies, specialist diplomas), first degrees (in-service BEd, BPhil, BSc (Educ)) and higher degrees with a taught element (MEd, MA (Educ)). In all cases, a student is required to have done some teaching and may well need to have a teacher's certificate. One implication of these criteria is that students will have a basic knowledge of psychology alongside practical experience.

Examples of topics considered are 'child development', 'definition and measurement of personality', 'recent advances in behaviour modification', 'micro-teaching techniques' and 'residential education—psychological con- siderations'. Higher degrees by course work frequently offer specialist courses in psychology. The range of topics in post-experience courses rests essentially on the interests of the staff but the pattern across colleges and universities defies classification.

In addition to lecture and seminar methods, students are sometimes required to prepare 'papers' for presentation to the group. Dissertations, so called to distinguish them from the more substantial and research-orientated thesis, are frequently required.

Higher Degrees by Research

Higher degrees by thesis leading to the MEd, MA (Educ) or PhD which are psychological in content usually require the candidate to have had experience in research techniques, but not always (though preferably) a basic knowledge of psychology. The special interests of the supervisor have a substantial influence on the student both in terms of the topic chosen and the direction of the methodology. The depth of knowledge is 'picked up' from the literature and contacts with other specialists in the same field. But it has to be admitted that there is a certain haphazardness about the range of contacts possible, especially when some of the degrees mentioned above can be carried out by part-time study whilst the individual is holding down a full-time job.

Professional Training as an Educational Psychologist

Whilst the courses offered to students for professional training as educational psychologists involve very few students when taken over the country as a whole, nevertheless, their service to education is vital. Most are full-time and lead to an MSc or MEd in educational psychology. The central objective of the majority of the courses is to provide training for those wishing to work as educational psychologists in the School Psychological Service, Child Guidance and other services. Those wishing to enter on such courses must already possess both a degree in psychology and some teaching experience.

The work covered falls into three broad categories of:

(a) an advanced theoretical kind in psychological, sociological and educational fields relevant to educational and child psychology;
(b) the principles and practice of psychological investigation and intervention; and
(c) professional practical training.

Under these headings we find such topics as, for (a), the development of normal and handicapped children, relationships between children, parents and teachers, learning and teaching, research design, statistics and assessment techniques. Under (b) we may find strategies of investigation, observation techniques (behavioural analysis, interviewing, experimental method), systems analysis approach, intervention systems for both individuals and groups, survey techniques. The professional practice in (c) consists of such topics as the role of educational psychologists in the LEA, the organization of the services, the ethical and practical aspects of an educational psychologist's work.

The methods of teaching adopted range from seminars, workshops, lectures and role-play simulations to placements (both short and long term) in special schools, centres, units and other places in the School Psychological and Child Guidance services. A dissertation is most often a requirement at the end of these programmes.

'General Interest' Courses

There is an extraordinary variety of courses which include educational psychology on offer both to professional groups and the public. These range from short seminars, half-day conferences to termly or yearly periods. Universities, colleges and polytechnics through Adult Education Departments or through special arrangements with the LEAs or DES (Department of Education and Science) are the usual centres which organize these. Most are for general interest; for example, some recent DES/Regional Short Courses organized at my present university included 'Organizing the Curriculum', 'Teacher-based Assessment', 'Towards a Policy of Language Development', 'Education of Backward Children' and 'Careers Guidance: Developments in Theory and Practice'.

Further areas which might well qualify as general interest programmes are the staff development courses provided by universities and polytechnics for their teachers. Occasional lectures, two- or three-day conferences or seminar sessions usually include themes of psychological interest such as learning and teaching, assessment, study methods (to include topics like remembering and forgetting) and motivation amongst higher education students.

The foregoing gives a rather sketchy indication of the most prominent ways in which psychology has found its way into educational contexts. Some are deliberate and intense courses leading to professional qualifications. Others are optional courses for those needing only a passing knowledge. But the total number of students involved in any one academic year is quite formidable.

WAYS IN WHICH THE CURRICULUM OF PSYCHOLOGY IN EDUCATIONAL CONTEXTS MIGHT DEVELOP

Curriculum formulation in psychology as applied to education both at a national (British Psychological Society Survey, 1962; Stones and Anderson, 1972) and institutional level (in university and college departments) has usually been done using the collected wisdom of those teaching the subject. Syllabuses are derived by sifting through 'what was' and 'what is' taught, or by handing on from tutor to tutor the content. In other words, we obtain our *syllabuses by consensus*. New ideas filtering through from the research gradually become added to the existing content, but this process is very slow.

But what influences the syllabus for, say, the training of teachers? We have already hinted at several. For example, trends in psychology begin to have an impact (usually several years after the introduction); professional pressure also shifts the emphasis from generation to generation. A good example of this is the recent upsurge in enthusiasm for behaviour modification programmes to meet a demand for the satisfactory control of behaviour, particularly deviant behaviour, in the classroom. Other 'in' topics at present include creativity, theories of instruction (Bruner, Ausubel, Gagné) and the controversies aroused by Jensen. As fashions develop, often through the *zeitgeist* or 'spirit of the time', they gradually find a place in the repertoire. Other concepts drop out of fashion or become modified. McDougall's instincts, enjoying a revival in the work of the ethologists such as Lorenz and Tinbergen, as well as in the motivation theory of Cattell (1957; Cattell and Child, 1975), and the 'memory is like a muscle and has to be exercised' view are but two. Thus, when we are looking into the crystal ball to speculate on the ways in which psychology as applied to education might develop, we have to take account of past and recent developments.

A second determinant of professional pressure has always been there in one form or another. The strongest and most persistent plea has rightly been for the contribution of psychology to bridge the gap between theory and practice. One central question, therefore, is what should count as *relevant* in psychology for education? Some find it easy to argue the case that any generalization about human behaviour would be of significance to a teacher, but this does tend to overrate the applicability of many findings in psychology to the special circumstances of the classroom. In any case, we are critically short of time and opportunity in education courses, particularly the Graduate Certificate in Education, and we must consequently be severely selective in course content.

There are those, like Ausubel (1953), Parlett (1974) and Bruner (1966) who see little of value in extrapolating from fundamental findings and who believe in a discipline called *educational psychology*. This involves action research in the classroom—looking at learning environments *as they exist.*

Ausubel (1953) has taken a very definite line in demarcating those aspects which are to be regarded as most fruitful to the teacher. He identifies three sources of information as 'basic science' research, 'extrapolated' research and 'applied' research. The term 'basic' is used as a contrast to the term 'applied'. According to Ausubel, 'the design of basic science research bears no *intended* relation whatsoever to problems in the applied disciplines, the aim being solely to advance knowledge . . . . This applicability is apt to be quite indirect and unsystematic.' The level of generality is also criticized as being too great for the particular problems facing a teacher with pupils. The second, extrapolated basic science research, 'satisfies the important criterion of relevance, but must still contend with the problem of level of applicability.' Often the research is cast in a form which is sufficiently simplified to enable uncomplicated models to be located. Unfortunately, these are often so far away from reality as to limit their value in classrooms.

The third, and now a cliché in education, is the *in situ* research—observing and analysing the behaviour of children and teachers in classrooms 'as they really are' (Clifford, 1976). Parlett (1974) in his call for more *illuminative evaluation* is attempting to adopt this suggestion of Ausubel. Parlett's aim in studying any innovatory programme is to discover:

> how it operates; how it is influenced by the various school situations
> in which it is applied; what those directly concerned regard as its
> advantages and disadvantages; and how student intellectual tasks and
> academic experience are most affected. It aims to discover and docu-
> ment what it is like to be participating in the scheme, whether as
> teacher or pupil, and, in addition, to discern and discuss the innova-
> tion's most significant features, recurring concomitants and critical
> processes.

Bruner says a theory of instruction should be central to educational psychology, and concern itself largely with how 'to arrange environments to optimize learning according to various criteria—to optimise transfer or retrievability of information, for example'. This may well be true, but the snag is
the near-intractable complexity of the task, particularly in the light of the
inadequate nature of our existing tools for observation of classroom events.
The extreme position of the approaches expounded by Ausubel, Parlett and
Bruner is the now familiar ethnomethodological one.

Somewhere between these extremes is an eclectic and pragmatic approach
using as many sources and forms of evidence or 'clues' as can be found. Psychology is still not in a fit state as a science, and I do not believe we can afford
to be dogmatic or obsessional about particular approaches at the expense of
others in the process of mapping out all aspects of human learning behaviour.
The syllabuses found in colleges and departments of education, generally
speaking, reflect this compromise by the varieties of strategies used in presenting
the subject. This point is well worth exploring in more detail because it is quite
important as a structural consideration in formulating a curriculum. Some
tutors tend to treat psychology in terms of well-defined areas such as human
ability, personality, language development, motivation, etc., and to deal with
each area separately, drawing out the strands which are relevant to the work
of the teacher. Others prefer to start with classroom themes rather than psychological domains and to talk of maladjustment, gifted children, learning
styles, the nature–nurture controversy, reading, discipline, discovery methods,
open plan classrooms, etc. A crude analogy of the different perspectives
suggested here is the 'sandwich cake model' where we imagine the layers one
upon another as representing the *domains* (personality, cognitive development,
etc.), and slices of the cake as representing *themes*. In the latter case we draw
upon certain aspects of each domain in order to build up a picture of individual
or group differences.

A common preference is a combination of both 'layer' and 'slice' approaches.
It would seem logical to present these in the same order as in making the sandwich cake—we lay down the layers first to establish the foundations of the

subject before cutting out slices. The 'general' textbook usually tries to satisfy the layer method, whilst specific texts, which have become very popular in the last ten years as several series of short specialist texts, commonly deal in slices. Attempting to do both these adequately in one text is obviously forbidding. But both are necessary perspectives which the tutor can do much to combine. Students find this exercise of drawing the elements together both relevant and salutary. Without this cross-referencing between the major areas of psychology and some of the pressing practical problems of classroom life, students grow to regard the subject as isolated units of knowledge.

In courses of initial training and further professional studies there is reasonable certainty that the syllabuses will become more 'classroom' directed. Greater place is, and will be, given to examining process and product variables. The upsurge of interest in recent years in cognitive and affective styles in children and teaching styles is evidence of this supposition. At face value process variables would seem to hold out a good deal of hope to practising teachers, so why have they not figured more significantly in courses? The basic reason is that processes cannot be observed directly. Using an analogy of a watch, we can hear the tick and see the time, but this tells us nothing about the mechanics of what we hear or see. To learn about the latter we would have to dismantle some part of the watch. When dealing with children, we can only observe effects from what we assume to be mental activities without knowing the precise nature of those activities. Unfortunately, we cannot dismantle a child's mind in this way. Consequently, our chief concern as teachers tends to be directed towards effects, on what the child is doing or has done rather than on causes, that is on how and why the child is doing. This is one of the drawbacks of IQ tests; they tell us something about the quantity of intelligent thought and very little about its quality.

It is not without significance that a recent influential research report by Bennett (1976) says more about the effects of classroom organization (or teaching style as he calls it) than about the modus operandi of learning processes on the performance of pupils.

So, if we cannot observe mental processes directly, what techniques are we left with? There are three alternatives:

1 we can ignore them and concentrate on input and output (that's stimulus and response) without making assumptions about intermediary processes as behaviourists would do;

2 we can make *ex post facto* deductions from the products of mental activity, as cognitivists or interaction analysts might do; or

3 we can make a direct assault on the neural system of the body in an attempt to connect brain or body functioning with mental behaviour (that is, what happens in the brain during problem solving), although even here we are

dependent upon linking overt action with whatever reactions are obtained from the neural probes—but what a daunting task.

Progress in this third alternative has been slow and singularly unhelpful to teachers. Lashley, probably one of the most famous psychophysiologists, was moved to remark that the brain is so complex and its division of labour so diffuse that learning ought to be impossible. Another question, incidentally, which the physiological approach raises is that at this level of analysis where does physiology end and psychology begin?

If, therefore, we want to speculate about the inner experience of human learning processes, and it seems the most likely direction in the foreseeable future, then we are left with the crude instruments of observation (experimental and ethological), or self-reporting, with all the limitations of methods which are one step removed from the scene of the action.

DEVELOPMENTS IN METHODS OF LEARNING AND TEACHING PSYCHOLOGY IN EDUCATION

Almost any method of communicating concepts which comes to mind is sure to be used somewhere at sometime. I have already alluded to many time-honoured techniques which, I believe, will continue to be used to greater or lesser extent for many years to come (lectures, seminars, textbooks, etc.). Ideas must be communicated, skills developed, thinking and reasoning encouraged, routines assimilated, personal development and satisfaction hoped for and a professional approach acquired by teachers and others concerned with the application of psychology to education. In this quest, new or revised techniques arise in response to changing attitudes. The mood of the times has undoubtedly accentuated the need for 'chalk-face' practical experience for those in initial training and for custom-made, pragmatic courses for those in teaching service (counselling, classroom interaction, behaviour modification). Apart from pressure from teachers, the LEAs are becoming more selective in the courses to which they will second teachers. Not that the number of students coming to read higher degrees of a theoretical kind has declined; such a move would be tragic for a profession which depends upon theoretical as well as practical knowledge. But at times when funds are scarce, the tendency is for it to be channelled towards outlets which are regarded as more 'urgent' and practical.

This surge towards classroom-based training and research has led to several developments which doubtless will expand in the coming years. The direct experience methods include taking children either in the classroom, in small groups or drawing out individuals in order to test out the psychological principles covered in theory. Sometimes the principles might be tried in isolation from curriculum content as with Piagetian stages experiments, or gaining experience in the administration and use of standardized tests. Generally, the principles are treated as part of a more complex pattern of classroom interaction. Examples of this can be found in a consideration of class management, assessment and curriculum planning, in small-group work with slow learners and reading groups or individuals as in career guidance.

In order to highlight certain aspects of this pattern, an innovation called 'micro-teaching' has appeared in recent years. As the term implies, a small portion of the teaching–learning process is taken, either in isolation over a short period so as to stimulate a piece of classroom practice (for example, question and answer sessions, or methods of keeping order) or as a slice of a whole lesson. The teaching is videotaped and a 'post mortem' held (Perrott, 1977). The technique of videotaping led to some interesting applications in exploring behaviour modification (Poteet, 1973). The effects of positive and negative reinforcement, the recording of token economy methods and the impact of modelling can all be captured on tape and analysed by students.

Practical work with a research flavour, but outside the conventional school practice, is expanding. In colleges and university departments there is an increasing amount of experimental work using personality and ability tests, learning experiments and occasionally psychological tests in perception and memory. In schools, more students are becoming involved in observation of child–teacher, child–child interaction. The 'child-study' has actually been with us for a long time, but it is still regarded by many as a most effective way of introducing students to the skills of observation, recording in detail the social, emotional and intellectual characteristics of a child and probably giving students one of the few opportunities they will ever get of making a depth study of childhood.

Simulation exercises have begun to find their way into both initial and in-service education. In one example, a school had been 'invented' (Selmes, 1974) along with staff and a set of problems which it was hoped would create a situation similar to the 'real thing'. For student-teachers the items were intended to provoke discussion about such factors as interrelations, assessment and examinations, difficult children and what to do with them, pastoral care and so forth. The purpose was 'to (i) explore the wide range of attitudes and opinions expressed, (ii) attempt to identify some of the reasons for these attitudes and (iii) to help self-understanding and, at the same time, to indicate some of the psychological knowledge (or concepts) which require further understanding'. For serving teachers these reasons might also include role-play as a head or deputy head dealing with correspondence, recalcitrant pupils, parent complaints and so on.

The rapid and unabated expansion of technological aids has generated a need for introductory courses in their use. In addition to a massive volume of visual and auditory machinery, there is some use made of teaching machines and computer-assisted learning and instructional devices. The principles underlying their application are most frequently dealt with in the psychology lectures. The aims are two-fold. One is to help the student to help others; the other is to help himself to self-instructional techniques.

A development which has been on the cards for several years is some form of industrial experience for teachers. Whether this is done as an addition to the school practice in the form of a 'works practice' by working in industry (sandwich course, in effect) during vacations is a matter of conjecture, but the pressure from parents and industry to provide a smooth and realistic transition for youngsters passing from school to work is increasing (Green Paper, 1977). The absence of industrial experience in many young teachers who may well be responsible for youngsters about to enter industry has not gone unnoticed. There is a vast, untapped reservoir of psychological knowledge relating to work conditions, relations between those at work, living in a technological society, coping with increasing leisure time, etc. Therefore, I see a growth in industrial placements, a greater involvement of industry where it involves educational affairs, more courses being developed for serving teachers which bear on the psychological aspects of 'the world of work', how a technological society survives, and the development of an education which enables youngsters to adapt to the changing patterns of work and leisure.

SOURCE TEXTS AND MATERIALS

The following annotated list of texts, materials and sources of information for intending teachers of psychology to students of education represents a scratch on the surface of all that is available. Textbooks alone which may be recommended for use by either teacher or taught will run into thousands. The list, therefore, is a starting point for further exploration.

The list is divided into textbooks, journals, source indexes, syllabuses and useful agencies.

Textbooks

There are plenty of textbooks in educational psychology on the market, written with both the lecturer and the student in mind. The American literature is very extensive, but these texts tend to be voluminous and not too closely related to examples of the system in the UK. Nevertheless, several colleges do use American texts, one or two of which are mentioned below. Only recent editions are included.

General

Too numerous to list, but here are a few recent publications:
Child, D. (1977). *Psychology and the Teacher*. London: Holt, Rinehart & Winston, second edition.

Child, D. (ed.) (1977). *Readings in Psychology for the Teacher*. London: Holt, Rinehart & Winston—a companion Reader for the core text mentioned above.

Cross, G. R. (1974). *The Psychology of Learning*. Oxford: Pergamon.

Lovell, K. (1974). *Educational Psychology and Children*. London: University of London, eleventh edition.

McFarland, H. S. N. (1971). *Psychological Theory and Educational Practice*. London: Routledge & Kegan Paul.

Morrison, A., and McIntyre, D. (1973). *Teachers and Teaching*. Harmondsworth: Penguin, second edition; and (1972). *The Social Psychology and Teaching*. Harmondsworth: Penguin. This attempts to deal with some important social psychological topics.

Mussen, P. H., Conger, J. J., and Kagan, J. (1974). *Child Development and Personality*. New York: Harper International. This book deals in some detail with developmental aspects of psychology relevant to teachers and teaching.

Sandström, C. I. (1976). *The Psychology of Childhood and Adolescence*. Harmondsworth: Penguin. Another popular developmental text.

Sauts, J., and Butcher, H. J. (eds) (1975). *Developmental Psychology*. Harmondsworth: Penguin. A Reader which draws together many well-known contributors to developmental psychology.

Texts in the form of a series

Basic Books in Education, Macmillan.
Exploring Education, National Foundation for Educational Research.
Psychology and Education, Open Books.
Students Library of Education, Routledge & Kegan Paul.
Theory and Practice in Education, Blackwells.
Unibooks, University of London Press.

Journals

Journals of interest to psychologists in education are abundant. Those specifically in psychology from Britain and America include:

The British Journal of Educational Psychology;
Journal of Educational Psychology;
Child Development;
Journal of Experimental Education;
Educational and Psychological Measurement;
Psychology Teaching, Bulletin of the APT;
Journal of Experimental Child Psychology.

Of those more broadly educational which contain papers of psychological interest, the following are amongst the best known in Britain:

Educational Research (NFER);
Research in Education (University of Manchester);
Educational Revi:w (University of Birmingham);
Educational Studies (Carfax Publishing Company);
Durham and Newcastle Research Review (Universities of Durham and Newcastle).

Source Indexes

Richmond, W. K. (1972). *The Literature of Education*. London: Methuen.
The British Education Index. London: The British Library, Bibliographic Services Division.
Register of Research into Higher Education. London: Society for Research into Higher Education.
Register of Educational Research in the United Kingdom 1973–76. Slough: National Foundation for Educational Research.

Syllabuses

The two major studies which looked at syllabuses in psychology of education have already been mentioned in the foregoing:

British Psychological Society (1962). *Teaching Educational Psychology in Training Colleges*. London: British Psychological Society.
Stones, E., and Anderson, D. (1972). *Educational Objectives and the Teaching of Educational Psychology*. London: Methuen.

Discussion of curriculum matters are also to be found in *Psychology Teaching*, the Bulletin of the Association for the Teaching of Psychology.

Some Useful Agencies

Below are given some addresses of agencies which deal with test materials, research reports and curriculum development:

Assessment of Performance Unit, Department of Education and Science, Elizabeth House, York Road, London, SE1 7PH.

British Educational Equipment Association, Sunley House, 10 Gunthorpe Street, London, E17 7RW.

Catalogue of Psychological Tests and Clinical Procedures, National Foundation for Educational Research Publishing Co. Ltd., 2 Jennings Buildings, Thames Avenue, Windsor, Berks., SL4 1QS

Central Bureau for Educational Visits and Exchanges, 43 Dorset Street, London, WIH 3FN.

Independent Assessment and Research Centre Ltd., 57 Marylebone High Street, London, W1H 3AE.

National Children's Bureau, 8 Wakley Street, London, EC1V 7QE.

Tests and Psychology, University of London Press, Saint Paul's House, Warwick Lane, London, EC4P 4AH.

Schools Council, 160 Great Portland Street, London, W1N 6LL.

REFERENCES

Adams, J. (1900). *The Herbartian Psychology Applied to Education*. London: Isbister.
Ausubel, D. P. (1953). The Nature of Educational Research. *Education Theory*, **3**, 314–320.
Bennett, N. (1976). *Teaching Styles and Pupil Progress*. London: Open Books.
British Psychological Society (1962). *Teaching Educational Psychology in Training Colleges*. London: British Psychological Society.
Bruner, J. S. (1966). *Toward a Theory of Instruction*. New York: Norton.
Cattell, R. B. (1957). *Personality and Motivation Structure and Measurement*. New York: World Book Co.
Cattell, R. B., and Child, D. (1975). *Motivation and Dynamic Structure*. London: Holt, Rinehart & Winston.
Catty, N. (1934). *The Theory and Practice of Education*. London: Methuen.
Clifford, B. (1976). Educational Psychology—To Be or Not To Be? *Psychology Teaching*, **4**, 39–44.
Compayré, G. (1890). *Psychologie Appliqué à l'Education* (trans. W. H. Payne, 1893). Boston: Health.
Fox, C. (1925). *Educational Psychology: Its Problems and Methods*. London: Kegan Paul, Trench & Trubner.
Green Paper (1977). *Education in Schools: A Consultative Document*. HMSO Cmnd. 6869.
Griffith, C. R. (1939). *Psychology Applied to Teaching and Learning*. New York: Farran & Rinehart.
Herbart, J. F. (1824). *Psychologie als Wissenschaft*, 2 vols. Unzer: Konigsberg.
Kennedy-Fraser, D. (1923). *The Psychology of Education*. London: Methuen.
Parlett, M. (1974). The New Evaluation. *Trends in Education*, **34**, 13–18.
Perrott, E. (1977). *Microteaching in Higher Education: Research Development and Practice*. Guildford: RHE Monographs, University of Surrey.
Poteet, J. A. (1973). *Behaviour Modification: A Practical Guide for Teachers*. London: Unibooks.
Ross, J. S. (1931). *Groundwork of Educational Psychology*. London: Harrap.
Sandiford, P. (1928). *Educational Psychology: An Objective Study*. London: Longmans, Green.
Selmes, C. (1974). The Use of Simulation Material in the Teaching of Psychology to Student Teachers. *Psychology Teaching*, **2**, 51–61.
Semeonoff, B. (1976). Understanding Psychology, a series in the periodical *Psychology Today*: Clareville Publishing, **2**, Nos. 1–10.

Stones, E., and Anderson, D. (1972). *Educational Objectives and the Teaching of Educational Psychology*. London: Methuen.

Sully, J. (1886). *The Teacher's Handbook of Psychology*. London: Longmans, Green.

Tudhope, W. B. (1942, 43). A Study of the Training College Final Teaching Mark as a Criterion of Future Success in the Teaching Profession. *British Journal of Educational Psychology*, **12**, 167–171 and **13**, 16–23.

Ward, J. (1926). *Psychology Applied to Education*. Cambridge: Cambridge University Press.

Welton, J. (1923). *The Psychology of Education*. London: Macmillan.

The Teaching of Psychology
Edited by J. Radford and D. Rose
© 1980 John Wiley & Sons Ltd.

16

Industrial, Commercial, and Public Service Contexts

CLIVE FLETCHER

INTRODUCTION

Teaching psychology to people in industry, commerce or public service generally means teaching them psychology as it relates to people at work. This particular aspect of the discipline is called occupational psychology in Britain and industrial or organizational psychology in the USA. Occupational will be the term preferred in this chapter as it has a broader range of implication than just the psychology of industry. As one of the three main lines of applied psychology (the others being the educational and clinical fields), occupational psychology has been clearly distinguishable as a specialism since World War I, which gave impetus to the application of psychological techniques by the demands that arose from it, e.g. for ways of selecting army personnel, or for investigating fatigue and accidents amongst munitions workers. Further progress was made in the use of psychology for studying and solving work problems after 1918, but it took another World War to achieve a further leap forward in the development of occupational psychology. World War II saw a much wider range of problems being tackled by psychologists, and their methods increased in sophistication as a result. The success achieved in such fields as selection and training during wartime was not lost on industry, which carried over and extended the role of the psychologist in the workplace in the years following World War II.

Today, the scope of occupational psychology might be described thus:

1 The analysis and description of jobs.   Discovering what is actually involved in a job and the skills and abilities needed to do it well is fundamental information for proper selection, training and appraisal of performance.

2 Selection and placement of staff.   Apart from the use of various selection procedures, such as interviews, tests, group discussion tasks and so on, this also involves the earlier stages of advertising posts, designing application forms and the process of allocating recruits to the jobs most suitable for them.

3 Vocational counselling.   School leavers and other young people come to mind usually in relation to this, but it is increasingly concerned with other groups such as redundant executives, the disabled and women returning to work after having a family.

4 Work design, or in some cases redesign.   A particular concern of ergonomics (the sub-specialism of occupational psychology that concentrates on 'fitting the job to the man') that entails the construction of working environments and equipment in such a way as to facilitate human performance while not detracting from the job satisfaction of the users.

5 Industrial relations.   Studying the communication and bargaining strategies and drawing whatever lessons that can be learned.

6 Industrial training.   The three main elements of the psychologist's contribution here are the identification of training needs, the development of training methods and the evaluation of training.

7 Motivation in work covers both the identification and study of what factors motivate people at work and the levels of satisfaction that arise from them.

8 Organizational development.   This area is growing in emphasis and includes communications, the analysis of organizational structure and climate and the development of interpersonal skills.

9 Safety and accident-prevention at work.   Both the ergonomic design of equipment to high safety standards and the attitudinal component of the problem are taken in under this heading.

10 Consumer research.   'Consumer' in the widest sense, including those affected by public service bodies, activities as well as people buying things. The psychologist may have a role in advertising, market research and attitude surveys, and selling.

Obviously there is a great deal of overlap between the areas listed above, but between them they cover just about all the endeavours of the occupational psychologist. For a fuller consideration of the field, see Warr (1978) and Davis and Shackleton (1976), or more comprehensively McCormick and Tiffin (1975). There is of course a strong relationship between the rest of psychology and its occupational specialization, and later in the chapter considerably more will be said about this relationship and its implications for teaching. For the moment it should be noted that the interaction is a two-way one, with occupational psychology drawing heavily on basic principles derived from the study of individual differences, group processes and so on, while in return contributing a lot to the basic psychological theories relating to areas such as skill, information processing, psychometrics and motivation. Something similar could be said of methodology too, but here occupational psychology has perhaps contributed rather little to 'formal' techniques of investigation while borrowing fairly heavily from other branches of applied psychology. However, occupational psychology operates in a very different environment from its parent discipline and has recently begun to focus on the broader aspects of its methodology more clearly in an attempt to increase its effectiveness; more of this later, as it has important implications for teaching psychology in this context.

Having identified occupational psychology as being that part of psychology most relevant to the title of this chapter, and briefly described it, we can now turn to the teaching of it. One of the first things that strikes one here is the diversity of groups who are taught this subject or parts of it, and the diversity of their needs. Psychology graduates are given formal postgraduate training in occupational psychology so that they may practice the full range of skills if so required; line managers encounter it on management training courses and want to relate it to the management of their subordinates; personnel managers have it as a sizable input to their professional training and will be heavily involved in many areas of occupational psychology; careers counsellors need to understand (amongst other things) the development of the individual, the nature of aptitudes and abilities and the use of psychological tests; engineering students frequently are taught the principles of ergonomic design; marketing executives seek a knowledge of motivation, attitudes and survey techniques; and so on. The range of places in which it will be taught is equally varied and will include universities, colleges and night schools, training departments of companies, management centres and hotel conference suites.

In discussing the teaching of psychology to these and other groups, we will concentrate on the needs of the group concerned, the content of the course and the techniques used. These will be dealt with first in relation to teaching occupational psychology to psychology students and then (at much greater length) to non-psychologist groups. The particular problems associated with teaching each of these two main types of student will be gone into later on in the chapter.

TEACHING PSYCHOLOGY STUDENTS

In both Britain and America, a first degree in psychology is seldom considered adequate training for actually working in an applied field. Most training in occupational psychology is done at postgraduate level. Indeed, in Britain this field of psychology is given very little attention at all at undergraduate level (Lowe, Bachler, Donaldson, Drewicz, Gill and Morrissey, 1977). Those courses that do offer some kind of undergraduate specialization in occupational psychology usually include one or more periods of attachment to organizations so that the students can relate the theory element of the course to practical experience—vital in teaching applied psychology. The postgraduate courses either weave into the timetable secondments enabling the student to get experience or offer part-time attendance so that the students may carry on a job and draw on the experience provided by that.

The content of the courses inevitably varies, and anyone involved in setting up such a course would be well advised to find out what is offered by existing courses. Some addresses connected with the main courses in British universities are given at the end of this chapter. A perusal of the structure and syllabus of each of these courses will give a good idea of what ground has to be covered and what is optional. A further input on this can be obtained from the Division of Occupational Psychology (of the BPS) in Britain and from the Division of Industrial and Organizational Psychology (of the APA) in America—again, the addresses to write to are given at the end of this chapter. These professional associations will give guidance on the requirements for courses to be recognized as adequate training in this field.

Little else will be said here about what specifically needs to be taught to this group of students—partly because the reader would be better served by sampling a range of ideas as suggested in the previous paragraph, and also because the outline of occupational psychology given earlier implies much of the basic course content in itself. However, one must make the distinction between the needs of students pursuing a course in occupational psychology as an element of their undergraduate degree and those attending courses designed to equip them as practitioners. For the former group, a sampling of the main topic areas (as given earlier) will probably suffice—in fact it will probably be as much as can be achieved in the time available. The practical element will not be important for this first group, whereas for the other group it will be an essential part of their training, particularly if they are full-time students who do not have the opportunity of developing and testing some of their skills in a job as the part-time students do. Thus, the techniques used in teaching undergraduate and postgraduate groups will differ sharply. The first group will probably be taught this topic in much the same way as the rest of their degree course ('chalk "n" talk' in all probability), while the others will clearly need techniques that facilitate both the acquisition of specific skills (e.g. in interviewing), and the development of their personal effectiveness in terms of the intervention process. This will involve a mixture of lectures and tutorials, case studies, project work, practical exercises (in interviewing, test administration and interpretation, and so on) under guidance and various experiential techniques (see Chapter 2).

The exact balance between the 'knowing' and 'doing' aspects of the course is something that must be decided by the tutors concerned, but if the course is a part-time one then the emphasis will almost inevitably fall on the 'knowing' element. It may in fact prove difficult to fit all this practical and theoretical work in on a course of the length envisaged, so an element of choice might be introduced in the form of a course unit system. This would entail students taking a 'core' course of essential material and then specializing in certain areas according to their interests, abilities and/or existing employment. Careful counselling of students at the time they make their decisions on what to specialize in is highly desirable. Incorporating a measure of choice in the course is a good thing anyway, and further increases student interest and involvement; the extent to which it can be built in, however, depends on the teaching resources available.

We have looked briefly at the teaching of occupational psychology to graduate and undergraduate psychology students. But relatively few courses of this kind seem to be starting up from scratch at the present time, and the greater need for help for those new to teaching this subject probably relates to teaching it on the expanding range of courses for the numerous other groups who have an interest in occupational psychology. It is to these that we now turn our attention.

TEACHING OTHER GROUPS

Reference has already been made to the diversity of interests and needs of the non-psychologist groups who are taught some occupational psychology. It would be impossible to give detailed consideration here of each potential audience, but what can be said is that the tutor must make an analysis of their needs concerning the psychology input as his first step. In some cases, this is largely predetermined by a set syllabus (as in the British Institute of Personnel Management Diploma, for instance). More often, the tutor will find that a degree of flexibility exists over the material to be presented. How does he make the choice that will best suit the needs of the students? By way of spadework, he could usefully read around the subject of training; some texts that might be found helpful are Davies (1971), Gagne and Briggs (1974) and Stammer and Patrick (1975). At much the same time, he will consult with any other people involved with the course, particularly course directors, to get clear what precisely the aims and objectives of the course as a whole are and how his particular section of it fits in with them—what are the students supposed to get out of it, and how are they intended to use the information, etc., they receive? He will also need to establish the *kind* of student he will be dealing with; their level of seniority, their educational level, whether they are voluntary attenders on the course or have been sent on it by their superiors, and so on. From all this a provisional framework should emerge which can again be discussed with others directly concerned with this part of the course. Finally, at the start of his session(s) with the students, the psychologist should, if possible, outline what he will be doing and how. Depending on the type of course and seniority of the students, he can invite them to express their own opinions on whether his intended approach seems to fit their needs or if any modifications are required. Clearly, if this is just one or two brief 'modules' of psychology, there would be little real time or opportunity to seek such suggestions, let alone act on them. If, however, this course (or this part of it) is of several days' duration or longer, then obtaining the students' participation and involvement in their own learning process is essential. Senior managers in particular are liable to 'mutiny' if they feel they lack any ownership of the course and that it is failing to meet their needs while taking up their hard-won time. This feedback process relates both to content and to teaching techniques and can be carried a stage further by the provision of some post-course evaluation; however, more about that later.

Having considered the problem of defining the students' needs in relation to the content of the course, we might, before going further, usefully make a distinction between two broad groups of courses. First, there are those courses of a more general nature, ranging from short management courses to such things as the IPM Diploma or the Diploma in Careers Guidance. These courses have varying amounts of psychological input amidst much other material. The second group consists of fairly short courses aimed at imparting some specific skill (e.g. appraisal interviewing). There are many courses of this kind where some or all of the teaching staff are psychologists and which are heavily based on psychological theory and research. Obviously these two groups of courses are not mutually exclusive—one finds specific skills being taught within the programmes of longer 'knowledge' courses—but it is helpful to distinguish between them here as they entail different approaches. Taking the longer, more general courses first, they often have broad titles like 'Management and Supervisory Skills' or 'An Introduction to Personnel Management' and include such topics as Leadership, Job Satisfaction, O & M work, Negotiation, Employment, Law and so on. The greater amount of time available and of material to be put over both permits and requires a diversity of teaching techniques. Almost invariably there will be some lecturing, and on long courses leading to some qualification this will be no great problem as the students tend to be younger and have a fairly clear idea of why they are doing the course (i.e. they are strongly motivated). But long hours of unremitting lectures are a daunting enough test of concentration even for undergraduates, let alone for managers and others who left formal education behind them some years ago. Where you have such an audience and they are attending a more general management course of the kind that organizations send people on for refresher or development training, there is no surer way of losing their interest than to present them with a series of formal lectures. To maintain motivation and interest, the students must be actively involved in acquiring the knowledge your diagnosis of their training needs has suggested they most require. The involvement can be through syndicate (small group) or individual work on case study material, business games (see Elgood, 1976; Gibbs, 1974) and discussion topics. Where some direct communication of material seems necessary, films can often be more 'invigorating' than lectures; some addresses for hiring training films is given in the Appendix to this chapter. But generally speaking, there should be at least as much of these other teaching methods timetabled as there is for lecturing. This is particularly important when the course is a residential one—the students rather quickly become 'institutional-ized' and the soporific effects of this are exacerbated by the steady drone of some lectures. And apart from maintaining the student interest, active learning techniques are essential if the students are to relate the psychological theory and findings to their own or similar situations—which must of course be one of the tutor's chief aims. With this in mind, he should choose his examples of studies and experiments (wherever he quotes these) so that they approximate as closely as possible to the work context of his students.

These general courses by nature often have rather general (even vague) aims, and the different elements within them (e.g. in a middle management course these might include interviewing skills, group and committee exercises, economic studies, employment legislation, organizational studies and indus-trial relations) are sometimes not well integrated. This makes effective liaison and collaboration with the course director particularly important, other-wise there may well be both needless duplication and a lack of any sense of continuity of material. Equally valuable is the information obtained from course evaluation. If the course as a whole is not evaluated, it is worth doing some evaluation just on your own contribution to it. This could take the form of a final 'wash-up' or plenary session at which queries are raised, lessons sum-marized and feelings about the course expressed. However, it is a less than ideal way of evaluating the psychological element, as it tends to be subject to various group conformity pressures. Much better is the anonymous completion of a single questionnaire asking the students to rate the various sessions in terms of how well taught they were, how relevant and useful they seemed and what improvements (if any) could be made in them. To ensure an adequate response, the questionnaire should be completed just before the last session of the course, though *ideally* it would be fitted in sometime after the course. The information you get from this will go some way to telling you whether your contribution to the course was received well and perceived as relevant. This helps reduce some of the uncertainty one sometimes feels about just what psychological input is most useful on courses of this type.

Moving on now to the other group of courses, those dealing with specific skills. Again, and by nature of the exercise, the emphasis is on practical work. There may be a great temptation to give a comprehensive presentation of psy-chological findings—if there is, resist it. Usually the time available on courses teaching the rudiments of interviewing, survey work, negotiating skills and so on is such that if anything is to be achieved, the emphasis must be on learning by doing. This is not to say that the findings of psychological research cannot be utilized—they can, but mainly in the form of straightforward advice on what to do and what not to do (the 'advice' may come early in the course as part of an introductory lecture, or in feedback from the psychologist to the student after the latter has completed some practical work). The main point about courses of this kind, however, is that much the greatest demand on the psychologist's skill is made by the need to give feedback to students on their performance, and to do so in a constructive and helpful way that will not lead to defensive reactions. This is too complex a topic to deal with here, but the reader will find Egan (1975) a useful book in this context. The courses which most commonly come into this category seem to be those concerned with interviewing of one kind or another, particularly selection and appraisal interviewing. For discussion of training courses in the former, the reader is referred to Lewis, Edgerton and Parkinson (1976), Keenan (1977) and Hackett (1978), while for the latter Anstey, Fletcher and Walker (1976) cover the ground. The occasional use of films instead of lectures has already been advocated, and in the case of selection and appraisal there are good training films available on hire at remarkably low cost in the UK from the Central Office of Information (the address of which is given in the Appendix).

This section has discussed the teaching of occupational psychology to the various interested groups and tried to indicate some general strategies that might be found helpful. Clearly, the main point is to tailor your approach as closely as possible *to* the needs of the group you are teaching. There are, however, a number of snags that the tutor will encounter, and these will now be discussed.

THE PROBLEMS

Some of the problems of teaching occupational psychology have been mentioned already, but the greatest ones as far as the two groups we started out with (psychologists and non-psychologists) are concerned have not been dealt with. These will be looked at here, firstly in relation to the psychologist group. For them, there are two related difficulties the tutor must think about. One is the gulf between academic and applied psychology, while the other is the need to help students develop the personal and professional competence they will require to cope with their future work environment.

Most occupational psychology is taught at postgraduate level, as was said earlier. This means that the students have already been given a thorough grounding in academic psychology. They will be well schooled in the scientific method, or at least in that peculiar variety of it that pervades psychology. Their expectations are that the usual approach involves one in making observations, formulating a hypothesis, designing the appropriately controlled experiment to test it, analysing the data and writing up the results in the generally accepted form for psychological research. This is a careful, thoughtful, fairly precise and often slow process. There may be some vague concessions made to the possibility of experimenter effects (Rosenthal, 1961) or towards recognizing the social demand characteristics of the experiment (Orne, 1962), but by and large their training provides a methodological approach that apes the physical sciences. The desirability or otherwise of this is a topic in itself and not appropriate for discussion here. However, what must be conveyed to the students of occupational psychology is the realization that this approach they have been taught so far is something of an ideal and is often impracticable, sometimes even undesirable, in this applied field (Heller, 1976). It is worth saying a little more on this as many occupational psychology texts do not make the problem very explicit. The fundamental point, of course, is that one cannot emulate laboratory conditions in most 'real-life' research settings. But this is not the only difference, and it may be helpful to list some other ways in which research in the occupational field varies from academic research:

(a) It often arises from the request of a client, who needs the information to solve some problem or make some decision. Much academic research arises from the interests of the researcher and the current literature.

(b) Partly as a consequence of (a), the applied research often has a much shorter timescale altogether—less scope for considering the problem, for reading the literature, for designing the study and for gathering the data than would be the case in more academic studies.

(c) The degree to which experimental controls can be built into the research will frequently be minimal in field studies; real-life situations can seldom be organized to suit the researcher because of the disruption this would cause.

(d) The analysis and writing-up of the research needs to be done in such a way that it takes account of the available time and of the client's statistical knowledge. Both of these imply a simpler approach than would be the case in academic research, and sometimes greater boldness in drawing conclusions.

It is essential that the tutor gets his students to understand that applied research, like politics, is very much the art of the possible. It may, through the demands of the situation and of the client, be more pragmatic in nature, but this does not mean that it simply becomes a watered-down version of the scientific approach. 'Action Research', as it is sometimes called, has techniques of its own (e.g. Heller, 1969) which the tutor will no doubt wish to mention as part of the course.

While there is no place for 'Holier than thou scientism' (Heller, 1976) in courses of this kind, the more vigorous approach put across at undergraduate level is certainly still valuable in many instances; the tutor has to be careful not to throw away the baby with the bath water. The ethos of scientific research is perhaps particularly worth fostering in relation to those (often substantial) elements of the occupational psychologist's work that involve skilled but routine functions like assessment, training and so on. There is a danger of slipping into an uncritical acceptance of tasks and techniques encountered in the non-research part of the work which might be offset by a continuing emphasis on scientific enquiry.

Bound up with all this is the environment the occupational psychologist will be working in and the skills needed to cope effectively with it. This is something that is not dealt with at all at undergraduate level, and is thus of concern to those teaching at the postgraduate level. The problem is that this is not something that lends itself easily to teaching—much of it really needs to come from first-hand experience. Perhaps an outline of the kinds of difficulties the occupational psychologist has to deal with will illustrate this. Most of them revolve round the relations with the client who employs the psychologist either permanently or temporarily. The psychologist may be brought in, for example, to run an attitude survey on some management innovation like Flexible Working Hours. Very often, the client's own ideas of what information is needed and how it is to be obtained are rather vague or poorly worked out. One of the first tasks for the psychologist, then, is to correctly diagnose what the problem (if there is one) seems to be, what is needed and how to go about it. To do this he may have to persuade the client to see things differently and negotiate with him the terms of reference for the project as a whole. The negotiation will have to take in other interested parties too. Using the example from above, a survey about flexible working hours, the trade union or staff association concerned will need to be consulted. For the success of the project, all those involved with it need to feel they have some degree of control and participation in it—to feel they 'own' it. When the data has been collected, the analysis and results must be written-up and presented in a way that: (a) is likely to be read at all; (b) is likely to be understood; and (c) is likely to be acted on. This usually involves close liaison with the client and other parties involved before anything is even written down. Besides specialist knowledge, all this requires considerable interpersonal sensitivity and competence. The applied psychologist is working in a highly political atmosphere where many different and often conflicting interests are at work. The classical academic notion of the data being 'neutral' is not one the occupational psychologist can adopt with an easy mind. Data mean different things to different people, and what might be very pleasing and acceptable data to management may be far from pleasing or acceptable to trade unions. Indeed, the latter may object to psychologists consulting their members at all in the course of a project—they may see it as an attempt by the psychologist (paid by management) to usurp the function of the union by consulting staff directly and representing their views. This in turn leads to the whole question of the ethics of applied psychology; is it right for the psychologist to undertake certain kinds of work, or to allow their skills to be used in the pay of one set of interests (e.g. management)? What are the limits of the psychologist's obligations to the individual and to the employing organization?

There are clearly many traps for the unwary occupational psychologist. How can the tutor help him during his training to avoid the worst pitfalls? As pointed out above, there is an element of learning 'the hard way' by confronting the problems on the job itself. Many little 'tricks of the trade' and 'survival measures' can be picked up this way (for instance, to prevent clients turning round at the end of an attitude survey and saying—as some do—'I could have told you all this myself anyway', ask them to *predict* the results of the survey in advance; they are never 100 per cent successful). But other things can be done on the course itself. First, experiential training (see Chapter 2) can help the student acquire a greater awareness of how he relates to others and they to him, as well as providing fresh insights into group interactions. Simulated negotiation exercises are also a possibility (Sisson, 1977). The tutor will also wish to direct his students towards texts that deal with the question of personal effectiveness, such as Argyris and Schon (1974), Egan (1975) and Walton (1969). All this, along with the usual seminar discussion, etc., should foster on awareness of the problems to be confronted and the kinds of skills needed by the practitioner. The ethical perspective on the work must also be taken into account, and the relevant code of conduct can be obtained from the professional associations of psychologists should the tutor not have a copy.

The difference between academic and 'action' research, along with the question of professional and personal competence are perhaps two of the greatest problems for the tutor training psychology graduates in the occupational specialization. One might infer that he will meet with a reasonable level of success only if he has himself had first-hand experience of the field he is talking about.

Turning now to the problems involved in teaching non-psychologist groups, three main ones come immediately to mind: their lack of basic psychological knowledge and concepts, their ideas and images of psychology and of psychologists, and their attitude to data and research. Dealing with them in that order, we will consider first the lack of basic psychological knowledge. This is slightly less of a problem than it was some years ago thanks to the wide-scale dissemination of psychological theories, concepts and techniques through the media and through the availability of many relatively inexpensive paperback psychology books. Also, many basic courses in other fields—for teachers, managers, social workers and others—include a grounding in fundamental psychological principles. However, just how well taught or remembered this is one frequently cannot tell to begin with, so if the occupational psychology course requires an understanding of some basic principles the tutor must make arrangements to cover them at the outset. First he will analyse precisely what does need to be explained and what can safely be left out. If quite a lot of basic psychology is needed, he has two options. One is to get the students to cover the ground in the form of pre-course reading, the other is to devote some of the early sessions of the course to this material. The former saves time, but one cannot always guarantee that the students have done the requisite reading. The latter is safer, but time-consuming. If the basic psychology needed is rather less than this, then it can probably be dealt with as and when the particular elements of it come up on the course (though again, if the students can be encouraged to read some psychology paperbacks beforehand, so much the better). In all cases the tutor should request his students to seek elucidation if they are in any doubt.

The second issue to be looked at here concerns the notions students have about psychologists and their discipline. Again, this is partly a function of their familiarity with psychology generally. The main types of erroneous reaction one seems to encounter might be classified thus:

(a) 'You are going to psychoanalyse me'.
(b) 'You read people's minds'.
(c) 'Psychologists are ivory-tower academics'.
(d) 'Psychologists are management lackeys' (and/or 'Do-gooders').
(e) 'They never tell you the truth about what they are doing and why'.

The initial attitude the students have towards psychology can markedly influence the way they receive the teaching, and it is in every tutor's interest to understand and detect his audience's notions about him and his subject as early as possible. Briefly running through the ones given above may help; many of them will be familiar to psychologists and even to students of psychology. The first simply reflects the ambiguity in the public's mind about the similarities and differences between psychologists, psychiatrists and psychoanalysts. Unfortunately, the media are of no help at all in clearing this up—in fact they frequently get them mixed up too. The second one is typical of the rather defensive reaction many people have, based on the notion of the psychologist as some kind of magician; it implies almost total ignorance of what is involved in the study of psychology. Amazingly, even well-educated and successful people sometimes come out with this kind of misapprehension. The third, (c) above, is one that is particularly characteristic of some managers, especially the lower-level or poorer quality ones in my experience. However, one encounters hints of it in many management groups, and those who have this attitude are quite likely to think that 'psychologists say what everyone knows in language that nobody understands'. The fourth view, (d), is one that is held by some trade unionists who suspect that he who pays the piper calls the tune; unfortunately, this particular image of the psychologist is not always totally erroneous. The last of these five reactions to psychologists is one that affects the applied psychologist in his normal work more than the teacher of occupational psychology. It arises from psychologists' lamentable track-record of deception of subjects in experiments. Often it is really desirable that people should not understand why studies are being carried out, for if they do they will alter their behaviour from what it would normally be. Quite apart from the fact that telling them the experiment is about something else or explaining nothing about its purpose, it frequently leads to other kinds of distortion, the whole idea of deception raises important ethical questions. But by now many individuals have the expectation that psychologists are less than honest about their operations, and this lack of trust is not entirely undeserved.

What can the tutor do about these essentially negative reactions that may interfere with what he wishes to communicate? His audience tells him something; looking at who they are beforehand, he might infer that a younger student group will be more open-minded (though not necessarily better informed) than older groups (e.g. middle-management level staff). Anyway, he will want to find out as much as he can about this group's acquaintance with psychology, in particular whether they have had any psychological input to any previous training and whether they are likely to have encountered psychologists in other aspects of their work. If they have had none, then he must be ready for just about anything. A pre-course reading list of short and readable psychology paperbacks is once more of great help, providing this is not too much of a luxury for the length of the course concerned. Reading of this kind will help dispel many of the more bizarre images and ideas. If the length of the course is such that this can be re-inforced in the early sessions with some further explanation of the role of the psychologist, so much the better.

Once the course has actually started, the tutor may feel it wise to take some soundings as to his students' attitudes to psychology. Informal conversation with them might produce some information on this, but probably the best thing to do is to involve the students as early as possible in some discussion topic that will allow them to express their ideas and feelings about the subject. This will give the tutor a much better idea of what he is dealing with. Incidentally, it would be a mistake to assume that all students are broadly favourable to psychology simply because they are on the course: some of them on management courses will have attended because they have to, some simply to get a qualification and some because other (non-psychology) elements of the course attracted them.

Involvement and participation of students in the course generally, as advocated earlier for other reasons, is a good safety-valve and also acts as a check on misunderstandings. The tutor should make clear at the start that queries or contributions from the students are welcome and can be raised at any time in the session. The other thing he can do to dispel any unfavourable or mistaken ideas about psychologists is to project himself and his discipline appropriately. For example, if he is faced by a no-nonsense, down-to-earth group of managers then they are more likely to listen to what he says and take note of it if he can convince them by the style and content of his teaching that he is equally rooted in reality (as pointed out earlier, studies as closely relevant to the situation of the audience help in this respect). One aspect of this is his own appearance— if he walks in looking like the stereotype academic, then anyone with the 'ivory-tower' image of psychologists will feel confirmed in his view. Unfortunately, some audiences (or parts of them) seem less inclined to listen to a teacher who they perceive as being 'not one of us'. If the tutor is really concerned about persuading the students of the validity of his views, theories, findings, etc., he will have to think about whether he will go down better dressed in a fashion likely to be more consistent with that of his audience.

No matter how he presents himself to audiences of this kind, the tutor needs to prepare himself for more questions, personal anecdotes and even sometimes hostility from these students than he is ever likely to get from undergraduates. More mature students are less backward in coming forward, so to speak. This sometimes makes the less confident tutor feel even more insecure, but it is usually a fairly healthy sign—at least they are listening!

In planning the course it is sometimes useful to try introducing material into the early sessions that will challenge existing beliefs and disconfirm some 'commonsense' notions and expectations. If you can do this early on, it will help break down any tendency to think 'Well, I could have told you that', which is a not unknown phenomenon. Asking the students to say what they would expect the findings from such-and-such a study to be before revealing them and showing how they do not conform to expectations can provide a salutary lesson.

One last point on the students' image of psychologists and their profession. So far only negative or incorrect attitudes and ideas have been mentioned. There are some students who are in quite the opposite direction, having an unrealistically high regard for psychologists (can there be such a thing, we ask ourselves in all modesty?!) or being over-swift in wanting to climb on to the latest psychological bandwagon. This is much less of a problem to deal with and is chiefly a matter of trying to give the students a critical perspective on psychological theory and research, particularly in relation to new developments. However, this raises the question of the students' interpretation of psychological findings in general, which is the fifth and last main difficulty in teaching non-psychologists that will be discussed here. It resolves into trying to steer students between the two extremes of believing nothing on the one hand and of enthusiastically accepting everything as gospel on the other. This can be a problem on conventional undergraduate courses in psychology, but it is more difficult still when teaching shorter courses to other groups. There is little time or scope for an adequate representation of academic debate on these shorter courses. Even if there were, it would often not be appreciated as many of the students would be looking for something to help them interpret, understand and deal with various problems in their work environment. Giving them a quick but nicely balanced debate on, say, the value of intelligence tests may breed more confusion and dissatisfaction than anything else. The danger is then that they will become overly sceptical and feel they can place their trust in nothing. Without the presentation of contrary or qualifying findings, however, the students may acquire an unrealistically simple view of the situation. Inevitably, this is a problem that each tutor has to solve for himself according to the type of course and student he is dealing with. In taking what seems to be the right balance, he will probably have to be flexible, adjusting his approach as he goes along and sees how the students are reacting. As a general point, however, one can say that description of too many research studies (or too much detail about a few of them) is unlikely to be very helpful. Whilst most undergraduate course lectures are heavily laced with empirical findings, the same kind of material in similar quantities given to older students on short courses tends to be either confusing or tedious (or both).

How can the tutor assess whether he has pitched his material at the right level and given his students a realistic appraisal of whatever the topic was? Some feedback will obviously be obtained during the course itself, but this can be added to by asking the students to make some post-course commitment based on the content of the course—in other words, asking the students at the end of the course to publicly specify some way in which they will actively use at least part of what they have learned in their normal working environment afterwards. If they cannot or will not do this, it may be that either they see no relevance of the material taught to them or that they simply have not been able to understand it well enough to relate to. If they can and do make such commitments, these will help the tutor decide whether people have received and utilized the information he put across in a desirable way. This of course is part of the wider question of deciding whether what is taught meets the students' needs, as was discussed earlier (p. 311). The evaluation or monitoring of the course advocated then can also help in gauging whether the right balance has been achieved in presenting the material, just as the post-course action commitments of the students can be used as another way of judging how well students' needs have been met.

SUMMARY AND CONCLUSION

The ways in which occupational psychology is taught in all its various settings could in many cases be generalized to teaching other elements of psychology in different spheres. Strangely, though, the approach taken still seems to be limited mainly to this one area of the subject. Perhaps it is not entirely appropriate to describe it as 'an approach' because it involves a number of techniques that vary according to the audience involved. However, it is possible to draw together the main themes of this chapter and to summarize the advice given. First, the needs of the students have to be studied and analysed, a process involving consultation with others connected with the course and also doing some fact-finding about the likely nature of the students. Once the content of the course is broadly decided on, the need for pre-course reading will be clear when appropriate. On the course itself, do not rely too heavily on lecturing as the method of teaching; adapt both the content and teaching techniques to the needs and reactions of the students. As far as possible, involve the students in their own learning experience. Seek, and be sensitive to, feedback on the relevance of the material being taught, how well understood it is and how you are coming across personally. Try to retain a degree of flexibility so that you can change at least a little of the content or timetabling of the course to suit the requirements of any particular course membership.

Occupational psychology, like other branches of the subject, is in a continual process of evolution. It undergoes many shifts in emphasis, not least because it seeks to remain relevant in a changing world. This, along with the emergence of new techniques and new research findings, means that the nature of what is taught (and how, and to whom) will change too. In recent years, for example, there has been a shift towards the perspective of organizational psychology. Speculating on the future is somewhat hazardous but it seems likely that there will be an increasing trend towards inter-disciplinary teaching and research in this area. Developments like equal opportunities legislation, the application of psychological ideas to accountancy and (as yet, only minimally) to economics, and the growth of environmental psychology will all probably contribute to changes in teaching. For example, anyone teaching selection or appraisal as topics can scarcely do so properly today without making some reference to employment legislation or the equal opportunities laws. The pooling of findings and ideas with industrial sociology is something that has been happening for a considerable time, and we may anticipate similar cross-fertilization of thought with other disciplines in future. Within psychology itself, there seems to be a greater realization amongst those working in the applied fields that they share many problems in common, particularly in relation to dealing and negotiating with other groups, be they in hospitals, schools or factories. This could conceivably lead to a wider teaching of occupational psychology within the framework of other applied psychology courses.

APPENDIX

The following addresses may be found useful in obtaining information:

(a) Information on course content and requirements in occupational psychology:

Department of Occupational Psychology, Birkbeck College, Malet Street, London, WC1E 7HX, UK.

Department of Behaviour in Organizations, University of Lancaster, Furness Cottage, Bailrigg, Lancaster, LA1 4YZ, UK.

University of Hull, MSc Course in Industrial Psychology, 26 Newland Park, Hull, UK.

MRC Social and Applied Psychology Unit, The University, Sheffield, S10 2TN, UK.

The Secretary, Division of Occupational Psychology, The British Psychological Society, St Andrews House, 48 Princess Road East, Leicester, LE1 7DR, UK.

The Division of Industrial and Organizational Psychology, The American Psychological Association, 1200 Seventeenth Street NW, Washington DC 20036, USA.

(b) Information on training films and other teaching aids:

Central Film Library, Government Building, Bromyard Avenue, Acton, London, W3 7JB, UK.

Video Arts Ltd., 205 Wardour Street, London, WIV 3FA, UK.

Management Training Ltd., Management House, Parker Street, London, WC2B 5PT, UK.

Management Games Ltd., 11 Woburn Street, Ampthill, Bedford, MK45 2HP, UK.

REFERENCES

Anstey, E., Fletcher, C., and Walker, J. (1976). *Staff Appraisal and Development*. London: Allen & Unwin.

Argyris, C., and Schon, D. A. (1974). *Theory in Practice: Increasing Professional Effectiveness*. London: Josey-Bass.

Davies, I. K. (1971). *The Management of Learning*. London: McGraw-Hill.

Davis, R., and Shackleton, V. J. (1976). *The Psychology of Work*. London: Methuen.

Egan, G. (1975). *The Skilled Helper*. California: Brooks/Cole.

Elgood, C. (1976). *Handbook of Management Games*. London: Gower Press.

Gagne, R. M., and Briggs, L. J. (1974). *The Principles of Instructional Design*. New York: Holt, Rinehart & Winston.

Gibbs, G. I. (ed.) (1974). *Handbook of Games and Simulation Exercises*. London: Spon.

Hackett, P. (1978). *Interview Skills Training—Role Play Exercises*. London: IPM Management Reports.

Heller, F. A. (1969). Group Feed-back Analysis: A Method of Field Research. *Psychological Bulletin*, **72**, 108–117.

Heller, F. A. (1976). Towards a Practical Psychology of Work. *Journal of Occupational Psychology*, **49**, 45–54.

Keenan, A. (1977). Selection Interview Training—An Individual-centred Approach. *J. Euro. Indust. Training*, **1**, 6, 7–9.

Lewis, C., Edgerton, N., and Parkinson, B. (1976). Interview Training—Finding the Facts and Minding the Feelings. *Pers. Mgt.*, May 1976, 29–33.

Lowe, G., Bachler, L., Donaldson, J., Drewicz, J., Gill, A., and Morrissey, M. (1977). Topic Areas in Psychology as Represented in British University Examinations. *Bull. Br. Psychol. Soc.*, **30**, 218–219.

McCormick, E. J., and Tiffin, J. (1975). *Industrial Psychology*. London: Allen & Unwin, sixth edition.

Orne, M. T. (1962). On the Social Psychology of the Psychological Experiment: With Particular Reference to Demand Characteristics and their Implications. *American Psychologist*, **17**, 776–783.

Rosenthal, R. (1961). On the Social Psychology of the Psychological Experiment: The Experimenter's Hypothesis as an Unintended Determinant of Experimental Results. *Am. Sci.*, **51**, 268–283.

Sisson, K. (1977). *Negotiating in Practice: Management Report*. London: Institute of Personnel Management.

Stammer, R., and Patrick, J. (1975). *The Psychology of Training*. London: Methuen.

Walton, R. E. (1969). *Interpersonal Peacemaking: Confrontations and Third-party Consultation*. London: Addison-Wesley.

Warr, P. D. (ed.) (1978). *Psychology of Work* (2nd edn). London: Penguin.

The Teaching of Psychology
Edited by J. Radford and D. Rose
© 1980 John Wiley & Sons Ltd.

17

The Context of a Third World Country

ROBERT SERPELL AND MUYUNDA MWANALUSHI

THE PRESENT STATE OF PSYCHOLOGY TEACHING IN THE THIRD WORLD

The Third World encompasses a majority of the world's nations and houses a majority of its people. The vast conglomerates of China and India take their place under this rubric along with small island communities. Institutions of higher learning in the Third World also cover a vast range both of size and age. We have not attempted, in preparing this chapter, to review the provisions that exist for the teaching of psychology in all these diverse places. Instead we will draw on our experience at the University of Zambia (UNZA) to illustrate some major issues which we believe have some generality of application across many other institutions in Third World countries.

The Student Population

Psychology in Zambia, as elsewhere in the world, is taught almost exclusively at the tertiary level of formal education. In Third World countries the pyramid of student enrollment tapers to a narrow peak at tertiary level. For instance in Zambia, from a base of 72,800 pupils enrolled in Grade 1 in 1962, the number of entrants to the University and other post-secondary institutions in 1974 was only 2800, less than 4 per cent of those who started out (Sanyal, Case, Dow and Jackman, 1976, p. 115).

Career Opportunities

The range of education available to this small elite is partly determined by a centralized policy of manpower development planning. On the attainment of its political independence in 1964, the Zambian nation numbered 108 university graduates and barely 1200 people with a complete secondary education among its indigenous population of about 3.5 million (Sanyal *et al.*, 1976, p. 57). The copper mining industry (the hub of the national economy which until recently accounted for more than half the Government's total recurrent revenue) and the civil service (including the teaching service) were staffed at the professional level predominantly by expatriate personnel. A crash programme of expansion of educational facilities was therefore instituted with the goal of supplying educated Zambian manpower to both of these key sectors of employment. Within the civil service the greatest demand in terms of numbers was for teachers and administrators, followed by medical practitioners, engineers and other technical professions. In 1975 a major economic crisis, long foreshadowed by economists, struck Zambia with a sharp fall in the international price of copper. As a result, a shift of emphasis took place in the planning of the economy, with high priority now being attached to agriculture. This has therefore now become another focus of demand for highly educated manpower.

Within this manpower planning framework, the principal demands for psychology teaching have been related to education and to industry, with a secondary demand related to health. These demands are expressed at three levels:

1 the immediate professional staffing of existing psychological services;

2 professional psychologists for the expansion of existing services; and

3 psychology as one component of the training programme for other professions.

We shall briefly discuss these in turn.

The Ministry of Education, the Ministry of Labour and Social Services and the Mining Industry Manpower Services Unit provide the three main employment opportunities for professional psychologists in Zambia. The Psychological Service of the Ministry of Education is responsible for the annual setting of two aptitude tests which carry a heavy weighting in the nationwide selection examination for admission to the secondary schools. This Service also attempts to co-ordinate career guidance activities across the secondary schools, and has been actively involved in planning for the establishment of facilities for special education. The Educational and Occupational Assessment Service (EOAS) of the Ministry of Labour and Social Services constructs the Zambia Advanced General Ability Test (ZAGAT) which is administered to all secondary school leavers. ZAGAT scores, Cambridge 'O' level School Certificate results and other records of school performance are stored by the EOAS on a central register to which *bona fide* employers have access for occupational selection. In addition this Service also mounts specialized selection exercises for government, parastatal and private organizations. The Mining Industry Manpower Services Unit (MIMSU) is also principally concerned with personnel selection, in addition to advising on the design of training and accident prevention pro- grammes for the mines.

All three of these organizations have been greatly preoccupied with the development and standardization of mental tests for use in educational and occupational selection, with the result that other pressing needs, such as special education, especially for the mentally handicapped, and the design of industrial working conditions, have not received their full attention.

Although the training of professional and academic psychologists is usually of special interest to teachers of psychology, it is important to recognize that they constitute only a small fraction of the demand in the employment sector. By far the largest group of students who need to study some psychology are those training for the teaching profession. Other groups for whom psychology has been prescribed or recommended as a component of their degree programme at UNZA are students for degrees in medicine and in business administration.

The curriculum needs of these students who do not intend to specialize in psychology are generally quite different from those aspiring to a career as a professional psychologist. This problem has been met at UNZA with two alternative strategies. Where the number of non-specialist students is relatively small, the less advanced courses within the specialist programme have been opened to non-specialists (e.g. biology, sociology and business administration students). Entry to the more advanced courses is made conditional on the successful completion of more elementary 'prerequisite' courses in psychology. On the other hand, with larger groups a more 'tailor-made' approach can be justified. Thus at UNZA two half courses in psychology are specially designed for the needs of medical students and two full courses for the needs of educa- tion students.

The effect of mounting specially tailored courses for particular professions is usually a fragmentation of the administrative base. At UNZA courses for medical students are still taught by members of the Psychology Department which is based in the School of Humanities and Social Sciences, but for some years the School of Medicine has expressed the desire to appoint 'its own' teaching staff to teach the programme. The School of Education at UNZA has already taken over the teaching of psychology to its students and includes a number of psychologists on its staff, and so do some other teacher-training institutions in the country. Such positions, of course, create another career prospect for graduates of UNZA who have specialized in psychology.

Curriculum Content

For the teaching of psychology to be responsive to the development priorities of a Third World nation requires not only recognizing the national priorities in respect of categories of manpower, it also calls for a curriculum which takes account of the peculiar psychological issues which will confront the graduate working in this particular society. Psychology as a science has emerged from the research and writings of a group of scholars most of whom were familiar only with Western cultures and Western societies. This poses a problem for the selection of reading material as we shall see below. More fundamentally, however, it places a great responsibility on the teachers of psychology in Third World countries to identify issues of special importance to the understanding of behaviour in the society in which their students have grown up, in which they are presently living and in which they will ultimately work.

Current approaches to this dimension of psychology teaching vary widely both in the range of variables they encompass and in the sources on which they draw. Many lecturers acknowledge the pedagogical value of citing topical anecdotes to illustrate phenomena which otherwise might appear remote from their students' experience. Such anecdotes may be supplemented in class discussion by inviting students to illustrate theoretical principles from their own observations. For expatriate lecturers who have recently arrived in the country such observations by students may quite often include unfamiliar phenomena. The success with which these are handled in discussion will depend in large part on the maturity and intelligence of the students. Systematic extensions of this approach have been tried out in several courses at UNZA, with lecturers inviting students to write descriptions of selected experiences, case studies or full autobiographical essays (cf. Bloom, 1972).

A more formal approach to incorporating student experience within the framework of psychology teaching is the mounting of demonstrations and class experiments. Most psychology courses at UNZA include some 'practical classes' in which either groups or individuals act as subjects in formal experiments. Where the expected results are obtained, these serve both as a means of highlighting theoretical material presented in lectures and reading material, and also as an introduction to research methods and statistics. But on the occasions when theoretically unexpected results are obtained, the interpretations available must often include cross-cultural differences between the present students and other populations from whom the theory has been derived. The logic of drawing such inferences is, however, notoriously complex (cf. Cole and Scribner, 1974; Goodnow, 1975; Serpell, 1976). For this reason alone a case can be made for the introduction of locally conducted studies into the curriculum at an early stage.

Local Research Material

Local psychological research available in Zambia is rather limited in extent— there is certainly much less than in India or Mexico, for instance—and our experience in this respect may therefore be less typical of the general situation in Third World countries than is the case for other parameters. The following major categories, however, are probably of general relevance to psychological research in the Third World. One category rather poorly represented in the Zambian literature is that of direct replications of experiments designed and first performed in More Industrialized Countries (MICs). Within this category we may distinguish those studies which yielded essentially identical results to those of the original (MIC) study and those which did not. The latter often give rise to follow-up studies. These fall into the second (and probably the largest) category of studies, designed to build on and extend knowledge established by MIC research, and firmly conceived within the general framework of a theory or theories developed in MICs. A third category, which like the first is rather poorly represented in the Zambian literature, comprises studies which are based on local theoretical innovations. These must, of course, ultimately take their place alongside MIC theoretical notions and be assessed by the same logical and empirical criteria. We will have more to say about them below.

Although any theory tends to generate scope for its own extension, the extensions of MIC psychological research most often found in studies in the second category listed above draw their inspiration from one of two kinds of consideration: (a) cross-cultural differences in the environment influencing child development; and (b) cross-national differences in priority social problems calling for applied research. The cross-cultural literature regarding human development provides an increasingly well articulated perspective on the first of these issues (see bibliography) and the Zambian research literature has contributed a number of empirical studies in this field (cf. Kingsley, 1977b). In the field of applied research the majority of local studies have been concerned with test development, reflecting the importance attached to educational and occupational selection by the existing professional services. The recognition of other local priorities has only recently begun to generate research in such areas as alcohol consumption, multi-lingualism, the generation gap, and the conservation of animal resources (Haworth and Mwanalushi, 1977; Serpell, 1977b; Mwanalushi, 1976; Schuster, 1976). Other issues of topical concern have only been related to psychology in the form of speculative discussion (e.g. malnutrition, road traffic accidents, worker participation in industrial decision-making, traditional healing practices and mob behaviour).

This patchy development of local psychological research in relation to social priorities gives rise to a teaching problem which is probably not unique to Zambia. On the one hand psychology teachers would like to situate their courses in a context of 'relevance', while on the other hand they would prefer to emphasize rigorously established research results. At the present stage of history, if they lean too far in the first direction they run the risk of presenting psychology as an armchair discipline which is lacking in empirical rigour. But if they confine themselves to well-established results, issues of local signifi-

cance dwindle to a small proportion of the total curriculum. The teaching programme at UNZA presently reflects an unstable compromise between these
two extremes. The broad framework of the programme reflected in course
titles (e.g. Basic Human Processes, Personality and Social Psychology; Cognitive and Perceptual Development; Skills; Mental Testing) implies a universalistic view of the discipline. But depending on the staffing of these courses from
year to year, the proportion of local material included in lectures and written
assignments may range from next to nothing up to more than 50 per cent.
One development of special importance has been the growing number of courses
in which students are given the opportunity not merely to carry out research
procedures but to generate their own topics for systematic, albeit preliminary,
investigation under academic supervision.

Before concluding this review of psychology teaching at UNZA we must
consider its contribution to the experimental Social Science Foundation
Course, which has now been mounted for four successive years in the School
of Humanities and Social Sciences. Centred around a theme which varied
from year to year, the course was intended to introduce first year students to
basic concepts in economics, political science, psychology and sociology,
and to the interlinkages and complementarity among the four disciplines.
Since all staff were expected to conduct seminars on all aspects of the course
a great deal of preparation was required. In addition the task of developing a
coherent approach from a multi-disciplinary base was extremely demanding.
In respect of the knowledge component of the course, psychology seemed to be
more difficult to integrate with the other disciplines than they were with each
other. The experiment as originally conceived has recently been discontinued,
and with effect from 1978 a modified, single-course version will be offered with
emphasis on methodology, concurrently with optional separate introductory
courses in each of the four disciplines.

A thoughtful evaluation of the course in its various forms has been written
by Shanks (1979). Other Third World universities contemplating such an
approach to Foundation Year teaching would do well to heed his warning that
an essential prerequisite for the continuing success of such a course is a high
degree of consensus among the staff involved regarding social science theory
and ideology.

SUGGESTIONS ABOUT THE DEVELOPMENT OF PSYCHOLOGY
TEACHING IN THIRD WORLD COUNTRIES

Most readers of this book will share an attitudinal bias which accords significance to the psychological dimensions of any social problem. This bias,
however, is seldom shared by policy-makers in the Third World or elsewhere.
They tend to perceive economic and political dimensions as relatively more
important. Very few politicians or administrators have received more than the

slightest exposure to contemporary psychological theory. Their image of the discipline is dominated by pathological phenomena such as psychotic behaviour, emotional crises and mental handicap, and perhaps a nodding acquaintance with the format of IQ tests. This narrow conception of psychology gives rise to an equally narrow view of how the discipline can contribute to the solution of social problems. The teacher of psychology must challenge this narrow view if for no other reason than that he cannot allow it to constrain the range of psychology he teaches.

Psychology and National Development

The task of explicating the full potential of psychology as a source of contributions to national development can be addressed in a variety of complementary ways. One might be described as delegation: although the teacher's immediate audience is quite small, these students will in turn have an opportunity to present to others a different image of psychology. Let us consider, for example, a student who is preparing for a career in industry. This student has a right to be taught the skills which his employers will expect. But in addition he should be encouraged to think about possible extensions of the role which is likely to be assigned to him on appointment. Three specific ways of doing this deserve mention:

1 the student should be made aware of activities undertaken by psychologists in industry elsewhere, which are not currently attempted in the student's own country. The advantages and difficulties inherent in introducing such additions to the work of a local industrial psychologist should be explored during training;
2 where techniques and approaches have been imported from outside, the student should be encouraged to evaluate critically their appropriateness to the local situation. A more radical appraisal may be possible for the student than for a person already in employment; and
3 a sociological perspective should be offered to the student on how he as a psychologist will operate within a social context. In particular the need to collaborate with (and to work through) colleagues with much fewer years of formal education than him- or herself requires emphasis. This in turn implies the need to cultivate skills of communication and management.

A second approach is participation in policy development and 'helping out'. This has been discussed elsewhere in relation to research objectives (Serpell, 1978). Third World academics are often called upon to participate in the formulation of policy and in its implementation in ways which are not open to those working in more industrialized countries. Such participation is more than a luxury or side-line for the teacher of psychology. It provides an opportunity for discussing and testing the practicality of his ideas concerning the issues listed as 1 and 2 above. Given the very limited resources for immediate systematic research, this kind of informal evaluation provides a valuable check on the 'armchair research' referred to above. In parallel to the teachers' opportunities for learning, these forays into the outside world provide occasions for psychologists to renegotiate with policy-makers the definition of their role and that of their students in national development.

Social Change and Cultural Relativism

Space does not allow us in this chapter to elaborate on all the unique qualities of psychology. We will therefore outline only one which has a special significance in many Third World countries. It is a commonplace that social change is accelerated in Third World countries, and students of every discipline face problems in relation to this facet of their environment. The problems have many dimensions. Especially salient in the Third World are the gross disparities across generations in access to the new technology, and the tendency for the traditional–novel continuum to coincide with the potentially independent continuum of indigenous-exotic. When we add that tertiary educational facilities are typically located in urban centres which command more than their share of the benefits of modern technology, a personal dilemma confronting most Third World tertiary students comes into focus.

These students are located in a setting which is both physically and culturally remote from that in which they grew up and in which their parents and less 'successful' contemporaries are still living. The prevalent ideology used to justify their educational endeavours is one of technological progress and national autonomy. How then do the students reconcile their desire to master a new and powerful technology with the desire to assert the legitimacy of a valued indigenous cultural tradition, when the technology is largely exotic and unknown to those individuals who best represent the cherished tradition?

In Zambia, as in many parts of Africa, the cognitive systems of much of the rural population are characterized by Christian values and traditional beliefs in supernatural and magical forces, and it is from this kind of home background that most university students have come. Some writers have argued that the combined effect of Christian values and traditional beliefs is an impediment to 'open-mindedness' of the cognitive system requisite for 'objective manipulation and detached analytic thought' characteristic of the scientific method which psychology has adopted (Bloom, 1976). Others, however, have noted that the models and procedures of the physical sciences have serious limitations when applied to the study of human experience (e.g. McGuigan, 1963; Orne, 1962; Rosenthal, 1965; Shotter, 1975).

Bloom (1976, p. 133) maintains that 'in Africa (as elsewhere) the major role of psychology is to demonstrate that a scientifically disciplined approach to the analysis and understanding of human behaviour offers an *alternative* to magical, religious and philosophical explanations. Thus, in their training as psychologists, students may develop intellectual and emotional conflicts' (our italics).

This dissonance, for the African student of psychology, is supposed to arise from the conflict between 'Western abstract thought and other traditional, supernatural modes' (p. 132). It seems to us that to contrast the 'scientific' and the traditional–supernatural modes in this manner may be both misleading and counter-productive. In the first place, supernatural beliefs are not peculiar to Africans (Jahoda, 1969). Second, there exist significant similarities between Western belief systems and African traditional beliefs (Horton, 1967a, 1967b; Okonji, 1975). Both systems speculate about the nature and causes of human behaviour; they are both involved in the business of prediction, control and change of behaviour; both speculate about the faculties of knowing, feeling and willing, etc. Thus, both systems 'hold theories of causation, both derive specific explanatory hypotheses from these theories and both carefully apply recognized tests to these hypotheses' (Marwick, 1974, p. 581). Moreover 'Africans, in the same way as Europeans, have appreciated and successfully based their routines of living on principles of causation [and] on the logical implications of ideas' (Forde, 1954, pp. x–xi). It seems reasonable, therefore, to consider these orientations as different perspectives or different levels of explanation which should be treated as complementary and not contradictory. Third, it has been found that, despite their real differences, the systems can co-exist in a single individual without evidence of cognitive dissonance (Jahoda, 1970). Our view of the role of psychology in this domain is that it should build on this cognitive potential for accommodating diversity. Rather than encouraging African students to reject, *in toto*, the African cosmological viewpoint (and thus to develop a 'closed' cognitive system), psychology teaching should aim to promote a sceptical and inquisitive open-mindedness.

A curriculum with this objective must seek to provide students with the conceptual tools to acknowledge multiple belief systems within a coherent framework. One such framework is the sociology of knowledge which traces the different beliefs to their various social origins. A relativistic psychology can supplement this framework by showing how different sets of assumptions are consistent with different interpretations of behaviour. We have found this exercise to be intellectually stimulating and illuminating for Zambian students in relation to such topics as parental care for infants, the assessment of intelligence and causes of mental illness. The last of these, for instance, constitutes an arena for two contrasting types of analysis, the medical models of MIC-trained psychiatrists and the spiritual models of local traditional healers. Most of our students have some first- or second-hand experience of traditional healing practices, and are well aware of their extensive clientele among the urban, educated population of Zambia (see Leeson and Frankenberg, 1977). Class discussions focused on the contrasting interpretations of a given cluster of symptoms by these practitioners and by the hospital psychiatrists enable each student to 'think through' a given line of reasoning based on certain premises without feeling emotionally affronted by the contradictions it may generate with some of his or her cherished beliefs. By acknowledging and discussing the potential scientific validity of their personal convictions, this approach to psychology seeks to enhance the personal development of the students with the promotion of insightful self-awareness and understanding.

In addition to providing students with a tool for analysing their own experience, a relativistic psychology has other advantages. Theoretical research is still very much dominated by Western models in the Third World. Among the students of today must be found the researchers of tomorrow. To emphasize in their teaching that current psychological theory owes much of its form and its content to the Western cultural foundations on which it has been built is to invite students to contemplate radical alternatives, some of which may eventually generate important new theoretical insights for a psychology more appropriate to behaviour in their own cultures.

SOME TEACHING METHODS OF PARTICULAR VALUE IN THE THIRD WORLD

We pointed out in the first section that psychology courses at UNZA attract a large number of students from different programmes with a variety of reasons for studying psychology. This varied background brings with it a marked heterogeneity of needs, requirements and expectations. We also noted that the cognitive systems of the student population tend to be dominated by Christian values and traditional beliefs in supernatural and magical forces (see the section about suggestions for the development of psychology teaching in Third world countries).

In teaching psychology, it is important to take account of both of these dimensions of students' backgrounds. This makes the task peculiarly challenging and stimulating but at times also frustrating. Effective teaching of the concepts, methods and insights of psychology under these circumstances demands the use of a wide variety of teaching methods including modifications of traditional methods. We now turn to an examination of these methods.

Lectures

Departments of psychology in the Third World are generally understaffed, and are obliged to rely heavily on lecturing. However, the traditional expository lecture has many limitations (Bloom, 1953; Bligh, 1962). Moreover in the Third World, teaching is often in a second language for both students and staff.

At UNZA, English is a second language for at least half the academic staff, who speak it in a wide variety of accents.

Because of these shortcomings of the traditional expository lecture, our experience suggests that 'mixed' methods of teaching during what is scheduled as a lecture period are more effective. This involves a mixture of the lecture with discussion and question sessions. With regard to questions emanating from the 'floor', it is often better that these be answered by other students and that the lecturer simply elaborate on what has been said and provide illustrations. Where no-one in the class seems to have understood the point and is therefore able to give a satisfactory answer, this gives the lecturer an opportunity to provide clarification which facilitates understanding before going on to the next topic. In some cases such questions reveal incomplete understanding of assigned reading material and the lecturer may find it necessary to explain such material to the class. The advantage of this approach consists in providing immediate *feedback* to both lecturer and students.

Seminars

Over the last few years the Psychology Department at UNZA has used the seminar as a teaching tool and Kingsley (1977a) has subjected it to systematic study. In general, the results have not been entirely satisfactory. There is a tendency for many students to approach the preparation of a seminar presentation in the same way they approach the writing of an essay, with the result that they usually end up reading out to the class what amounts to an essay without apparently having thoroughly mastered the material. Nevertheless the potential benefits of the seminar seem to us to make it worth devoting further efforts to developing it as a teaching mode. One potential benefit of special importance, in addition to facilitating learning through active participation, is the opportunity for students to develop teaching and communication skills. These skills are essential not only for teachers but also for almost all graduate, professional personnel in the Third World (including psychologists), since they will often be called upon to 'educate' their fellow workers in the nature and value of new ideas and techniques. Furthermore the seminar creates an atmosphere in which students feel free to challenge and question one another's opinions more readily than those of a lecturer especially on issues about which little empirical information is available, such as the role of traditional healers, the social functions of supernatural beliefs, language usage, etc., thereby providing very valuable insights into such phenomena.

Experiments and Demonstrations

Exercises in the design and execution of experiments provide an excellent setting in which to instil discipline and sharpen observational skills. Students are introduced in this context to the principles of analysing relevant variables, controlling as many as possible, to the exercise of caution in assigning causal roles to variables and to the use of inferential statistics in drawing conclusions. One difference between experimentation in the Third World and other contexts lies in the materials used in experiments. Many an experimenter trained in the West has found it frustrating to carry out experiments in the Third World due to the non-availability of 'conventional' materials for experiments. This situation calls for inventiveness on the part of the instructor to find comparable substitutes from locally available materials, as well as to select relevant topics and culturally relevant social contexts for conducting experiments.

Experiments also serve the function while introducing students to the scientific method, of demystifying the scientific model itself. As they engage in various experimental activities they come to realize that the experimental approach has much in common with everyday modes of thought as well as having certain limitations. This is particularly important since students in the Third World are less likely than students in MICs to encounter laboratory-type situations outside the university.

Teaching Through Research

Underwood (1957) has emphasized the importance of imparting to students skills in research methodology. In the Third World, as well as imparting these skills, student participation in research is seen as a useful teaching method since it gives students the opportunity to learn by experience. This is important because, unlike students elsewhere, many of our students are, immediately upon graduation, called upon to assume challenging roles as administrative or research officers who are expected to apply their newly acquired skills to a wide range of complex problems (cf. Gardiner, 1975).

Of course, student participation in research activity has other benefits for both the students and the staff. For the students, it gives them the opportunity to feed into their study programme ideas and issues which are not acknowledged in the foreign literature (on which we have to rely for so much of our teaching in the Third World). For the staff, particularly foreign staff (who tend to be in a majority in many departments of psychology in the Third World, especially in Africa), it provides them with the opportunity to learn from their students about the social context in which they are teaching and to which the student often has greater access than the staff. In the Department of Psychology at UNZA teaching through research is therefore considered highly desirable and an increasing emphasis is placed on active student participation in research. In higher level courses students are required to carry out research projects as part of their learning and this contributes to their continuous assessment.

USEFUL MATERIALS FOR TEACHING PSYCHOLOGY IN THE THIRD WORLD

Laboratory Facilities

The University of Zambia had the rare opportunity in 1967 to plan a psychology laboratory from scratch with fairly generous funding (see Heron, 1969). The building and equipment which resulted have been in operation, at the time of writing, for about ten years. We will attempt in this section to highlight those specialized features of the design which have been most and least successful in the hope that other departments in the making elsewhere in the Third World may learn from our experience.

A laboratory serves both teaching and research functions and the UNZA laboratory has many strengths as a research base, but our concern here will only be with the teaching functions. From this point of view, the most intensively and effectively used features of the building in our experience have been the lecture room with its projection facilities for slides and films and the demonstration rooms. We have made extensive use of the films produced by the American Psychological Association and the slides published by McGraw-Hill (see bibliography). It is perhaps worth noting that the physical set-up for implanting an electrode in the brain or for conditioning a pigeon is less likely to be part of a student's general background experience in a Third World university than in a MIC. Hence the special importance we attach to the use of these visual aids. The observation chamber, with large one-way screens looking into both adjacent rooms, has also been extensively used for observational studies.

Another potentially important facility, the set of cubicles, has been somewhat under-utilized. Departments planning for the future would do well to note that facilities for individualized practicals will only yield their full potential in conjunction with a fairly low student–staff ratio. Also somewhat under-utilized for teaching has been the animal room. The back-up facilities for breeding and maintaining a colony of caged animals call for a good deal of administrative work. The only lecturers likely to undertake such work are those for whom the exercise can be linked to a research interest. Here too, then, a strategic factor emerges from our experience: departments planning a psychology laboratory would do well, in our view, to decide on whether laboratory animal research is to become a priority focus in the department's work. If not, an animal room, if included in the plan, is probably doomed to be chronically under-utilized. Two subsidiary facilities in our laboratory deserve special mention: the photographic dark-room and the capacious stores for equipment. Both of these have been fully utilized and constitute assets envied by other departments at UNZA.

In our stores, in addition to general purpose equipment such as tape-recorders, cameras and timers, we have also built up a stock of raw materials for the construction of special purpose apparatus. In our view strenuous efforts need to be made at the level of planning to create an environment in which individual lecturers and students take responsibility whenever possible for the construction, repair and maintenance of the department's equipment. One effect of such a policy would be to divert attention from sophisticated electronic devices towards 'sealing-wax and string' apparatus. We would see this as consistent with the general demand in the Third World for 'appropriate technology' (cf. Schumaker, 1973). Of course, certain industrially produced devices such as calculators, projectors, tape-recorders and cameras convey unique advantages, and we would not advocate giving up these. But many other items of the apparatus needed in any psychology laboratory can be quite easily constructed with wood, aluminium and cardboard, and space should be allocated in the planning of a laboratory for such activities to take place.

An important omission of which we have become conscious in our own facilities is a completely dark room. This needs to be large enough for several people to move around in it both in front of and behind the displays for visual perception experiments. It is notoriously difficult to black out a room completely for such purposes unless it was properly designed. It is therefore well worth including at the initial stage of the architect's plan.

Reading Materials

As a preface to this section it should be noted that the availability of books cannot be taken for granted in most Third World countries, and still less so of journals. Our department is fortunate in having built up a good holding of many of the psychological periodicals during a time when funds were available in relative abundance. Since the beginning of Zambia's economic crisis there has been increasing pressure to discontinue the library's subscriptions to a number of these. The relatively small size of the market for academic publications in Zambia means that commercial booksellers are very cautious about importing such books on speculation. Lecturers are thus forced to rely more heavily than in MICs on mail advertisements for keeping track of the latest publications in their field.

If university lecturers are hampered in their access to publications, it will be very apparent that most of the students when they graduate will experience this shortage to an even greater degree. As a result they will be forced to rely to a great extent on the personal libraries they build up while they are at university. It is thus incumbent on the staff to pay special attention to the selection of useful texts to be ordered by the university bookshop for students to purchase.

In discussing the value of involving students in research activities we made reference to the fact that most literature in the Third World is from the West and written for audiences in such contexts. In fact, present-day psychology is still largely Western-oriented in its methods, concepts and theories. Much of the literature is of uncertain relevance to situations prevailing in the Third World and therefore of limited usefulness to students in such contexts. Selecting reading materials is therefore problematic.

Three kinds of books appear to go some of the way towards meeting this problem. These are: (a) books aimed specifically at Third World audiences; (b) textbooks with a world-wide perspective; and (c) textbooks on cross-cultural psychology. Very few books on psychology in English of which we are aware fall into category (a). El-Abd (1973) and Wickert (1967) both appear to have prepared their books with an African audience in mind. But we would hesitate to include Read (1959) or Wober (1975) since although these books have a clearly regional focus they are addressed at least as much to Western as to African audiences. Even if such books were more widely available, however, they would only be recommended in conjunction with other texts, because of the danger of parochialism. Thus category (a) books should be tempered with other-context-specific literature so as to provide a much broader perspective on human behaviour. Moreover, this may provide some incentive to Third World students to engage in research in their contexts and write about their own experiences thereby contributing to the growing body of knowledge about man and helping to make psychology a more dynamic science of human behaviour.

At the present stage of development of psychology, a world-wide perspective is extremely difficult to adopt. Thus books in category (b) represent a very ambitious and probably risky undertaking. It is probably for this reason that very few such books have been attempted. Whittaker's (1976) introductory text makes a considerable impact with its international variety of photographs, but the research on which the text is based remains more narrowly Western than sheer availability dictates.

We have already hinted at the relevance of our third category of possible reading material, books on cross-cultural psychology. Suffice it to say here that even those authors who favour a universalistic approach (e.g. Brislin, Lonner and Thorndike, 1973; Rohner, 1975) cannot fail to acknowledge the issue of cultural relativism. We have noted in the bibliography some of the outstanding features of the various books available in this field.

FURTHER INFORMATION USEFUL TO INTENDING PSYCHOLOGY TEACHERS IN THE THIRD WORLD: AN ANNOTATED BIBLIOGRAPHY

In order for this section to double as a reference list for citations earlier in the chapter, we have listed publications in alphabetical order of the authors. But in order to draw attention to the category of materials which we consider of special relevance for teaching psychology in a Third World country, we have

confined these to a separate, initial list, with a general reference list included at
the end.

Multi-cultural, Cross-cultural and Regional (African) Perspectives

This listing is more comprehensive for cross-cultural materials than for the
other two categories. We have made no attempt to include regional materials
for other continents than Africa, since this would greatly enlarge the scope
of this short bibliography. Throughout the list IACCP* stands for the International Association of Cross-cultural Psychology.

Awoni, J. O. (1973). The Teaching of Psychology in a Developing Country—
Nigeria. Paper presented at the 1st African Regional Conference of
the IACCP*, Ibadan, Nigeria, 2–7 April 1973. This short paper argues the
case for a 'sandwich' course, allowing students to gain professional experience before completing their formal training. It is based on the experience
of the Psychology Department at the University of Nigeria at Nsukka.

Berry, J. W., and Dasen, P. R. (eds) (1973). *Culture and Cognition: Readings
in Cross-cultural Psychology*. London: Methuen. An excellent, annotated
selection of twenty-five papers, including many of the most seminal cross-
cultural studies of the 1960s. Suitable for upper level undergraduate courses;
available in paperback (see Price-Williams, 1969).

Berry, J. W., and Lonner, W. J. (1975). *Applied Cross-cultural Psychology*.
Amsterdam: Swets & Zeitlinger. Proceedings of the 2nd International
IACCP* Conference, containing fifty-five short papers and a list of sixty-
four more with the authors' addresses. Useful as reference material for
lecturers.

Bloom, L. (1972). Some Values and Attitudes of Young Zambians Studied
Through Spontaneous Autobiographies. *African Social Research*, **14**,
288–300.

Bloom, L. (1976). Psychology and Higher Education in Africa. *African Social
Research*, **22**, 131–146. A well-written provocative paper based on the
author's experience as a lecturer in Nigeria, South Africa and Zambia.
We take issue with some of his views in the second section of this article.
Instructive reading for Third World lecturers.

Brislin, R. W., Lonner, W. J., and Thorndike, R. (1973). *Cross-cultural Research
Methods*. New York: Wiley. A systematic presentation suitable for postgraduate students.

Brislin, R. W., Bochner, S., and Lonner, W. J. (eds) (1975). *Cross-cultural
Perspectives on Learning*. New York: Halsted/Wiley. A very diverse set of
thirteen papers by some of the leading American researchers in cross-
cultural psychology, addressing their favourite themes (not all related obviously to 'learning'), and by one Pakistani on the adjustment problems of
foreign Muslim students in Pakistan. Reference material for postgraduate
students and lecturers.

Bruner, J. S., Olver, R., Greenfield, P. M., *et al.* (1966). *Studies in Cognitive Growth*. New York: Wiley. Eleven empirical studies set in the theoretical context of Bruner's Harvard team. This book is exceptional in situating without effort some African studies (by Greenfield in Senegal) within a 'mainstream' theoretical context (closely related to Piaget's work). Something of a classic by now, the book is still valuable reading for upper level undergraduates and postgraduate students.

Cole, M., Gay, J., Glick, J. A., and Sharp, D. W. (1971). *The Cultural Context of Learning and Thinking*. London: Methuen. A carefully reasoned, thoughtful account of a series of empirical studies among the Kpelle of Liberia. This book is a milestone in the development of cross-cultural psychology. Mandatory reading for postgraduate students in this field, it is probably too specialized for most undergraduates.

Cole, M., and Scribner, S. (1974). *Culture and Thought*. New York: Wiley. This is probably the best available introductory book on cross-cultural psychology, although its focus is exclusively cognitive. Starting with a historical account of Western thinking on the subject, it reviews empirical studies carefully, albeit highly selectively and ends with a lucid exposition of methodological problems. Suitable for undergraduate courses; available in paperback.

Cronbach, L. J. C., and Drenth, P. J. D. (eds) (1972). *Mental Tests and Cultural Adaptation*. The Hague: Mouton. These proceedings of an important conference in Istanbul contain fifty papers from a very broad spectrum of nations, focused on the limitations of conventional, Western style mental tests for use in other cultural settings. Abbreviation has made some of the text very dense. Suitable for postgraduate and professional courses in educational and industrial psychology in the Third World.

Dasen, P. R. (ed.) (1977). A valuable collection of Piagetian studies by Third World scholars in their home cultures, in *Piagetian Psychology: Cross-Cultural Contributions*. New York: Gardner Press.

Dawson, J.L.M., and Lonner, W. J. (eds) (1974). *Readings in Cross-cultural Psychology*. Hong Kong: University Press. Proceedings of the 1st International IACCP Conference, containing short papers and a list of more with the authors' addresses. Useful as reference material for lecturers.

Deregowski, J. B. (1973). Illusions and Culture. In: Gregory, R. L., and Gromrich, E. H. (eds). *Illusion in Nature and Art*. London: Duckworth. This well-illustrated chapter contains a detailed review of empirical studies on cultural variations in the perception of pictures (not only geometrical illusions). The book, which contains other good chapters on visual perception, is suitable for undergraduate and postgraduate courses.

El-Abd, H. A. (1973). *Educational Psychology Research and the African Teacher*. Cairo: Dar El-Hana. A mixed bag purporting to introduce educational research to African teachers, this volume contains detailed accounts of three empirical studies by the author in Uganda, as well as an elementary chapter on statistics and some general advice to teachers. The book does not review other psychological research in Africa. Reference material for lecturers and students.

Evans, J. L. (1970). *Children in Africa: A Review of Psychological Research.* New York: Teachers College Press. This slim volume reports in eclectic detail a number of studies, without a clear effort at integration. Reference material for lecturers.

Forde, D. (ed.) (1954). *African Worlds: Studies in the Cosmological Ideas and Social Values of African Peoples.* Oxford: Oxford University Press. A collection of nine anthropological studies. Reference material for lecturers.

Fox, L. K. (ed.) (1967). *East African Childhood.* Oxford: Oxford University Press. This volume grew out of a course in Human Learning and Development at Makerere University in 1964–65. It contains personal accounts of their childhood experience by members of three East African Societies— the Baluyia, the Acholi and the Akamba—along with comments and observations about traditional child-rearing practices and how these were changing in the authors' generation.

Gardiner, H. W. (1975). An Unopened Pandora's Box for Developing Countries: The Challenge of Teaching through Research. In: Berry, J. W., and Lonner, W. J. (eds). *Applied Cross-cultural Psychology.* Amsterdam: Swets and Zeitlinger, pp. 265–270.

Gay, J., and Cole, M. (1967). *The New Mathematics and an Old Culture.* New York: Holt, Rinehart & Winston. A more popular precursor to the volume by Cole, Gay, Glick and Sharp (1971), this slim paperback is suitable as supplementary reading for undergraduates.

Goodnow, J. J. (1976). The Nature of Intelligent Behaviour: Questions Raised by Cross-cultural Studies. In: Resnick, L. B. (ed.). *The Nature of Intelligence.* New York: Wiley, pp. 169–188. A thought-provoking chapter in a useful volume, suitable for postgraduate and advanced undergraduate students.

Haworth, A., and Mwanalushi, M. (1977). A Study of Community Response to Alcohol-Related Problems in Zambia. University of Zambia: mimeo.

Heron, A. (1969). The Establishment of a Department of Psychology in an African University. *International Journal of Psychology*, **4**, 153–157.

Horton, R. (1967a). African Traditional Thought and Western Science—I. From Tradition to Science. *Africa*, **27**, 50–71.

Horton, R. (1967b). African Traditional Thought and Western Science—II. The Closed and Open Predicaments. *Africa*, **27**, 155–187.

IACCP Cross-cultural Psychology Newsletter. A forum for news and discussion, this quarterly newsletter includes useful lists of recent publications.

International Journal of Psychology. One of the three main journals publishing cross-cultural psychological research.

Irvine, S. H., Sanders, J. T., and Klingelhofer, E. L. (1970). *Human Behaviour in Africa: A Bibliography of Psychological and Related Writings.* University of Western Ontario: mimeo. A list of 2310 entries under fourteen headings, together with an author index.

Jahoda, G. (1969). *The Psychology of Superstition*. London: Allen Lane. A well-documented and provocative account of the phenomenon of superstition among peoples of different cultural backgrounds.

Jahoda, G. (1970). Supernatural Beliefs and Changing Cognitive Structures among Ghanaian University Students, *Journal of Cross-cultural Psychology*, **1**, 115–130.

Journal of Cross-cultural Psychology. One of the three main journals publishing cross-cultural research.

Journal of Social Psychology. As above.

Kiev, A. (1972). *Transcultural Psychiatry*. Harmondsworth: Penguin. Such value as a book with this coverage might have is seriously undermined by its style. What level of credibility can it have for an African student who reads on p. 19: 'Particularly stressful, for example, is the loss of culture that is experienced by the educated yet still semi-primitive marginal African, who has become a member of a partially urbanized and Westernized society'?!

Kingsley, P. R. (1977a). Student Grade Thyself: Some Experiments in Student Evaluation of Seminar Presentations at the University of Zambia. Publication of the University of Zambia Psychology Association, University of Zambia, Lusaka: mimeo.

Kingsley, P. R. (1977b). Psychology in Zambia: A Bibliography. *HDRU Reports*, **26**, University of Zambia, Lusaka: mimeo. Lists 345 publications and limited circulation reports of which 325 appeared since 1965.

Kluckholn, C., and Murray, H. A. (1956). *Personality in Nature, Society and Culture*. New York: Alfred A. Knopf, second edition. Most of the material in this book is now somewhat dated but provides useful insights into an area of psychology which until recently was a preserve of anthropologists, namely 'culture and personality'. The editors have done a good job of integrating anthropological and psychological literature.

Leeson, J., and Frankenberg, R. (1977). The Patients of Traditional Doctors in Lusaka. *African Social Research*, **23**, 185–234.

Levine, R. A. (1973). *Culture, Behaviour and Personality*. Chicago: Aldine. This book provides an authoritative review of this very extensively researched area, as well as presenting the author's own new theoretical position. Suitable for advanced undergraduate and postgraduate students.

Lloyd, B. B. (1972). *Perception and Cognition: A Cross-cultural Perspective*. Harmondsworth: Penguin. A scholarly review of research in this area. Suitable for postgraduate students and lecturers.

Luria, A. R. (1976). *Cognitive Development: Its Social and Cultural Foundations*. Cambridge, Mass.: Harvard University Press. A leisurely account of empirical research conducted in 1931–32 among central Asian communities of the USSR. The book is replete with verbal protocols and discusses many of the classic methodological problems of cross-cultural cognitive research. Reference material for advanced students and lecturers.

Marwick, M. (1974). Is Science a Form of Witchcraft? *New Scientist*, **63**, 578–581.

Munroe, R. L., and Munroe, R. H. (1975). *Cross-cultural Human Development*. Monterey, California: Brooks/Cole. The authors of this book acknowledge some of its major weaknesses. Although strongly universalistic in theoretical orientation, the book tends to stress a modern-Western/ traditional-non-Western dichotomy. The illustrations reinforce this bias by portraying non-Western children in scanty attire and dramatic situations. In addition the authors adopt a 'strong inference' approach which leads them to play down methodological problems in favour of a sometimes simplistic clarity. Stylistically suited to undergraduate readers, this book requires supplementation with other materials, such as Cole and Scribner (1974).

Mwanalushi, M. (1976). Adolescent Stress in Zambia. Paper presented at the Third International Conference of the International Association for Cross-cultural Psychology, Tilburg University, The Netherlands, July 12–16 1976.

Nweze, A. A. (1973). A Nigerian Student Thinks about Psychology. Paper presented at the 1st African Regional Conference of the IACCP, Ibadan, Nigeria, 2–7 April 1973. This articulate account of an undergraduate student's impressions of psychology stresses the problems of grappling with the discipline's theoretical diversity, and argues the need to resolve a conflict between Western and African modes of thought, similar to that posited by Bloom (1976). See our contrary views on this subject in the second section of this article.

Okonji, M. O. (1975). African Approaches to the Study of Behaviour. In: Berry, J. W., and Lonner, W. J. (eds). *Applied Cross-cultural Psychology*. Amsterdam: Swets & Zeitlinger.

Poortinga, Y. H. (ed.) (1977). *Basic Problems in Cross-cultural Psychology*. Amsterdam: Swets & Zeitlinger. Proceedings of the Third International Conference of the International Association for Cross-Cultural Psychology. A selection of thirty-eight papers, including four on methodological issues in cross-cultural research which should be of interest to upper-level undergraduate and graduate students as well as to cross-cultural researchers. Also listed are ninety-three additional titles with the author's addresses.

Price-Williams, D. R. (ed.) (1969). *Cross-cultural Studies*. Harmondsworth: Penguin. An excellent selection of twenty-three papers, which does not overlap with Berry and Dasen (1973). Unlike the latter volume, this one includes studies on achievement motivation and Freudian hypotheses. Suitable for undergraduate courses.

Price-Williams, D. R. (1975). *Explorations in Cross-cultural Psychology*. San Francisco: Chandler & Sharp. Seven chapters which cover in depth the many serious methodological and ethical problems confronting psychology as it strives to encompass cultures outside the Western tradition. Mandatory reading for prospective lecturers and researchers in the Third World.

Read, M. (1959). *Children of Their Fathers: Growing up among the Ngoni of Malawi*. New York: Holt, Rinehart & Winston. This book introduces Ngoni child-rearing practices and values, and traces the important events and stages of development from infancy to adulthood among the Ngoni. Particular emphasis is placed on traditional methods of education, personality formation and preparation for adult roles, as well as the impact of schools and churches, as new institutions of education.

Rohner, R. P. (1975). *They Love Me, They Love Me Not: A World-wide Study of the Effects of Parental Acceptance and Rejection*. New Haven, Conn.: HRAF Press. An ambitious empirical study combining several different research methods to reach a strongly universalistic conclusion. Valuable reference material for lecturers and postgraduate students.

Sanyal, B. C., Case, J. H., Dow, P. S., and Jackman, M. E. (1976). *Higher Education and the Labour Market in Zambia: Expectations and Performance*. Paris and Lusaka: UNESCO and University of Zambia.

Schuster, R. H. (1976). Lekking Behaviour of Kafue Lechwe. *Science*, **192**, 1240–1242.

Segall, M. H., Campbell, D. T., and Herskovits, M. J. (1966). *The Influence of Culture on Visual Perception*. New York: Bobs-Merrill. A classic, multi-cultural study of geometrical illusions. Reference material for undergraduate and postgraduate students.

Serpell, R. (1976). *Culture's Influence on Behaviour*. London: Methuen. A brief introduction to cross-cultural psychology with emphasis on cognitive process, on methodological problems and on social implications. Reviewed informatively by Bennett, S. M. (1977). *Child Development Abstracts and Bibliography*, **51** (1 and 2), 71–72. Suitable for undergraduate students.

Serpell R. (1977a). Need for a New Direction: Psychology in Africa. *Reviews in Anthropology*, **4**, 153–161. A critical and discursive review of Wober's (1975) book.

Serpell, R. (1977b). Linguistic Flexibility in Urban Zambian Schoolchildren. *HDRU Reports*, **27**. University of Zambia, mimeo.

Serpell, R. (1978). The Nuts and Bolts of Relevance: How Academic Psychologists Interact with Society in Zambia. *IACCP Cross-cultural Psychology Newsletter*, **12**, pp. 5–9. A contribution to a debate within this magazine concerning the social relevance of psychology in Third World countries.

Shanks, I. P. (1979). The Social Science Foundation Course 1974 to 1978, School of Humanities and Social Sciences: A Critical Analysis. University of Zambia, Educational Research Bureau.

Topics in Culture Learning. A series of occasional volumes published by the Culture Learning Institute of the East–West Center, Hawaii. Less technical in style than the academic journals, these volumes contain valuable reference material for advanced students and lecturers.

Vernon, P. E. (1969). *Intelligence and Cultural Environment*. London: Methuen. A classic research report by an eminent educational psychologist of a cross-cultural study of intelligence, this book contains a clear statement of his influential theoretical position. Reference material for undergraduate and postgraduate students.

Whittaker, J. O. (1976). *Introduction to Psychology*. Philadelphia: W. B. Saunders, third edition. A basic, general introductory textbook, attractively designed for easy reading with numerous captions and illustrations. In addition to showing a concern with the social relevance of psychological issues, this book is quite exceptional among its genre in containing photographs of people of many different races and cultures engaging in a variety of activities. For Third World students, however, a lot more of the non-Western-based research deserves inclusion in an introductory course.

Wickert, F. R. (1967). *Readings in African Psychology*. Michigan State University: African Studies Center. A collection of fifty-one short pieces from Francophone Africa. Most of the papers are on applied topics, first published in French in the 1960s. The scope includes mental testing, personnel selection, industrial relations, attitudes, child development and psychopathology. Useful reference material for advanced undergraduate and postgraduate students.

Wober, M. (1975). *Psychology in Africa*. London: International African Institute. A detailed, critical review of more than 600 studies, this book sets out to demarcate the weaknesses of research in Africa to date as well as pointing the way to some neglected topics. For a critical review, see Serpell (1977a). Valuable reference material for advanced students in Africa.

Films

American Psychological Association films (16 mm sound, 30 minutes each): *No. 1 Focus on Behaviour*, *No. 2 The World We Perceive* (includes Gibson and Walk's 'visual cliff' and Witkin's BAT, EFT and RET), *No. 3 Brain and Behaviour*, and *No. 5 Learning about Learning* (includes experiments by Skinner, Harlow, Spence, Kendler and Kendler). Marketed by RTV International Inc., 405 Park Avenue, New York, NY 10022, USA.

ACKNOWLEDGEMENT

We are indebted to Phillip Kingsley for his valuable critique of an earlier draft and for drawing our attention to some important issues which we had overlooked.

REFERENCES

This section contains references cited in the text, which have not been included in the bibliography above.

Beard, R. (1972). *Teaching and Learning in Higher Education*. Harmondsworth: Penguin.

Bligh, D. A. (1972). *What's the Use of Lectures?* Harmondsworth: Penguin.

Bloom, B. S. (1953). Thought Processes in Lectures and Discussions. *Journal of General Education*, **7**, 160–169.

McGraw-Hill—Slide Group for General Psychology by James B. Maas, Cornell University (300 35 mm colour transparencies covering a wide range of topics).

McGuigan, F. J. (1963). The Experimenter: A Neglected Stimulus Object. *Psychological Bulletin*, **60**, 421–428.

Orne, M. T. (1962). On the Social Psychology of the Psychological Experiment: With Special Reference to Demand Characteristics and Their Implications. *American Psychologist*, **17**, 776–783.

Rosenthal, R. (1965). The Volunteer Subject. *Human Relations*, **18**, 389–406.

Schumaker, E. F. (1973). *Small is Beautiful*. New York: Harper.

Shotter, J. (1975). *Images of Man in Psychological Research*. London: Methuen.

Underwood, B. J. (1957). *Psychological Research*. New York: Appleton-Century-Crofts.

Author Index

Subject Index